The Sustainable Development of Port Group

Bo Lu

The Sustainable Development of Port Group

Evaluation and Management

Springer

Bo Lu
School of Economics and Management
Dalian University of Technology
Dalian, Liaoning, China

ISBN 978-981-97-2377-5 ISBN 978-981-97-2378-2 (eBook)
https://doi.org/10.1007/978-981-97-2378-2

This research is funded by the Key Project of Philosophy and Social Science Foundation of China [Grant Number 20&ZD129]; the National Natural Science Foundation of China under [Grant Number 72073018; 72261147705].

This Springer imprint is published by the registered company Springer Nature Singapore Pte Ltd.
The registered company address is: 152 Beach Road, #21-01/04 Gateway East, Singapore 189721, Singapore

Paper in this product is recyclable.

Contents

Chapter 1
The Connotation of Regional Port Group and Environmental Coordinated Development

1.1 The Role of Port Group in Economic and Social Development

With the continuous development of port economy, the problems of disorderly expansion and vicious competition among ports in the region due to similar port resources and overlapping hinterlands are becoming increasingly prominent. These problems not only result in low operating efficiency of ports, but also hinder the rapid development of regional economy. Therefore, the optimization and integration of port groups can alleviate the competition for resources and cargo sources among ports, promote the rational flow of resources within the region, and optimize port investment and construction activities. In the process of port group optimization and integration, regional supply chains and transportation networks are also being optimized and integrated, promoting the coordinated development of ports and regions, and is the inevitable choice for promoting regional economic development and maintaining the sustainable development of the port industry. For this reason, in recent years, our country has actively promoted the integration of regional port groups, especially in optimizing resource allocation and port functions, in order to improve port competitiveness and port scale benefits.

The resource allocation of regional port clusters contributes to the improvement of operational efficiency and market competitiveness of port enterprises. The marketization of port resource allocation prevents port enterprises from monopolizing the construction and operation of port resources, thus prompting port enterprises to improve their own operational efficiency in order to secure more port resources and development space. All port enterprises operate on a marketized platform, and the operational efficiency of port enterprises becomes the fundamental goal of enterprise development. The optimization of port resource allocation essentially changes the integrated planning, construction, and operation of ports under the management system where the port government and enterprises are not separated, into a marketized allocation of ports under the national port layout plan. Resources and technology,

B. Lu, *The Sustainable Development of Port Group*,
https://doi.org/10.1007/978-981-97-2378-2_1

under the marketized allocation mechanism, will inevitably converge towards ports with development potential, promoting the construction and development of ports, and thus promoting the structural adjustment and optimization of the port industry (Ge et al. 2017).

Therefore, the supply and demand relationship of port resources is well coordinated under the marketized allocation mechanism. Port layout, port functions, and port services are also optimized, improved, and enhanced due to market competition for resource allocation, thereby enhancing the core competitiveness of the port cluster and promoting economic and social development. Regional port clusters guide accurate investment towards core port technologies, enhance the comprehensive strength of port clusters, and maximize benefits. The marketized allocation of resources by regional port clusters lays the foundation for the establishment of a marketized investment and financing system for port development. Under the market mechanism pursuing maximum investment returns, funds will be invested in port infrastructure and improve the completeness of the infrastructure, thereby expanding port capacity. At the same time, marketized resource allocation is beneficial to guide funds towards port hinterland transport facilities, thereby achieving the goal of enhancing the competitiveness of the port logistics chain.

Due to market competition pressure, port investors always focus on how to improve the quality of port assets, and mastering and improving the core technology of the port logistics chain is an effective means to improve the quality of port assets. Therefore, marketized resource allocation will guide funds towards core port technologies. The integration of regional port clusters drives the economic development of the hinterland. Regional port clusters have increased the investment in the construction of the transport system, making each port an important water and land transport hub. The port transport system is the channel that connects the port with its serviceable hinterland, determines the level of cargo source, and is an important condition for the survival and development of the port (Dong et al. 2018).

The construction of the port transport system promotes the connection construction between the hinterland transport system and the port area, effectively improves the port's radiation capacity, expands the range of the port's economic hinterland, connects more railway branch lines and roads with the port area, improves the railway and road transport channels, ensures railway transport capacity, and connects urban roads with the port area to establish a comprehensive port transport system. It promotes the development of multimodal transport at each port, makes the connection of multimodal transport smoother, improves the efficiency of cargo transshipment, and drives the economic development of hinterland cities. The scale benefits of regional port clusters have strengthened the competitiveness of hinterland regional enterprises in the international market. The integration of port cluster resources will focus on the needs of hinterland economic development, allocate cargo sources of each port according to the resource needs of the hinterland, clarify the functional positioning and division of labor of each port, and lay a resource foundation for the economic development of its hinterland.

At the same time, it also creates a core brand for the port area to promote the market development ability of the hinterland region. The brand effect of enterprises is far less than the regional brand effect that aggregates the advantages of most enterprises in the region. The Lingang Industrial Zone in Zhuhai City, Guangdong Province, has used the regional brand dominated by the petrochemical industry to harvest cooperation invitations from companies around the world, attracting more suppliers and investors, greatly promoting the economic development of the industrial zone. Each port can also learn from the experience, establish a port brand that is in line with its own reality, realize the synergistic value creation of the port and hinterland economic development, and achieve the effect of "1 + 1 > 2".

Later, on the basis of integrating natural resources and economic resources, the port cluster will also pay more attention to the driving and radiation effects of port resource integration on hinterland economic development, focusing on the economic development of hinterland-related enterprises and port logistics parks, helping to improve the collection and distribution system, and boosting the economic development of the hinterland region. Currently, 17 provinces and cities in our country have established provincial-level port groups. In addition, the coordinated development of regional port clusters, three world-class port clusters (Bohai Rim, Yangtze River Delta, Guangdong-Hong Kong-Macao Greater Bay Area port cluster) are also forming. The Ministry of Transport continues to guide and promote the coordinated development of regional port clusters and further deepen the integration of resources of provincial port groups, organize and implement good port service capacity improvement projects, to play a more powerful service guarantee role in promoting regional economic coordinated development and building a modern industrial system.

1.2 Problems Related to the Coordinated Development of Regional Port Clusters and the Environment in China

The negative impact of port operations on the environment increases with the growth of throughput. Port operations have direct and indirect impacts on the environment, and regulators, shippers, and port authorities have been working to address this issue in recent years. The main environmental impacts are air and water pollution, due to the energy demand of port operations, noise and light intrusion cause the consumption of fossil fuels (Jiang 2023).

The discharge of ballast water, dredging operations at the port, waste disposal, and oil spills can all potentially pollute the waters near the port. Large ships have large amounts of water in their ballast tanks to stabilize the ship. When cargo is removed, water is pumped into the ship to compensate for changes in cargo weight distribution. After the cargo is loaded, the ballast water is discharged.

When ballast water is discharged in different areas (pumped in at one port and released at another), environmental problems arise; it can lead to unintentional invasions of non-native species. These microorganisms can disrupt aquatic ecosystems and cause health problems. Similar problems can also occur in the transport process of non-native organisms through hull fouling. When dredging operations are carried out to increase the depth of the port, the aquatic environment is also negatively affected. Finally, waste generated on board must be disposed of in a harmless manner, and ports are expected to provide waste disposal solutions. Oil leaks can occur anywhere along the ship's route, including near the port, causing serious environmental consequences.

Ships, cargo handling equipment, and port superstructures have altered the appearance of the surrounding port environment, causing visual intrusion or aesthetic pollution. Added to this is the noise generated during port operations, as well as light pollution during night operations, all of which have a severe negative impact on nearby residents, particularly in terms of sleep deprivation and increased stress.

Noise is a serious issue in today's transportation, especially noise from aircraft. To address the noise issue of airport operations, authorities have adopted several strategies. For example, changing the way aircraft enter the airport, steeper descents to minimize impact on residents, and adopting new technologies on aircraft engines. A similar situation exists in the maritime sector; however, for ports, the main source of noise pollution is from dock and inland operations, not the ships themselves. Another very different environmental issue of port operations is the noise impact of maritime transport on marine mammals.

Air pollution in ports is the result of vehicle and cargo movement (ships, cargo handling equipment) and has both local and global consequences. Various types of pollutants are emitted, some of which affect local air quality, while others are forcing factors for climate change (Xin 2022). Currently, dealing with air pollutants is the most pressing issue that port authorities, shippers, and regulators are trying to address through most existing policies and port measures. The next section reviews academic research in the field of port environmental impacts, focusing mainly on emissions. The coordinated development of regional port clusters and the environment in our country is an important issue.

As an important part of our country's marine economy, regional port clusters play a significant role in promoting local economic development and international trade. However, the development of port clusters also faces challenges of environmental protection and sustainable development.

(1) Pollution Control and Prevention

The construction and operation of port clusters may generate a large amount of wastewater, exhaust gas, and solid waste, which pose threats to the surrounding environmental quality and biodiversity. The development of port clusters often accompanies a large amount of ship transportation and cargo handling activities, which generate a large amount of exhaust gas, wastewater, and solid waste. How to control and reduce the emission of pollutants, and prevent pollution to the surrounding environment, is an important issue, so pollution control and prevention should be strengthened.

We should strengthen the environmental access and supervision of port enterprises, increase the management of environmentally sensitive enterprises, and ensure that enterprises meet the national and local environmental protection requirements in technology and equipment. Strengthen the construction of environmental protection facilities within the port cluster, including wastewater treatment plants, exhaust gas treatment facilities, etc., to ensure that the emissions within the port are effectively treated and purified. Strengthen the monitoring of the water, air, and soil environment of the sea and land around the port cluster, timely detect and respond to potential pollution sources and environmental problems, and protect the safety and health of the surrounding ecological environment.

(2) Ecological Protection and Restoration

The construction and operation of port clusters often require extensive activities such as large-scale land reclamation, dredging, and river channel modification. These activities may pose threats to marine ecosystems and coastal wetlands, causing potential damage to the natural environment. Therefore, it is a problem that needs to be addressed on how to protect and restore the ecological environment during the construction and operation of ports. Hence, it is necessary to strengthen ecological protection and restoration. A robust ecological compensation mechanism should be established to compensate for ecological losses caused by port construction, and ecological protection should be incorporated into port construction planning and project evaluation. Efforts should be made to strengthen the ecological restoration and protection of coastal areas around port clusters, including the protection of coastal wetlands and the restoration of marine ecosystems, to promote the coordinated development of port clusters and surrounding ecosystems. It is also necessary to strengthen the monitoring and assessment of the ecological environment of port clusters, regularly assess and monitor the ecological environment of port clusters, identify and resolve potential problems in a timely manner, and promote the sustainable development of port clusters.

(3) Water Resource Utilization

Port operations require a large amount of water resources, including those used for maintaining navigation channels for ships entering and leaving ports, loading and unloading goods, and washing dock facilities. Therefore, it is a problem that needs to be addressed on how to use water resources reasonably and reduce the consumption of surrounding water resources (Wang et al. 2023). Hence, it is necessary to improve the efficiency of water resource utilization. Promote the use of water-saving equipment and technology to reduce the consumption of water resources by port activities. At the same time, strengthen water resource management to ensure the rational and efficient use of water resources in port clusters.

(4) Noise and Vibration

Mechanical equipment and ship activities in port operations can generate noise and vibration, affecting surrounding residents and the ecological environment. Therefore, it is a problem that needs to be addressed on how to control and reduce the impact of noise and vibration, and ensure the quality of life of surrounding residents. Hence, it is necessary to establish noise and vibration control measures. Develop noise and vibration control standards, adopt noise reduction and vibration reduction measures, and reduce the impact of port activities on surrounding residents and the ecological environment.

(5) Low-carbon

Development and Green Transition The development of port clusters often involves a large amount of energy consumption and carbon emissions, which pose challenges to addressing climate change and promoting green low-carbon transition. Therefore, promoting the low-carbon development and green transition of port clusters is an important way to achieve the coordinated development of port clusters and the environment. It is necessary to increase the use and development of clean energy, promote the energy structure transformation of port clusters, reduce the dependence on traditional energy, and improve energy utilization efficiency. Strengthen the greening transformation of logistics and transportation, promote the use of electric vehicles and new energy vehicles, and reduce carbon emissions from port clusters and transportation links. Strengthen the energy-saving and carbon reduction work within the port clusters, promote energy-saving and environmentally friendly equipment and technology, and reduce the energy consumption and environmental impact of port clusters (Li 2017).

In conclusion, the coordinated development of regional port clusters and the environment in our country is a complex and important issue. By strengthening pollution control and prevention, ecological protection and restoration, and low-carbon development and green transition, a positive interaction between port clusters and the environment can be achieved, promoting sustainable development. The government, enterprises, and all sectors of society should work together to form a joint force to promote the coordinated development of regional port clusters and the environment in our country.

1.3 Requirements for the Coordinated Development of Port Clusters and the Environment in China in the Future

The requirements for the harmonious development of China's future port clusters and the environment involve multiple aspects, including environmental protection, sustainability, and economic development. Specifically, a port cluster refers to a group of ports in a certain area that are geographically close, have similar or identical economic hinterlands, and rely on similar external conditions such as transportation. This is a manifestation of the enhancement of regional port functions and competitiveness, and it is also an important way to rationally allocate regional port resources and improve the efficiency of hinterland services.

Harmonious development of port clusters and the ecological environment refers to the virtuous cycle of harmonious relationships formed by the mutual coordination of port cluster development and the ecological environment, in order to achieve simultaneous improvement of economic and ecological benefits of port cluster development. It includes two levels of coordination, one is the coordinated development between ports within the port cluster, and the other is the coordinated development of the entire port cluster as a whole with the ecological environment. Its short-term goal is to protect or improve the regional ecological environment while achieving rapid development of the port cluster, ensuring that the development of the port cluster does not exceed the carrying capacity of the regional ecological environment; its ultimate goal is to achieve sustainable development of the port cluster. This chapter summarizes the relevant requirements for the harmonious development of China's future port clusters and the environment from four aspects: ecological protection, sustainable development, economic development, innovation, and technology.

1.3.1 Ecological Protection Requirements

To minimize the impact of port operations on the surrounding ecosystem, ports must strictly comply with national and local environmental laws and regulations. Specifically, ports should develop and implement environmental management plans, including waste disposal, water quality monitoring, and air quality control, to ensure the effectiveness of environmental protection measures.

In the development process of port and shipping enterprises, it must be recognized that environmental damage is irreversible. The concept of "ecology first, green development" must be fully implemented. Rather than construction at the expense of ecological damage, all construction should be based on the implementation of environmental protection requirements, with the protection of the environment and ecology as the main premise. When formulating construction plans, port construction units should follow relevant planning and policy requirements, especially the requirements of the "Notice of the State Council on Strengthening Coastal Wetland Protection and Strictly Controlling Reclamation" and the "Notice on Strengthening the Planning and Construction of Coastal and Inland Ports and Channels to Further Standardize and Strengthen Resource Element Guarantee". When determining needs, they should minimize the occupation of sea areas, ensure the scientific and realistic nature of the plan, rather than blindly pursuing the expansion of scale or excessive consumption of future resource needs.

Through the implementation of the above measures, we can ensure the harmonious development of port construction and the ecological environment, and achieve a virtuous cycle. This will help protect the ecological environment, enhance the level of sustainable development of ports, and provide good support for future economic development.

1.3.2 Economic Development Requirements

Port development should be coordinated with national strategies and regional economic development plans, play a supporting role in trade and logistics, and promote domestic and foreign trade. Ports should improve operational efficiency, optimize port infrastructure, reduce logistics costs, and enhance port competitiveness.

The optimization and integration of port clusters can help alleviate competition for resources and cargo between ports, promote the rational flow of resources within the region, and drive the coordinated development of ports and regions. At the same time, the construction of port infrastructure and logistics networks can strengthen connections with the inland economic hinterland, serve the economic hinterland, and promote the internal circulation of the economy. By forming economies of scale through industrial agglomeration, ports can enhance their international competitiveness and influence; according to market needs and industry development trends, guide port enterprises to strengthen technological innovation and industrial chain expansion, and adopt appropriate policies and support measures to accelerate the transformation and upgrading of the port economy. These measures will help improve the industrial structure upgrade and transformation of our country's port industry, laying a solid foundation for future sustainable port development. Optimize port operation processes: adopt energy-saving technologies, establish intelligent management systems, and enhance operational efficiency.

1.3.3 Requirements for Sustainable Development

Ports should be committed to sustainable development, including improving resource utilization efficiency, reducing energy consumption, and reducing carbon footprint. The construction of green ports should be promoted, adopting environmental protection technologies and green energy to reduce negative impacts on the environment.

Sustainable development is a guiding ideology for resolving the contradiction between humans and the Earth's environment. It must meet the needs of contemporary people without impairing the ability of future generations to meet their needs. Sustainable development must adhere to the three basic principles of ecological sustainability, social and cultural sustainability, and economic sustainability. In the future development process of port clusters, attention needs to be paid to issues such as resource utilization efficiency. For example, ports should improve resource utilization efficiency, manage and use water, land, energy and other resources reasonably, and avoid waste and excessive consumption; reduce energy consumption, take energy-saving measures, optimize energy use, and reduce energy consumption. This can be achieved by using efficient equipment and technologies, improving port operation processes, and reducing energy demand; reducing carbon footprint, reducing greenhouse gas emissions, and controlling carbon footprint. Ports can use clean energy, such as solar and wind energy, to reduce dependence on fossil fuels. In addition, electric vehicles, low-carbon transportation and other environmental protection measures can be promoted. By meeting the requirements for sustainable development, ports can achieve the dual goals of economic development and environmental protection, providing a more sustainable port operation model for the future.

1.3.4 Innovation and Technology Requirements

Ports should actively adopt the latest science and information technology, improve the level of intelligent and automated operations, and reduce resource waste. Promote the digital transformation of ports, achieve information sharing and resource collaboration, and improve overall efficiency. Strengthen technological innovation and promote the construction of smart ports. Vigorously apply artificial intelligence, the Internet of Things, autonomous driving, and geographic information systems, etc., to improve the comprehensive production efficiency and safety of port operations. Promote the deep integration of information technologies such as the Internet, the Internet of Things, and big data with port services and supervision, deepen the information openness and sharing and business collaboration between governments and enterprises, and between departments. Relying on informatization, focus on port smart logistics, dangerous goods safety management, etc., strive to innovate the logistics service model with the port as the hub, safety monitoring and supervision methods, promote the realization of the port logistics operation system's "cargo-single system, information-network communication", and gradually form the port dangerous goods safety management system's "data in one library, supervision in one network".

These requirements reflect the Chinese government's expectations for the future development and environmental coordination of port clusters, emphasizing the balance of environmental protection, sustainability, and economic benefits. These requirements help ensure the sustainable development of the port industry while reducing adverse environmental impacts. At the same time, this also helps Chinese ports maintain competitiveness and leadership on the global stage.

1.4 Purpose and Significance of This Study

With the advancement of global economic integration, the mode of port competition has changed, and the regional development of ports has become a common trend in the development of our country's coastal ports.

The optimization and integration of port clusters is an important means to promote the regional development of ports. By improving the layout and structure of port clusters and promoting the integration of regional supply chains, port clusters can improve resource utilization and international competitiveness in the process of regionalization, scaling, and specialization. In 2006, our country's former Ministry of Transport announced the "National Coastal Port Layout Plan", dividing our country's coastal ports into five major port clusters: the Bohai Sea, the Yangtze River Delta, the Southeast Coast, the Pearl River Delta, and the Southwest Coast. In recent years, with the development of economic trade and the planning and construction of port infrastructure, the logistics services and infrastructure of our country's five major port clusters have been gradually improved, and the competition between individual coastal ports has gradually transformed into competition between port clusters. The optimization and integration of port clusters is an important means to achieve the scaling, range, and agglomeration of ports, enhance the competitiveness of port clusters, and optimize the layout and structure of regional ports, and promote the upgrading of port industrial structures. The optimization and integration of our country's coastal port clusters is of great significance to the realization of the "Belt and Road" initiative, and also plays an important role in building the "new development pattern of domestic and international dual circulation" proposed by General Secretary Xi Jinping.

However, a series of activities in the process of port optimization and integration may have adverse effects on the regional ecological environment. In September 2019, the Central Committee of the Communist Party of China and the State Council issued the "Outline for Building a Strong Transportation Country", making green development, conservation and intensification, low-carbon environmental protection, and strengthening transportation ecological environment protection and restoration the key tasks of building a strong transportation country. At present, our country is about to start the "Fourteenth Five-Year Plan" to fully build a modern socialist country. The main goals of our country's economic and social development during the "Fourteenth Five-Year Plan" period not only include "new achievements in economic development", but also "new progress in ecological civilization construction".

In such an era, the optimization and integration of our country's port clusters should also pay attention to coordination with the environment and achieve the common development of regional port integration and ecological civilization construction. From the planning policies of our country's port regional integration development, it can be seen that there is still a certain gap between the current development status of our country's coastal port clusters and the goal of building green ports and achieving coordinated development of ports and the environment. By improving the integration strategy of port clusters, optimizing the logistics network of port clusters, and promoting the digital transformation of port enterprises, port clusters can achieve coordinated development with the environment during the optimization and integration process. The optimization and integration of port clusters is of great significance to our country's optimization of the logistics network and the implementation of the "Belt and Road" and economic "dual circulation". Ports in our country's coastal areas are densely distributed, and ports in nearby areas often have problems of overlapping hinterlands, homogeneous service types, and fierce competition. The optimization and integration of port clusters can bring three changes to our country's coastal ports: first, enhance regional resource utilization efficiency and optimize port investment and construction decisions; second, promote the common development of ports and regions; and third, promote the optimization of the industrial structure of port clusters.

The optimization and integration of port clusters can alleviate competition for resources and goods between ports, promote the rational flow of resources within the region, and optimize port investment and construction activities. In the process of port cluster optimization and integration, regional supply chains and transportation networks are also being optimized and integrated, promoting the coordinated development of ports and regions. Through the integration of regional supply chains, ports are developing towards specialization and scale, which promotes the upgrading and transformation of port industrial structures.

With the construction of port infrastructure and logistics networks in the process of port cluster optimization and integration, China's coastal ports can enhance their connections with the inland economic hinterland and enhance their ability to serve the economic hinterland. This is of great significance for stimulating China's domestic demand and promoting the "internal economic cycle". In addition, ports can form economies of scale through industrial agglomeration, which is beneficial to enhance the international competitiveness and influence of China's port clusters, and promote the implementation of the "external economic cycle" and the "Belt and Road Initiative".

The optimization and integration of port clusters is an important means for coastal ports to adjust their layout structure, improve port resource utilization efficiency, promote the integration of regional supply chains and logistics networks, and promote the development of coastal ports towards large-scale, specialized, and scaled directions. It plays an important role in enhancing the international competitiveness of China's coastal ports and enhancing the service capabilities of China's coastal ports to inland areas. The optimization and integration of port clusters and the construction of regional ecological environment influence each other. In the process of port cluster optimization and integration, attention should be paid to the coordination of port cluster development and regional ecological environment.

However, due to issues related to policy standards, data sharing platforms, and port competition patterns, there are still risks of inconsistency with the goals of regional ecological environment construction in China's port cluster optimization and integration activities. By improving the strategy of port cluster optimization and integration, optimizing regional logistics networks, promoting the digital transformation of ports, the infrastructure within the port cluster can be improved, the competition pattern between ports can be adjusted and improved, and the mechanism for collaborative cooperation within the region can be established. These measures are of great significance for promoting the coordinated development of port clusters and the environment.

Therefore, this book starts from the perspective of system science, and conducts research on the evaluation and governance of the coordinated development of regional port clusters and the environment, which will help the coordinated development of China's port clusters and the ecological environment, and achieve the goal of sustainable development of China's regional port clusters.

1.5 Research Methods and Technical Routes of This Book

1.5.1 Research Methods

This book mainly studies the coordinated development of port clusters and the environment, involving many levels and fields, such as carbon footprint, environmental carrying capacity, system dynamics, etc. Therefore, it has studied literature from various aspects, clarified the current research status in this field, and also provided a theoretical basis for further research in the following text.

Specifically, this book draws on existing theoretical research results, analyzes the relevant mechanisms and influencing factors of the formation of existing green, ecological, or energy-saving ports, and uses methods such as attribution decomposition analysis and LMDI decomposition to construct a multi-level, multi-dimensional low-carbon port driving and influencing factor set. It reveals the coordination path between the port and the environment, explores and analyzes the linear and non-linear relationships between various factors and between factors, constructs a comprehensive formation mechanism of low-carbon ports based on the Gamma distribution function of surface driving factors and deep influencing factors, and uses scenario simulation methods for analysis. Secondly, this book aims to minimize the comprehensive cost of low-carbon port investment, with constraints such as the upper limit of port low-carbon investment, and uses tools such as stochastic processes and optimization decision theory to establish a low-carbon port carbon emission reduction investment optimization model, seeking the best investment plan. In this process, this book comprehensively uses quantitative and qualitative analysis methods, through comparative analysis, case analysis, etc., to propose corresponding suggestions from the industry level and port level. When conducting related research, further analysis is carried out in combination with examples, such as the regional port group pollutant emission estimation model, regional port group carbon footprint estimation model, etc. In addition, this book also opens a separate chapter to analyze the cases of domestic and foreign port group and environmental coordination governance, and gives relevant insights and suggestions in the following chapters.

1.5.2 Technical Route

See Fig. 1.1.

The first chapter mainly introduces the role of port groups in economic and social development, as well as the problems and future requirements for solving problems between regional port groups in our country and coordinated development with the environment at the current stage, and also introduces the research content methods and technical routes of this book.

The second chapter mainly introduces the theoretical basis of this book's research, involving the theory, mechanism, influencing factors of regional port groups and

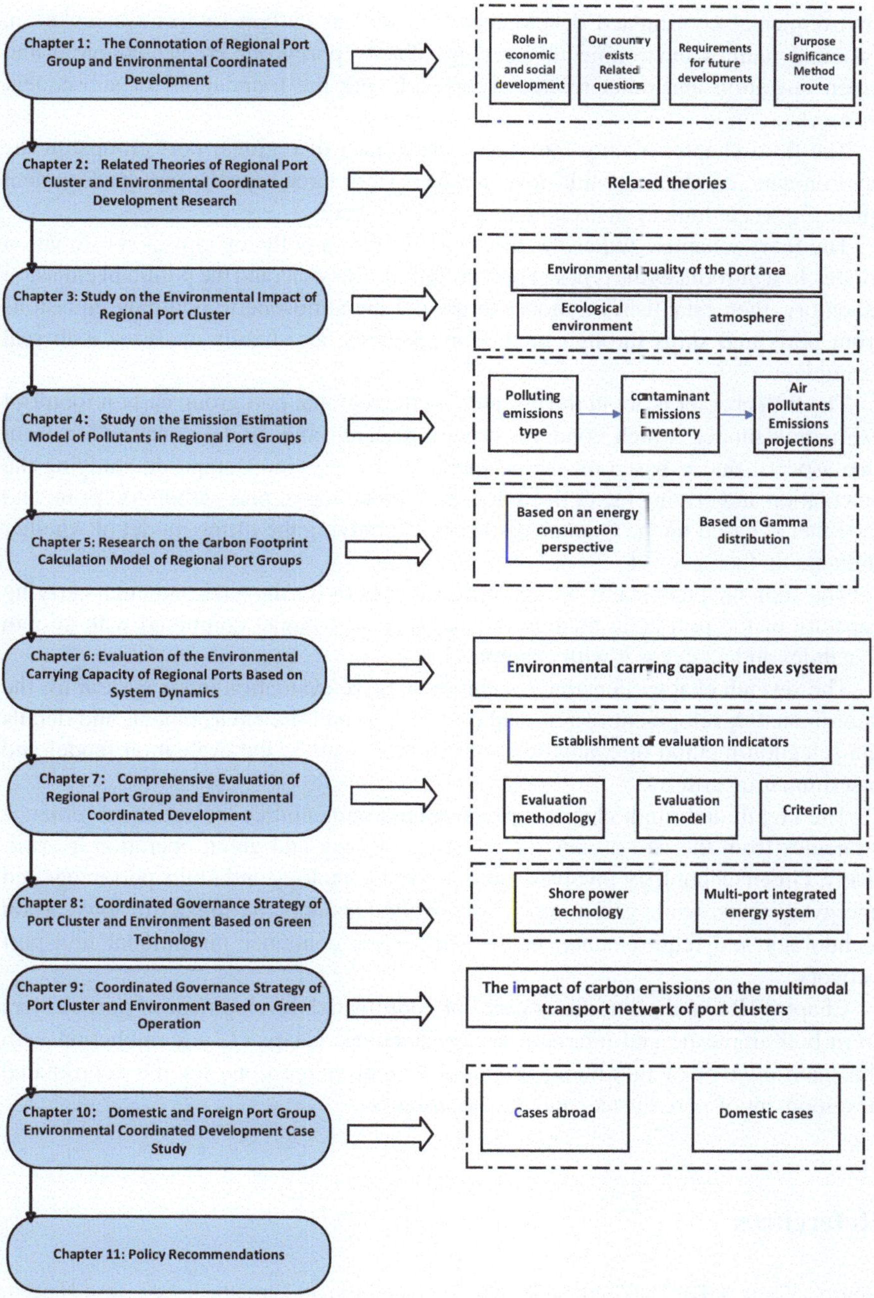

Fig. 1.1 Technical route map

environmental coordinated development, as well as carbon footprint calculation, system dynamics, environmental carrying capacity, port group green technology and green operation and other related theories, laying the foundation for subsequent research.

The third chapter mainly introduces the impact of regional port groups on the environment, conducting multi-level analysis from three aspects: port environment quality, port ecological environment, and atmosphere.

The fourth chapter studies the regional port group pollutant emission estimation model, first introduces the types of port pollution emissions and the pollutant emission inventory, then establishes a model to predict the atmospheric pollutant emissions from ports and ships through prediction methods, and finally analyzes with real examples.

The fifth chapter is about the research on the regional port group carbon footprint estimation model, which conducts related research and model construction from two aspects: one is based on the perspective of energy consumption, studying the calculation and driving factor decomposition modeling of port carbon footprint, and the other is based on the Gamma distribution, studying the fitting model of whether influencing factors exist.

The sixth chapter establishes an indicator system for the environmental carrying capacity of the port area, then establishes a related model combined with system dynamics and analyzes it with examples.

The seventh chapter constructs a comprehensive evaluation index system for the coordinated development of regional port groups and the environment, and details the selection method of evaluation indicators as well as the evaluation model and discrimination criteria.

The eighth and ninth chapters propose environmental coordination governance strategies from the two aspects of green technology and green operation, respectively. Green technology involves shore power technology and multi-port integrated energy systems, while green operation mainly considers the impact of low-carbon technology and requirements on the port area's container multimodal transport network.

Chapter 10 mainly introduces cases of coordinated development of port clusters from both domestic and international perspectives. Chap. 11, in conjunction with the main content of this book, proposes several suggestions for the coordinated development of port clusters and the environment.

References

Dong G, Zheng S, Lee PTW (2018) The effects of regional port integration: the case of Ningbo-Zhoushan Port. Transp Res Part E: Logistics Transp Rev 120:1–15

Ge Y, Hao Y, Cao G (2017) Analysis on the strategies and measures for the deep integration development of ports in the post-port resource integration era. China Water Transp 17(12)

Jiang K (2023) Current situation and development strategies of ecological port construction in China. Port Technol 11:16–19

Li N (2017) Problems and suggestions on port resource integration in China. Port Economy
Wang M, Ji M, Wu X, Deng K, Jing X (2023) Analysis on evaluation and spatial-temporal evolution of port cluster eco-efficiency: case study from the Yangtze river delta in China. Sustainability 15(10):8268
Xin M (2022) Review and future focus of port cluster collaborative development research. China Bus Rev 22:106–109

Chapter 2
Related Theories of Regional Port Cluster and Environmental Coordinated Development Research

2.1 Theoretical Basis of Regional Port Cluster and Environmental Coordinated Development

The theoretical basis of regional port cluster and environmental coordinated development is the logical starting point of the theory of regional port cluster and environmental coordinated development, the cornerstone of all theories of regional port cluster and environmental coordinated development, the theoretical basis for the necessity, rationality and feasibility of sustainable development of port clusters, and the action guide for the practice of sustainable development of port clusters. However, the research on the theoretical basis of regional port cluster and environmental coordinated development is a blank in the current theoretical research on regional port cluster and environmental coordinated development, which has adverse effects on the deepening of people's understanding of regional port cluster and environmental coordinated development, the perfection and maturity of the theory of regional port cluster and environmental coordinated development, and even the sustainable development of port clusters. Therefore, the research on the theoretical basis of regional port cluster and environmental coordinated development is an important direction and content of the theoretical research on regional port cluster and environmental coordinated development.

The theory of ecological economics provides the theoretical basis for correctly understanding the interaction between regional port cluster and environmental development, the theory of synergy provides the systematic method for correctly understanding the intrinsic connection between regional port cluster and environment, the theory of sustainable development provides the theoretical basis for understanding the relationship between regional port cluster and environment, and the theory of coordinated development of port cluster and ecological environment is based on the theory of ecological economics, synergy theory and sustainable development theory, systematically studying the relationship between regional port cluster

B. Lu, *The Sustainable Development of Port Group*,
https://doi.org/10.1007/978-981-97-2378-2_2

development and environment. Through the study of the contradictory relationship between regional port cluster development and environment, the relationship between the two is transformed from restrictive to promotive, and the contradiction is finally unified. On the basis of the impact of regional port cluster development on the environment not exceeding the environmental carrying capacity, the regional port cluster continues to develop rapidly, thus promoting the continuous growth of regional economy.

2.1.1 Ecological Economics Theory

Famous ecological economist Robert Costanza believes: "Ecological economics is a science that comprehensively studies the relationship between ecological systems and economic systems. These relationships are the root of many pressing issues faced by humanity today (such as sustainability, acid rain, global warming, species extinction, wealth distribution, etc.), and existing disciplines cannot adequately study these relationships between ecological systems and economic systems."

Ecological economics is a science that studies the laws of system movement in accordance with ecology, economy, and society. It is different from traditional economics and ecology, and is not a simple combination of economics and ecology. Ecology studies the interdependence between animals and plants in nature, economics mainly studies the interdependence between commodities, while ecological economics focuses on the study of the relationship between humans and nature. The theory of ecological economics believes that the essence of human economic activity is to transform and process materials and energy in the ecological system into various products that can meet human needs. These products, after being consumed through human production and life, eventually return to the natural ecological system in the form of waste. Human economic activity is just a process of material circulation, energy flow, and information transmission in the natural ecological system. It depends on the natural ecological system and at the same time acts against the natural ecological system. All economic activities and even human activities are based on the operation of the natural ecology, and the process of economic development cannot be separated from this ecological system foundation.

The role of the ecosystem can be summarized as providing resources and purifying environmental pollution. Without these two major functions of the ecosystem, economic and social development is out of the question. The relationship between ecology and economy is intricate and complex. They complement each other, blend with each other, and create conditions for each other. The economy draws from nature for development, and economic development can in turn regulate and coordinate natural forces. If people over-exploit resources and pollute the environment, it will inevitably cause damage to the natural ecological system, and even destroy the natural environment for human survival. The unity of contradictions between ecology and economy warns us that if humans follow the laws of ecological economics, protect and build a good ecological system, then economic development will have a guaranteed foundation. The basic contradiction of the ecological economic system is due to the increasing contradiction between the limited supply of resources in the natural ecological system and the unlimited demand of humans.

Based on the review of representative definitions of ecological economics, Pan Hong et al. (2010) believe that ecological economics is an economic science that studies and solves ecological economic problems, explores the operating laws of ecological economic systems, aims to complete the process of economic ecologization and ecological economization in the coupling process of ecological systems and economic systems, and ultimately achieves coordinated development of the two major systems in a mutually agreed direction.

This definition has the following four basic characteristics:

First, ecological economics is a social science, an economic science within social sciences. Although it is based on some natural laws, especially ecological laws, ecological economics explores these laws from an economic perspective. To put it further, under the premise of the action of ecological laws, ecological resources have a certain degree of scarcity (the other causes of scarcity of ecological resources mainly come from incorrect human intervention), and ecological economics is under the given ecological law conditions, explaining the thoughts and principles of the best allocation of scarce ecological resources.

Second, ecological economics is problem-oriented, that is, it starts with ecological economic problems. Ecological economics is not pure theoretical economics from theory to theory, but rises from practice to theory, and then guides practice with theory. It is both practical and theoretical applied theoretical economics.

Thirdly, ecological economics must summarize some ecological economic laws based on some core categories. If there are no rules to follow, then ecological economics will lose its scientific nature, and therefore will have no reason to exist.

Fourthly, the goal of ecological economics is to achieve the ecologicalization of the economy, the economization of ecology, and the coordinated development between the ecological system and the economic system.

The so-called ecologicalization of economy requires that any economic activity must follow both economic and ecological laws, establishing economic development on a basis that does not harm the environment, intended to achieve the process of transitioning from "environmentally destructive" to "environmentally friendly". In practice, the transition from a "black economy" and "white economy" to a "green economy" is the concrete process of the ecologicalization of the economy.

The so-called economization of ecology means that all items in nature cannot only be considered for their ecological value, but also their economic value. They cannot be treated as freely usable items, but as valuable ecological resources. The phrase "green water and green mountains" turning into "gold mountains and silver mountains" is a vivid description of the economization of ecology. In the context of the economization of ecology, protecting the ecology is protecting productivity.

2.1.2 Synergy Theory

Synergy theory was established by Haken. He pointed out that the "synergistic effect" of the interrelation between various subsystems within a system can also make the entire system move from disorder to order, which is when order parameters appear. The cooperation and competition between order parameters eventually lead to only a few order parameters dominating the system's further move towards synergy and order. Synergistic effects determine the characteristics and laws of system phase transitions, achieving system self-organization. Synergy theory uses a combination of dynamics and statistics to study open systems that exchange matter and energy with the external environment. The motion state of each subsystem in the system is determined by the independent motion of the subsystem and the synergistic motion caused by the direct association of the system. When the former dominates, the system tends to work in a disordered state. However, when the external "control variable" of the system reaches a certain limit, the energy of the subsystem's association is greater than the energy of the subsystem's independent motion, so the subsystem's independent motion is hindered. At this time, the subsystem's operation must comply with the coordinated motion formed by the association.

The entire Earth system or ecological economic system of humanity is a very complex system. In the current development, due to human influence, the entropy of this system is increasing disorderly. If no measures are taken or the current economic development method is not changed, this system will eventually move towards disorder and lead to extinction. Therefore, according to the evolution law of the system, we should use synergy theory to solve problems from the interrelation of various subsystems within the human ecological economic system, so that the entire ecological economic system can achieve sustainable development.

Synergy theory is based on control theory, information theory, system theory, and mutation theory, studying the mechanisms and laws of open systems forming ordered structures through the synergistic effects of internal subsystems. Synergy theory views all research objects as "systems composed of components, parts, or subsystems". These subsystems interact with each other through the exchange of matter, energy, or information. Through this interaction between subsystems, the entire system will form a holistic effect or a new type of structure.

Synergy theory believes that despite the different properties of various systems, there is a relationship of mutual influence and cooperation between each system in the entire environment. Any system is composed of several elements, but the system is not a simple addition of the constituent elements. Instead, it is realized through the organization and order of the elements interacting and connecting with each other. The overall function of the system is greater than the sum of the functions of each element, and new functions will not be produced in the isolated state of each element.

Synergy is a self-organizing ability inherent in any complex system and is the internal force that forms the orderly structure of the system. In complex systems, there is a nonlinear interaction between elements. When external control parameters reach a certain threshold, the elements interconnect and interrelate, replacing their relative independence and mutual competition to dominate, thereby demonstrating coordination and cooperation. The overall effect is enhanced, and the system moves from a state of disorder to a state of order, that is, "synergy leads to order". The orderliness of a system is formed by the synergistic action of the elements within the system. The synergistic action of the system is not completed in one or two times, but is a new synergistic action that is constantly carried out at new levels in motion.

Whether from the natural world or from the social field, harmony, synergy, and cooperation are necessary conditions for all aspects to develop and make progress. Synergistic cooperation, like contradiction and struggle, is the internal driving force for the world to exist and develop, which is the synergy of the development and change of things. Synergy theory reveals the relationship between the elements within and between systems, which has important practical significance for production and life.

2.1.3 *Stakeholder Theory*

The term "stakeholder" originated from the 16th-century Western bet on a certain activity, "stake". It was not until three centuries later that "stakeholder" developed into a theory, the "stakeholder theory". In 1963, scholars from Stanford University first clearly proposed this term to define the group of people closely related to the enterprise, that is, "the group without whose support the organization could not survive".

Stakeholder theory developed gradually in Western countries around the 1960s. Its influence rapidly expanded after the 1980s, beginning to affect the choice of corporate governance models in countries like the UK and the US, and promoting the transformation of corporate management methods. The emergence of stakeholder theory has a profound real-world background.

The emergence and development of stakeholder theory are inseparable from the real background of the enterprise after the 1960s. From a macroeconomic perspective, since the late 1960s, economies like the UK and the US, where companies adhere to "shareholder supremacy", have encountered unprecedented difficulties in the real economy. However, the economies of Germany, Japan, and many Southeast Asian countries, which more reflect the thought of "stakeholder theory", have risen rapidly.

After the 1980s, the logic of "shareholder supremacy" in traditional concepts was seriously challenged from both theoretical and practical aspects, and the arrangement of corporate ownership became a theoretical problem in front of economists and jurists. Now, people have increasingly clearly realized that a company is actually a "state-dependent" economic entity, a collection of social relations centered on ownership. The owners of the company's residual rights have been continuously expanding outward, from the shareholders of the past to other stakeholders, including managers, workers, customers, suppliers, banks, communities, etc.

Another more important reason that prompted the Western academic and business communities to start paying attention to stakeholder theory is that global companies began to generally encounter a series of real problems around the turn of the century, mainly including corporate ethical issues, corporate social responsibility issues, environmental management issues, etc. These issues are closely related to whether the company considers the interests of stakeholders when operating, and urgently require the business and academic communities to provide satisfactory answers.

This concept first made people realize that a company is not an isolated entity, but rather, there are many interest groups around it that relate to the company's survival and development. The classic work "Strategic Management: A Stakeholder Approach" by the famous American economist Freeman not only sparked academic discussions about stakeholders, but also initiated the application of stakeholder theory in practice. Freeman attempted to reveal the interactive relationship between stakeholders and corporate strategic management, and defined stakeholders as "any group or individual who can affect or is affected by the achievement of the organization's objectives". Later, he further defined stakeholders as "those who benefit or are harmed by the company's activities, and whose rights are respected or violated by the company's activities". The merit of this definition lies in its revelation of the interactive relationship between stakeholders and corporate organizations, and more importantly, it creates conditions for stakeholders to participate in corporate strategic management activities. The pioneering nature of Freeman's research lies mainly in his successful application of stakeholder theory analysis methods to corporate strategic management, and his programmatic and operational explanation of the application techniques and implementation mechanisms of this method. Since then, Freeman and his successors have continuously supplemented and perfected this theory, forming a relatively complete and feasible theoretical framework based on practical verification, and widely applying it to the practice of corporate strategic management, achieving good results and receiving widespread attention.

2.1.4 Sustainable Development Theory

In 1987, Mrs. Brundtland, Prime Minister of Norwayd, in her report "Our Common Future" to the United Nations World Commission on Environment and Development, which she chaired, defined sustainable development as "development that meets the needs of the present without compromising the ability of future generations to meet their own needs". This definition was widely accepted and reached consensus at the United Nations Conference on Environment and Development in 1992.

Some scholars in our country have supplemented this definition as follows: sustainable development is "development that continuously improves the quality of life and environmental carrying capacity of the population, meets the needs of the present generation without damaging the ability of future generations to meet their needs, and meets the needs of a region or a country without damaging the ability of people in other regions or countries to meet their needs".

Sustainable development is a development model or guiding ideology proposed by mankind to face the increasingly depleted resource problem and the increasingly tense environmental problem. Sustainable development is development that meets the needs of the present without compromising the ability of future generations to meet their needs. In other words, this kind of development cannot only pursue immediate and short-term benefits at the expense of the foundation for long-term development, it must balance long-term and short-term benefits, with development at its core.

The concept and implementation program of sustainable development, once proposed, was recognized by all sectors of the world, and became the rule of the "natural–social–economic" system operation of the century, being incorporated into various economic plans and development plans. On the one hand, it became the choice of national development strategic goals, on the other hand, it became the standard for diagnosing the healthy operation of the country.

Sustainable development must follow three basic principles: ecological sustainability (development must be consistent with basic ecological processes, biodiversity, and the maintenance of biological resources); social and cultural sustainability (improving people's control over their lives, maintaining and enhancing community individuality and cultural diversity, and achieving development in harmony with community culture and values); economic sustainability (effective management and use of resources, sustained economic growth, and leaving enough development space for future generations).

The important indicators of sustainable development are the sustainable use of resources and the improvement of the ecological environment. Sustainable development is the economic construction and development of various social undertakings under the conditions of strict control of population growth, improvement of population quality, sustainable use of resources, and protection of the ecological environment. Only by continuously improving and enhancing the ecological environment while developing the economy can it be considered sustainable development. At the same time, sustainable development requires the correct handling of the relationship between man and nature, fundamentally changing people's traditional unsustainable production methods, consumption methods, and thinking methods with new ideas, new perspectives, and new technologies of sustainable development, and establishing economic, social, resource, and environmental unified thinking and behavioral norms.

The concept of sustainable development was first formally discussed at the United Nations Human Environment Seminar held in Stockholm in 1972. This seminar jointly defined the rights enjoyed by mankind in creating a healthy and vibrant environment. Since then, countries have been committed to defining the meaning of sustainable development, and hundreds of definitions have been proposed, covering international, regional, local, and specific sector levels. Sustainable development is the result of mankind's reflection on the process of industrial civilization, a rational choice made by mankind to overcome a series of environmental, economic, and social problems, especially global environmental pollution and widespread ecological destruction, and their imbalanced relationships. "Economic development, social development, and environmental protection are interdependent and mutually reinforcing components of sustainable development."

The Communist Party of China and the Chinese government also pay great attention to this issue: The World Environment and Development Commission first expounded the concept of sustainable development in the "Our Common Future" report in 1987, which received widespread consensus from the international community. In 1991, China initiated the "Conference of Ministers of Environment and Development of Developing Countries" and issued the "Beijing Declaration". In June 1992, the Chinese government solemnly signed the Environment and Development Day at the World Summit in Rio de Janeiro. On March 25, 1994, the State Council of the People's Republic of China passed the "China 21st Century Agenda". To support the implementation of the "Agenda", the "China 21st Century Agenda Priority Project Plan" was also formulated. In 1995, The CPC Central Committee and The State Council of the People's Republic of China regard sustainable development as a basic national strategy, and call on the people of the whole country to actively participate in this great practice.

The definition of sustainable development contains two basic elements or two key components: "needs" and "limits" to needs. To meet needs, the first is to meet the basic needs of the poor. The limitation to needs mainly refers to the limitation that endangers the ability of future environmental needs, once this ability is broken, it will endanger the atmosphere, water bodies, soil, and organisms in the natural system that supports the life of the earth. The key factors determining the two basic elements are:

(1) Redistribution of income to ensure that natural resources are not exhausted for short-term survival needs;
(2) Reducing the vulnerability of mainly poor people to natural disasters and plummeting agricultural product prices;
(3) Universally providing basic conditions for sustainable survival, such as hygiene, education, water, and fresh air, protecting and meeting the basic needs of the most vulnerable people in society, and providing equal opportunities and freedom of choice for all people, especially the poor.

At the end of the 1960s, humans began to pay attention to environmental issues. On June 5, 1972, the United Nations convened the "Human Environment Conference", proposed the concept of "human environment", passed the Human Environment Declaration and established the Environmental Planning Agency.

Sustainable development is a new way of human survival. This way of life not only requires reflection in the environmental living areas mainly based on resource utilization and environmental protection, but also needs to be reflected in the economic and social life that serve as the source of development. Implementing a sustainable development strategy must adhere to some basic principles:

Firstly, the principle of fairness. Sustainable development emphasizes that development should pursue fairness in two aspects: one is the fairness of the current generation, that is, equality within the generation. Sustainable development needs to meet the basic needs of all people and give everyone the opportunity to fulfill their desire for a better life. The reality of today's world is that while some people are affluent, one-fifth of the world's population lives in poverty; developed countries, which make up 26% of the global population, consume 80% of the world's energy, steel, and paper. This world of wealth disparity and polarization cannot achieve sustainable development. Therefore, we need to give the world fair distribution and development rights, and consider poverty eradication as a particularly priority issue in the process of sustainable development. The second is intergenerational fairness, that is, equality between generations. We must recognize that the natural resources on which humans depend for survival are limited. The current generation must not, by its own development and needs, compromise the conditions that generations of mankind have met their needs, natural resources and the environment. We need to give every generation the right to fairly use natural resources.

Secondly, the principle of sustainability. The core idea of the sustainability principle is that human economic construction and social development cannot exceed the carrying capacity of natural resources and the environment. This means that sustainable development not only requires fairness between people, but also fairness between humans and nature. Resources and the environment are the basis for human survival and development. Without resources and the environment, there is no way to talk about human survival and development. Sustainable development advocates development based on the protection of the Earth's natural systems, so development must have certain limiting factors. The rate at which human development depletes natural resources should fully consider the criticality of resources and should not harm the natural systems that support Earth's life, such as the atmosphere, water, soil, and organisms. In other words, humans need to adjust their lifestyles and determine their consumption standards according to the principle of sustainability, rather than overproduction and overconsumption. Once development destroys the material basis for human survival, development itself will also decline.

Thirdly, the principle of commonality. Given the differences in history, culture, and development levels of countries around the world, the specific goals, policies, and implementation steps of sustainable development cannot be the same. However, as a global development goal, sustainable development embodies the principles of fairness and sustainability, which should be commonly adhered to. To achieve the overall goal of sustainable development, we must take global joint actions and recognize the integrity and interdependence of our home, the Earth. Fundamentally, implementing sustainable development is to promote harmony between humans and between humans and nature. If everyone can sincerely act according to the "principle of commonality", then there can be a mutually beneficial relationship between humans and between humans and nature, thereby achieving sustainable development.

The core theory of sustainable development is still in the process of exploration and formation. The currently emerging schools of thought can be roughly divided into the following categories:

(1) Theory of Sustainable Resource Utilization

The epistemological basis of the sustainable resource utilization theory school is that whether human society can sustainably develop depends on whether the natural resources on which human society depends for survival and development can be used forever. Based on this understanding, this school is committed to exploring theories and methods for sustainable use of natural resources.

(2) Externality Theory

The epistemological foundation of the externalities theory school is: it believes that the root cause of the worsening environment and the emergence of unsustainable development phenomena and trends in human society is that humans have always regarded nature (resources and environment) as "public goods" that can be enjoyed for free, not recognizing the economic value of natural resources, and excluding natural inputs from the economic accounting system in economic life. Based on this understanding, this school is committed to exploring the theory and method of incorporating natural resources into the economic accounting system from an economic perspective.

(3) Intergenerational Wealth Fair Distribution Theory

The epistemological foundation of the Intergenerational Wealth Fair Distribution Theory school is: it believes that the root cause of the emergence of unsustainable development phenomena and trends in human society is that contemporary people have excessively occupied and used the wealth that should belong to future generations, especially natural wealth. Based on this understanding, this school is committed to exploring the theory and method of fair distribution of wealth (including natural wealth) between generations.

(4) Three Production Theories

The epistemological foundation of the Three Production Theories school is: the material basis for the sustainable development of human society lies in whether the material flow in the world system composed of human society and the natural environment is smooth and forms a virtuous cycle. They divide the material movement of the world system composed of humans and nature into three major 'production" activities, namely human production, material production, and environmental production, and are committed to exploring the theory and method of harmonious operation between the three major production activities.

2.2 Definition of Regional Port Cluster and Environmental Coordinated Development

Regional port cluster and environmental coordinated development refers to the process of port construction, planning, and integration, which not only focuses on the growth of port economic benefits but also on the growth of environmental benefits, achieving the common development of port integration and environmental construction.

The optimization and integration activities of the port cluster may have an impact on the regional environment of the port cluster. These impacts have both positive and negative aspects. On the one hand, the optimization and integration of port resources can promote the intensive and economical use of port resources, practice the concept of low-carbon, environmentally friendly, and sustainable port production. At the same time, the optimization and integration of the port cluster also promote regional integrated development, strengthen the connection between regions, and are conducive to the joint governance and protection of the environment across regions. On the other hand, the process of port cluster optimization and integration may include a series of port construction activities, such as port relocation, expansion, layout structure adjustment, etc., these construction activities may have adverse effects on the surrounding atmospheric environment and water resources of the port.

2.2.1 Concept of Regional Port Cluster and Environmental Coordinated Development

Regional port cluster and environmental coordinated development refers to the virtuous cycle of harmonious relationship between the development of the regional port cluster and the environment, while improving the economic and ecological benefits of the development of the regional port cluster.

The coordinated development of the regional port cluster and the environment includes two levels of coordination: the first level refers to the coordinated development among the ports within the port cluster; the second level refers to the coordinated development of the port cluster as a whole with the environment. Its short-term goal is to achieve rapid development of the port cluster while the regional environment is well protected or continuously improved, and the development of the port cluster does not exceed the carrying capacity of the regional environment. Its ultimate goal is to achieve the sustainable development of the port cluster.

The coordinated development of regional port clusters and the environment not only emphasizes the development speed and scale of the port clusters, but also emphasizes that while the quantity indicators of port cluster development are growing, the quality indicators of port cluster development are improving, and the development of port clusters and the environment are efficiently mutually beneficial. The concept can be understood from the following aspects: the development level of the port cluster improves, the environment improves, at this time it can be considered that the regional port cluster and the environment are well-coordinated; the development level of the regional port cluster improves, the environment suffers a certain degree of damage, but this damage is within the capacity of the environment, at this time it can also be considered that the regional port cluster and the environment are coordinated; the development level of the port cluster improves, the impact of the development of the port cluster on the environment has exceeded the capacity of the environment, at this time it is considered that the regional port cluster and the environment are uncoordinated; the development of the port cluster stagnates, regardless of whether the environment is damaged, the regional port cluster and the environment are uncoordinated.

2.2.2 *The Connotation of Coordinated Development of Regional Port Clusters and the Environment*

The coordinated development of regional port clusters and the environment has the following connotations:

(1) The development of the port cluster is the core of the coordinated development of the regional port cluster and the environment

Isolating the relationship between the development of the port cluster and the environment, ignoring the protection of the environment, and unilaterally pursuing the rapid development of the port cluster is a one-sided and undesirable development view. However, in the system of coordinated development of regional port clusters and the environment, the port cluster is the main body of development, and the development of the port cluster is the premise of their coordinated development and plays a decisive role in achieving their coordinated development. Therefore, the development of the port cluster is the core of the coordinated development of the regional port cluster and the environment.

(2) The environment and the development of the port cluster restrict each other

The environment provides various production resources for the development of the port cluster. The increase or decrease in the quantity and quality of the production resources provided by the environment directly affects the scale and growth rate of the provision of production materials, and then affects the improvement of the development level of the port cluster. The natural resources provided by the environment are limited. The quantity, type, and quality of natural resources such as water, energy, and electricity in the environment cannot fully meet the development requirements of the port cluster, which will to some extent affect and restrict the development of the port cluster. During the development of the port cluster, a certain amount of waste is always discharged into the environment, and the environment has the function of diffusing, storing, and assimilating waste. Using this function can reduce the cost of artificial waste treatment. After the environment is polluted and damaged, it not only causes huge economic losses to society, but also the exhaustion of environmental resources limits the development of the economy, thus causing the development of the port cluster to stagnate.

(3) Accurately handle the relationship between port cluster development and the environment

The development of the port cluster is in a certain environmental system, and the huge pressure of port cluster development on the environment and port environmental issues have become the main difficulties and prominent contradictions in the global development of port clusters. Correctly handling the dialectical relationship between port cluster development and the environment has very important theoretical and practical significance in the coordinated development of regional port clusters and the environment. The dialectical relationship between the regional port cluster and the environment has the characteristics of spatiotemporal variability, therefore, the methods of dealing with the relationship between port cluster development and the environment should be studied according to different regions and different periods in practice.

2.2.3 *Characteristics of Coordinated Development of Regional Port Clusters and the Environment*

From the understanding of the concept and connotation of coordinated development of the regional port cluster and the environment, it can be seen that it has the following characteristics:

(1) Coordination. This coordination is reflected in the organic whole composed of certain quantities and structures between the development of the port cluster and various elements of the environment, which can harmonize and cooperate appropriately.
(2) Temporality and spatiality. In terms of time, under different levels of economic development, the urgency of the requirements for the development of the port cluster and the understanding of the impact of the environment on the quality of human life are different, and the coordination standards change with the economic development of a country. In terms of space, different countries and regions have different understandings of the coordinated development of regional port clusters and the environment.
(3) Controllability. The coordinated development movement of the regional port cluster and the environment is regular. Humans, by understanding the regularity of its movement, use scientific technology, adopt various economic measures and policies, laws and regulations, and other effective macro-control means to regulate and control its development and change process, making the coordinated movement between the regional port cluster and the environment develop towards the goals of human social development.
(4) Relative stability and absolute dynamism. From a cross-sectional perspective, the coordinated development of the regional port cluster and the environment is a state where the port cluster and the environment develop together to reach a coordinated state. It has relative stability, but from a longitudinal perspective, the port cluster subsystem in a coordinated state, driven by the continuous upgrading of human economic development needs, will continuously evolve to a higher level. Correspondingly, the environmental subsystem may be promoted by the port cluster subsystem to continuously enhance its carrying capacity, and the environment may further improve, thus continuously promoting the coordinated development to a higher level, showing dynamism. In this sense, it is more appropriate to say that coordinated development is a process of constantly evolving to a higher level rather than a state. Therefore, we can also say that the coordinated development of the port cluster and the environment is sustainable.

(5) Phased. Looking at the evolution process of the relationship between the development of the port cluster and the environment, it has gone through the original coordination phase, the uncoordinated phase, and is evolving towards the relatively coordinated phase and the coordinated development phase.

2.3 Mechanism of Coordinated Development of Regional Port Cluster and Environment

2.3.1 Dimensions of Coordinated Development of Ports and Environment

Policy environment. Ports are the strategic fulcrums and important hubs of China's "Belt and Road" initiative, and General Secretary Xi Jinping has always paid attention to and cared about port development. Since the 18th National Congress of the Communist Party of China, he has visited more than 10 domestic and foreign ports. In January 2019, during his inspection of Tianjin Port, he specifically pointed out: "We must aim far and strive to build a world-class smart port and green port to better serve the construction of the Belt and Road." In November 2019, the Ministry of Transport and the National Development and Reform Commission and other departments jointly issued the "Guidelines on Building World-Class Ports", which clarified measures to accelerate the construction of green ports, among which building a clean and low-carbon port energy system is one of the core tasks of port carbon reduction.

Economic Environment. Global economic integration means that the interests of developed countries and some developing countries are closely linked through shortened time and space. This interdependence is facilitated by various factors, including international trade, market integration, technological innovation, and a series of issues to be addressed. Due to the positive role of economic globalization, resources are optimally allocated worldwide, leading to rapid development in international trade. At the same time, the distribution and integration of global resources have promoted the comparison and development of competitiveness, creating a new model of the international economy. The development of transnational trade has driven the formation of international markets, and the continuous improvement of international division of labor and the optimization of global resource allocation have further improved production efficiency. In terms of the international economy, the global economy will remain in a weak growth mode for a long time, the overall economic recovery is still slow, the potential risks are significant, and the impact of the financial crisis shows a long-term trend. In this situation of weak global economic recovery, it is inevitable to bring about a new change to the global shipping industry. The depressed market has accelerated the major restructuring process of shipping companies, directly promoting the development of ports towards deep-water and hub ports. In terms of the domestic economy, the economy shows signs of stable growth, but with the continuous decline of traditional growth momentum and the pressure of global economic rebalancing, the problem of overcapacity in the manufacturing industry and the irrational economic structure will become more prominent. The economy needs a lasting internal driving force to maintain growth. Considering the position of ports under economic conditions and the attached industries, ports will still be the key development area. At the same time, combined with the mission of various countries in environmental protection and resource allocation, the regionalization of ports and coordinated environmental development will continue to advance.

Social Environment. On the one hand, with the continuous improvement of living standards, people's pursuit of material life gradually changes to the pursuit of a better life concept and lifestyle. The change in consumption concept prompts the essence of consumption content to change, especially with the change in consumption methods and payment methods, service consumption and experiential consumption become hotspots, and the added value of port services will become a new trend in port development. At the same time, under the promotion of the "domestic demand-based" national strategy, new demands will be generated for the port transportation system. The popularity of global environmental awareness makes consumers' green preferences increasingly high, they are more willing to pay for green additional services, which also promotes the coordinated development of port groups and the environment.

Technological Environment. To achieve the goal of building resource-saving and environmentally friendly ports, regional port groups should always adhere to the concept of green and low-carbon development, while continuously developing and applying green energy-saving technologies. As an important task to achieve a green ecological port group, the control of pollutants and the achievement of pollution emission standards have always been the focus of port environmental protection work. To reduce pollution emissions from ships docking at ports, shore power technology should be promoted.

2.3.2 *Internal Coordinated Development Mechanism of Port Environment*

Firstly, promoting the "Green+" intelligent construction of ports. The development of modern ports is mainly achieved through the integration of port business and innovative technology, which drives the transformation of port industrial structure, economic structure, and operational structure, and promotes the upgrade of the port ecological system. "Green+" intelligent ports refer to the application of intelligent port equipment driven by technology, the reconstruction of port production business, management models, and business models, thereby enhancing port value through resource integration. Port clusters need to plan ahead and layout in advance, utilizing modern technology and automated machinery, integrating new generation technologies such as big data, the Internet of Things, 5G, artificial intelligence, etc., into practical applications in the actual production business of Dalian Port, including but not limited to automated loading and unloading at the dock, equipment control through instructions, intelligent tallying, remote monitoring, etc., to improve port work efficiency. By using an open and shared digital platform, innovating new business models for "Green+" intelligent ports, improving port management, operations, systems, etc., establishing standard collaborative work mechanisms, improving operational efficiency, and creating a more intelligent operating environment.

Secondly, perfecting the "Green+" port distribution system. The distribution system is one of the core competencies of port development "Green+", by strengthening strategic layout and implementing corresponding measures through port connectivity and hinterland accessibility, reasonably planning and expanding the port hinterland, strengthening connectivity and accessibility with the economic hinterland, it is necessary to coordinate planning in transportation, logistics, etc., and improve corresponding infrastructure and tools. Reshape the logistics network "cargo-driven multimodal transport", merge goods to analyze the urgency of cargo transportation, determine the mode of transportation according to the urgency, and also transport some non-urgent goods in a cheaper, cleaner but slower way, to minimize the total operating cost and promote the coordinated development of regional port clusters and the environment.

Thirdly, accelerating the construction of the 'Green+" information chain of ports. Improve the construction of the "Green+" unified transportation information platform, promote the platformization of business, management and other elements, vigorously popularize the application of digital intelligent terminal equipment, and accelerate the standardization of port information collection. Using internet innovative thinking and blockchain technology to build an integrated network platform, transitioning from traditional information models to supply chain innovation models, promoting the digitalization of logistics information, and providing security for logistics transportation capabilities and information security. The information chain integrates and connects the closeness of information between each link, and synchronously shares the data of each link, forming a complex information network, developing into a central node that integrates and processes various economic, information, and services, quickly integrating the information of various parts of the logistics node, and achieving traceability, monitoring, collaborative operations, and management of the transportation process. It helps users understand and control the comprehensive logistics information of the port, assists in meeting the needs of port users, and comprehensively improves the efficiency of each operation link.

2.3.3 External Coordination and Cooperation Mechanism of Port Environment

Formulate a win–win cooperation and location-specific development strategy. The formulation of the port cluster optimization and integration strategy should be adapted to the national "Belt and Road" initiative and the economic "dual circulation". On the one hand, it encourages regional ports to establish a win–win cooperation pattern, enhance the service capacity of coastal ports for our inland areas, and international competitiveness. On the other hand, the formulation of the strategy should be adapted to the economic development status and geographical location characteristics of different regions, achieving division of labor and differentiated development of the port cluster. The development strategy of the port cluster should not only include the strategy for economic development but also the development strategy for the ecological environment protection of the port cluster. In the process of formulating the strategy, the final and phased goals of port cluster optimization and integration and environmental coordination should be clarified to ensure that economic growth is always adapted to ecological environment protection.

Build a data sharing and technological innovation information system. Information sharing plays an important role in port cluster optimization, integration, and cross-regional environmental governance. The shared data platform can link ports, other multimodal transport suppliers, goods supply places, demand places customers, shipping companies, and other supply chain activity-related parties together, promote the rational flow of logistics, information flow, and capital flow, improve the efficiency of supply chain operations, and enhance the competitiveness of the port cluster. At the same time, the shared data platform can provide support for the coordination evaluation of ports and the environment, record the production status of ports, resource usage status, and the impact of port activities on the environment.

2.4 Factors Influencing the Coordinated Development of Regional Port Clusters and the Environment

Ports, as important hubs of the transport network, play an increasingly important role in promoting regional economic development and global trade. However, with the continuous growth of global maritime volume, ports produce a large amount of pollutants such as sulfur oxides, nitrogen oxides, particulate matter, etc. during the production process, which not only damage the ecological environment but also have adverse effects on human health. Against this background, the concept of green ports was born.

The so-called green port refers to a port or dock that, in the process of production operation and providing port services, adheres to the concept of resource conservation and environmentally friendly development, actively fulfills social responsibilities, comprehensively adopts technologies and management measures conducive to resource and energy conservation, environmental and ecological protection, and climate change response, and meets the requirements of the corresponding green port level standards.

Green ports focus on environmental protection and achieve the maximization of port economic benefits on the basis of maintaining a good production and living environment. The development of green ports not only needs to meet the needs of environmental protection but also needs to improve its social and economic benefits. The economic and social benefits of the port cannot exceed the carrying capacity of the port's ecological environment, and a balance between the two needs to be found. In this sense, the green port is a developing concept.

With the coordinated development of regional port clusters and the environment, jointly building a green port cluster has become a consensus among ports in the region. The main influencing factors include the construction of green port cluster infrastructure, the construction of green port cluster logistics network, and the construction of green port cluster logistics network.

2.4.1 Construction of Green Port Cluster Infrastructure

Focusing on the construction of functional infrastructure, we aim to establish the cornerstone of green port development. To avoid dust pollution during operations, reduce diesel combustion particles and greenhouse gas emissions, and improve port air quality, we should vigorously promote projects such as "oil to electricity" and "oil to gas". At the same time, to maximize the recovery and reuse of ballast water and prevent the overflow of coal-containing wastewater into the sea, we can increase investment in new ballast water recovery devices. By transforming the sewage network and connecting the treated water source with the ballast water tank, ecological wetlands, and ecological lakes, we can form an intelligent circulation system for the ecological water system through the use of intelligent control systems.

Focusing on the construction of ecological infrastructure, we should prioritize the transformation of green port development. We need to address common issues in traditional ports such as dust from open-air stockyards and material transfer processes, and improve air quality monitoring in ports. We should introduce new dust suppression facilities, implement greening experiments, plant vegetation in artificial lakes, and add automatic air quality monitoring stations. By monitoring indicators such as nitrogen dioxide, sulfur dioxide, carbon monoxide, PM_{10}, PM2.5, we can scientifically reflect the atmospheric conditions of the port, accurately identify the sources of pollutants, and effectively prevent and control air pollution in the port.

Focusing on the construction of smart infrastructure, we aim to enhance the efficiency of green port development. We should accelerate the construction of port automation, port informatization, and port data construction, further tap into the value creation ability of port stockyards, and use big data analysis technology to reflect the visualized, intuitive and concrete port operation status, thereby improving decision-making efficiency.

2.4.2 Green Port Group Logistics Network Construction

The construction of a green port logistics network mainly includes three tasks.

Firstly, clarify the division of labor and positioning of ports in the logistics network, implement differentiated development strategies for ports in the region, thereby alleviating resource competition between ports in the same region, and promoting the rational allocation of regional resources and the common development of ports.

Secondly, improve the construction of the port and city layout network. Affected by the adjustment of port industrial structure and urbanization, the layout planning of ports and cities is constantly changing. Optimizing the layout planning of port cities can help reduce the adverse effects of port activities on cities, alleviate the competition for spatial resources between ports and cities, and achieve coordinated development of ports and cities.

Thirdly, strengthen the construction of multimodal logistics networks. On the one hand, compared with road transport, water-rail transport has the advantages of larger transport volume, lower transport cost, and less environmental pollution. Promoting the development of water-rail transport is of great significance to regional environmental protection. On the other hand, multimodal transport can effectively solve the "last mile" problem in the logistics network, enhance the connection between ports and ports, ports and the economic hinterland, promote the integration of port supply chains, and achieve regional coordinated development.

2.4.3 Green Port Group Energy-Saving and Low-Carbon Technology

China's ports are actively promoting the research and development and promotion of low-carbon technologies, including the use of shore power supply system technology for wheel berthing, LNG new energy power port equipment projects, bulk cargo terminal yard LED high pole light green energy-saving lighting projects, terminal lifting equipment energy feedback solutions, container iron-water intermodal demonstration projects, port energy online monitoring systems, and green buildings. Under the promotion of shore power technology, several ports in our country have actively invested in the research of green, low-carbon, and smart ports, forming a large number of leading green and low-carbon technologies such as ship shore power, port high-power LED lights, energy feedback, iron-water intermodal information platform, energy management, and green buildings, and have tried to industrialize them.

However, due to the lack of timely and effective science and technology policies as support, our country has not yet systematically carried out the construction of low-carbon technology innovation, so it cannot play the due normative and compulsory role for enterprises and the government, and to some extent indirectly affects the development process of low-carbon technology innovation. Therefore, our government should establish and improve the science and technology policy to promote low-carbon technology innovation as soon as possible.

Science and technology policy is the key and guarantee to promote the innovation of low-carbon technology in our country's green port group. The development of low-carbon technology innovation cannot be separated from the guidance and support of science and technology policy. Science and technology policy and low-carbon technology innovation provide guarantees and support for the development of a low-carbon economy, and the development of a low-carbon economy is based on the innovation of low-carbon technology and science and technology policy. In the face of opportunities and challenges brought about by competition in the development of a low-carbon economy, continuously improving our country's science and technology policy for low-carbon technology innovation will provide greater guarantees for our country to achieve the development of a low-carbon economy, create a "resource-saving and environmentally friendly" society, and thus enhance our country's overall competitiveness internationally.

2.5 Theories Related to the Calculation Method of Carbon Footprint of Regional Port Groups

The formation mechanism and investment optimization research of low-carbon ports involve the theory of the low-carbon development stage of our country's ports, the theory of port carbon footprint calculation, LMDI decomposition theory, Gamma distribution function, random optimization decision and other basic theories.

2.5.1 Theory of Low-Carbon Development Stage of Ports in Our Country

The low-carbon development of our country's ports has roughly gone through three historical stages according to the time dimension, namely the self-development stage (1987–1993), the exploration and practice stage (1994–2009), and the policy support stage (2010–present) (Nini 2015), as shown in Fig. 2.1. The criteria for stage division include the following three points: First, it refers to the change of carbon footprint indicators of our country's ports. Second, it refers to the historical changes of low-carbon construction policies in our country's port industry. Third, it refers to the development process of low-carbon port construction in our country from nothing to something, from unintentional to autonomous (Liu et al. 2017).

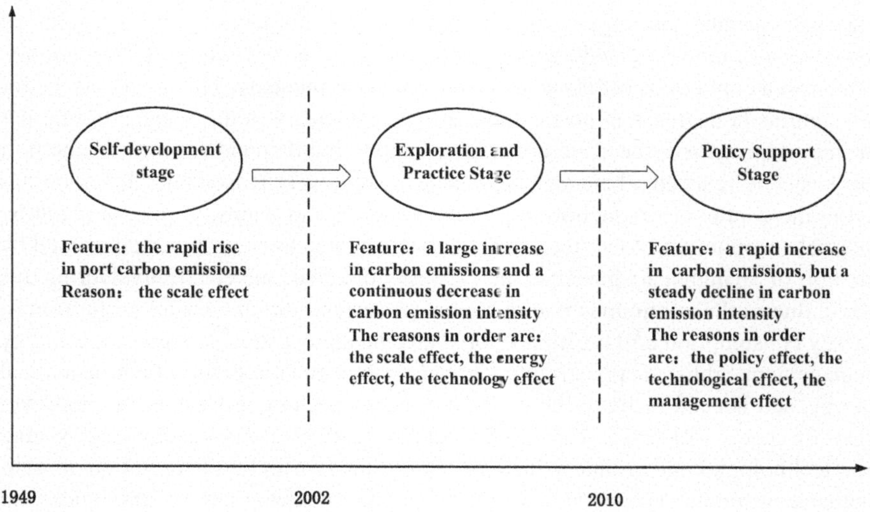

Fig. 2.1 Division of China's port low-carbon development stage

(1) Stage 1: Self-development stage (before 2002)

The division of this stage is mainly based on: First, the low-carbon concept and proactive practice of China's port industry have not yet formed. Second, there is a lack of special policy support for low-carbon port construction. In the self-development stage, China's ports do not yet have a concept of low-carbon development, let alone implement special low-carbon practice activities. The main feature of this stage is the rapid rise in port carbon emissions, and the main reason for this phenomenon is the scale effect of port operations. Because at this stage, with the implementation of China's reform and opening-up policy, the foreign economy is growing rapidly, and the scale of China's port cargo throughput business has greatly increased, resulting in a corresponding large increase in port carbon emissions. On the other hand, as the actual production scale of the port is getting closer to the actual demand capacity, it is gradually moving towards a scale economy state, the effect of the scale economy is gradually revealed, leading to a significant decrease in port carbon emission intensity. In summary, during this period, the expansion of China's port production scale has a very obvious effect on reducing its carbon emission intensity.

(2) Stage 2: Exploration and Practice Stage (2003–2009)

This stage is different from the self-development stage, the main difference is that the port actively explores port carbon emission reduction construction. Of course, this stage still lacks special policy support for low-carbon port construction. Since 2003, China's ports, especially coastal ports, have relied on their own strengths and characteristics to explore low-carbon construction, and have achieved significant results. During this stage, China's export economy continued to maintain a high growth rate, the large-scale expansion of port production, and a significant increase in throughput, leading to a continuous large increase in port carbon emissions and a continuous decrease in carbon emission intensity. The main reasons for the significant decrease in port carbon emission intensity in this stage are, in order of importance: First, the scale effect. The supply and demand capacity of the port has basically reached a balanced state, and the relatively reasonable allocation has led to the continuous reduction of port carbon emission intensity brought about by the scale economy. Second, the energy effect. The main energy types consumed by the Port of Shanghai are gasoline, diesel, heavy oil, coal, and electricity. During this stage, due to the continuous rise in energy prices and the increasing proportion of energy consumption costs, China's ports have taken measures to strengthen energy management, adjust energy structure, greatly reduce the direct use of petrochemical energy, and instead increase the use of electricity, thereby promoting the improvement of energy efficiency. Third, the technology effect. Ports adopt energy-saving new technologies and products, increase the elimination and transformation of high-energy-consuming equipment, actively adopt energy-saving new technologies, and the unit energy consumption of port production has undergone a gratifying change.

(3) Stage 3: Policy Support Stage (2010–present)

The most significant feature of this stage is the implementation of national low-carbon port support policies. In 2009, our government made a commitment at the Copenhagen Global Climate Change Conference to vigorously develop a green economy. In 2010, the "Eleventh Five-Year" plan for transportation for the first time proposed the construction of a low-carbon transportation system. In 2011, our country's "Twelfth Five-Year Plan" identified the transportation industry as one of the three major energy-saving and low-carbon emission industries; the "Twelfth Five-Year Development Plan for Transportation" emphasized the core position of ports in green and low-carbon transportation. In 2012, the Ministry of Transportation issued the "Twelfth Five-Year Plan for Controlling Greenhouse Gas Emissions in the Transportation Industry", clearly stating that the carbon dioxide emissions per unit of port production throughput will decrease by 10% compared to 2005, marking the official entry of our country's low-carbon port construction into the policy support stage. In 2012, the Ministry of Transportation issued a notice on organizing the pilot management of regional and thematic special funds for energy conservation and emission reduction in transportation, proposing Tianjin Port, Lianyungang Port, Qingdao Port, and Shekou Port as pilot units for "low-carbon port construction", marking a new stage in our country's low-carbon port construction. Against this backdrop, during this stage, our ports showed a rapid increase in total carbon footprint, but a steady decline in port carbon emission intensity. In recent years, the slowdown in our country's economic development has also slowed the growth of Shanghai Port, and port carbon emissions have correspondingly grown rapidly. The main reasons for the steady decline in port carbon emission intensity are: firstly, the policy effect. In 2012, the Ministry of Transportation issued the "Guiding Opinions on Port Energy Conservation and Emission Reduction Work", which clarified the measures and directions for low-carbon port development from the use of clean energy, experience and innovation in energy-saving and emission-reduction technologies, and energy-saving and emission-reduction management systems; it also released the "Green Low-Carbon Port Evaluation Indicator System", guiding the awarding and arrangement of port energy conservation and emission reduction related work and the application for special funds for port energy conservation and emission reduction. Ports are subject to increasingly strict supervision in terms of environmental protection, dust control, and safe production, and environmental protection investment continues to increase. Secondly, the technological effect. Coastal ports actively explore new models of "energy conservation and emission reduction" and "reducing consumption and increasing efficiency", constantly accelerating the independent research and development and transformation application of new energy-saving and environmentally friendly technologies and processes in port practice, and the use of oil-to-electricity, ship shore power technology, and LNG and wind energy and other clean energy sources, are vigorously promoted in low-carbon port construction. Thirdly, the management effect. Coastal ports improve the refinement of "low-carbon" management, strengthen the design and management of energy conservation and emission reduction in port planning and operation processes, strengthen port informatization construction, improve energy conservation and emission reduction performance assessment measures, increase the management supervision of energy conservation and emission reduction, and promote energy conservation and emission reduction and low-carbon popular science activities, so that the concept of low-carbon is integrated into port planning, construction, production, and operation processes.

2.5.2 *Port Carbon Footprint Process Calculation Theory*

Calculating the carbon footprint of ports is an important and effective way to evaluate greenhouse gas emissions from ports. The Port Carbon Footprint Guidance Document released by the International Association of Ports and Harbors (IAPH) provides global ports with guiding principles for carbon footprint accounting, analysis, and trend tracking for the first time.

(1) Carbon Footprint Measurement

From existing research and practical operations, the current port carbon footprint measurement methods mainly include two categories: one is absolute measurement, which includes the total port carbon footprint (generally converting the emissions of other greenhouse gases into carbon emissions), carbon dioxide, chemical oxygen demand, sulfur dioxide, etc. The other is relative measurement, such as the comprehensive indicators of port unit cargo throughput carbon footprint, greenhouse gas emissions per unit of freight volume (passenger), and greenhouse gas emissions per unit of cargo value, such as Villalba and Gemechu (2011) using the two indicators of greenhouse gas emissions per unit of freight volume and emissions per unit of cargo value to measure and evaluate the greenhouse gas emissions of the Port of Barcelona in 2008.

Details on the summary of port carbon footprint measurement methods can be seen in Table 2.1.

(2) Carbon Footprint Process Accounting Method

At present, the main method in port carbon footprint research is process analysis accounting, which obtains energy consumption and related energy carbon emission coefficient data through port production activity inventory analysis, and then calculates the port carbon footprint and unit cargo or container throughput carbon footprint within a certain period (Peng 2012).

The port carbon footprint process analysis accounting method is shown in Fig. 2.2. The specific explanation is as follows:

The first step is to determine the source of port carbon footprint energy consumption. Based on the definition of the scope of carbon footprint calculation, the work of accounting is carried out. The sources of port carbon footprint include the carbon footprint generated by energy consumption in the process of port production, loading and unloading, warehousing, and transportation, involving mainly diesel, gasoline, electricity, coal, natural gas, etc. According to the different types of energy, the

Table 2.1 Port carbon footprint measurement

Index type	Specific index representative
Absolute index	Total carbon footprint, carbon dioxide, chemical oxygen demand, sulfur dioxide, etc.
Relative index	Greenhouse gas emissions per unit of freight volume (passenger), and greenhouse gas emissions per unit of cargo value; Transport turnover of operating vessels CO_2; Port production unit throughput CO_2, etc.

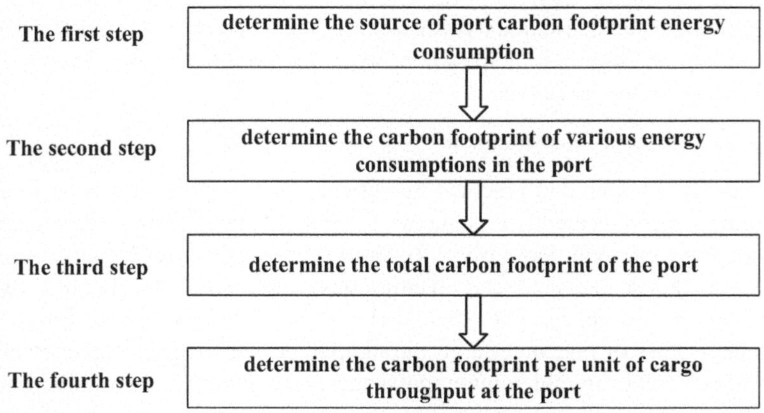

Fig. 2.2 Framework of port carbon footprint accounting process

carbon footprint generated by energy consumption is divided into direct carbon footprint and indirect carbon footprint. The direct carbon footprint is the amount of CO_2 produced by terminal energy consumption (such as diesel, fuel oil, gasoline, natural gas, etc.), and the indirect carbon footprint is the amount of CO_2 produced by electricity consumption. Therefore, determining the source of port carbon footprint energy consumption is to statistically summarize the consumption of various types of energy by the port according to various activities within a certain period. It should be pointed out that the carbon emissions of the port are closely related to the port operation process. Various types of port business and their business volume release carbon footprints of different scales and proportions through the energy consumed by key links and equipment in the operation process. In practice, port loading and unloading operations are the main link, and its bridge cranes, tire-type lifting and other loading and unloading machinery are the main sources of port carbon emissions. In addition, handling, stacking and other operations will also produce a lot of carbon emissions.

The second step is to determine the carbon footprint of various energy consumptions in the port. The carbon footprint of a certain energy consumption in the port equals the consumption of a certain energy in the port over a certain period multiplied by the corresponding carbon emission coefficient. For the accounting of direct energy carbon footprints such as diesel and fuel oil, their carbon emission coefficients can be obtained by querying the 2006 IPCC National Greenhouse Gas Inventory Guidelines established by the United Nations World Meteorological Organization and the Environmental Planning Agency. As for the accounting of carbon footprints generated by indirect energy such as electricity, since it is converted from coal, natural gas, nuclear energy, etc., the carbon emission coefficient cannot be obtained directly, and the baseline carbon emission factor of the regional power grid where the port is located needs to be used instead.

The third step is to determine the total carbon footprint of the port. By summing up the various energy consumption carbon footprints obtained in the second step, the total carbon footprint of the port within a certain period is obtained. Once the total carbon footprint of the port is determined, it can be used to understand the specific structure of the port's carbon footprint and the corresponding measures to be taken subsequently.

The fourth step is to determine the carbon footprint per unit of cargo throughput at the port. The carbon footprint per unit of cargo throughput at the port equals the total carbon footprint of the port divided by the corresponding cargo throughput or container throughput, which is used to measure the intensity of the port's carbon footprint emissions. In practice, some ports, in response to global climate change and to gain reputation and enhance corporate competitiveness in fulfilling social responsibilities, have adopted measures such as using cleaner energy, developing and applying energy-saving and emission-reducing technologies and equipment, strengthening management and improving the level of production organization, effectively reducing the CO_2 emission intensity of container terminals

2.5.3 Carbon Emission LMDI Decomposition Theory

Currently, there are mainly two methods for the decomposition analysis of carbon footprint driving factors: Structural Decomposition Analysis (SDA) and Index Decomposition Analysis (IDAP). Among them, Structural Decomposition Analysis is a relatively static analysis method based on input–output tables and their data. Index Decomposition Analysis was first proposed by Boyd et al. (1987), which is a more dynamic analysis method that expands the differential of each explanatory variable, with the reporting period or base period index value of other explanatory variables as weights. Index Decomposition Analysis is based on the Kaya identity, decomposing the target variable into the product of multiple factor variables. Index Decomposition Analysis can be further divided into methods based on Divisia, Laspeyres, etc., each of these models has its own characteristics and uses.

Scholars Ang and Liu (2001) further proposed the Logarithmic Mean Divisia Index Decomposition Method (LMDI) based on the Divisia Index Decomposition Analysis. Subsequently, Ang and his collaborators continuously improved the LMDI method. This method assumes that changes in energy consumption or carbon footprint can be decomposed into several interrelated influencing factors. By constructing an extended Kaya identity and making corresponding transformations, the contributions of each complexly related factor are separated, providing a basis for further research analysis and related policy decisions. The characteristic of LMDI factor decomposition analysis is that it can simultaneously analyze coexisting parallel and nested influencing factors, that is, it can analyze the influencing factors of carbon emissions from both horizontal and vertical perspectives: horizontally, it can decompose total energy consumption into energy consumption of economic production sectors, transportation, and residential consumption; vertically, it can analyze the impact on energy consumption from the dimensions of scale, structure, and technology.

By comparing the advantages and disadvantages of various forms of factor decomposition methods from theoretical foundations, adaptation range, application convenience, and result expression, it is believed that the LMDI method satisfies factor reversibility, can effectively eliminate residual items, and compared to other methods that still have residual items after decomposition or improper decomposition of residual items, this method has higher accuracy and can make the model more persuasive. Due to the advantages of the LMDI analysis method, such as complete decomposition without residual items, ease of application, and consistency of multiplication and addition decomposition, it has outstanding advantages among various factor decomposition methods and is therefore widely used in the analysis field of internal causes and action intensity of carbon footprint growth. For example, Ang (2007) and others used LMDI to decompose the total emissions of carbon dioxide in China and the world, showing that this method has good consistency and completeness. Ye and Lei (2009) used the LMDI decomposition method to decompose the influencing factors of the overall energy intensity of the industry into four aspects: energy substitution, industry adjustment, department adjustment, and energy utilization technology change.

Carbon emission LMDI decomposition method can be further divided into two types: LMDI I decomposition and LMDI II decomposition, and both have multiplication decomposition and addition decomposition modes, among which:

LMDI I multiplication decomposition mode:

$$\begin{aligned} D_{xk} &= \exp\left[\sum_i \frac{L(V_i^T, V_i^0)}{L(V^T, V^0)} \ln\left(\frac{x_{k,j}^T}{x_{k,j}^0}\right)\right] \\ &= \exp\left[\sum_i \frac{L(V_i^T, V_i^0)/(\ln V_i^T - \ln V_i^0)}{L(V^T, V^0)/(\ln V^T - \ln V^0)} \ln\left(\frac{x_{k,j}^T}{x_{k,j}^0}\right)\right] \end{aligned} \tag{2.1}$$

where, V is the carbon emission variable, which is affected by multiple factors x_i. The subscript i represents the category of carbon emission variables. T represents the period.

LMDI II addition decomposition mode:

$$\Delta V_{xk} = \sum_i L(V_i^T, V_i^0) \ln\left(\frac{x_{k,j}^T}{x_{k,j}^0}\right) = \sum_i \frac{V_i^T - V_i^0}{\ln V_i^T - \ln V_i^0} \ln\left(\frac{x_{k,i}^T}{x_{k,i}^0}\right) \tag{2.2}$$

where, the parameter meaning is the same as above.

LMDI II multiplication decomposition mode:

$$D_{xk} = \exp\left[\sum_i \frac{L(w_i^T, w_i^0)}{\sum_j L\left(w_j^T, w_j^0\right)} \ln\left(\frac{x_{ki}^T}{x_{ki}^0}\right)\right] \tag{2.3}$$

where, $w_i^T = V_i^T / V^T, w_i^0 = V_i^0 / V^0$.

LMDI II addition decomposition mode:

$$\Delta V_{xk} = \sum_i \frac{L(w_i^T, w_i^0)}{\sum_j L\left(w_j^T, w_j^0\right)} L(V^T, V^0) \ln\left(\frac{x_{ki}^T}{x_{ki}^C}\right) \tag{2.4}$$

where, the parameter meaning is the same as above. Because the results of the two decomposition methods are very close, but the calculation process of the LMDI II decomposition method is more complicated, so it is not widely used. The LMDI I decomposition method has become the most popular carbon emission driving factor decomposition method, and its addition decomposition method is easier to promote and apply, and can be used to establish an energy decomposition index system, provide data support for the formulation of energy-saving policies, evaluate the effect of energy-saving work, and is conducive to in-depth comparison of energy efficiency in different regions.

2.5.4 Gamma Distribution Function Theory

The Gamma distribution is a continuous probability function in statistics and is a very important distribution in probability statistics. The Gamma distribution assumes that the random variable The waiting time required for the nth event to occur has a density function:

$$f(x,\delta,\tau) = \frac{\delta^T}{\Gamma(\tau)} x^{\tau-1} e^{-\delta x}\ x > 0 \tag{2.5}$$

where, $\Gamma(\tau) = \int_0^\infty t^{\tau-1}e^{-t}dt\sqrt{a^2+b^2}$, the parameter τ is called the shape parameter, and δ is called the inverse scale parameter.

The characteristic function of the Gamma distribution is:

$$\psi(t) = \left(1 - \frac{it}{\delta}\right)^{-\tau} \tag{2.6}$$

The mean and variance of the Gamma distribution are respectively:

$$E(X) = \frac{\tau}{\delta} \tag{2.7}$$

$$Var(X) = \frac{\tau}{\delta^2} \tag{2.8}$$

The "exponential distribution" and "χ^2 chi-square distribution" are special cases of the Gamma distribution:

(1) When the shape parameter is $\tau = 1$, the Gamma distribution is an exponential distribution with parameter κ, $X \sim Exp(\kappa)$;
(2) When $\tau = n/2, \delta = 1/2$, the Gamma distribution is a χ^2 chi-square distribution with n degrees of freedom, $X \sim \chi^2$(n);

In addition, the Gamma distribution and the Poisson distribution are consistent in mathematical form, but the Poisson distribution is discrete and the Gamma distribution is continuous. It can be intuitively considered that the Gamma distribution is a continuous version of the Poisson distribution on the set of positive real numbers.

The probability density function and failure rate function of the Gamma distribution depend on the value of the shape parameter τ:

(1) When $\tau < 1$, $f(x,\delta,\tau)$ is a decreasing function;

(2) When $\tau = 1$, $f(x, \delta, \tau)$ is a decreasing function;
(3) When $\tau > 1$, $f(x, \delta, \tau)$ is a unimodal function.

The Gamma distribution is widely used in fitting non-negative data, including business decisions, insurance claims, traffic flow fitting, income distribution, image segmentation, continuous cumulative wear of mechanical equipment, medical accidents and other fields. It has been deeply practiced, and even highly valued and applied in the latest artificial intelligence and deep learning (Wang et al. 2020).

2.5.5 Stochastic Optimization Decision Theory

In reality, various random variables are often encountered in optimization decision problems. These random variables directly affect the reliability of the optimization results. Incorporating these uncertainties into the optimization decision model is referred to as a stochastic optimization decision model. Stochastic optimization decision problems are a type of optimization decision problem. Compared to deterministic optimization problems, they specifically involve optimization decision problems with random factors and require the use of tools such as probability statistics, stochastic processes, and stochastic analysis. These random factors include environmental random factors, uncertain factors of control variables, uncertain factors of decision target values, etc. (Calafiore et al. 2006).

For a given system $f(z)$, define the random variable ξ_j. Introduce a random variable ξ_j into the system objective function, and the expression of the system objective function changes to $f(z, \xi_j)$. The stochastic optimization decision model is then:

$$\min f(z, \zeta_j)\ z \in R$$
$$s.t. \begin{cases} g_i(z, \zeta_j) \le 0 \quad \forall i \\ \zeta_j \in \Omega \quad j \in \{1, 2, \ldots, l\} \end{cases} \tag{2.9}$$

In Eq. (2.9), ξ_j is the random variable of the given optimization model, Ω is the set of all random parameters, l is the total number of scenarios, R is the set of real numbers.

The first method to deal with random factors is the expected value method, which replaces the random factors with their expected values and transforms the problem into a deterministic problem. That is, the constraint condition containing the random variable $g_i(z, \xi_j) \le 0$ is transformed into the expectation of the constraint condition, as follows:

$$\min f(z, \zeta_j)\ z \in R$$
$$s.t. \begin{cases} E[g_i(z, \zeta_j)] \le 0 \quad \forall i \\ \zeta_j \in \Omega\ j \in \{1, 2, \ldots, l\} \end{cases} \tag{2.10}$$

The second method is to consider the optimization problem in a probabilistic sense. For example, considering the optimization problem under a confidence level, the problem is transformed into an optimization problem with probability constraints or chance constraints. That is, the optimal solution satisfies the constraint condition with a probability greater than a certain confidence level, as follows:

$$\begin{aligned} &\min\ f(z, \zeta_j)\ z \in R \\ &s.t. \begin{cases} \text{Prob}[g_i(z, \zeta_j) \le 0] \ge 1 - \lambda \quad \forall i \\ \zeta_j \in \Omega \quad j \in \{1, 2, \ldots, l\} \end{cases} \end{aligned} \tag{2.11}$$

where, $\text{Prob}[g_i(z, \zeta_j) \le 0]$ represents the probability that the constraint $g_i(z, \xi_j) \le 0$ holds, $1 - \lambda$ represents the confidence level.

The advantage of the second method over the expected value method is that it takes into account the impact of various risks, but the disadvantage is that it makes the problem more difficult to handle. Equations (2.9)–(2.11) represent the optimization model of random variables in the constraint conditions. For the optimization model of random variables in the objective function, and the optimization model of random variables in both the objective function and constraint conditions, their forms and solution methods are largely similar.

2.6 Port Group Environmental Carrying Capacity Based on System Dynamics

2.6.1 Theories Related to Port Environmental Carrying Capacity

"The Port Law of the People's Republic of China" defines a port as: an area composed of clearly defined waters and land, with functions such as ship entry and exit, berthing, passenger embarkation and disembarkation, cargo loading and unloading, transshipment, and storage. A green port is a port whose economic and social development does not exceed the carrying capacity of the natural system.

Ports are not only a specific economic concept, but also a specific geographical and regional concept. Any waters suitable for port construction are undoubtedly rivers, lakes, and seas with good water transport conditions. People take advantage of superior natural water transport conditions, choose deep water areas suitable for berthing various types of ships, plan and build docks, and gradually form busy port economic areas, driving the economic development of the entire city (Yu et al. 2007). Some ports have become regional, national, and international shipping centers. In this sense, the role of ports in regional and national economic development is irreplaceable by other industries. However, from the perspective of ecological environment protection, if the ecological environment protection of the port is not paid attention to, it will destroy the ecological environment of the region and endanger the human living environment.

In terms of port sustainable development research, some progress has been made, such as the concepts of "green port", "port competitiveness" and the proposal of port planning environmental assessment.

A "green port" is a sustainable development port that achieves a good balance between environmental impact and economic benefits.

"Port competitiveness" is the comparative ability of port enterprises in the market competition process, through the integration and optimization of their own elements and the interaction with the external environment, in terms of occupying the market, creating value and maintaining sustainable development relative to other ports (Qian 2007a, b).

Port planning environmental assessment refers to the analysis, prediction and evaluation of the environmental impact of port planning and its alternatives, proposing mitigation measures to mitigate, avoid or eliminate the adverse impact of port planning on the ecological environment, and applying the evaluation conclusions to the planning decision-making process (Rong et al. 2006a, b).

The above research has defined and discussed some aspects of port sustainable development (such as economic aspects, environmental aspects, etc.), but lacks a comprehensive definition of port environmental carrying capacity. The definition of port environmental carrying capacity is complex, because the port is a composite environment, including not only natural ecology, but also humanistic economy, and it is closely related to people's lives and inseparable from social development (He et al. 2007).

Port environmental carrying capacity is a recently emerging research field, and there is no consensus on its exact definition. When defining port environmental carrying capacity, various factors should be considered and it should be defined from the perspective of sustainable development. The port environment refers to the whole composed of various ecosystems composed of natural and other human factors, and indirectly, potentially, and long-term affects human survival and development. When defining port environmental carrying capacity, the following factors should be considered:

① The definition of port environmental carrying capacity should consider the maximum development capacity of port resources.

② The definition of port environmental carrying capacity should consider the maximum support capacity for social and economic development under the premise of rational use and optimal allocation of port resources.

③ The definition of port environmental carrying capacity should consider its ability to support the maximum scale of socio-economic development and a certain number of people with a certain standard of living.

Based on the above definition of carrying capacity, combined with the definition of ports in the "Port Law of the People's Republic of China", and integrating the existing research on sustainable development of ports, this study defines port environmental carrying capacity as: within a certain period and range, the potential ability of the port ecosystem to maintain its own health and stable development under normal conditions, and the ability to bear various human social, economic, and living activities. It can be seen as a representation of the suitability of the port environmental system structure and regional socio-economic activities.

The subject of port environmental carrying capacity is port resources, and the objects are population, ecological environment, and socio-economy. The port environmental carrying capacity treats the ecological environment as the carried body, considers it alongside the population and socio-economic systems, and highlights the distribution and coordination relationship of these objects to port resources.

The meaning of port environmental carrying capacity can be understood from the following aspects:

(1) Temporal evolution. The port environmental carrying capacity should reflect the support capacity of the port, the carrying subject, for the carried objects under different locations, times, living conditions, and levels of scientific and technological development. Due to the definition of carrying capacity being limited within a certain time and space, the temporal evolution must be considered when considering the connotation of port environmental carrying capacity. With the continuous changes in the port situation at different times, different models or evaluation methods are used, and the resulting port environmental carrying capacity is also different. Since ports cannot exist without socio-economics, they are influenced by various factors. When defining port carrying capacity, it must be discussed within a certain time frame to accurately describe the evaluation results. The carrying capacity of ports for population, ecological environment, and economy at different times is different, which also reflects the idea of sustainable use of port environmental carrying capacity and sustainable social development.

(2) Socio-economic connotation. When defining the general environmental carrying capacity, the main consideration is the internal connections of the ecosystem, which are mostly related to nature. Ports are products of human civilization development to a certain stage and are closely related to socio-economic development. Therefore, when defining, more consideration should be given from the "human-centered" perspective. When studying its carrying capacity, the focus should be on the connection between the port and economic development, allowing the port to better serve economic development.

    The socio-economic connotation of port environmental carrying capacity is mainly reflected in the technical ability of humans to develop port resources, the level of transportation in its hinterland, the level of industrial development, the economic level of the hinterland, and the supply capacity of resources and energy such as water and electricity in the hinterland. It is possible to improve the port environmental carrying capacity by adjusting the industrial structure and improving the technical level without increasing the consumption of natural resources.

(3) Connotation of sustainable development. Sustainable development is China's environmental protection strategy. The development and utilization of port resources should be sustainable and should not allow the load of the current port environment to exceed its carrying capacity, otherwise, such development is unsustainable. Therefore, the definition of regional port resource carrying capacity should reflect the ability of regional port resources to continuously supply the social system.

In addition, the sustainable connotation of port environmental carrying capacity should also be reflected in the continuous enhancement of port resource carrying capacity, which should be manifested as a growth in carrying capacity driven by technological progress.

The port environmental carrying capacity has the following characteristics:

(1) Temporality and Spatiality. The port environment system changes over time, and correspondingly, its carrying capacity also changes. Similarly, the differences in ecological and social environments within different geographical ranges will affect the size of the corresponding environmental carrying capacity. Therefore, the definition of environmental carrying capacity should be limited to a certain time and spatial range. A too large span of time and space will cause deviations in the calculation of port environmental carrying capacity, which will have a negative impact on the correct evaluation of port environmental carrying capacity and the formulation of port development planning (Che 2012).
(2) Objectivity and Subjectivity. The objectivity of port environmental carrying capacity is mainly manifested in the fact that within a certain time and spatial range, the port's environmental carrying capacity objectively exists and can be calculated through models and algorithms. It is a manifestation of the suitability between the environmental system structure and the socio-economic system. The subjectivity of port environmental carrying capacity is manifested in that when people use different standards, models, and algorithms, the actual or relative values of the calculated port environmental carrying capacity are not exactly the same, but they all characterize the port's environmental carrying capacity, which varies according to the methods subjectively adopted by people.
(3) Socio-economic nature of port environmental carrying capacity. Previous studies on environmental carrying capacity have focused more on the consideration of ecosystems, while this book studies the port environmental carrying capacity. Ports are the product of human society's development to a certain stage, are service-oriented enterprises centered around human activities, and are inseparable from socio-economic activities. Therefore, the study of port environmental carrying capacity should involve its association with socio-economics. This association is mainly reflected in the economic and technological capabilities of humans to develop port resources, the level of water and electricity resources used by various sectors of society, the optimization of resource allocation by society, etc. The port environmental carrying capacity can be improved by adjusting the industrial structure and developing economic and technological levels without increasing the amount of natural resources.

(4) Sustainability of port environmental carrying capacity. Currently, China's development policy for ports requires that ports should sustainably develop port area resources and should not operate beyond their capacity within the range that the port environment can support and accommodate. The continuous improvement of the port's ecological environment and the innovation of production facilities and technologies should also be sustainable, which is beneficial to further strengthen the port's environmental carrying capacity.

2.6.2 System Dynamics Theory

System dynamics is an important branch of economic mathematics, first created by Professor Jay W. Forrester of the Massachusetts Institute of Technology. Initially introduced into the industrial field, the use of system dynamics has gradually expanded, especially for studying macro complex system problems, such as the rise and fall of cities, the interrelationships between people, economy, society, natural resources, and ecological environment. System dynamics has gradually developed into a relatively mature discipline.

System dynamics is based on systems theory and draws on the essence of control theory, information feedback theory, nonlinear theory, organizational theory, large system theory, and decision theory. System dynamics believes that system behavior is mainly determined by its internal structure. Once the internal structure and trends are mastered, the system's behavior pattern can be predicted. System dynamics emphasizes starting from the microstructure inside the system, fully considering the relationships between various factors inside the system and between the system and the external environment. On the premise of grasping the internal mechanism, basic structure, and variable relationships of the system, it analyzes the characteristics and dynamic behavior of the system. The core of the system dynamics model is a set of first-order differential equations with time delay, which is convenient for studying nonlinear and time-varying problems (Fig. 2.3).

Diagram System dynamics modeling utilizes system flow diagrams, which are composed of three elements: state variables, rate variables, and information. State

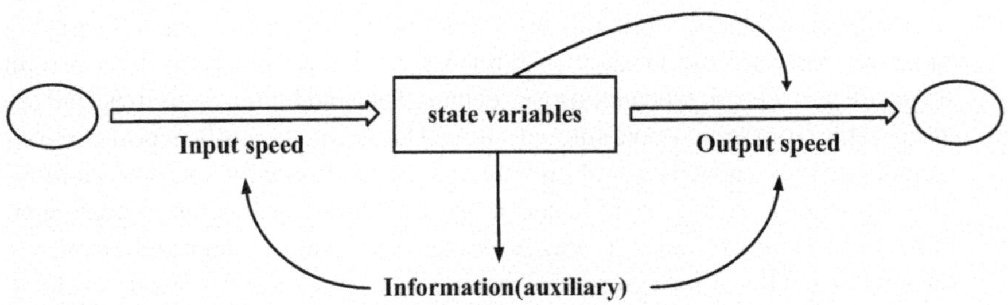

Fig. 2.3 Basic system structure

variables reflect the accumulation of variables over time, determining the characteristics and behavior of the system. Rate variables reflect the input or output speed of accumulated variables, determining the speed of state variable changes. System flow diagrams can clearly reflect the internal cause-and-effect feedback relationships within the system, with the relationships between each variable quantified through variable equations.

The characteristics of system dynamics are as follows:

(1) System dynamics can conduct comprehensive research on complex large systems at both macro and micro levels.
(2) The main research objects of system dynamics are open systems with self-organizing and dissipative structural properties.
(3) System dynamics is a method of analyzing and solving problems that combines qualitative and quantitative aspects, emphasizing system analysis, system thinking, synthesis, and inference. It tries to use "whitening" technology to relatively "improve" poor structures, and its model simulation belongs to structure–function simulation.
(4) The models of system dynamics are standardized, with variables classified according to the basic structure of the system, facilitating clear communication of ideas and handling of complex problems by users.

The process of system dynamics modeling can generally be divided into five steps: system analysis, structural analysis, establishment of a standard model, model testing and evaluation, and model simulation and policy analysis.

(1) System Analysis

The main task of system analysis is to analyze actual problems and determine system boundaries. It involves a thorough investigation and study of the actual situation of related systems, determining research problems and modeling objectives, defining system boundaries, identifying main variables, and understanding the behavior and trends of these main variables.

(2) Structural Analysis

The purpose of structural analysis is to analyze the feedback mechanism of the system and dissect the hierarchical structure of the system. It involves determining the overall and local mechanisms and causal relationships of the system, dividing the system into sub-blocks or subsystems according to the principle of system decomposition, defining the variables within the system and determining the relationships between them, drawing the system's cause-and-effect feedback relationship diagram, and determining the polarity and main loop of each loop.

(3) Establishment of a Standard Model

Based on the cause-and-effect feedback relationship diagram, a system flow diagram is drawn to quantify the system structure. The system's state variables, rate variables, auxiliary variables, and constants are determined, the relationships between variables are quantified, standard variable equations are established, and table functions are assigned values.

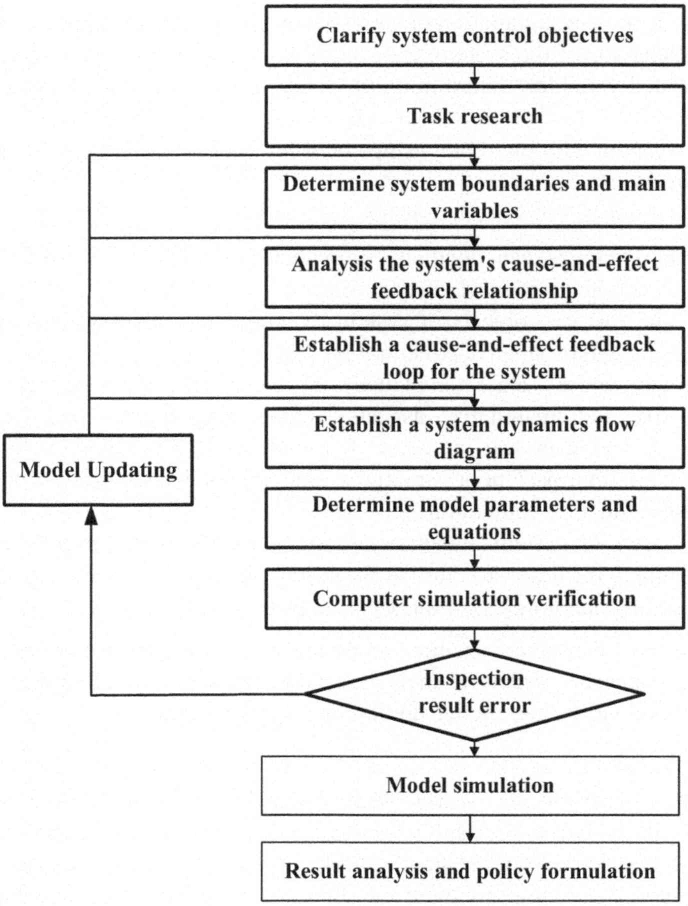

Fig. 2.4 The modeling process of system dynamics

(4) Model Testing and Revision

The system dynamics model is run using software to check the validity and error of the results. If the model's results differ significantly from reality, one should return to the previous steps to check and modify the problem, then simulate and test again. This process is repeated, continuously correcting and improving until the model's accuracy meets the requirements.

(5) Model Simulation and Policy Analysis

The established system dynamics model is used for simulation, seeking feasible countermeasures for system problems, establishing simulation test plans and running them one by one, comparing and analyzing to select the best decisions that can effectively solve system problems (Fig. 2.4).

2.7 Comprehensive Evaluation of the Coordinated Development of Regional Port Groups and the Environment

2.7.1 Selection of Evaluation Indicators for the Coordinated Development of Regional Port Groups and the Environment

Analyzing the indicator system of traditional construction project environmental impact assessment, according to the characteristics of port master planning and the status and role of planning environmental impact assessment in China's environmental impact assessment system, the evaluation indicators of port master planning environmental impact assessment include natural environment indicators (water environment, atmospheric environment, sound environment and other 5 environmental elements), resource indicators (water resources, shoreline resources and land resources and other environmental elements), and social environment indicators (transportation, economic development, infrastructure and other environmental elements). Based on the above analysis, resource and environmental evaluation indicators are preliminarily screened.

Due to the macro-level position of regional port cluster planning above construction projects, which has a certain dynamic development, the information it can provide is also macro. Therefore, the technical methods of planning environmental impact assessment should meet the uncertainty and complexity of planning. The technical methods currently used in environmental impact assessment can be roughly divided into two types, one is adopted in the environmental impact assessment of construction projects, such as: various methods of identifying impacts (inventory, matrix, network analysis), describing the basic status quo, environmental impact prediction models, etc.; the other is used in economic sectors, planning research, which can be used for planning environmental impact assessment methods, such as: various forms of scenario and simulation analysis, regional prediction, input–output method, geographic information system, investment-benefit analysis, environmental carrying capacity analysis, etc. This chapter introduces individual evaluation methods for the above two types of technical methods.

(1) Project EIA evaluation method. Although the planning environmental impact assessment differs from the project environmental impact assessment in terms of evaluation objectives, methods, and depth of accuracy, they have certain similarities in procedures and basic ideas. Therefore, planning environmental impact assessment can learn from many technical methods in traditional project EIA, such as environmental mathematical model method, analogy analysis method, environmental impact inventory, environmental impact matrix, etc.
(2) Foreign strategic environmental impact assessment methods. Many foreign countries have accumulated a lot of practical experience in strategic environmental impact assessment and have formulated laws in this regard. Planning

environmental impact assessment is a type of strategic environmental impact assessment, so the method of strategic environmental impact assessment can also be used in the overall planning environmental impact assessment of ports, such as simulation analysis, regional prediction, scenario analysis, etc.

(3) Regional environmental impact assessment method. Regional environmental impact assessment is based on regional development planning, and port master planning is also concentrated in a certain area, so the port master planning environmental impact assessment has commonality with regional environmental impact, so the evaluation process can use more mature methods in regional environmental impact assessment, such as geographic information system, remote sensing, landscape simulation, graphic overlay, etc.
(4) DPSIR model evaluation method. This method is a widely used evaluation indicator system conceptual model in the environmental system, which divides the evaluation indicators characterizing a natural system into five types: Driving forces, pressure, state,impact, and responses, each type is divided into several indicators.

In the specific selection of regional port clusters and environmental coordination development indicators, the focus of the evaluation methods also varies, and should be comprehensively analyzed and investigated, while drawing on domestic and foreign port environmental impact assessment research, and the setting of indicators in actual work. First, select evaluation information from the original data, then determine the evaluation indicators through theoretical analysis, expert consultation, and public participation, and supplement and adjust according to the actual situation in the progress of port environmental impact assessment work, and finally improve into a formal port environmental impact assessment indicator system.

2.7.2 Principles for Constructing Evaluation Indicators for Regional Port Clusters and Environmental Coordination

The construction of evaluation indicators for regional port clusters and environmental coordination should pay attention to the environmental impact brought by planning on the region and resource sustainable development, as well as the interrelationships within the sustainable development system. Whether the indicator system is scientifically, reasonably, and systematically established directly affects the quality and effect of the indicator evaluation. Therefore, when selecting and establishing the indicator system, it is necessary to consider the problem as comprehensively and systematically as possible. The construction of evaluation indicators for regional port clusters and environmental coordination should follow the following principles:

(1) Principle of Scientificity

All scientific research requires scientificity as a basic requirement, and scientificity is also an important principle for establishing all indicator systems. The construction of indicators should reflect scientificity, the establishment of indicators should be reasonable, the concepts should be clear, and the definitions should be clear, that is, they can reflect the actuality, essence, and laws of the project, and are convenient for data collection and collection. On the basis of scientificity and rationality, it is necessary to accurately reflect the connotation and requirements of planning EIA, which is conducive to making the information fed back by the indicators objectively and truly reflect the development and changes of the system, so as to facilitate people's adjustment and control of strategic planning.

(2) Targeted and Comprehensive Systematics

According to the connotation of environmental impact economic evaluation, the establishment of the indicator system should fully consider the environmental losses and environmental economic benefits obtained by the port construction project. The established indicator system should be a complete, systematic, and comprehensive evaluation system, with a complete hierarchical structure and strong overall evaluation capabilities. Evaluation indicators should be closely linked with environmental factors to achieve quantitative standards. At the same time, the selection of indicators should also adapt to all-round needs, ensuring the pertinence and comprehensiveness of the planning environmental assessment indicator system.

(3) Principle of Hierarchy

The environmental coordination evaluation indicator involves the population, resources, and environment as the research object of the system, which has a relatively complex hierarchical structure, so the setting of indicators for planning environmental impact evaluation should also meet the requirements of hierarchy. The principle of hierarchy requires that environmental coordination evaluation indicators should have a clear hierarchical structure, which is conducive to reflecting the environmental impact of planning at different levels.

(4) Principle of Operability

The purpose of the economic analysis of the environmental impact of port construction projects is to serve the government's macro decision-making and project optimization, so the established indicators should have strong operability and implementation. The current statistical system in our country is still imperfect, and the data statistics at the grassroots level are not comprehensive and often do not conduct relevant statistics, which increases the difficulty of scientific research. Therefore, in the process of constructing the indicator system for port planning environmental impact evaluation, it should strictly follow the principle of operability and establish indicators from the perspective of feasibility. Improving the operability of the planning environmental assessment indicator system is also conducive to reducing work time and improving work efficiency.

(5) Principle of Combining Qualitative and Quantitative

Quantitative indicators are convenient for grading and comparison of research objects, but their indicators cannot significantly express in terms of comprehensiveness and correlation. Therefore, in order to fully guarantee the implementation of the evaluation, some qualitative indicators should also be appropriately used for comprehensive evaluation, so as to meet the basic requirements of combining qualitative and quantitative aspects.

(6) Principle of Independence and Comparability

There may be certain connections between the layers of indicators and between the indicators themselves, but they should be classified according to the results of environmental impact analysis to avoid overlap between indicators due to measurements from different perspectives. That is, a category of indicators represents a substantive content and has relative independence. At the same time, the evaluation indicator system considers the comparability of projects. For the same type of port projects, detailed comparisons and analyses can be made, and for different types of port projects, macro comparisons and analyses can be made at the same level.

2.7.3 Factors Involved in the Evaluation Indicator System of Regional Port Clusters and Environmental Coordination

The construction of the environmental coordination evaluation indicator system involves the ecological environment quality, resource and energy utilization, and socio-economic development of regional port clusters. This chapter will expand on the factors involved in these three benchmark layers.

(1) Ecological Environment Quality

Port planning includes the construction of port terminals, the development of portside industries, and other aspects of construction and development. The impact of planning on the environment is mainly reflected in five aspects: water, atmosphere, sound, solid waste, and ecology.

① Water Environment Quality

According to the relevant requirements in the "Technical Specifications for Environmental Impact Assessment of Port Construction Projects" and the analysis of the impact of port construction in our country on water environment quality, the main impacts of port shoreline resource development on the water environment are: the release of nutrients from bottom mud materials caused by water dredging projects;

oily wastewater; runoff rainwater, washing water and leakage containing coal and mineral wastewater from dry bulk cargo yards; box washing wastewater; domestic sewage; the impact of the development area on the surrounding water dynamic conditions.

② Atmospheric Environment Quality

The atmospheric environment quality of port planning environmental assessment mainly includes controlling air pollutant emissions and protecting regional air environment quality. The atmospheric environment quality selects the total annual emission of pollutants per ten thousand tons of throughput as the driving force indicator; the pressure indicator is mainly the annual emission of air pollutants; the daily average concentration of regional air pollutants, the impact range of air pollutants, the range of regional air quality standards, and the proportion of the area exceeding the standard in the regional area are selected as the main status indicators of this evaluation indicator system; the response indicator of atmospheric environment quality selects the compliance emission rate of major air pollutants.

③ Sound Environment Quality Indicators

The sound environment quality will effectively control the regional environmental noise level and improve the sound environment quality as environmental protection goals. In the selection of sound environment quality indicators, no driving force indicators were chosen, the main reason being that it is difficult to express the noise pressure on the evaluation area in a quantitative form. The status indicators mainly include the day and night noise values at the port boundary, the day and night noise values of the port road, the range of sound environment standards in the development area, and the proportion of the area exceeding the noise standard in the regional area. The response indicators mainly include the compliance rate of port road noise and the compliance rate of noise in the evaluation area.

④ Solid Waste

In the environmental impact assessment of port planning, the environmental impact of solid waste refers to the impact of the garbage generated by the production of the port, ship production, and daily life in the evaluation area on the regional ecological environment. The environmental impact of hazardous waste in port planning should be given special attention. The environmental goal of solid waste management aims to reduce the generation rate of solid waste as much as possible, improve the efficiency of solid waste treatment, and achieve resource utilization and reduction of solid waste. The driving force index selects the amount of solid waste generated per ten thousand tons of throughput; the pressure index selects the annual emission of solid waste, per capita solid waste generation, and annual generation of hazardous solid waste; the impact index selects the rate of solid waste treatment and disposal, and the rate of harmless treatment and disposal of hazardous waste; the response index selects the rate of waste sorting and collection and resource utilization, and the comprehensive utilization rate of solid waste.

⑤ Ecological Environment Quality

The goal of ecological environment quality protection should comprehensively reflect the ecological environment characteristics of the port area ecosystem. The proximity of the port area to sensitive targets is selected as the driving force index; the ratio of biodiversity index before and after planning is selected as the pressure index, and the ratio of vegetation coverage before and after planning is the state index; the area of nature reserves and its proportion of the total area of the region is selected as the impact index; the response index selects the greening rate of the port area.

(2) Resource and Energy Use

China's policies on resource utilization require port planning to pay attention to resource utilization. The level of land, shoreline, water resource development and utilization, energy consumption level, etc. are included in the evaluation system. These indicators are related to the current level of resource utilization in China's industry and future development policies.

① Land Resources

Land is the basis for human construction activities and life, and is a very precious natural resource. However, land resources are not infinitely available. Under the multiple effects of human activities and various natural factors, they will continue to degrade and even be lost. The impact of port planning on land resources is mainly reflected in the occupation of land and reclamation projects, and the destruction of soil and vegetation. The driving force index of land resources selects the amount of land occupied by the development area and the amount of land occupied in ecologically sensitive areas as evaluation indicators, selects the area of available reserve land in the evaluation area as the state index, and selects the ratio of reclaimed land area to the area of land occupied by development and the rate of land degradation treatment as response indicators.

② Water Resources

Port production is mainly the process of cargo loading and unloading in the port area and ships. The supply and demand of water resources is a prominent environmental issue in port planning. The daily water consumption in the evaluation area is selected as the driving force index for water resource utilization. To reflect the water supply situation in the development area, the per capita water resource in the area is selected as the state index; the water recycling rate in the port area and adjacent industrial areas is selected as the response index. Port planning should consider coordinating reasonable water resource allocation with local departments, and on the other hand, through comprehensive utilization of seawater, recycling and other measures to alleviate the pressure of port development on urban water resource utilization, and in combination with regional water resource conditions, plan the industrial structure reasonably to achieve water saving, scientific and efficient water use.

③ Shoreline Resources

The issue of shoreline resources is a key focus in the process of port planning and development. Whether shoreline resources can be sustainably utilized will profoundly impact the sustainable development of port construction. In the selection of driving force indicators for the sustainable use of shoreline resources, the proportion of developed port shoreline resources to natural shorelines, the length of developed shoreline resources to the original other functional shorelines, and the proportion of developed deep-water shorelines to the total length of deep-water shorelines are chosen as evaluation indicators. From a sustainability perspective, suitable port shoreline resources should be reasonably reserved as strategic resource reserves for future port development. Therefore, the reserved shoreline length is chosen as the status indicator for sustainable development of port shoreline resources.

(3) Socio-economic Development

The development of ports has its unique development model and industrial structure, and relative indicators are generally chosen for evaluation. For example, on the economic development level, the industrial economic density is chosen as the status indicator for port development, and the average annual growth rate of total port output value is chosen as the response indicator. On the social development level, the proportion of environmental protection investment in fixed asset investment, the contribution to regional industrial structure adjustment, and the impact on fishery production are chosen as response indicators for evaluation. At the same time, the management requirements of rapid planning, such as environmental management requirements for port planning implementation and resident environmental satisfaction, etc. To achieve sustained, rapid, coordinated, and healthy development of the national economy, it is necessary to innovate development and management models, and environmental input and management level is an important content. The establishment of an indicator system can reveal regional environmental background characteristics, reflect port environmental load, resource utilization, and planning implementation management requirements, and is one of the important contents of planning evaluation. Through the establishment and analysis of specific related indicators (including quantitative and non-quantitative), and the accessibility analysis of these indicators, the planning evaluation work will be targeted and effective, and it is also conducive to the implementation of environmental protection policies and specific technical measures.

The rationality and completeness of the evaluation indicator system are key to the strategic environmental impact assessment of port shoreline resource development. Establishing a comprehensive strategic environmental impact assessment indicator system based on the actual situation of port shoreline resources in various places will play a positive and crucial role in reasonably evaluating the environmental impact of port shoreline resource development and environmental protection.

2.8 Theories Related to Green Technology of Port Groups

2.8.1 Overview of Green Technology of Port Groups

Green technology innovation, also known as ecological technology innovation, is a type of technology innovation, generally referred to as green technology innovation aimed at protecting the environment. Green technology innovation is the only way for sustainable development of enterprises. Increasing the intensity of green technology innovation, increasing technology innovation investment, and technically transforming old equipment, high-pollution, high-emission process systems will provide new economic growth points for enterprises, while also taking on the due responsibility for the coexistence of humans and nature. Green technology and low-carbon economy have become the trend, and port development will consider energy conservation and environmental protection more. Green technology innovation aimed at energy conservation, environmental protection, and low-carbon development has been accepted by more and more people and is the inevitable strategic direction for China's future port development. Emphasizing the construction of green ports will become a trend, and this article introduces four types of green technologies for port groups.

(1) High-voltage Shore Power

The implementation of high-voltage shore power helps to improve the air environment around the port, reduce water pollution, and establish an environmentally friendly corporate image. It can lower the electricity costs during berthing and the maintenance costs of the ship's own power generation facilities. It optimizes the energy structure, reduces the pollution to the environment by auxiliary power generation of berthed ships, ensures high utilization of the high-voltage ship shore power system, and explores a mature business cooperation model for port-ship shore power projects. The goal is to achieve full coverage of high-voltage shore power construction for container terminal ships. This mainly includes: modification of the terminal bridge, installation of shore power box transformers, laying of high-voltage cables, reasonable distribution of shore power junction boxes, meeting the power supply needs of ships at any berth in the port area, and ensuring stable power supply.

The high-voltage shore power system mainly includes the following three parts: shore power supply system, cable connection equipment, and ship power receiving system. The shore power supply system supplies power to the connection point near the ship after frequency conversion and transformation of the AC power from the port high-voltage substation. Cable connection equipment refers to the cables and equipment connecting the shore power box and the ship's power receiving device, which should be easy to use, quick to connect, and convenient for cable storage. Cable connection equipment can be installed on the ship, on the dock, or on a barge. The ship power receiving system refers to the power receiving system permanently installed on the ship, mainly including cable winches, ship transformers, and related electrical management systems.

High-voltage shore power generally chooses local grid power as the input source, and its output process needs to be appropriately converted to better meet the needs of different ships. The basic ship power system in our country is 380 V/50 Hz or 440 V/ 50 Hz, while the main power frequency of ships internationally is 60 Hz, and the voltage is basically 6.6 kV or 440 V. In general, the main substation of high-voltage shore power mainly plays the role of frequency conversion and transformation, and then transmits it to the shore power box on the dock through the cable on the dock, and finally delivers the power to the docked ship.

Currently, high-voltage shore power systems mainly have high-low–high and high-high transformation schemes. The power system voltage level of high-voltage ships and low-voltage frequency conversion schemes is 6.6 kV/11 kV. The input voltage of the high-voltage shore power system is 6 kV/10 kV. Through the step-down transformer, the input voltage can be reduced to 380 V or 690 V, and then the low-voltage inverter converts it from 380 V/50 Hz or 690 V/50 Hz to 440 V/60 Hz AC, and the output is converted into 6.6 kV/11 kV required by the ship through the step-up transformer. The step-down transformer needs to choose the storage location according to the actual situation, which can be stored on the barge at the dock or directly on the ship. For high-voltage ships and high-voltage frequency conversion schemes, the basic principle of the scheme is: the high-voltage inverter can convert 6 kV/50 Hz or 10 kV/50 Hz AC into 6 kV/60 Hz or 10 kV/60 Hz, and then the step-up transformer converts 6 kV/60 Hz or 10 kV/60 Hz into 6.6 kV/60 Hz or 11 kV/60 Hz, directly supplying power to the ship. Figure 2.5: High-voltage ship and low-voltage frequency conversion scheme. Figure 2.6: High-voltage ship and high-voltage frequency conversion scheme.

(2) RTG "oil to electricity" conversion

Since RTG uses diesel generators for power and operates intermittently, according to statistics from relevant ports, after the RTG engine starts, the actual time used for loading and unloading work is only 41.5%, and the other 58.5% of the time is idle consumption. A single RTG consumes 15.0–15.5 L of diesel per hour during idle

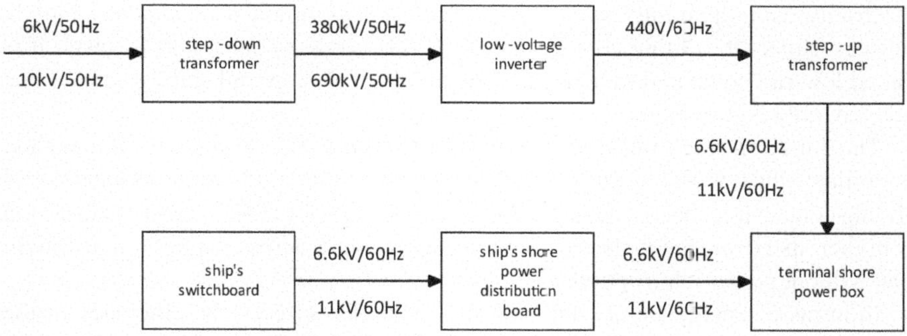

Fig. 2.5 High-voltage ship and low-voltage inverter program

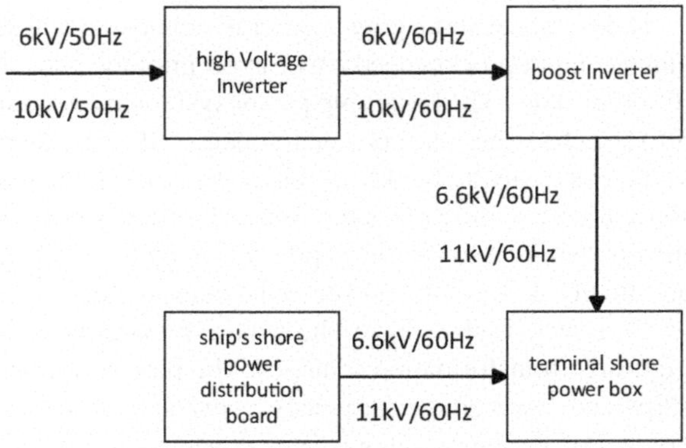

Fig. 2.6 High-voltage ship with high-voltage inverter program

time, resulting in high energy consumption, high operating costs, heavy pollution, and large idle consumption. In contrast, the operating cost of E-RTG is only one third of that of diesel-powered RTG, and it produces less exhaust gas, noise, and oil and water leakage during operation, greatly saving energy and reducing environmental pollution.

Currently, there are three main methods for RTG "Oil to Electricity" conversion in container handling, namely cable drum, low-rail sliding contact line, and high-rail sliding contact line.

The first is the cable drum method, which requires adding a cable drum, power cable plug and socket, and power selection switch to the tire crane. The tire crane can use city electricity for normal operation. The cable drum method is a way for E-RTG to carry a cable for power connection. The structure (the equipment itself) of E-RTG powered by the cable drum method is more complex (and heavier) than that of E-RTG powered by the sliding contact line method, and the cost per unit is higher.

The second is the low-rail sliding contact line method, which requires adding a transformer, low-rail tower, sliding contact line, collector pole, power selection switch, etc. to the tire crane for power supply. The low-rail is a way to connect to electricity using a sliding contact line, which is a common way to power mobile devices. Since the sliding contact line for E-RTG power connection is lower, it is called low-rail compared to high-rail. The pillars of the low-rail sliding contact line are generally 3–4 m high.

The third is the high-rail sliding contact line method. The power receiving method is similar to the low-rail sliding contact line method, basically the same as the low-rail sliding contact line, but because the sliding contact line for E-RTG power connection is higher, its advantage is that the equipment can work across the field in a straight line without power interruption.

In terms of energy saving and emission reduction effects, the efficiency of the above three methods is almost the same, but in the cable drum scheme, as the length of the used cable increases, it will cause a larger voltage drop and relatively larger power loss. All three methods use city power. When using normal electric power supply, all three have no exhaust gas and noise emissions, truly achieving environmental protection effects. Generally, ports will choose the most suitable "Oil to Electricity" scheme based on their own characteristics.

(3) Automated Container Terminal System

The automated container terminal is a major innovation in the field of intelligent port management, and the construction of an automated container terminal system can also promote the development of green ports. It mainly includes automated guided vehicles, automated loading vehicles, and automated stacking cranes. Semi-automated container terminals are divided into open yard and closed yard types: open yard terminals allow personnel and vehicles to enter, and often use the "gantry crane with outreach + trailer" process system; closed yard terminals prohibit personnel and vehicles from entering, and often use the "automated gantry crane + straddle carrier" process system. The newly built semi-automated container terminals mostly adopt the closed yard type.

The fully automated container terminals that have been built in the world mostly use the traditional "automated gantry crane + straddle carrier" process system. To improve the overall loading and unloading efficiency of the system, newly built terminals often optimize the process, for example, the "shore crane + automated straddle carrier + automated gantry crane" and "shore crane + automated guided vehicle with self-lifting function + automated gantry crane" process systems currently have ongoing application projects.

"The Automated Rail Crane + Automated Guided Vehicle" process system is set up on the shore with shore cranes (mostly dual-trolley shore cranes) responsible for ship loading and unloading. The automated guided vehicles are responsible for the horizontal transportation of containers on the shore, and the automated rail cranes are responsible for the loading and unloading of containers in the yard and the container distribution. This type of process system is aimed at achieving full automation of container terminal operations, with representative terminals including ECT, CTA, and Euromax terminals.

The "Outreach Rail Crane + Tractor" process system is set up on the shore with shore cranes responsible for ship loading and unloading, tractors responsible for the horizontal transportation of containers on the shore and in the yard, and outreach rail cranes responsible for yard container loading and unloading. This type of process system is aimed at achieving semi-automated operations at container terminals, with representative terminals including Hong Kong International Container Terminal, Hanjin Terminal, and Gaoming Terminal.

The "Automated Rail Crane + Straddle Carrier" process system is set up on the shore with shore cranes responsible for ship loading and unloading, straddle carriers responsible for the horizontal transportation of containers on the shore, and automated rail cranes responsible for the loading and unloading of containers in the yard and the container distribution. This type of process system has a comprehensive positioning, suitable for semi-automated container terminals, while reserving technical transformation space for fully automated container terminals. Representative terminals include Virginia Container Terminal, Busan New Container Terminal, and

London Gateway Terminal. Other forms of process systems, in addition to the above-mentioned automated container terminal process systems, there are also process system forms based on rail distribution systems and vertical storage yard systems in the world. However, due to issues such as their technical maturity and construction costs, they are still in the conceptual design stage.

(4) Intelligent Precise Dust Suppression Technology

The traditional manual watering method is upgraded to an intelligent computer control system, which carries out efficient data transmission through optical cables connected to the bus control box near the equipment, achieving intelligent watering monitoring and management. The host computer of this system can realize real-time monitoring and automatic fault alarm of the spraying equipment, and manually or automatically control the spraying equipment according to actual needs. In addition, it can automatically control according to changes in factors such as wind speed and time, and automatically adjust the spraying equipment according to different seasons and scenes. Operators can carry out remote real-time monitoring, greatly reducing labor intensity and production costs.

2.8.2 *Overview of Domestic and Foreign Port Energy System Engineering*

Research on port energy in developed countries abroad is mainly reflected in green ports. As early as 2004, the Port of New York-New Jersey began to implement the port environmental management system. The UK, Australia, Japan and other countries all have mature experiences in building green ports. The practice of foreign green ports is mainly reflected in planning and infrastructure construction, developing and using clean energy, and implementing green management in ports. China has also achieved some results in port energy-saving development. Ports such as Shanghai Port, Tianjin Port, Qinhuangdao Port, Shenzhen Port, and Qingdao Port have all carried out research and application related to green ports, mainly in environmental protection and energy-saving technology transformation. At present, domestic related research and applications are mainly reflected in informatization and automatic loading and unloading. Ports with advanced management have logistics information, production management, equipment management and other information platforms.

(1) Foreign Port Energy System Engineering Case

① Port of Los Angeles, USA

The Port of Los Angeles in the United States is the second largest port in the country, located at the top of San Pedro Bay on the southwest coast of California, on the eastern side of the Pacific Ocean. The Port of Los Angeles includes 15 bulk/general cargo berths, 36 container berths, and 14 oil terminal berths. Loading and unloading equipment includes various shore cranes, container cranes, floating cranes, gantry cranes, mobile cranes, loading bridges, and roll-on facilities. Among them, the maximum lifting capacity of the container crane is 40 t, the floating crane is 350 t, and it also includes oil pipelines with diameters of 150–300 mm. The container terminal can stack 25,000 standard containers. The port area has once berthed an oil ship with a load of 220,000 t, the oil tank capacity reaches 500,000 t, and the open storage yard area reaches 1 million m^2.

The Port of Los Angeles has been built into a world-leading modern multi-functional electrified port, and the port area includes various factories, enterprises, and related research institutions. In 2020, the Port of Los Angeles put into operation 6 hydrogen energy transfer tractors, becoming the first port to apply hydrogen energy vehicles. After large-scale electric energy substitution and clean energy substitution for port equipment, the Port of Los Angeles has become a typical representative of the port comprehensive energy supply system where the energy system and logistics system are coupled, with electricity as the core and various forms of energy coexisting.

② Port of Esbjerg, Denmark

According to the statement of the Port of Esbjerg, it has reached a cooperation agreement with the Danish Labor Fund, which will provide funds to help the port expansion. Among them, $850 million will be used to increase the capacity of the port's offshore wind turbine production base, and the project is expected to be completed by 2027; about $100 million will be used to build carbon capture and storage, power conversion and other infrastructure, planned to be put into operation by 2028; in addition, about $70 million will be used to promote the development of multi-modal facilities such as road and rail transport at the port, strengthen the connection between Esbjerg Airport and sea and land transport, and this plan is expected to be realized by 2032. The remaining funds will be used to promote the development of green fuels and improve logistics flexibility.

③ Port of Esbjerg

The Port of Esbjerg is located in the North Sea region of Europe and is one of the main bases supporting the development of offshore wind power industries in many European countries. In January 2023, the Port of Esbjerg signed a partnership agreement with several ports in Belgium, the Netherlands, Germany, and other countries, hoping to solve the problem of insufficient port capacity for offshore wind expansion, while jointly promoting the construction of offshore wind farms in European countries.

The Portsmouth International Port (PIP) on the south coast of the UK announced that the port will trial a new smart energy system, which will include a new energy storage solution. The system will involve designing and building a dual-chemistry battery technology project, which is specifically designed to meet the port's requirements. The project will work in conjunction with advanced management software to help optimize port energy use, reduce emissions, and improve air quality. This project is very forward-looking, as the port's electricity demand is constantly increasing with ships using more shore power and adopting electric propulsion systems. Therefore, it is necessary to develop a system that can provide more electricity without relying on expensive grid upgrades.

(2) Case Studies of Energy System Engineering in Chinese Ports

① Tianjin Port

The world's first zero-carbon smart green energy system dock has been connected to the grid for power generation at Tianjin Port. This is the first "wind-light-storage-load integration" smart green energy project in China's ports, marking a new step in the construction of green ports in Tianjin Port and leading the industry's green and low-carbon development in a new mode. As the world's first "smart zero-carbon" dock, all dock loading and unloading equipment, horizontal transport equipment, and production auxiliary equipment are driven by electricity, and 100% of energy consumption comes from the "wind-light-storage-load integration" system. Tianjin Port fully utilizes the excellent wind energy and solar energy in the port area to build distributed photovoltaic and wind power projects.

The installed capacity of wind power and photovoltaic power generation systems that have been put into operation has reached 42.55 MW, generating about 90 million kWh of green electricity annually; it can reduce carbon emissions by about 75,000 tons each year, equivalent to planting 210,000 trees. The proportion of green electricity in the entire port has reached 14%, ranking first among ports nationwide. At the same time, Tianjin Port uses advanced energy monitoring technology, and energy consumption is 17% lower than traditional automated container terminals, taking the lead in achieving "zero emissions" of carbon dioxide on both sides of energy production and consumption.

② Qinhuangdao Port

Since 2015, Hebei Port Group has begun to accelerate the promotion and use of green and low-carbon technologies such as ship shore power, and promote the construction of shore power for port containers and specialized berths for dry bulk cargo of 50,000 tons and above. In 2017, the Ministry of Transport issued the "Port Shore Power Layout Plan", requiring more than 50% of the built container, passenger and roll-on/roll-off ship, cruise ship, 3,000-ton and above passenger transport and 50,000-ton and above dry bulk cargo specialized berths in the main ports along the coast and inland rivers and ports within the ship emission control area to have the ability to provide shore power to ships by the end of 2020. According to the plan, Hebei Port Group plans to invest nearly 70 million yuan to build 8 sets of multi-electric, standalone ship shore power systems with a capacity of 1250 kVA in the East Port Area of Qinhuangdao Port. In November 2018, the shore power system of Qinhuangdao Port, which ranks among the top, successfully supplied power to the cargo ship connected to the grid at berth 905# of the Coal Fifth Phase, marking that Qinhuangdao Port has high-voltage shore power supply capability.

③ Yangshan Deep-Water Port

The Shanghai Yangshan Deep-Water Port was opened on December 10, 2005, located in the rugged archipelago outside the mouth of Hangzhou Bay, including Xiaoyangshan Island, Donghai Bridge, and Yangshan Free Trade Port Area. It is the world's largest intelligent container terminal. At present, the main port area of Yangshan Port has completed equipment electrification, and some port areas have achieved unmanned operations. In 2016, the cargo throughput of Yangshan Port reached 702 million tons, and the container throughput was 37.13 million TEUs, maintaining the world's first for seven consecutive years since 2010.

Yangshan Port mainly includes energy operation port area and container loading and unloading port area. The energy operation port area includes a liquefied natural gas receiving station and a submarine gas pipeline, which can import 3 million tons of liquefied natural gas each year. At the same time, Yangshan Port is also the largest finished oil transshipment base in the Far East, planning to build a 1900-m-long oil product dock operation area. After the project is completed, it can store 2.7 million m^3 of finished oil. The container loading and unloading port area is mainly in the North Port Area and West Port Area, with a planned deep-water shoreline of 10 km, more than 30 berths, and can load and unload the world's largest Panamax container ships. A variety of cargo types, rich energy sources, and extremely high levels of intelligent operation make Yangshan Deep-Water Port a pioneer in the field of green port comprehensive energy systems in China.

④ Rizhao Port

Rizhao Port is the eighth largest port in China and a significant global hub for energy, raw materials, and container transshipment. The port mainly handles goods such as containers, ores, timber, grains, edible oils, crude oil, natural gas, and coal. Rizhao Port's annual electricity consumption exceeds 100 million kilowatt-hours, equivalent to over 40,000 tons of standard coal and 27,000 tons of carbon emissions. It also has fuel load, natural gas load, and cold and heat loads. Moreover, Rizhao Port is rich in sunlight and wind energy, has great potential for electrical equipment transformation, and its various load demands have complementary conditions, making it an appropriate demonstration area for low-carbon port energy use.

Currently, Rizhao Port is promoting the "Fourteenth Five-Year" plan for green and low-carbon ports. On the energy supply side, it is developing renewable and low-carbon energy; on the energy consumption side, it is achieving port energy electrification and decarbonization. Ultimately, it aims to build a comprehensive energy network with multiple energy coupling and complementarity, forming a smart energy solution for the port. By investing in photovoltaics, wind power, combined heat and power units, and energy storage equipment in Rizhao Port in stages, it aims to replace port energy with clean electricity. By gradually introducing gas-powered heavy trucks and electric heavy trucks, it aims to replace port energy with electricity.

2.9 Theories Related to Green Operation of Port Groups

2.9.1 Composition of the Hinterland Container Transport System of Port Groups

Since the 1960s, container freight transport has been widely used in modern goods transport due to its high efficiency, high benefits, and high safety. The vigorous development of international container transport by sea marks the beginning of the containerization era in global goods transport. With the improvement of container transport facilities and modern management, multimodal transport of containers has gradually emerged, creating conditions for "door to door" transport of goods. Since the 1980s, Western countries have begun to vigorously develop multimodal transport and containerization of goods due to their significant advantages in efficiency, cost reduction, safety and reliability, and low-carbon environmental protection.

Port-hinterland multimodal transport refers to a multimodal transport mode that combines sea transport with road and rail transport, with the port as the core. In the port-hinterland multimodal transport network, the port, as an important node in global trade transport, bears the important function of sea-land transshipment. In the transport process between the port and the hinterland, goods are transported in containers, realizing the standardization of transport tools and improving the efficiency of loading and unloading. For the hinterland container transport system of the port, it is the beginning or continuation of sea transport of goods in the inland part, mainly undertaking the freight transport task between inland hinterland cities and coastal hub ports. Table 2.2 elaborates on the constituent elements of the hinterland container transport system of the port group.

2.9.2 Theories and Methods Related to Green Operation of Port Groups

Multimodal Transport Path Optimization is a key content in the optimization of Multimodal Transport Operation Service Network. It relies on the actual infrastructure network, considering various factors, to allocate transport resources more reasonably and effectively. Path optimization is a comprehensive research direction involving Transportation Organization, Operations Research, and Systems Science.

Foreign scholars proposed a method to solve the multimodal transport path selection problem in fuzzy environments, to deal with the uncertainty of marginal costs. They proposed an algorithm based on the fuzzy shortest path and flow increment loading, which is an adaptation of the Bellman-Ford algorithm, enabling it to quantitatively handle uncertainty factors on its original basis. They also used the Sioux Fall network, which is suitable for multimodal transport problems, to verify the efficiency of this method. Koohathongsumrit et al. (2021) proposed a comprehensive

Table 2.2 Components of a containerized transport system in the hinterland of a port complex

Constituent element	Description of elements
Major players in transportation services	(a) Shipper: Also represents the owner of the goods, which generates the demand for transportation of goods in the hinterland; plans and organizes the process of transportation of goods, and whose main decision-making task is the selection of the mode of transport and route of transportation of containerized goods in the inland segment (b) Carrier: For the implementation of specific transport services and tasks, such as road transport enterprises, railroad transport enterprises and waterway transport enterprises, etc., whose main task is to provide means of transport and transport services will be on time and safe delivery of goods (c) Service facility manager: Refers to the entire transport network or service facilities managers, such as coastal container port terminals, inland intermodal terminals, inland waterless ports and multimodal transport corridors and other builders and managers; its main task is to optimize the service facilities and transport corridors so as to improve their own or the network's level of service (d) Governmental management organization: Refers to national or regional governments and industry administrations, etc., whose main task is to consider the social, economic and environmental impacts of transportation through administrative means, financial subsidies, formulation of relevant policies, etc., in order to promote its development in a sustainable direction
Principal relationships	(a) CY (Cntr Yard, Container Yard): CY refers only to the container yard in the container terminal, and may not refer to the container yard elsewhere (b) DR (Door): Shipper or CNEE (consignee) factory or W/H (warehouse) gate (c) CFS (Cntr Freight Station, Container Freight Station): mainly for LCL cargo services, it is the place where LCL handles the handover. Its main functions are: for export cargo, from the consignor to pick up the goods, the flow of goods in the same direction of assembly in the cabinet; on the import of cabinets, is responsible for dismantling the cabinet and delivery to the consignee. Most of the CFS is located in the port or near the port area, a few set up inland, known as the Inland Depot
Transportation services facilities	(a) Coastal container port terminals: Playing the role of a hub port in international intermodal container transportation, they connect the land portion of cargo transportation with the sea portion (b) Inland waterway transit node: Mainly refers to inland waterway transit ports, it is the key node of public water transit and iron water transit, with land and water projects and other corresponding supporting facilities, some ports are also supported by railroad into the port facilities, mainly for the container cargo to provide loading and unloading, transit, storage and other services (c) Inland Railway Transshipment Node: Also known as "waterless ports" or "inland ports", it is a key node in the inland area with alternative port services and the ability to provide public-rail transit services

(continued)

Table 2.2 (continued)

Constituent element	Description of elements
Type of transportation	(a) Road transportation: Transportation services are provided by road transportation enterprises (b) Waterway transportation: Transportation services are provided by container shipping companies (c) Railway transportation: the State Railway Administration and port authorities provide container liner transportation services
Carrier	(a) Container trucks: can provide door-to-door service, not suitable for long-distance and high-volume transportation (b) Container ships: suitable for large-volume, long-distance transportation, with poor security and punctuality (c) Container railroad train: suitable for large-volume transportation, with high security and punctuality
Forms of transport organization	(a) Direct trucking: direct road transportation between seaports and hinterlands using trucks (b) Public-water intermodal transport mode: short-distance road transport between the hinterland and inland river ports, and long-distance, high-volume waterborne container ship transport between inland river ports and seaports, so that a public-water intermodal transport corridor is formed between the seaport and the hinterland (c) Public-railway intermodal transportation mode: short-distance road transportation between the hinterland and the inland anhydrous port, and longer-distance, high-volume railroad train transportation between the anhydrous port and the seaport, thus forming a public-railway intermodal transportation corridor between the seaport and the hinterland
Mode of delivery of goods	(a) Door-to-door (DOOR-DOOR): the consignor's warehouse will transport the containerized goods to the consignee's warehouse (b) Door-to-door handover (DOOR-CY): the consignor's warehouse will transport the containerized goods to the terminal yard at the port of discharge (c) Door to station delivery (DOOR-CFS): the consignor's warehouse will be transported to the discharge port container freight station or inland freight station (d) field to field handover (CY-CY): from the loading port terminal yard containerized goods to the discharge port terminal yard (e) field to door handover (CY-DOOR): the loading port terminal yard containerized cargo to the day ¨ ground consignee's factory or warehouse (f) field to station handover (CY-CFS): the loading port terminal yard containerized cargo to the port of discharge container freight station or inland cargo terminal (g) station to door handover (CFS–DOOR): containerized cargo from the terminal container freight station or inland freight station will be transported to the consignee's warehouse or factory (h) station to field handover (CFS–CY): the terminal container freight station or inland freight station will be transported by the containerized cargo to the port of discharge terminal yard (i) Station to Station Handover (CFS–CFS): the containerized cargo is transported by the terminal container freight station or inland freight station to the consignee's terminal container freight station or inland freight station

Note Summarized according to the "Research on Optimization of Hinterland Container Multimodal Transport Network Considering Carbon Emissions" framework based on the Fuzzy Risk Assessment Model (FRAM), Data Envelopment Analysis (DEA), and Multi-Criteria Decision Making (MCDM) to address the varying risks in multimodal transport networks, providing a basis for risk prediction in route selection in fuzzy environments.

There are also many Chinese studies on the path of multimodal transport services. For example, Pei and Lu (2020) and others mainly targeted the different preferences of various participants in multimodal transport, analyzed their needs and satisfaction from the perspectives of consignors, carriers, and the government, and established a combined satisfaction-based transport network model, enabling transport path design planning to be accepted by participants at multiple levels. Wen (2021) and others conducted a comprehensive analysis of economies of scale, transport costs, transport time, and capacity constraints in hub-and-spoke networks, constructed a multimodal freight transport network model, and demonstrated the importance of the construction of feeder channels to the transport network.

In the topology of multimodal transport networks, points and lines are the basic elements of the network. Domestic and foreign scholars' designs for the topology of multimodal transport networks mainly include direct links, corridors, hub-and-spoke, connected hubs, static routes, and dynamic routes. Multimodal transport network optimization includes facility location problems, hub location problems, competitive location problems, etc. This paper divides the relevant theoretical research into two parts: the strategic planning level and the tactical planning level of the multimodal transport network.

(1) Strategic Planning Level of the Multimodal Transport Network

The strategic level planning of the multimodal transport network mainly solves the hub location problem and network design problem in the network.

First, the main research task of the hub location problem is to determine the location and number of multimodal transport hub nodes and the merger of non-hub nodes to hub nodes. The basic models for this problem are mainly divided into P-median problems, P-center problems, and coverage problems. With scholars' in-depth research on location problems, location models have developed a series of extended models such as hierarchical location problems, location-allocation problems, multiple coverage problems, multi-objective location problems, and random location problems. In addition, depending on the different ways of merging non-hub nodes to hub nodes, the hub location problem can be divided into: single assignment problems, multiple assignment problems, r assignment problems, and hierarchical assignment problems.

Second, the design of the multimodal transport network is related to the configuration of infrastructure, which includes multiple aspects. The most representative is the hub-and-spoke network design model and related extended models, as well as the network layout optimization problem for transport channels.

(2) Tactical Planning Level of the Multimodal Transport Network

The tactical level planning of the multimodal transport network mainly solves the network flow planning problem and the service network planning problem of transport.

First, network flow planning is composed according to a predetermined network structure and transportation mode, comprehensively optimizing the movement of goods flow in the network. It usually aims to minimize total transportation costs, and the optimization decision content includes the reasonable combination of transportation modes and optimal paths. Therefore, the optimization of multimodal transport network paths is an important aspect of this problem. It can be seen as an extension of the vehicle routing problem, and the solution algorithms are similar. Common solution methods include: exact algorithm class (such as branch and bound method, Dijkstra's algorithm, sequential optimization method, etc.), heuristic algorithm class (such as genetic algorithm, ant colony algorithm, taboo algorithm, etc.) or using efficient solution software (such as Lingo, Cplex, Matlab, etc.).

Second, service network planning emphasizes the design of transportation services in the multimodal transport network based on existing transportation resources. That is, while optimizing the transportation path, decision-makers also need to determine the design of transportation services on the path, such as service frequency, service capacity, service time or service pricing, etc. This type of problem can be divided into static service network design and dynamic service network design, the latter further incorporates the consideration of the time dimension based on the former. The solution algorithms for this type of problem are mainly completed by precise solution of mathematical models and computer simulation methods.

References

Ang BW, Liu FL (2001) A new energy decomposition method: perfect in decomposition and consistent in aggregation. Energy 26(6):537–548

Ang BW, Liu N (2007) Negative-value problems of the logarithmic mean Divisia index decomposition approach. Energy Policy 35(1):739–742

Boyd G, McDonald JF, Ross M et al (1987) Separating the changing composition of US manufacturing production from energy efficiency improvement: a Divisia index approach. Energy J 8(2):77–96

Calafiore G, Dabbene F (2006) Probabilistic and randomized methods for design under uncertainty. Springer, Berlin, pp 381–414

Che F (2012) Research on environmental carrying capacity based on sustainable development—taking Liaoning Province as an example. Liaoning University Shenyang

He Y, Meiting S et al (2007) Discussion on the environmental planning of Tianjin Green Port. Environ Prot 380:69–71

Koohathongsumrit N, Meethom W (2021) An integrated approach of fuzzy risk assessment model and data envelopment analysis for route selection in multimodal transportation networks. Exp Syst Appl 171:114342

Liu C, Wang X (2017) Problems and countermeasures in the green and low-carbon development of China's ports. Water Transp Manage 2017(03):21–24

Lv R, Lin J, Xu H (2006) Research on the environmental impact assessment index system of port planning. Mar Environ Sci 2:92–95
Lv R, Lin J, Xu H (2006) Research on the evaluation index system of port planning environmental impact. Marine Environ Sci 25(2):38–39
Nini W (2015) China's port energy saving and emission reduction "thirteenth five-year" outlook. China Ports 9–11
Pan H, Li E (2010) Ecological economics. Jilin University Press
Pei X, Lu Y, Zhang C (2020) Multimodal transport path model and its algorithm based on comprehensive satisfaction. Traffic Inform Saf 38(1):136–144
Peng C (2012) Port carbon emission accounting method—a case study of the 2010 carbon footprint report of Jurong Port in Singapore. Port Econ 7:5–9
Qian S (2007a) Preliminary exploration of port sustainable development. China Water Transp 7(4):181–182
Qian S (2007b) Preliminary exploration of port sustainable development. China Water Transp (Acad Edn)4:181–182
Villalba G, Gemechu ED (2011) Estimating GHG emissions of marine ports-the case of Barcelona. Energy Policy 39(3):1363–1368
Wang F, Huang J, Liu Z (2017) Port management and operation: emerging research hotspots and progress. J Manage Sci 20(5):111–126
Wang B, Li D, Qin P et al (2020) Traffic flow time series segmentation model based on Gamma distribution. J Dalian Univ Technol 60(3):293–299
Wen X, Lu Y, Xiang X (2021) Framework and application of freight network optimization model for multimodal transport. Logist Technol 40(01):67–72, 82
Ye L, Lei W (2009) Decomposition analysis of the influencing factors of China's industrial energy intensity change—based on the LMDI decomposition method. J China Univ Min Technol (Soc Sci Ed) 66–70
Yu J, Wang Z, Zou P et al (2007) Fuzzy evaluation of comprehensive quality of port projects. J Guangzhou Maritime College 15(1):22–25

Chapter 3
Study on the Environmental Impact of Regional Port Groups

3.1 The Impact of Ports on the Environmental Quality of the Port Area

3.1.1 The Impact of Ports on the Nearshore Marine Environment

The use of the sea for transportation, seabed engineering, sea reclamation, and special uses all involve construction. For example, port construction and land reclamation can lead to a reduction in tidal volume, deterioration of water quality, siltation in harbors, and a decrease in marine ecological functions. It can also occupy the coastline, reducing and damaging the living space and foraging grounds of organisms. Ship navigation and the noise it generates, dredging of harbour pools and waterways will all have an impact on and damage marine organisms (Ke 2022).

In addition, accidental oil spills from port vessels will have a devastating impact on the marine ecosystem. With the accelerated development of coastal areas, the petrochemical industry is intensive, the port transportation is busy, and the nuclear power industry is distributed along the coastline, which leads to an obvious increase in the risk of catastrophe in the marine environment and a relative concentration of risk sources (Chen and Zhang 2014). The ecological crisis triggered by the crude oil leakage caused by the explosion of 716 oil storage tanks in Dalian Xingang, as well as the environmental disaster triggered by the explosion of dangerous goods in Tianjin Xingang, are always sounding the alarm for us.

At the same time, dredged spoils may become a source of pollution; dredging depths in channels and harbors may change water currents and salinity, thus affecting waterfront industries. Buildings, wharves, breakwaters and other buildings may cause erosion or alluvial deposition in certain waters; channel changes may affect tides and the speed of sea currents; shading of inlet channels or harbor pools may result in complex wave reflections and refluxes; and the construction of port facilities

B. Lu, *The Sustainable Development of Port Group*,
https://doi.org/10.1007/978-981-97-2378-2_3

such as warehouses, roads, and yards is a potential threat to the surrounding waters. Ship discharges, discharges of ballast water, bilge water and domestic sewage not only have a direct impact on the water quality of the harbor, but also upstream and downstream of it; paints or other compounds used to maintain and clean ships that prevent the attachment of bilge seabirds have a significant impact on bilge seabirds. Cargo spillage, any spillage of cargo, especially toxic cargo, can have a significant impact on the environment; spillage of bulk terminal storage can also have a significant impact on the environment.

The bays and estuaries where ports are located are good places for organisms to grow, reproduce, and return. However, the construction of port docks changes the shoreline and hydrodynamic conditions, affecting migratory animals, spawning grounds, and growth areas, as well as the aquaculture industry and fisheries, to some extent, damaging the ecological environment of local waters.

In addition, suspended matter, domestic sewage, and oily water generated by port loading and unloading operations can increase the turbidity of local waters, cause eutrophication of local water bodies, and damage the living environment of aquatic organisms to a certain extent.

Areas far from the mainland, where the water and sand environment is less disturbed by human activities, are in a state of dynamic equilibrium over the long term. When external conditions change slightly, it can cause changes in erosion and sedimentation in the sea area, and various marine engineering constructions are the main factors causing these new changes, i.e., the impact of marine engineering construction on the hydrodynamic environment (Zhang et al. 2018).

Research shows that before and after port construction, the direction of the tidal current at the front of the project does not change much and is consistent with the direction of the island boundary. In the area where the shoreline is recessed, significant changes occur during periods of rapid rise and fall of the water. Analysis of sediment movement and seabed erosion and sedimentation changes shows that the alongshore current generated by waves does not cause siltation in the port and can be disregarded. The tidal current may cause siltation in the port, but the amount of siltation is small.

For Tianheng Island and Green Island, it is found that the hydrodynamics before and after the completion of the wharf has not changed much outside the wharf area of 500m, and the tidal current field and residual current field of the waters around the wharf have changed and the hydrodynamics have weakened in the vicinity of the wharf, in addition to the reduction of part of the sea area by enclosing the sea to make fields. The change of hydrodynamics in the sea area near the wharf will be unfavorable to the transport of pollutants in the nearby sea area, and it is necessary to strengthen the management of pollutants discharged from the wharf area to protect the water quality environment in the wharf area (Yuan et al. 2003).

Marine resources are an important part of the natural resources on which mankind relies for its survival, and in addition to providing mankind with huge physical objects such as marine life, seabed minerals and oil and gas, its naturally large bodies of water also provide mankind with environmental resources. The environmental capacity of water refers to the maximum load of pollutants that a water body can accommodate under the specified environmental objectives, and its size is related to the characteristics of the water body, water quality objectives and pollutant characteristics. The environmental capacity of near-shore waters is ultimately a water environmental capacity, the size of which is jointly determined by the hydrodynamic characteristics of the waters to which it belongs, the functional zoning of near-shore waters and the characteristics of pollutant discharges. With the rapid development of economy and society, people's resource utilization of near-shore sea area is increasing, especially the construction of port area is more common, this kind of construction is often a large amount of works, and it involves the reclamation of land, which changes the distribution of the natural shoreline of the local near-shore sea area, and the hydrodynamic characteristics of seawater tides, waves, etc. within a certain range will be affected, which will affect the environmental capacity.

Studies have shown that the construction of port projects in near-shore areas has changed the shape of the coastline, weakened the tidal dynamics of the surrounding sea area, weakened the effects of pollutant diffusion and migration, and reduced the environmental capacity (Hao 2016). The closer the construction site is to the sea area, the stronger the effect of the weakening of tidal dynamics is, and the greater the decrease in environmental capacity is; while the sea area far away from the construction site has a limited impact on the tidal dynamics characteristics of the sea area, and therefore the environmental capacity there is very little affected.

3.1.2 Impact of Ports on Land Environment

Ports are the link between land and sea. While promoting trade and economic development, they also have a certain impact on the surrounding land environment.

Firstly, port construction requires a large amount of land. The construction of port facilities such as docks, yards, and warehouses often requires a large area of land. This may cause the original land ecosystem to be destroyed and biodiversity to decrease. To solve this problem, port managers can choose to plan port land use reasonably, try to retain and restore the local natural ecosystem, such as through afforestation, wetland protection, etc., to achieve a win–win situation for ecological protection and economic development.

Secondly, port operations produce pollutants such as wastewater and waste oil. In port transportation activities, the wastewater and waste oil discharged by ships, as well as the daily wastewater treatment discharge of port facilities, may cause pollution to the surrounding water bodies. To solve this problem, port managers should establish comprehensive wastewater and waste oil treatment facilities for effective treatment and discharge control. In addition, they should strengthen monitoring and law enforcement to ensure that port companies operate in compliance with regulations and strictly prohibit illegal discharge and dumping of waste.

Thirdly, port activities can lead to air pollution. Processes such as port loading and unloading operations, and the combustion of transportation vehicles, can produce a large amount of emissions, such as sulfur dioxide, nitrogen oxides, particulate matter, etc., causing pollution to the surrounding air quality. To reduce this impact, green port construction and operation can be promoted. For example, introducing clean energy supply, promoting electric vehicles and shore power supply systems to reduce emissions of air pollutants. In addition, port managers can also require ships to use low-sulfur fuel to reduce exhaust emissions.

Fourthly, ports are one of the potential pathways for biological invasions. With the development of international trade, ports have become important channels for the invasion of alien species. These species may be brought into the port through ship ballast water, sediments, etc., causing damage to the local ecosystem. To prevent biological invasions, port managers can strengthen species monitoring and management, establish quarantine measures and biosecurity systems. Regular inspections of ship ballast water and sediments, timely cleaning and handling of potentially carried alien species, can prevent invasion risks.

Lastly, port operations generate noise and vibration. Noise and vibration are generated during the start-up, docking and operation of mechanical equipment, vehicles and vessels in ports, causing disturbance and even harm to neighboring residents, wildlife and plants. To minimize the impact of noise and vibration on the environment, port managers should strengthen noise and vibration monitoring and take appropriate protective measures. For example, port facilities should be reasonably planned and set up, low-noise mechanical equipment should be used, and vehicle speed and routes should be controlled to reduce the spread of noise and vibration.

The impacts of ports on the terrestrial environment mainly include land use, water pollution, air pollution, biological invasion, and noise and vibration. In response to these problems, port managers need to adopt a series of environmental protection measures, including rational planning of land use, construction of wastewater treatment facilities, implementation of green port construction, strengthening of species monitoring and management, and control of noise and vibration, in order to realize sustainable development of ports and protection of the ecological environment. At the same time, the government and society should also strengthen their supervision and participation to jointly promote the green development of the port industry (He and Luo 2018).

3.2 Impact of Ports on the Ecological Environment of the Port Area

3.2.1 Main Ecological Issues Caused by Port Construction and Development

(1) Impact on the surrounding terrestrial ecosystems

Port construction requires a large amount of land for construction, and it is necessary to plan the coastal land for internal use. During the construction process, considering safety and durability, construction materials with high hardness such as masonry, concrete, and reinforced concrete are generally chosen. However, these materials have very obvious negative impacts. They will linearize the planar shape of the river very much, and the cross-section of the river channel will become very regular, making it impossible for the surrounding natural environment to achieve effective biological succession. Water, air, soil, and organisms are all cut off. Such treatment will destroy the entire ecological environment along the river bank, and ecological diversity cannot be guaranteed, which will bring about very serious ecological disasters (Yu 2023). After the port is put into use, during the loading, unloading, storage, and transportation of solid bulk cargo, there will inevitably be a large amount of dust, oil, bulk liquid chemicals, and other dangerous substances. These substances will form a large amount of volatile gases, and at the same time, they will emit a large amount of pollutants. The large machinery and vehicles operating in the port will produce strong noise. These are the main sources of ecological pollution, which bring huge negative impacts to the entire port environment (Tian 2023).

(2) Impact on the surrounding aquatic ecosystem

The natural attributes of the river bank are bound to be more complex than the land environment, and the ecosystem is more susceptible to damage and more fragile. After the port is put into use, it will not only affect the hydrology and sediment of the entire port area, but also directly affect the tides, waves, and river flooding. Flood dikes and other protective measures will have a serious impact on the water bodies of the entire region, changing the effects of tides and waves, and causing changes in the migration of silt and pollutants in the sediment (Long 2022). The most serious impact on the entire regional ecosystem after the port is put into operation is the deterioration of water quality. Ships operating in the port are likely to inadvertently discharge a large amount of pollutants into the water, causing serious water pollution, which is the most direct impact on the environment. Specifically, the most obvious pollution in the port environment is sediment pollution and the impact of ships on biological communities; during the inspection or salvage of ships, oil leaks and other pollution situations are likely to occur; ship transportation can lead to the discharge of some waste and cause water pollution, and there are also some dangerous goods scattered and leaked due to ship accidents.

3.2.2 Impact of Sea Enclosure and Reclamation Projects on the Port Ecological Environment

Large-scale sea enclosure and reclamation directly change the coastal structure and tidal movement, affecting tidal differences, water flow, and waves and other hydrodynamic conditions; for estuaries, after the estuary is reclaimed, the river channel is narrowed, the tidal wave deformation is intensified, and the maximum ebb flow speed and ebb section tidal volume decrease (Liu 2023). Large-scale sea enclosure and reclamation activities directly change the hydrodynamic conditions of the bay, reducing the water's ability to carry sand, accelerating the siltation of the bay, and leading to changes in the shore beach.

Research shows that the reclamation activities along the coast of Ling Shan River estuary in South Korea have led to a decrease in tidal backwater, an increase in tidal range, and exacerbated flood disasters during typhoons. Using a wave numerical model to analyze the changes in wave elements in the waters near Caofeidian, Tianjin Port, and Huanghua Port in the Bohai Bay, the results show that after the construction of engineering structures, the effective wave height decreases, especially in the harbor pool and tidal channels. Based on the Bohai hydrodynamic model, the simulation of intensive sea use on tides found that changes in the coastline caused the semi-diurnal tide nodal point in the waters near the Yellow River Sea Port to gradually shift southeastward, the amplitude of the semi-diurnal tide in Laizhou Bay decreased, and the amplitude in the three major bays increased. Simulating the changes in tidal currents and wind wave characteristics before and after the Bohai Bay reclamation project, the results show that the distribution of sand content in the Bohai Bay shows a trend of decreasing under normal dynamic conditions, decreasing in nearshore areas under strong dynamic conditions, and increasing in the sea area in front of the building. Using numerical simulation methods to predict the impact of reclamation projects on the surrounding sea areas from four aspects: tide level, tidal current, waves, and suspended sand concentration, the results show that in the sea area blocked by the project, the effective wave height of the waves decreases, the sand-lifting ability decreases, and the suspended sand concentration in the nearby sea area also decreases (Li et al. 2023).

Reclamation directly changes the type and sedimentary characteristics of sediments in adjacent sea areas. The originally single fine-grained sedimentation area dominated by tidal action has become a mixed sedimentation of coarse and fine grains, the sediment sorting becomes worse, the frequency curve presents an irregular multi-peak type, and some even cover all the fine-grained sediments, becoming local coarse-grained sediments. The filling area severely changes the seafloor topography, destroys the seafloor environment, and causes new seafloor and coastal erosion or siltation. In 1984, the reclamation project in Rishan Bay on the west coast of South Korea built a 8 km long seawall at the bay mouth, causing significant changes in the sedimentation process of the low tide beach (Lv et al. 2023).

The study of sedimentation in northern Liaodong Bay shows that human activities are an important influence on changing and reshaping the modern sedimentation pattern in northern Liaodong Bay. Reclamation has reshaped the coastal morphology and spatial distribution pattern, restricting the ability of coastal shallow-water materials to participate in modern sedimentation and indirectly affecting the change of sedimentation rate, the dynamical differentiation of detrital minerals, and the enrichment and diffusion of heavy metal elements. The impact of the large-scale offshore artificial island construction in Longkou on the surface sediments is characterized by the obvious transport effect of the long-term implementation of the large-scale reclamation project on the sediments with grain size less than 63 μm, while the transport effect on the sediments with grain size larger than 63 μm is less influential. The analysis of the grain size and clay mineral composition and distribution characteristics of the surface sediments in the Caofeidian nearshore area shows that the long-term implementation of the reclamation project has a more obvious effect on the distribution of finer particles in the surface sediments, and the distribution characteristics of illite, kaolinite and chlorite are closely related to the hydrodynamic changes caused by the reclamation (Wang and Zhang 2023).

Reclamation projects reduce the water exchange capacity and pollutant self-purification capacity of the sea area, and activities such as aquaculture, port terminals and port-related industries formed by reclamation increase the discharge of pollutants in the sea area, and the superposition of the two effects leads to the continuous deterioration of the near-shore water environment and environmental pollution of the bottom mud.

Research on the distribution characteristics and formation mechanism of the low-oxygen zone in the bottom layer of the Bohai Sea shows that the low-oxygen zone has a north–south “double-core” structure, which is basically consistent with the structure of the double-centered cold water, and the seasonal stratification of seawater in the central part of the Bohai Sea and its blocking of the dissolved oxygen are the key physical mechanisms for the generation of low-oxygen zones, and the generation of the low-oxygen zones is a result of the drastic change of the ecosystems of the Bohai Sea and the centralization of its manifestations.

Elemental arsenic content in the bottom sediments in the northern shallow sea area of Liaodong Bay is high, and the high value area is distributed in Jinzhou Bay and its vicinity, and the bottom sediment pollution in Jinzhou Bay is mainly caused by frequent reclamation activities and discharge of pollutants from land-based sources into the sea. The study of heavy metal pollution caused by reclamation in Bohai Bay shows that the contents of Cu, Cd and Pb in sediments in 2011 were higher than those in 2003, and the situation of heavy metal pollution tends to be more serious, the high value areas of Cu, Zn and Cd are concentrated in the central waters of Bohai Bay, and the high value areas of Pb are concentrated in the near-shore estuaries and the central and southern parts of Bohai Bay. Evaluating the ecological impacts of intensive sea use, it is found that the integrated index of habitat quality in the western and southern nearshore waters of Laizhou Bay is lower than that in the central and eastern parts of the Bay, and the main pollution factors of the water quality are inorganic nitrogen, reactive phosphate, and COD, in which the content of inorganic nitrogen exceeds the first class standard of the water quality of the sea. Evaluation of heavy metal pollution and potential ecological hazards in the Caofeidian reclaimed area showed that the average content of five heavy metals in the surface sediments near the reclaimed area was higher than the background value of heavy metals in Bohai Bay sediments, and Hg was the main pollutant in the surface sediments, which was a strong ecological hazard.

Reclamation projects have occupied a large number of coastal mudflat wetlands, completely altering the natural properties of the wetlands and leading to the basic disappearance of their ecological service functions (Li et al. 2023). Coastal mudflats and estuaries are key habitats for fish spawning and migrating, migratory birds foraging, and rare plants and animals, but reclamation has led to a massive reduction in the number of wetland biological populations and even to near extinction, completely altering the ecosystem's structure, and seriously decreasing the function of ecological services.

The study shows that: large-scale reclamation in Dalian City has led to the loss of offshore wetlands, ecosystem degradation, and reduction of biodiversity; the loss of ecological services such as ecological diversity, climate regulation, air and water quality regulation, and other ecological services caused by the Caofeidian reclamation project occupying the mudflat wetlands amounted to 47.36 million yuan per year; the loss of ecosystem service value of wetlands caused by reclamation in the northern coastal area of Weifang was 1.02 × 104 million yuan/a, with a loss of 1.06 million yuan hm-2a-1 per unit area. 1.04 million yuan/a, and the loss per unit area was 1.06 million yuan hm-2a-1. The study on the impact of reclamation activities in the Yellow River Delta on the organic carbon content of vegetation in coastal wetlands found that the vegetation types in areas with strong reclamation activities, such as Dongying Harbor and Pile 5, were relatively homogeneous, and that the reclamation activities changed the key environmental factors for vegetation growth and caused the vegetation elements to be more complex, and the vegetation elements to be less complex. The intensity of reclamation activities in the 1970s–80s, 1990s and 2000–2010 exceeded the carrying capacity of the Yellow River Delta wetland ecosystem and showed an increasing trend (Zhang et al. 2022).

The processes of marine land extraction, blowing and burying in the reclamation project have brought about drastic changes in offshore substrate conditions and benthic survival conditions in the sea area, resulting in the loss and fragmentation of benthic habitats, deterioration of the benthic environment, reduction in the number of benthic organisms, change in the structure of the community, and reduction in biodiversity. An analysis of the environmental and ecological impacts of suspended sediments generated by reclamation in Dalian's Lingshuiwan found that changes in seabed sediments and seawater quality have affected marine ecosystems, with numerous benthic organisms and plankton migrating, dying or even becoming extinct as a result of changes in habitat and breeding environments. Changes in habitat elements such as shoreline, mudflat, and nearshore shallow sea have a significant impact on the community structure of macrobenthos in the nearshore waters of Bohai Bay, and the environmental changes caused by the reclamation project are unfavorable to the survival of mollusks and crustaceans, resulting in a decrease in the number of species and a reduction in diversity. Reclamation projects have prominent impacts on marine living resources such as benthic organisms, plankton, fish eggs and larvae, swimming animals, etc. For example, arkshells and tetraodontiform clams show vertical migration behavior after being buried, and the mortality rate gradually increases with the increase of burial depth, and the sensitivity of larvae to the suspension gradually increases with the prolongation of the exposure time of suspended matter. Reclamation exacerbated the loss of benthic habitats, reduced species diversity, and average biomass and abundance in the Yellow Bohai Sea, while offshore benthic habitat loss and fragmentation led to significant changes in benthic faunal distribution patterns.

Marine fishery resources are an important foundation for the sustainable development of China's marine economy, but large-scale reclamation occupies and destroys the "three fields and one pass", which, along with pollution of the aquatic environment, overfishing and climate change, are the main causes of the degradation of fishery resources. The impact of large-scale reclamation on marine fishery resources is very serious, mainly manifested in the following: the construction of the project has caused permanent changes in the properties of the sea, leading to a decline in water quality, loss of benthic habitats, a decline in biodiversity and biomass, affecting the entire food chain and leading to the degradation of coastal ecosystems; leading to a reduction in the amount of tidal flux, deterioration in the ability to exchange water, and significant changes in the physical conditions of the coastal zone such as hydrodynamics, sediment and salt, thus causing the degradation of fishery resources spawning grounds, roping grounds, and the physical condition of the coastal zone. The hydrodynamic and sedimentary environment changes lead to changes in the material circulation process, which indirectly leads to the deterioration of the environmental quality of the surrounding marine areas, and indirectly leads to the degradation of the coastal ecosystem. The changes in hydrodynamic and sedimentary environments lead to changes in material circulation processes, which indirectly lead to the deterioration of environmental quality, ecological degradation and damage to biological resources in the surrounding waters.

The Caofeidian reclamation project has had a huge impact on coastal tides and currents, especially by blocking shallow tidal channels, drastically altering the surrounding topography and sediment erosion and siltation, causing damage to the coastal environment, ecology and resources, and even having a significant impact on the material transport and fish migration of the entire Bohai Sea. Reclamation has increased the content of suspended substances in near-shore waters and reduced the quality of the water environment, leading to the degradation of near-shore fishery resources; at the same time, restrictions on fishing have forced the cessation of a number of fishing operations and aquaculture industries, which to a certain extent has seriously affected the economy and livelihoods of local fisherfolk, and has put the local space for fishery development under pressure from unprecedented transfers.

Scientific and reasonable reclamation activities can provide a large amount of land resources for coastal economic and social development, meet the development of port terminals and port-related industries, provide space for aquaculture and salt production, etc., thus bringing new economic growth points to the local area, promoting the healthy, diversified and sustainable development of the regional economy, and upgrading the region's economic strength and social development level. However, blind, excessive and disorderly reclamation has many drawbacks, and has brought a great impact on the development of traditional industries and low-carbon economy, especially marine aquaculture, marine salt production, marine transportation and marine tourism.

For example, reclamation occupies the space for the development of aquaculture and salt industry, and due to the change of hydrodynamic conditions and the discharge of wastes and pollutants, the concentration of suspended solids in seawater increases, the quality of the water environment and benthic environment decreases, and the number of zooplankton and flora decreases drastically, which seriously affects the yield of aquaculture and the environment of the salt industry; the reclamation is generally located in the near-shore waters and estuarine entrances to the sea, such as shallow waters, which are often the areas where shipping is very prominent. These areas are often areas with very prominent shipping functions. Reclamation changes the hydrodynamic conditions of the sea and reduces the amount of tidal flow, resulting in siltation of sediment in bays and estuaries, siltation of ports, etc., which affects the navigation of shipping vessels, resulting in a decline in the function of waterways, and damage to the function of harbors and their economic benefits, and even necessitating the selection of new harbors.

Reclamation has led to an increase in the risk of natural disasters in the coastal zone and the oceans, as well as an increase in the vulnerability of the ecological environment, a decrease in the carrying capacity of resources and the environment, and an intensification of the contradictions between the economic and social system and the natural environmental system. Reclamation has changed the hydrodynamic conditions of the sea, causing sedimentation and siltation, weakening the wave dissipation capacity of offshore shallow waters, exacerbating the destructive effects of storm surges and other marine disasters, and directly affecting offshore protection projects; the concentration of suspended solids and eutrophic substances in the water has increased, and the water environment of the surrounding areas has deteriorated, with frequent occurrence of ecological disasters such as red tides and jellyfish and a great threat to the health of marine biodiversity and ecosystems. Reclamation breaks the balance of the dependence between land and sea, impedes the coordinated development of land and sea, changes the curved natural shoreline into a straight artificial shoreline, reduces the size of bays and estuaries, obstructs the channels leading to the sea, affects the descent of floodwaters, and alters the characteristics of the water cycle between the surface and the subsurface.

Reclamation encroaches on and destroys the natural wetlands along the coast, destroying the feeding grounds of animals, leading to the endangerment of many rare species and the destruction of many valuable coastal tourism resources; highly polluting, heavy metal-rich and other toxic substances are enriched in shellfish and fish, which are enriched through the food chain, and pose a great threat to the health of human beings. Reclamation has led to the loss of value of marine resources, intensified conflicts among different stakeholders, and easily caused social instability: reclaimed land has caused the disappearance of sandy beaches, mudflats, and other resources, and many fishermen are unable to continue to engage in marine fishery production and their income has decreased significantly, and in the absence of proper placement and transfer of surplus labor, it is easy to intensify social conflicts at a certain level; the management of marine resources involves multiple government departments, and there are often problems of sectoral interests and jurisdictions. The management of marine resources involves a number of government departments, and there are often differences in sectoral interests and jurisdictions, which can easily lead to contradictions and conflicts between departments and regions.

3.2.3 *The Impact of Alien Species Invasion on the Ecological Environment of Ports*

Invasive species refer to species that are introduced from their original habitats to new ecosystems, posing threats to the biodiversity, ecological functions, and the survival and reproduction abilities of local species in the new ecosystems. In the ecological environment of the port area, the invasion of alien species may have serious impacts, including competition and predation pressure on local species, destruction of the food chain, and changes to habitats (Fu et al. 2022).

Firstly, the invasion of alien species may lead to increased competition and predation pressure on local species. Some alien species have strong competitive abilities and adaptability (Cao 2021a, b). They compete with local species for survival resources, such as food, habitats, and breeding grounds, leading to a decrease or even extinction of local species. At the same time, some alien species may become new top predators, exerting predation pressure on local species and disrupting the balance of the original food chain. This increase in competition and predation pressure may have a negative impact on the stability and biodiversity of the port area's ecosystem.

Secondly, the invasion of alien species may cause damage to the food chain in the port area. The food chain in the port area is an interconnected and interdependent ecosystem composed of multiple species. When alien species invade, they may directly or indirectly interact with existing species, affecting the reproduction, migration, and food chain relationships of the original species, leading to the breakdown and disruption of the food chain. This will result in changes to the functions of the ecosystem, such as reducing the ability to purify water, destroying habitats, and so on, thereby having a profound impact on the ecological environment of the port area.

Thirdly, the invasion of alien species may change the structure and characteristics of habitats in the port area (Su 2023). Some alien species have strong adaptability and rapid reproduction abilities. They may find suitable conditions for survival and reproduction in the new ecosystem, gradually changing the structure and characteristics of the habitat. For example, some invasive plants may form dense single-species communities, replacing the original plant communities, leading to a decrease in habitat diversity; some invasive animals may change the physical and chemical characteristics of the soil, affecting the growth and distribution of local vegetation. This change in habitat may render the port area's ecosystem unable to provide the original ecological services, such as water source protection, soil conservation, and climate regulation.

Lastly, the invasion of alien species may disrupt the ecological balance and stability of the port area. The port area's ecosystem is a complex balance system, subject to the interaction and regulation of various biological and non-biological factors. When alien species invade, they may disrupt the original ecological balance and have a negative impact on the stability of the ecosystem. For example, some alien species may cause the spread of diseases, leading to a decrease in the number of local species; some alien plants may release toxic substances, having adverse effects on local plants and animals. This disruption of the ecological balance may lead to the collapse and loss of function of the entire port area's ecosystem.

The invasion of alien species has had significant impacts on the ecological environment of the port area, including competition and predation pressure on local species, destruction of the food chain, changes to habitats, and disruption of ecological balance and stability (Luo 2023). To mitigate these impacts, it is necessary to strengthen the prevention and control of alien species invasion, improve risk assessment and monitoring capabilities, strengthen species management and control, enhance scientific research and technical support, strengthen international cooperation and information sharing, and jointly promote the protection and sustainable development of the port area's ecological environment.

3.2.4 *Impact of Channel Excavation/Dredging on the Ecological Environment of the Port Area*

(1) Impact on River Habitat

Channel dredging operations, including stone dumping, sinking, and casting permeable frames, can cause local changes or disappearance of the aquatic environment in the construction area (Kang and Xu 2017). For example, the hardening of riverbank lining isolates the soil from the water, blocking direct contact between river water organisms, microorganisms, and the land, reducing the river's self-purification ability. In addition, stone dumping and sinking can increase riverbed roughness, forming underwater obstacles in the river. These obstacles can create turbulent wake flows, which over time can form artificial fish reef effects, providing refuge or habitats for migratory organisms.

Channel excavation and dredging can cause water to become stirred and turbid, causing suspended matter to float in the water, leading to changes in water quality. These suspended substances can affect the transparency of the water and the process of photosynthesis, impacting the photosynthetic productivity and biodiversity of the underwater ecosystem. In addition, suspended matter may also affect the dissolved oxygen content, nutrient salt concentration, and pH value of the water, affecting the growth and reproduction of aquatic organisms.

During channel excavation and dredging, a large amount of sediment and silt will be stirred up and suspended in the water, forming suspended matter and causing sediment transport (Feng and Guo 2023). These suspended substances may be transported to other areas under the action of water flow, causing changes in the distribution and composition of coastal and marine sediments. This change may affect the habitat and food chain structure of benthic organisms, further affecting fishery resources and ecosystem stability.

(2) Impact on Plankton

The stone dumping and sinking operations of channel dredging can disturb the original balance of the construction water body. On one hand, it can increase the concentration of suspended matter in the construction water area in a short time, reducing the number of plankton in the construction water area. The suspended matter produced by channel dredging operations is mostly sticky silt, which can cause filter-feeding plankton that can only distinguish particle size to die due to ingestion of excessive silt. On the other hand, the increase in the concentration of suspended matter in the operation water area can reduce the light transmittance of the water, hinder the photosynthesis of some algae and other planktonic plants, reduce the total amount of planktonic plants in the water area, and in the long term, affect the number of fish that feed on planktonic plants.

(3) Impact on Benthic Organisms

Excavation and dredging of shipping channels may lead to ecosystem destruction. For example, when ecologically important habitats (e.g., coral reefs, seagrass beds, wetlands, etc.) are damaged or directly buried, there may be a serious loss of biodiversity and ecological functions. In addition, waterway engineering activities may also lead to the displacement and damage of marine organisms, negatively affecting the productivity and sustainability of fishery resources such as fish, shellfish and crustaceans (Xie and Zhuang 2017).

Some organisms inhabiting stony and sandy beaches in the river channel have poor relative motility, and the benthic organisms on the ground surface of the direct riverbed will be buried during the process of rock-throwing and sinking and discharging during the construction operation of the channel dredging, resulting in the reduction of benthic organisms' numbers and populations. The impact of loss of benthic organisms during the construction period is categorized into permanent and temporary occupancy; the occupied area below the dry water platform is calculated according to temporary occupancy, and the loss is calculated by three times, and the area above the dry water platform is calculated according to permanent occupancy, and the loss is calculated by 20 times. The impacts of the channel dredging project on the aquatic environment also include the number and population of fish and rare wildlife. In addition, while analyzing the environmental impact, the current status of pollution source strength should be specifically calculated and predicted to provide a realistic basis for good environmental protection work in the later stage. Usually the pollutants of waterway dredging are suspended matter, and the suspended matter source strength produced by dredging and mud throwing is predicted according to the calculation formula recommended by the "Environmental Impact Assessment Specification for Inland Navigation Construction Projects" (JTJ227-2001), which predicts the total amount of suspended matter source strength produced by different operation modes.

3.3 Impact of Ports on the Atmosphere

3.3.1 Types of Air Pollutants from Ports and Ships

The prosperity of the water transport industry, while bringing huge economic benefits to our country, has also exacerbated the air pollution problem along the channel and surrounding port areas. The fuel consumption caused by ship power devices continuously emits nitrogen oxides (NOx), sulfur dioxide (SO_2), hydrocarbons (HC), carbon monoxide (CO), volatile organic pollutants (VOCs), fine particulate matter (PM) and other toxic and harmful pollutants, as well as greenhouse gases such as carbon dioxide (CO_2), into the atmosphere.

Research shows that ship emissions have become the third largest source of air pollution in our country after industrial waste gas and vehicle exhaust, and are also an important source of air pollutants in our port cities. According to the "China Mobile Source Environmental Management Annual Report 2019", in 2018, the national ship emissions of SO_2, HC, NOx, PM were 588,000 tons, 89,000 tons, 1.511 million tons, and 109,000 tons, respectively, accounting for 98.33%, 11.68%, 26.88%, and 24.49% of the national non-road mobile source emissions.

Specifically, the activity areas of inland waterway vessels often adjoin towns and village residential areas, where the population is relatively concentrated, and lack the sea-oriented diffusion transfer areas of seaports. Their pollution directly affects the air quality of urban environments and the health of terrestrial residents. Typically, particulate matter is formed by condensation of hundreds of volatile and semi-volatile substances on carbon cores. Excessive inhalation can cause inflammation in the body and lead to asthma and cardiopulmonary diseases. Research by Zhang Yan and others shows that in Shanghai, the impact of ships on urban air is mainly caused by inland waterway vessels, whose pollutant emissions account for about 40–80% of the total ship emissions. NOx can cause symptoms such as coughing, respiratory infections, and asthma, and reduce lung function, especially in children. Even short-term exposure to NOx can cause coughing and sore throat. In addition, NOx and olefin hydrocarbons can form highly toxic photochemical smog under intense ultraviolet radiation, causing strong irritation to the human eye and respiratory system, and possibly causing bronchitis and lung infections. SO_2 easily combines with water to form sulfurous acid, which has a strong irritant effect on the human mouth and nasal mucosa. If the concentration of SO_2 in the air is too high, it can cause symptoms such as difficulty breathing, redness of the respiratory tract, and chest tightness. After encountering water vapor, it forms sulfuric acid smog, which stays in the atmosphere for a long time, causing greater harm to humans and the environment. Port operations are closely related to ship transportation. As the volume of water transportation increases, port business continues to grow, and the environmental problems caused by port operations are further highlighted. The dust generated from the storage and operation of various bulk cargo yards is increasingly polluting the environment. Port dust is one of the main components of total suspended particulate pollution in our country's port cities. The continuous growth of the throughput of bulk liquid organic chemicals and bulk liquid fuel oil at the dock leads to a corresponding increase in port VOCs emissions. The large number of port operation machinery and feeder vehicles also face huge pressure for energy conservation and emission reduction.

At present, the emissions of atmospheric pollutants from ships and ports have become an important source of air pollution in the near-port areas of our country. As the emissions from land fixed sources and road motor vehicles are gradually effectively controlled, the impact of emissions of atmospheric pollutants from ships and ports on the regional atmospheric environment and ecosystem is becoming increasingly prominent. The prevention and control of atmospheric pollution from ships and ports is also attracting more and more attention from the academic community, the government, and the public, and is gradually becoming a new research hotspot.

3.3.2 *Emission Situation Under Different Operating Conditions of Ships*

For the construction of the emission inventory, it involves ship activities near and within the port, including entering the port, maneuvering, berthing, and leaving the port. By adding up all the activity stages of each ship berthed at the port and their respective fuel consumption, an estimate of the environmental footprint of port maritime operations can be obtained. These data can be provided by the port authorities or by AIS data services that collect ship location and speed. The main activities can be described by the mode of ship arrival at the port and the berthing time of each stop. Ports tend to release reports on their short-term expected traffic, which, combined with a comprehensive dataset of visiting vessels and berthing times, can be used to obtain a comprehensive analysis of emissions within the port.

When ships navigate in inland waterways and enter and exit ports, their speed will change accordingly, resulting in different navigation states when the ship's speed varies. The navigation state of the ship determines the operating state of the diesel engine. To make the calculation results of the atmospheric pollution emission inventory more accurate and the spatiotemporal distribution characteristics more apparent, it is necessary to calculate the emissions of atmospheric pollutants under different navigation states separately. The emission inventory study of the Port of Long Beach in the United States and SmithTWP and others divided the navigation conditions into four different driving modes according to the navigation speed of ocean-going ships, namely cruising state (speed $>$ 12kn), slow speed state (8kn $<$ speed $\leq$ 12kn), maneuvering state (1kn $<$ speed $\leq$ 8kn), and berthing state (speed $\leq$ 1kn). Due to the complex hydrological environment of inland waterways, narrow channels, and slower speed compared to the open ocean environment, this paper divides the navigation state of ships in this area into the following four types based on the navigation speed characteristics obtained from the public AIS data on the Internet: cruising condition, low-speed cruising condition, port maneuvering condition, and berthing

Table 3.1 Classification of navigation states

Running condition	Basis of judgment
Cruises	Speed>8 kn
Low-speed cruise	3kn< speed $\leq$ 8kn
In-port maneuvering	1kn< speed $\leq$ 3kn
Mooring (of a ship)	Speed $\leq$ 1 kn

condition. The determination basis for each navigation condition is shown in the following table.

Determination of ship dynamic activity level information The ship activity level data required for the establishment of the air pollutant emission inventory of inland waterway ships in Jiangsu section of Beijing-Hangzhou Canal are mainly the activity time and engine loading factor of each operating condition of the ship. Vessel operating conditions can be roughly divided into three kinds of mooring traveling, normal navigation, and mooring; according to the literature and relevant marine personnel's visit, for the inland waterway vessels navigating on the Beijing-Hangzhou Canal, their complete operating conditions should include the conditions of going out of port, normal navigation, waiting to enter the locks, entering the locks, waiting to exit the locks, exiting the locks, entering the port, mooring, etc.; in each condition, the main and auxiliary engines of the vessel are operating as in Table 3.1.

Ships will produce different emissions under different conditions. Below are some common ship conditions and their emissions (Cao 2021a, b):

(1) Cruising condition

During navigation, ships mainly provide power by burning fuel. At this time, the main pollutants emitted by ships include nitrogen oxides (NOx), sulfur dioxide (SO_2), particulate matter (PM), and carbon monoxide (CO). The amount of emissions depends on the type of fuel of the ship, combustion efficiency, and load, among other factors.

(2) Port condition

During port berthing, ships usually need to keep running to maintain power supply, air conditioning systems, etc. At this time, ships may use fuel with a higher sulfur content or burn liquid fuel through a generator set. Therefore, under port conditions, the content of sulfur dioxide (SO2) and particulate matter (PM) emitted by ships is usually higher.

(3) Start-stop process

During the start and stop of the engine, the concentration of pollutants emitted is usually higher. This is because during the start-up process, the engine is in a non-steady state, and during the stop process, unburned fuel and carbon residues may be emitted into the atmosphere.

(4) Refueling and cargo loading and unloading conditions

During refueling and cargo loading and unloading, ships may release volatile organic compounds (VOCs). These compounds may have a negative impact on air quality, and some VOCs may also be toxic and carcinogenic.

It should be noted that there are many specific factors affecting the emission situation of ships, including the type of ship, engine technology, sailing speed, and the fuel used. In order to reduce the atmospheric pollution emissions of ships, when designing and operating ships, it is necessary to consider using cleaner fuels, using emission control devices, promoting shore power supply, and strictly complying with relevant environmental protection regulations and standards.

To reduce the impact of ship emissions on the environment, the International Maritime Organization (IMO) and various governments have formulated a series of ship emission standards and control measures. For example, the IMO's international convention stipulates the emission limits of ships and requires ships to use low-sulfur fuel or adopt other emission reduction technologies. In addition, some regions and ports have also established stricter emission standards, requiring ships to treat exhaust gas and wastewater when entering the port to reduce the impact on the surrounding environment (Table 3.2).

3.3.3 *Emissions Under Different Port Operation Processes*

Once the ship is berthed, a series of loading and unloading of goods and passenger boarding and disembarking operations are carried out at the port according to the dock and ship type. When it comes to Ro-Ro terminals, vehicles need to move quickly from the ship to the yard, and vice versa, while trailers need to be moved by special yard equipment or truck trailer combinations. In the case of container terminals, due to the need for more yard equipment, yard operations are more complex. Stopford (2009) defines a dock as consisting of several berths, each berth is served by one or more ship-to-shore (dock) cranes capable of lifting up to 40 tons of containers. These cranes are usually installed on tracks, moving along the dock, positioned at the required position relative to the berthed ship. They are classified by lifting capacity and the maximum size of the container ship that can be handled. The main types are Panama cranes, which can handle ships 12–13 containers wide, post-Panama cranes (18 containers), and super post-Panama cranes, which can handle 25 containers, to handle the largest container ships.

Container terminals require a large storage space to store containers that may stay in the port for several days. Ideally, the place where containers are stacked should be close to the berth for quick unloading. This area is usually referred to as the yard, where containers are stored in multi-layer stacks, and for ports with very limited area resources, up to 12 layers of containers can be reached (for example, Hong Kong). The transportation between the dock and the yard varies depending on the size of the port, throughput, and available resources. The most commonly used

Table 3.2 Operating conditions and main engine status

Operating condition		Host state	Auxiliary machinery
Coasting	Leave harbor	Vessel started, main engine switched on, vessel speed increased to normal inland waterway speed	Part of the auxiliary engines are closed, the ship's electricity mainly comes from the battery or generator driven by the main engine to generate electricity, the battery is mainly driven by the main engine to start the generator charging solar panels charging: a small portion of the use of auxiliary engines
	Inbound	Vessel decelerates from normal voyage to docking with main engine on	
Normal passage		The main engine runs smoothly and the ship basically maintains a certain speed	
In and Out gates	Waiting to enter the gate	Ship moored in the wrong place, main engine off, no air pollutant emissions	
	Inlet sluice gate	The inlet gate opens and ships queue up to enter the gate in turn, the process of the mainframe is turned on	
	Waiting to exit the gate	Inlet gate closed, ship's main engine shut down	
	Out of the gate	Main engine on. Ship speeding up. Turning into the channel for normal navigation	
Mooring (of a ship)		Vessel is in docked condition, main engine is off, no air pollutant emission	Some ships turn on auxiliary engines for ship's electricity: some ships turn off auxiliary engines and use batteries or shore power to supply ship's electricity

machines are forklifts, front-moving stackers, chassis trailers, straddle carriers, and automated guided vehicles (AGV). Once the dock crane unloads the container from the ship (in the case of chassis and AGV boxes, the container is placed on top of the platform), these vehicles will pick up the container and move it to a place close to the storage stack, and vice versa. Cargo handling equipment needs to move containers horizontally and vertically at the stacking place (container reshuffling).

Typical machinery includes:

Rubber tired gantry (RTG), which is flexible, but puts a high load on the road surface.

Rail mounted gantry (RMG), more suitable for larger stacks, but more expensive.

Automated stacking cranes, although the purchase and maintenance costs are high, they reduce labor costs.

Containers destined for the mainland must first be moved from the container stack in the yard to the container stack on the mainland, and then they will be loaded onto locomotives or heavy trucks. These actions in the yard are usually performed by stacker cranes.

The last (or first process) occurs at the gate where export containers leave the port for inland destinations, and import containers arrive separately. The busiest terminals use advanced information technology to reduce congestion at the boarding gates and waiting times for trucks. As shown in Fig. 12.3, gate operations are a significant contributor to the production of most types of pollutants.

In all the above processes of moving containers, a large amount of energy is required. The source of this energy depends on the equipment used, whether it consumes fossil fuels (such as diesel engines), relies on electricity provided by the grid, or is a hybrid system. Estimates of energy demand can be completed by analysis calculations, which are based on the horizontal and vertical movement of containers from one place to another, using basic energy models (equipment specifications, container mass, movement speed, and height difference are necessary inputs) or simulation tools.

Different operational processes in the port can affect ship emissions. Here are the possible emissions under different operational processes in the port:

(1) Loading and unloading of ships

During the process of loading and unloading ships, machinery such as cranes, transport equipment, and cargo handling machinery may be involved. These devices are usually driven by diesel engines, so they emit pollutants such as nitrogen oxides (NOx), particulate matter (PM), and carbon monoxide (CO) during operation.

(2) Refueling of ships

When ships need to refuel, the fuel supply is usually carried out by oil tankers or refueling ships. During the refueling process, volatile organic compounds (VOCs) and other gaseous pollutants may be released into the air. These pollutants have a certain impact on air quality.

(3) Operation of refrigerated cabins

When operating refrigerated cabins for goods in the port, refrigeration equipment and refrigerants are usually used. If the equipment is old or poorly maintained, refrigerant leaks may occur. Some refrigerants, such as hydrochlorofluorocarbons (HCFCs) and hydrofluorocarbons (HFCs), are greenhouse gases that have a destructive impact on the atmospheric ozone layer.

(4) Port power supply

To reduce ship emissions in the port, some ports provide shore power supply systems, allowing ships to use shore power during berthing without the need for engine operation. This power supply method can reduce the emission of carbon dioxide (CO2) and harmful gases from ships.

To reduce pollutant emissions during port operations, a series of measures can be taken, such as using low-sulfur fuel, installing emission control equipment, maintaining good operation of equipment, and regularly checking refrigeration equipment to prevent leaks. In addition, promoting shore power supply systems is also one of the effective ways to reduce ship emissions. These measures help improve the port environment and reduce ship emissions under different operational processes.

At this stage, our country has not fully realized the harm of ship emissions and the importance of air pollution control. The main problems currently include the following aspects:

(1) The management system is chaotic, and the division of functions is unclear. At present, there are many departments involved in ship pollution. Although the functions of each department have been divided, there is still overlap, leading to a situation where "everyone is in charge, but no one is in charge." For example, both the Ministry of Environmental Protection and the National Ocean Administration have the function of supervising and managing the marine environment, but the leading and coordinating departments have not been clearly defined.
(2) The total amount of air pollutant emissions from ports and ships is unclear. There are a large number of motorized fishing boats with significant air pollutant emissions. However, due to the constraints of the overall domestic development level and different management methods, the management level of motorized fishing boats is low, and the work of preventing and controlling air pollution from motorized fishing boats is still a blank. Only a few cities have carried out emission inventory research, and the total amount of air pollutant emissions from ships and ports nationwide and their impact have not yet been mastered.
(3) There is still a significant difference between China's domestic ship emission control areas and international emission control areas (ECA). At present, the International Maritime Organization (IMO) has approved the establishment of four sulfur oxide emission control areas in the Baltic Sea, North Sea, North America, and the Caribbean Sea of the United States. Ships entering these areas should use fuel with a sulfur content not higher than 1000 ppm from January 1, 2015. However, the deadline for China's domestic ship emission control areas to fully use fuel with a sulfur content not higher than 5000 ppm is only one

year ahead of the global implementation deadline (January 1, 2020) required by Annex VI of the International Convention for the Prevention of Pollution from Ships (MARPOL Convention, with China and over 150 other contracting states accounting for 98% of the world's total shipping tonnage), and no nitrogen oxide emission control requirements have been proposed.

(4) The issue of marine fuel quality supervision is prominent. Although the "Air Pollution Prevention Law" requires that inland and river-sea direct ships should use standard diesel. In addition, starting from this year, the Pearl River Delta, Yangtze River Delta, and Bohai Sea (Beijing-Tianjin-Hebei) water area ship emission control areas have begun to implement low-sulfur fuel control requirements, and supporting policies for low-sulfur fuel supply and quality supervision must be introduced. At present, the threshold for the production of marine fuel oil in China is low, the source of crude oil is complex, it is difficult to guarantee the quality of oil, the market is still to be standardized, the supervision task is large, and the supervision means are insufficient.

(5) There is a lack of pollution prevention infrastructure, and the utilization rate is low. At present, many ports' facilities, equipment, and materials for receiving and treating ship pollutants, dust prevention, oil gas recovery, pollution surveillance and monitoring, and emergency handling of pollution accidents do not meet the needs; there is also a lack of effective ship and port environmental monitoring, energy efficiency monitoring systems, etc. Due to technical limitations, the utilization rate of established infrastructure such as shore power is not high, resulting in waste of resources.

References

Cao Z (2021a) Analysis of the harm of foreign species invading illegally with cross-border carry-on items and mailed items. Qual Saf Inspection Test 31(05):53–55

Cao Y (2021b) Study on emission inventory and characteristics of typical regional ships and port area atmospheric pollutants. Shanghai University

Chen X, Zhang J (2014) The impact of sea area use on the nearshore sea area environment—a case study of Hainan Island. Ocean Dev Manage 31(07):97–99

Feng D, Guo Y (2023) The main environmental impacts and preventive measures of cutter suction dredgers in channel dredging projects. Popular Standard 11:121–122+128

Fu W, Huang H, Zhang H et al (2022) Current status and suggestions on the construction of foreign invasive species prevention and control standard system in China. J Biosaf 31(01):87–93

Hao W (2016) The impact of port area construction on the environmental capacity of nearshore sea areas. Enterp Technol Dev 35(08):64–65

He C, Luo X (2018) The application of ecological restoration technology in port construction. China Water Transp 11:70–71

Kang Q, Xu X (2017) Environmental impact assessment and countermeasures of channel dredging engineering. Environ Dev 29(05):41–42

Ke Y (2022) Analysis of pollution control and environmental protection strategies in Nearshore Sea areas. Resour Conserv Environ Protect 05:16–19

Li L, Li Y, Gao J (2017) Experience in pollution prevention and control of ships and ports in the United States and suggestions for China. Environ Sustain Dev 42(05):111–115

Li X, Yue Q, Hu H et al (2023) Impact of reclamation activities on marine environment and biological resources and countermeasure suggestions. Mar Dev Manage 40(02):105–114
Liu Q (2023) Research on the impact evaluation of reclamation projects on the surrounding marine environment. China High-tech 09:111–112+124
Long L (2022) Research on the ecological impact and countermeasures of port and channel engineering construction. Pearl River Water Transport 24:63–65
Luo J (2023) The harm and countermeasures of foreign species invasion in China—taking Canadian goldenrod as an example. Trop Agric Eng 47(03):159–161
Lv H, Zhang S, Song D et al (2023) Changes and loss assessment of environmental capacity in Qinzhou Bay, Guangxi under the pressure of large-scale reclamation and land-based pollution. J Oceanogr 45(02):139–150
Su B (2023) Research on the prevention and control of foreign species invasion at ports based on holistic governance theory. Shanghai Customs College
Tan J (2023) Research on the temporal and spatial distribution characteristics of regional ship atmospheric pollution emission inventory based on AIS. Chongqing Jiaotong University
Tian Y (2023) Analysis of the impact of port shipping operations pollutants on the ecological environment. China Navig Wkly 18:51–53
Wang R, Zhang G (2023) Spatiotemporal analysis of tidal wave characteristics in Macao under the influence of reclamation. People's Pearl River 44(02):76–80+114
Xie J, Zhuang F (2017) Discussion on the impact and preventive measures of channel construction on marine ecological environment. Jiangxi Build Mater 18:164–165
Yu C (2023) Research on the ecological impact and countermeasures of port and channel engineering construction. 06:43–45
Yuan D, Lou, A, Li F et al (2003) Numerical study on the impact of Tianheng Island and Lvdao Wharf construction on the hydrodynamics of nearby waters. Mar Sci 12:62–65+70
Zhang G, Luo X, Lu C et al (2022) Study on the impact of reclamation projects on the hydrodynamics of Macao and nearby waters. Mar Eng 40(04):34–43
Zhang Y, Gong Y, Zhang X et al (2018) Numerical study on the impact of Zhangjiashan Island wharf construction on the hydrodynamic environment of Nearshore Sea areas. Environ Prot Circular Econ 38(06):27–33+38

Chapter 4
Study on the Emission Estimation Model of Pollutants in Regional Port Groups

4.1 Main Port Types and Pollution Emission Types

Docks are essentially facilities within the port, providing several berths for handling ships and exchanging goods and/or passengers. A port may have many different types (and sizes) of docks, each with a main operator responsible for various operations. Docks consist of dry and wet infrastructure, superstructures, cargo handling equipment, and human resources. Wet infrastructure is defined as the port basin, where one or more berths can receive ships. The pavement of the storage area, the roads within the dock, the crane tracks, and the foundation of the drainage system are all part of the dry infrastructure. Superstructures refer to buildings in the terminal, sheds, and all other covered storage spaces. Cargo handling equipment and human resources vary depending on the type and scale of the dock. Therefore, the main types can be divided into the following: Ro-Ro docks, liquid bulk cargo docks, dry bulk cargo docks, ferry docks, multi-purpose docks, container docks (Tan et al. 2014).

The negative impact of port operations on the environment increases with the growing throughput. In recent years, port operations have direct and indirect environmental impacts that regulatory agencies, shippers, and port authorities have been trying to address. The main environmental impacts are air and water pollution, depletion due to port operations, noise, and light pollution, and fossil fuel emissions. The discharge of ballast water, dredging operations in the port, waste disposal, and oil spills can all cause pollution in the waters near the port (Chen et al. 2017).

Large ships carry a lot of water in their ballast tanks to stabilize the ship. When goods are removed, water is pumped in to compensate for changes in the distribution of cargo weight. After the cargo is loaded, the ballast water is discharged. Environmental problems arise when ballast water is discharged in different areas (pumped in at one port and released at another), which may lead to unintentional invasions of non-native species. These microorganisms can disrupt aquatic ecosystems and cause health problems. Similar problems may also occur when non-native organisms are transported through hull fouling. The aquatic environment is also negatively affected

B. Lu, *The Sustainable Development of Port Group*,
https://doi.org/10.1007/978-981-97-2378-2_4

when dredging operations are carried out to increase the depth of the port. Ships, cargo handling equipment, and port superstructures change the appearance of the environment around the port, causing visual intrusion or aesthetic pollution (Song 2014).

Coupled with the noise generated during port operations and light pollution during night operations, these have a serious negative impact on nearby residents, especially in terms of sleep deprivation and increased stress (Wan et al. 2013). Noise is a serious problem in today's transportation, especially noise from aircraft. To address the noise problem of airport operations, authorities have adopted various strategies. For example, changing the way aircraft enter the airport, steeper descents to minimize the impact on residents, and adopting new technologies on aircraft engines. There are similar situations in the maritime sector; however, for ports, the main source of noise pollution is dock and inland operations, not the ships themselves. Another very different environmental issue for port operations is the impact of maritime transport noise on marine mammals (Ye et al. 2001).

Air pollution in ports is the result of vehicle and cargo movement (ships, cargo handling equipment) and has both local and global consequences. Various types of pollutants are emitted, some of which affect local air quality, while others are forcing factors for climate change. Currently, dealing with air pollutants is the most pressing issue that ports, shippers, and regulatory agencies are trying to address through most existing policies and port initiatives.

4.2 Port and Ship Air Pollutant Emission Inventory

Our country is a nation with a dense network of waterways, numerous lakes, and abundant shipping resources. Waterway transportation, with its advantages of large transport capacity, low transport cost, high energy utilization rate, relatively small environmental impact, and less land resource occupation, plays an irreplaceable role in our country's transportation system, forming a comprehensive transportation system together with highways, railways, pipelines, and air transport.

The prosperity of the water transport industry, while bringing huge economic benefits to our country, has also exacerbated the air pollution problem along the shipping routes and surrounding port areas (Wang et al. 2007). The fuel consumption caused by ship propulsion systems continuously emits toxic and harmful pollutants such as nitrogen oxides (NOx), sulfur dioxide (SO_2), hydrocarbons (HC), carbon monoxide (CO), volatile organic pollutants (VOCs), and fine particulate matter (PM), as well as greenhouse gases such as carbon dioxide (CO_2). Studies have shown that ship emissions have become the third largest source of air pollution in our country after industrial waste gas and vehicle exhaust, and are also an important source of air pollutants in our port cities (Gu et al. 2017).

In particular, inland ship activity areas are often adjacent to towns and village residential areas where the population is relatively concentrated, and lack the sea-oriented diffusion transfer areas of seaports, so their pollution directly affects the air quality of urban environments and the health of land residents. Typically, particulates are formed by the condensation of hundreds of volatile and semi-volatile substances on a carbon core, and excessive inhalation can cause inflammation in the body and lead to asthma and cardiopulmonary diseases (Yin et al. 2017). Relevant research by Zhang Yan and others shows that in Shanghai, the impact of ships on urban air is mainly caused by inland ships, whose pollutant emissions account for about 40%-80% of total ship emissions. NOx can cause symptoms such as coughing, respiratory infections, and asthma, and also reduce lung function, especially in children, even short-term exposure to NOx can cause coughing and sore throat (Xu et al. 2019). In addition, NOx and olefinic hydrocarbons form highly toxic photochemical smog under intense ultraviolet light, causing strong irritation to the eyes and respiratory system, and may cause bronchitis and lung infections. SO_2 easily combines with water to form sulfurous acid, which has a strong irritant effect on the human mouth and nasal mucosa. If the concentration of SO_2 in the air is too high, it can cause symptoms such as difficulty breathing, redness of the respiratory tract, and chest tightness, and after encountering water vapor, it forms sulfuric acid smog, which stays in the atmosphere for a long time, causing greater harm to people and the environment.

Port operations and ship transportation are closely related. With the increase in water transportation volume, port business continues to grow, and the environmental problems brought about by port operations are further highlighted (Feng et al. 2019). The dust generated by various bulk cargo yards during storage and operation is increasingly polluting the environment. Port dust is one of the main components of total suspended particulates pollution in the atmospheric environment of our country's port cities. The continuous growth of the throughput of bulk liquid organic chemicals and bulk liquid fuel oil at the dock has led to a corresponding increase in port VOCs emissions. The large number of port operation machinery and collection and distribution vehicles also face huge pressure for energy conservation and emission reduction. At present, the emissions of atmospheric pollutants from ships and ports have become an important source of air pollution in the near-port areas of our country. As the emissions from land fixed sources and road motor vehicles are gradually effectively controlled, the impact of emissions of atmospheric pollutants from ships and ports on the regional atmospheric environment and ecosystem is becoming increasingly prominent. The prevention and control of atmospheric pollution from ships and ports is attracting more and more attention from the academic community, the government, and the public, and is gradually becoming a new research hotspot.

4.2.1 Port and Ship Air Pollutant Information Collection

The fine division and accurate acquisition of basic static information and activity level information of the main air pollution sources of ships and ports are the basis for establishing a high time–space resolution emission inventory of air pollutants

(Peng and Qiao 2014). This paper addresses the difficulty of obtaining static information and activity level data for inland river ships in our country, explores the establishment of a full-caliber data structure for the ship inventory of Dongdu Port, and conducts detailed surveys of ship activity level data and basic information data, ultimately obtaining highly accurate basic static information and activity level data for Dongdu Port ships. For coastal ships, the same acquisition method as existing research results is adopted—the Maritime AIS system, which provides detailed information on Dongdu Port ships. For the main air pollution sources in the port area, relevant static information and activity level information were obtained through various methods such as questionnaire surveys, field surveys, partial parameter measurements, and literature research, in order to provide data support for the subsequent accurate construction of the emission inventory.

(1) Regional ship static information and dynamic activity level information

① Static information

Ship quantity and type. According to the statistics and analysis of the visa information of ships entering and leaving Dongdu Port area from Xiamen Maritime Bureau, there were a total of 13,963 ship times entering and leaving the port area in 2017, with no inland river ships. Through analysis, this paper divides the ships arriving at Dongdu Port into six categories: bulk carriers, general cargo ships, container ships, oil ships, tugboats, and other ships. In 2017, the number of container ship arrivals at Dongdu Port was the highest, accounting for 50.05% of the total ship arrivals, followed by general cargo ships and bulk carriers, accounting for 30.84% and 11.39% respectively, and the proportion of oil ships, tugboats, and other ship arrivals was relatively small.

Ship engine power. The maximum continuous rated power of the main engine of the ship arriving at Dongdu Port is obtained one by one based on the full ship list and ship visa data of the ship arriving at Dongdu Port provided by Xiamen Maritime Bureau in 2017, which is not detailed here. When estimating the emission volume of the ship's auxiliary engine, the auxiliary/main engine power ratio experience coefficient in existing research in Hong Kong and the United States is mainly referred to, and its ratio coefficient is shown in Table 4.1.

Table 4.1 Auxiliary/main engine power ratio coefficient boiler power

Ship type	Auxiliary rated power/main engine rated power
Bulk carriers	0.222
General cargo ships	0.191
Container ship	0.220
Tanker	0.211
Tug	0.222
Other ships	0.257

Boilers are used for heating fuel oil, lubricating oil, onboard domestic water, main engine cylinder heating, driving auxiliary machinery, and other miscellaneous onboard uses. When the ship is sailing normally at sea, the boiler is shut down in most cases. This is because the ship is equipped with an exhaust gas waste heat boiler, which can absorb the heat of the ship's main engine exhaust gas, replace the normal operation of the boiler, and provide the heat required on board. Therefore, when the ship is sailing normally at sea, the boiler is shut down. This article uses boiler load power data provided by Entec research, as shown in Table 4.2. The oil tanker needs the boiler to provide steam to drive the liquid cargo pump and the inert gas blower, which increases the load of the boiler. The boiler output power of the oil tanker is also higher than that of other types of ships.

② Dynamic activity level data

Ship operation time. The operation time of ships in various operating conditions in the Dongdu port area is mainly obtained based on the timestamp (TimeStamp) information in the AIS information, which is not detailed in this article.

Load factor. The load factors of the main engine and auxiliary engine refer to the research results of the United States and Hong Kong, as shown in Tables 4.3 and 4.4.

(1) Main atmospheric pollution source information

① Overview of port loading and unloading docks

According to actual surveys, there are a total of 6 docks in the Dongdu port area, namely Haitian Dock, Xiayu Dock, Shihushan Dock, Guomao Dock, Lugong Dock,

Table 4.2 Boiler load power (unit: kW)

Ship type	Navigation status	Slow	Shore driving	Passing status
General cargo ships	0	137	137	137
Container ship—1000	0	241	241	241
Container ship—2000	0	325	325	325
Container ship—3000	0	474	474	47%
Container ship—4000	0	492	492	492
Container ship—5000	0	630	630	630
Container ship—6000	0	545	S6	545
Container ship—7000	0	551	55%	551
Container ship—8000	0	525	525	S25
Container ship—9000	0	547	547	547
Other container ships	0	600	600	600
Bulk carriers	0	132	132	132
Tanker	0	371	171	3000
Tug	0	0	0	0
Other ships	0	137	137	137

Table 4.3 Ship main engine load factor

Ship type	Vessel navigation status		
	Cruising status	Drive slowly	Mooring and driving
Bulk carriers	0.5	0.361	0.031
General cargo ships	0.496	0.123	0.02
Container ship	0.5	0.296	0.024
Tanker	0.5	0.382	0.023
Tug	0.5	0.569	0.02
Other ships	0.50	0.454	0.023

Table 4.4 Ship auxiliary engine load factor

Ship type	Vessel navigation status			
	Cruising status	Drive slowly	Mooring and driving	Moored status
Bulk carriers	0.17	0.27	0.45	0.22
General cargo ships	0.13	0.25	0.5	0.17
Container ship	0.17	0.27	0.45	0.22
Tanker	0.13	0.27	0.45	0.67
Tug	0.17	0.27	0.45	0.22
Other ships	0.17	0.27	0.45	0.22

and Xianma Dock. Each dock is operated by Xiamen Haitian Container Co., Ltd., Xiamen Xiayu Dock Co., Ltd., Xiamen Guomao Dock Co., Ltd., Xiamen Shihushan Dock Co., Ltd., Xiamen Xianma Dock Co., Ltd., and Xiamen Lugong Petrochemical Co., Ltd. Among them, Xiamen Haitian Container Co., Ltd. and Xiamen Xiayu Dock Co., Ltd. have merged into Xiamen Container Dock Group Co., Ltd. In 2017, the main operating goods and throughput of the above-mentioned dock operating companies are shown in Table 4.5.

② Fuel consumption of operating machinery

In 2017, the fuel consumption of operating machinery of each dock operating company in the Dongdu port area is shown in Table 4.6. Among them, Xiamen Lugong Petrochemical Co., Ltd. mainly operates liquid bulk (finished oil) goods, mainly using pipeline transportation, without fuel-operated machinery.

③ Total freight volume and fuel consumption of feeder vehicles of each dock company

In 2017, the total freight volume and fuel consumption of feeder vehicles of each dock company in the Dongdu port area are shown in Table 4.7.

Table 4.5 Overview of Dongdu Port area loading and unloading docks in 2017

	The name of the pier	Running a company	Mainly engaged in goods	Throughput	Remark
1	Skypier	Xiamen Haitian Container Co., Ltd	Container	3.86 million TEU	At present, the two companies have been merged into Xiamen Container Terminal Group Co., Ltd
2	Xiangyu Wharf	Xiamen Xiangyu Wharf Co., Ltd			
3	Guomao Terminal	Xiamen International Trade Terminal Co., Ltd	Dry bulk and miscellaneous pieces	2.13 million tons	
4	Shihushan Wharf	Xiamen Shihushan Wharf Co., Ltd	Dry Bulk (Coal & Ore)	6.48 million tons	
5	Modern docks	Xiamen Modern Terminal Co., Ltd	Dry bulk and miscellaneous (sand and gravel, steel, fertilizers)	7.66 million tons	
6	Luyong Wharf	Xiamen Luyong Petrochemical Co., Ltd	Liquid Disperse (Refined Oil)	440,000 tons	

Table 4.6 Fuel consumption of operating machinery of dock companies in Dongdu Port Area in 2017

	Name	Dock cargo	Fuel consumption (t)
1	Xiamen Container Terminal Group Co., Ltd	Container	3709.2
2	Xiamen International Trade Terminal Co., Ltd	Dry and miscellaneous	270.6
3	Xiamen Shihushan Wharf Co., Ltd	Dry loose	220
4	Xiamen Modern Terminal Co., Ltd	Dry and miscellaneous	149
Total			4348.8

④ Parameters related to bulk cargo dock yard Particle size multiplier

The particle size degree of dust from loading and unloading, wind erosion, and road dust in the bulk cargo dock yard is based on the values in the "Technical Guidelines

Table 4.7 Total freight volume and fuel consumption of feeder vehicles of dock companies in Dongdu Port Area in 2017

	Name	Dock cargo	Total vehicle traffic (10,000 tons)	Fuel Consumption (t)
1	Xiamen Container Terminal Group Co., Ltd	Container	3860	680.9
2	Xiamen International Trade Terminal Co., Ltd	Dry and miscellaneous	648	81.6
3	Xiamen Shihushan Wharf Co., Ltd	Dry loose	766	93.2
4	Xiamen Modern Terminal Co., Ltd	Dry and miscellaneous	213	3.8
5	Name	Dock cargo	44	3.7
Total			5531	863.2

for the Compilation of Dust Source Particle Emission Inventories (Trial)", as shown in Table 4.8.

Moisture content of stockyard materials. This article is based on the results of the typical material moisture content measurement, see Table 4.9.

Road dust load. This article focuses on the measurement results of road dust load, see Table 4.10.

Table 4.8 Multiplier of particle size generated during loading and unloading process

Fugitive dust generation sources	TSP	PM_{10}	$PM_{2.5}$
Loading and unloading dust	0.74	0.35	0.053
Wind erosion and dust	1.0	0.5	0.2
Dust is raised from the roads around the yard	3.23	0.62	0.15

Table 4.9 Measurement results of typical bulk material moisture content

The type of item	Coal	Ore	Sand
Moisture content (%)	4.8	3.5	3.0

Table 4.10 Measurement results of typical material road dust load

Dust load	Coal	Ore	Sand
g/m^2	10.7	7.8	8.5

Threshold friction wind speed of wind erosion dust. The threshold friction wind speed of wind erosion dust comes from the reference "Technical Guide for the Compilation of Dust Source Particle Emission Inventory (Trial)", see Table 4.11.

Control efficiency of control measures. The control efficiency of dust control measures during loading and unloading, wind erosion, and road dust in this article refers to the "Technical Guide for the Compilation of Dust Source Particle Emission Inventory (Trial)", see Tables 4.12, 4.13 and 4.14.

Activity level data of bulk cargo terminal stockyard. The activity level information such as the loading and unloading volume, stockpile surface area, and traffic flow around the stockyard of the bulk cargo terminal enterprises in this article can be found in Table 4.15.

⑤ Liquid bulk terminal related parameter information

This study uses the American TANKS4.0.9 model software to calculate the VOCs emissions from the storage tanks of the bulk cargo terminal one by one. The specific tank information, meteorological information, stored liquid information, etc. are directly input into the software for calculation, and will not be detailed here. The saturation coefficient during the loading process. The saturation coefficient during the

Table 4.11 Reference values of threshold friction wind speed

Yard materials	Threshold friction wind speed (m/s)
Coal piles	1.02
Iron slag, slag (subgrade material)	1.33
Uncovered coal piles	1.12
Coal pile scraper or bulldozer track	0.62
Coal dust piles	0.54
Iron ore	6.3
Coal gangue	4.8

Note a in the table represents open-pit coal mine; b represents light coverage; c represents power plant

Table 4.12 Control efficiency of stockyard loading and unloading dust control measures

Control measures	TSP controls efficiency (%)	PM_{10} controls efficiency (%)	$PM_{2.5}$ controls efficiency (%)
Continuous sprinkling operation at the conveying point	74	62	52
The three sides of the building stockpile are covered by a fence with a porosity of 50%	90	75	63

Table 4.13 Control efficiency of stockyard wind erosion dust control measures

Stockpile nature	Control measures	TSP controls efficiency (%)	PM_{10} controls efficiency (%)	$PM_{2.5}$ controls efficiency (%)
Stockpiles	Sprinkle regularly	52	48	40
	Chemical mulching agents	88	86	71
Coal piles	Sprinkle regularly	61	59	49
	Chemical mulching agents	86	85	71
Construction stockpiles	Covered with a woven cloth	78	76	64

Table 4.14 Control efficiency of paved road dust source control measures

Control measures	Control objects	TSP controls efficiency (%)	PM_{10} controls efficiency (%)	$PM_{2.5}$ controls efficiency (%)
Sprinkle 2 times/day	All paved roads	66	55	46
Spray dust suppressant	City roads	48	40	30
Vacuuming (without vacuum)	Branch	8	7	6
	Main road	13	11	9
Vacuuming and sweeping (with a vacuum installed)	Branch	19	16	13
	Main road	31	26	22

loading process in this article is based on the research results of the US Environmental Protection Agency (EPA), see Table 4.16.

Liquid bulk terminal cargo loading and unloading and pipeline transportation activity volume. According to the statistical analysis of the survey questionnaire, the activity volume of liquid bulk terminal cargo loading and unloading and pipeline transportation in Dongdu Port area can be found in Table 4.17.

4.2.2 Emission Factors of Port and Ship Air Pollutants

Emission factors are tools that attempt to establish some connection between the concentration level of pollutants discharged into the atmosphere and their corresponding pollution source activities. Similar to the collection of air pollution source information, the accurate selection of emission factors has a positive impact on the precise construction of the emission inventory. Using emission factors that match the actual situation of the research area is an important condition for constructing a high-precision emission inventory. The "Manual of Industrial Pollutant Generation

Table 4.15 Activity level information of bulk cargo terminal enterprises

	Bulk cargo companies names	活动水平信息				
		Project	Loading and unloading(t/a)	Pile surface area(m^2)	The average length of the road around the yard (km)	The traffic flow of the road around the yard(辆/年)
1	Xiamen Shihushan Wharf Co., Ltd	Coal	5,680,000	260,000	2	142,000
		Ore	800,000	127,800	1.4	20,000
		Sand	0	0	0	0
		Subtotal	6,480,000	387,400	3.4	162,000
2	Xiamen Modern Terminal Co., Ltd	Coal	0	0	0	0
		Ore	1,010,998	49,200	1	25,275
		Sand	4,761,650	126,600	1.5	119,041
		Subtotal	5,772,648	175,800	2.5	144,316
3	Xiamen International Trade Terminal Co., Ltd	Coal	0	0	0	0
		Ore	0	0	0	0
		Sand	982,254	10,000	1.3	24,556
		Total	982,254	10,000	1.3	24,556
Total		Coal	Coal	260,000	2	142,000
		Ore	Ore	177,000	2.4	45,275
		Sand	Sand	136,600	2.8	143,597
		Total	Total	573,600	7.2	330,872

Table 4.16 Saturation coefficient during the loading process

Transmitters	Type of operation	Saturation factor (s)
Fuel tankers	Submersible filling to clean empty oil drum (tank) (with oil and gas recovery)	0.5
	Generally, a single submersible filling is carried out into the oil drum (tank)	0.6
	Vapor balanced and submersible filling to oil drums (tanks)	1
	Splash filling to clean empty drums (tanks)	1.45
	Generally, single cargo splash loading	1.45
	Vapor pressure balanced and splash water filling oil drums (tanks)	1
oil tanker	Submersible Loading: Small boats	0.2
	Submersible Loading: Large Ships	0.5

Table 4.17 Total activity volume of liquid bulk cargo in the storage and transportation link of the liquid bulk terminal

Storage and transportation	Luyong Wharf		Modern docks		Total number of activities (t)
	Cargo type	Activity level (t)	Cargo type	Activity level (t)	
Loading process	Diesel fuel	190,000	Cooking oil	24,000	464,000
	Gasoline	250,000			
	Subtotal	440,000			
Shipment process	/	/	Cooking oil	18,000	18,000
Pipeline conveying process	Subtotal	880,000	Cooking oil	84,000	964,000
Total	2,560,000		168,000		2,728,000

and Emission Coefficients" issued by the Ministry of Ecology and Environment of China (formerly the Ministry of Environmental Protection) in 1996, for the first time, constructed a database of emission factors applicable to fixed emission sources, but the emission factors involved are relatively few.

Currently in the field of emission inventory research, the determination of emission factors often refers to foreign literature. However, the emission factors in foreign references are generally determined based on local conditions, which may not match the actual situation of the air pollution sources involved in this paper. Therefore, this paper determines the emission factors of relevant pollution sources in the research area through fuel quality testing and research, ship emission on-board testing, and comprehensive domestic and foreign literature research, providing a research basis for the subsequent construction of an emission inventory that is highly accurate and in line with the actual situation of the research area. Analysis of the measured data of the emission factors of atmospheric pollutants from ships in the Dongdu Port area:

Instantaneous emission characteristics of ship atmospheric pollutants

In terms of the instantaneous emission characteristics of flue gas flow and smoke temperature, Fig. 4.1 shows the instantaneous emission variation characteristics of typical ship flue gas flow and temperature under different working conditions. It can be seen that: when the ship leaves the port, the ship's emission smoke temperature and flow both show unstable fluctuations, and the frequency of fluctuations is high; at the beginning of the lock entry, the ship's smoke temperature and flue gas flow are at a relatively low and stable level, and later show large fluctuations; during the lock exit stage, the ship's flue gas temperature shows a continuous upward trend, while the ship's flue gas flow also gradually shows an upward trend after a rapid rise and then a sharp drop at the beginning; during the normal sailing stage of the ship, the flue gas flow and flow speed are very stable, with the smoke temperature roughly stable at 200 °C, and the flue gas flow roughly stable at 180 L/s; at the beginning of

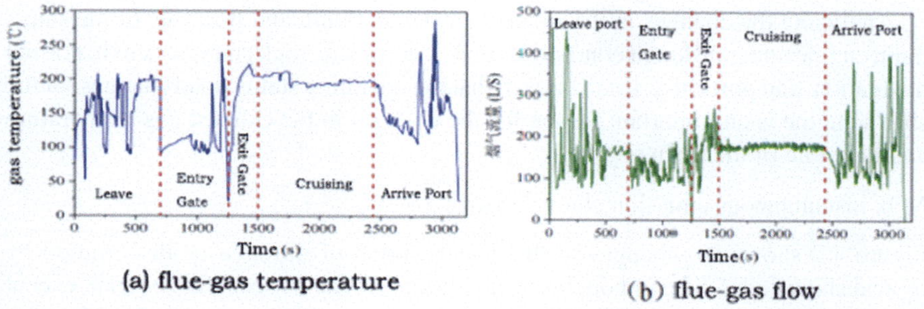

Fig. 4.1 The instantaneous emission characteristics of exhaust gas flow and temperature under typical ship conditions

the port entry stage, the ship's smoke temperature continues to drop, and the flue gas flow is also at a relatively low level, and later the smoke temperature and flue gas flow are both in a state of fluctuation.

Analyzing the reasons, it mainly has to do with the engine operating conditions of the ship under various circumstances: During the departure phase, the ship's main engine starts, and the ship sails out at a slower speed. To avoid collision with other ships, the crew needs to constantly change the engine load to adjust the ship's course and speed, causing the ship's exhaust gas temperature and flow rate to fluctuously vary. After entering the safe waterway, the ship begins to accelerate until it reaches normal navigation status. At this time, the ship's main engine is operating under high load, and both the ship's exhaust temperature and flow rate rapidly increase. At the beginning of the lock entry, the ship slowly enters the lock, and the ship's main engine is under a lower load, with the ship's exhaust gas temperature and flow rate at a relatively low level. After entering the lock chamber, the crew adjusts the ship's course and speed by constantly changing the engine load in order to adjust the ship's position and tie the ropes to the lock walls or the mooring posts of adjacent ships. At this time, the ship's exhaust gas temperature and flow rate fluctuate continuously. Once the ship has docked, the main engine is shut down to wait for the lock exit. During the lock exit phase, the ship's main engine restarts and continues to accelerate until it reaches normal navigation status. At this time, the ship's main engine is operating under high load, and both the ship's exhaust gas temperature and flow rate continue to rise. When the ship accelerates to the normal navigation phase, the ship proceeds at a stable speed, and the ship's exhaust gas temperature and flow rate are at a relatively stable level. Under the port entry conditions, the ship first continuously decelerates from the normal navigation speed, the ship's main engine load gradually decreases, and the ship's exhaust gas temperature and flow rate also gradually decrease. When about to dock at the port, the crew often intermittently increases the main engine power to adjust the ship's course and speed to avoid collision with other ships during the docking process. At this stage, the ship's exhaust gas temperature and flow rate are also fluctuating.

Analyzing the changes in the exhaust gas temperature and flow rate of the ship's main engine under different conditions such as departure, lock entry, lock exit, normal navigation, and port entry, it can be seen that the operating status (load changes) of the ship's engine is an important reason for the changes in the exhaust gas temperature and flow rate of the main engine.

NOx instantaneous emission characteristics

Figure 4.2 shows the changes in the concentration of nitrogen oxides emitted by typical ships under different operating conditions. It can be seen that: overall, except for the normal navigation phase, the concentration of NOx in the ship's exhaust is at a relatively stable level, while in other operating conditions, the concentration of NOx in the ship's exhaust fluctuates greatly around a certain concentration value. Usually, the NOx emissions from marine diesel engines are produced during the combustion process in the fuel cylinder. There are mainly three mechanisms for its production: (1) The nitrogen elements in the fuel combine with oxygen during combustion to produce fuel-type NOx; (2) Nitrogen and oxygen in the air react to produce thermal NOx under high temperature conditions; (3) The intermediate products of fuel combustion in the rich mixture area react with N_2 in the air to produce instantaneous NOx. In actual operation, the load of the ship's main engine is the main reason affecting the concentration of NOx emissions. Usually, the larger the main engine load, the greater the concentration and emission rate of NOx.

When the ship leaves the port, the crew intermittently increases the main engine power to adjust the ship's course and speed, causing significant fluctuations in the main engine load. As a result, the emission concentration of NOx fluctuates accordingly. In the later stage, when the ship enters a safe waterway and begins to accelerate continuously, the load of the ship's main engine continues to rise, and the combustion temperature in the cylinder also gradually increases. Therefore, the emission concentration of NOx from the ship rapidly increases, and the overall emission concentration of NOx is relatively high. During the lock entry phase, the ship begins to enter the lock at a slower speed, the main engine load is relatively low, and the NOx concentration

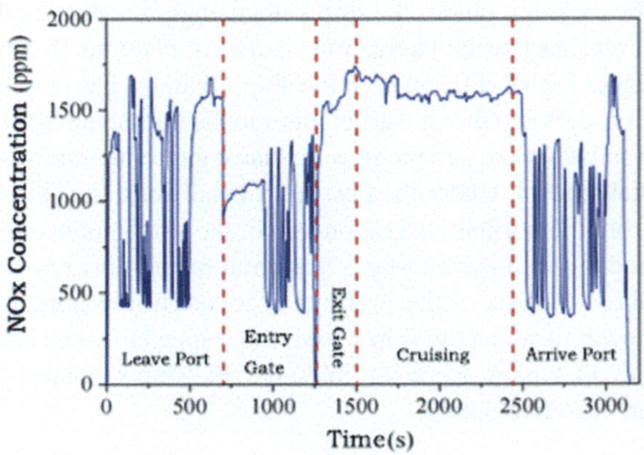

Fig. 4.2 The instantaneous emission characteristics of NOx under typical ship conditions

remains at a relatively low level (about 1000 ppm). After entering the lock chamber, the crew increases the main engine power to adjust the ship's position, causing significant fluctuations in the main engine load and NOx emission concentration, but the overall NOx emission concentration at this stage is relatively low. During the lock exit phase, the ship is in a continuous acceleration phase, similar to the port departure acceleration phase, the ship's main engine load increases, and the NOx concentration continues to increase. During normal navigation, the ship proceeds at a relatively stable speed and load. At this time, the continuous high temperature and oxygen-rich conditions make the ship's NOx emission concentration at a relatively high and stable level, with the NOx emission concentration generally stable at around 1500 ppm. The ship's port entry phase has certain similarities with the ship's departure, that is, near the berth, the crew constantly changes the main engine load to adjust the ship's course and speed, causing the NOx concentration to fluctuate. In addition, the continuous deceleration before berthing causes the NOx concentration to be in a continuous decline in the early stage.

The analysis of the changes in NOx concentration in the ship's main engine exhaust under different conditions such as departure, lock entry, lock exit, normal navigation, and port entry shows that the NOx concentration in the exhaust is relatively low under low load. The operating status of the ship's engine (load change) is an important reason for the change in NOx concentration in the main engine exhaust. That is, by adjusting the load of the ship's engine, the NOx concentration in the main engine exhaust can be partially controlled.

PM Instantaneous Emission Characteristics Particulate matter (PM) has always been one of the main emissions from marine diesel engines, with its composition mainly consisting of black carbon, sulfates, ash, and soluble organic components (SOF), etc. To explore the emission status of particulate matter under various operating conditions in the Dongdu Port area, ELPI is used to test the concentration of particulate matter in the ship's exhaust. Figure 4.3 shows the instantaneous changes in typical ship PM emissions under different operating conditions. Similar to NOx, the PM emission concentration of the ship fluctuates during the departure, lock exit, and port entry conditions, and the overall PM emission concentration is relatively high. In the early stage of the lock entry phase, the PM emission of the ship is at a low level, and in the later stage, it shows a large fluctuation. During stable navigation, the PM emission concentration of the ship is basically stable at a relatively low level of 220 mg/m^3. The reason for the change in PM concentration is generally due to the change in the load of the ship's engine.

Typically, diesel particulates (soot particles) are the products of hydrocarbon fuel cracking in a high-temperature, oxygen-deficient environment. Their formation usually involves several stages: pyrolysis, nucleation, surface growth and coagulation, polymerization, and oxidation. Pyrolysis is the controlling step in soot formation, where fuel undergoes cracking to form polycyclic aromatic hydrocarbons in a high-temperature, oxygen-deficient environment. These hydrocarbons continuously dehydrogenate and polymerize into carbon-based core particles. These core particles grow into 10–30 nm soot particles through collision coagulation and surface reactions, allowing gaseous hydrocarbons and other soluble organic components,

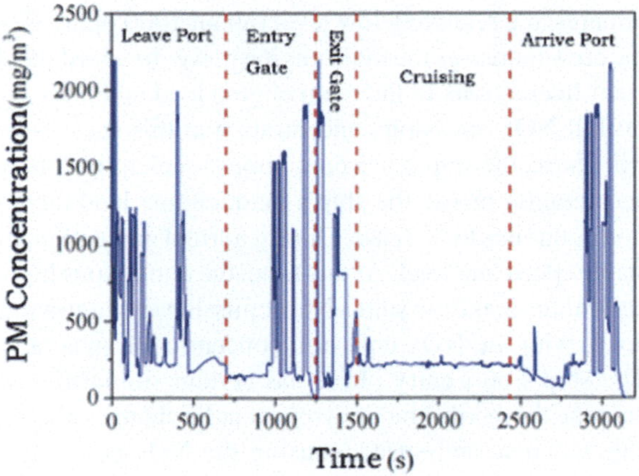

Fig. 4.3 The instantaneous PM emission characteristics of typical ship conditions

sulfates, and other components to condense on their surface. Finally, they aggregate into chain or globular soot particles.

The concentration of PM in the exhaust is directly related to the main precursor of soot particle formation in the flue gas—carbon core particles. During normal navigation, the engine operates stably, the cylinder temperature is relatively high, and the air–fuel ratio remains at a relatively high level, leading to more complete fuel combustion, which is not conducive to the formation of carbon core particles. Accordingly, the concentration of soot particles in the flue gas is relatively low. At the beginning of the lock entry, due to the ship's relatively stable and low speed into the lock, the ship's load is low, the air–fuel ratio is large, and the cylinder smoke temperature is relatively low. The low-temperature oxygen-rich state is not conducive to the cracking and dehydrogenation of fuel to produce carbon core particles, resulting in a relatively low PM concentration. During port entry and exit and later stages of lock entry, the PM concentration in the exhaust intermittently peaks. This is due to the intermittent increase in engine load due to the ship's operation, leading to an increase in engine fuel injection, a sudden decrease in the air–fuel ratio, and combustion in the cylinder moving towards an oxygen-deficient direction. This results in more soot particles being emitted before they can be oxidized, causing a sharp increase in PM concentration. During the lock exit, the ship is accelerating, the load is large, and the engine fuel injection increases, leading to an oxygen-deficient state in the cylinder due to rich fuel, reducing combustion efficiency and causing incomplete combustion, which in turn leads to a relatively high PM concentration.

(2) Emission factors of ships under different conditions

Figure 4.4 shows the average NOx emission rate and average emission factor for each driving condition of the test ship. Overall, the ship has a higher NOx emission rate during normal steady navigation, port entry and exit, and lock exit. The lock entry condition has a lower NOx emission rate due to the ship's slow travel for most of the time and lower engine load. However, the emission factor is roughly the same as

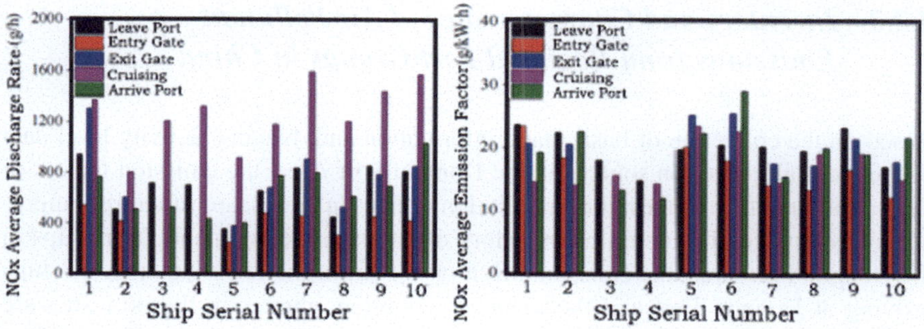

Fig. 4.4 The NOx emission rate and emission factor of the test ship in the Dongdu Port area

other conditions. This is because during lock entry, the main engine is under low load, combustion efficiency decreases, and the amount of brake fuel consumed increases, leading to an increase in the NOx emission factor of the ship's main engine.

(1) PM emission rate and emission factor of the test ship

Figure 4.5 shows the PM_{10} emission rate and emission factor of 10 test ships. It can be seen that during normal navigation and lock entry, the emission of particulates is relatively low, while the emission factor of ships during port entry and exit and lock exit is relatively high, which overall conforms to the combustion law of diesel engines.

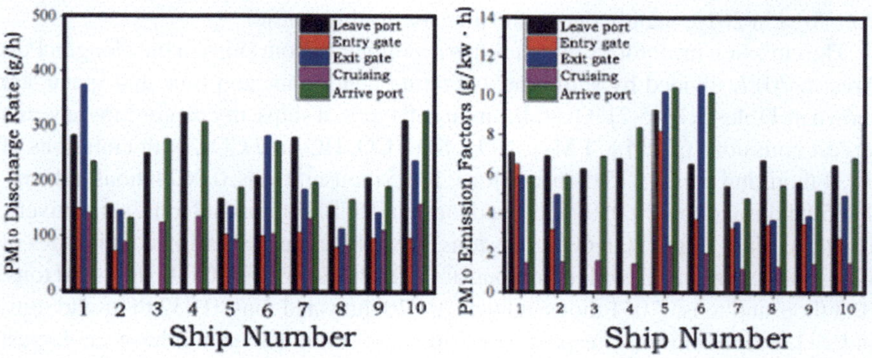

Fig. 4.5 Test of PM_{10} emission rate and emission factor of ships in Dongdu Port area

4.2.3 Inventory and Characteristics of Air Pollutant Emissions from Regional Port Groups in China

Based on the collection of basic static information and dynamic activity level data of the main air pollution sources in the Dongdu Port Area, the emission factors of various pollutants from the main air pollution sources in the research area are comprehensively studied. The emission inventory of atmospheric pollutants from ships in the Dongdu Port Area, the emission inventory of atmospheric pollutants from ships arriving at Dongdu Port and the main air pollution sources in the port area are established using methods such as estimating ship engine power. The emission characteristics and spatiotemporal distribution characteristics of atmospheric pollutants under different static information and dynamic activity level data are systematically analyzed, and the uncertainty analysis of the emission inventory is carried out. On the basis of strengthening the understanding of the emission characteristics of pollutants in the research area, the accuracy of the subsequent simulation research results is improved, and the effectiveness of the proposed control measures for ship and port air pollutant emissions is ensured.

(1) Emission Inventory of Atmospheric Pollutants from Ships in Dongdu Port Area

In 2017, ships in the Dongdu Port Area emitted a total of 0.163 thousand tons of PM_{10}, 0.144 thousand tons of $PM_{2.5}$, 16.55 thousand tons of NOx, 0.0780 thousand tons of SO_2, 0.107 thousand tons of CO, 0.0487 thousand tons of HC, and 660.71 thousand tons of CO_2. The emissions of PM and NOx were higher than the results of Cai Jun and others for the emissions of PM and NOx from ships in the Dongdu Port Area in 2010, mainly due to the increase in ship traffic.

The emission inventories of atmospheric pollutants from ships in the Dongdu Port Area in 2017, divided by ship type, operating conditions, and time and space, are shown in Tables 5.18–5.21. Overall, among all types of ships, dry cargo ships have the largest emissions of PM_{10}, $PM_{2.5}$, NOx, SO_2, CO, HC, and CO_2, with emissions of 0.131 thousand tons, 0.115 thousand tons, 13.25 thousand tons, 0.0624 thousand tons, 0.0859 thousand tons, 0.0390 thousand tons, and 528.17 thousand tons, respectively. The third-class ships (200–600 gross tons) have the largest emissions of all types of atmospheric pollutants, with emissions of 0.106 thousand tons, 0.093 thousand tons, 10.8 thousand tons, 0.051 thousand tons, 0.070 thousand tons, 0.032 thousand tons, and 431.9 thousand tons, respectively. Ships in normal navigation have the largest emissions of atmospheric pollutants, with emissions of 0.145 thousand tons, 0.127 thousand tons, 15.8 thousand tons, 0.074 thousand tons, 0.101 thousand tons, 0.046 thousand tons, and 628.9 thousand tons, respectively. The total emissions of PM_{10}, $PM_{2.5}$, NOx, SO_2, CO, HC, and CO_2 from ships within the range of ports along the line are 71.29 tons, 62.77 tons, 295.21 tons, 16.24 tons, 24.56 tons, 10.60 tons, and 13,291.65 tons, respectively. The total emissions of PM_{10}, $PM_{2.5}$, NOx, SO_2, CO, HC, and CO_2 in the Dongdu Port Area are 1448.16 tons, 1273.08 tons, 15,798.55 tons, 741.99 tons, 1012.90 tons, 459.11 tons, and 628,917.60 tons, respectively. The total emissions of PM_{10}, PM2.5, NOx, SO_2, CO, HC, and CO_2 at the ship lock are 114.14 tons, 100.37 tons, 456.08 tons, 22.11 tons, 35.48 tons, 17.59 tons, and 18,499.86 tons, respectively (Tables 4.18, 4.19, 4.20 and 4.21).

(2) Characteristics of Atmospheric Pollutant Emissions from Ships in Dongdu Port Area

The proportion of ship emissions by type, operating conditions, and spatiotemporal distribution characteristics in the Dongdu Port area are shown in Tables 4.22, 4.23 and 4.24.

Among all types of ships, dry cargo ships are the type with high pollutant emissions, contributing to about 80% of the total emissions from ships in the Dongdu Port area in 2017. Tugboats come next, contributing to about 14% of all types of pollutant emissions. Ships within the 200–600 tonnage range contribute the most to atmospheric pollutant emissions, with a contribution rate of about 65% for all types of pollutants. These characteristics are consistent with the research results of Xu Wenwen and others on the emission of atmospheric pollutants from inland

Table 4.18 Emission inventory of main pollutants from different types of ships

Ship type	Total emissions (t/a)						
	PM_{10}	$PM_{2.5}$	NO_x	SO_2	CO	HC	CO_2
Dry cargo ships	1308.09	1149.99	13,249.17	623.54	858.64	389.67	528,166.35
Chemical tankers	52.88	46.48	548.92	25.76	35.63	16.24	21,849.91
Tug	233.02	204.91	2324.86	110.17	150.00	67.48	93,137.53
Tanker	17.46	15.37	192.48	9.71	13.29	6.95	8120.00
Container ship	5.85	5.15	62.55	3.07	4.23	1.88	2580.86
Other ships	16.29	14.32	171.84	8.09	11.15	5.07	6854.45
Total	1633.59	1436.23	16,549.83	780.34	1072.94	487.30	660,709.11

Table 4.19 Emission inventory of main pollutants from ships of different tonnages

Ship tonnage distribution		Total emissions (t/a)						
		PM_{10}	$PM_{2.5}$	NO_x	SO_2	CO	HC	CO_2
First	> 1600 t	5.84	5.14	55.40	2.63	3.75	1.73	2233.88
Second-class	600–1600 t	230.64	202.77	2254.16	106.79	149.99	68.55	90,439.68
Third class	200–600 t	1058.01	930.13	10,848.28	509.88	699.06	316.79	431,918.17
Fourth-class	50–200 t	305.70	268.82	3050.83	144.55	197.77	90.28	122,233.47
Fifth class	< 50 t	33.39	29.38	341.17	16.48	22.36	9.95	13,883.88
Total		1633.59	1436.23	16,549.83	780.34	1072.94	487.30	660,709.11

Table 4.20 Emission inventory of main pollutants from ships in different operating conditions in Dongdu Port area

Ship driving conditions		Total emissions(t/a)						
		PM_{10}	$PM_{2.5}$	NO_x	SO_2	CO	HC	CO_2
Normal sailing	Host	1444.45	1269.67	15,639.53	730.78	998.58	453.90	620,029.95
	Auxiliary	3.71	3.41	159.01	11.20	14.31	5.21	8887.65
	Total	1448.16	1273.08	15,798.54	741.98	1012.89	459.11	628,917.60
Mooring and driving	Host	68.68	60.37	183.38	8.36	14.49	6.94	7041.48
	Auxiliary	0.04	0.04	1.75	0.12	0.16	0.06	97.73
	Total	68.73	60.41	185.13	8.49	14.65	7.00	7139.21
Access gates	Host	113.20	99.50	415.54	19.26	31.84	16.26	16,234.08
	Auxiliary	0.95	0.87	40.54	2.86	3.65	1.33	2265.77
	Total	113.50	99.78	428.29	20.16	32.98	16.68	16,946.55
Berth	Auxiliary	2.57	2.36	110.08	7.76	9.91	3.60	6152.44
Total emissions	Host	1626.32	1429.54	16,238.46	758.40	1044.91	477.11	643,305.51
	Auxiliary	7.27	6.68	311.38	21.94	28.03	10.20	17,403.59
	Total	1633.59	1436.23	16,549.83	780.34	1072.94	487.30	660,709.11

Table 4.21 Emission inventory of main pollutants from ships in ports along the line in Dongdu Port area

Port	Total emissions(t/a)						
	PM_{10}	$PM_{2.5}$	NO_x	SO_2	CO	HC	CO_2
Xuzhou	13.52	11.90	52.99	2.87	4.47	1.97	2357.73
Suqian	6.29	5.53	22.57	1.25	2.07	0.95	1025.12
Huai'an	9.62	8.47	36.91	2.02	3.09	1.35	1653.93
Yangzhou	5.25	4.62	22.75	1.26	1.92	0.83	1027.94
Zhenjiang	6.15	5.42	26.63	1.48	2.19	0.93	1205.95
Changzhou	12.96	11.41	58.61	3.25	4.72	1.98	2648.19
Wuxi	2.91	2.56	13.38	0.74	1.09	0.46	605.47
Suzhou	14.61	12.86	61.37	3.39	5.02	2.14	2767.32
Total	71.29	62.77	295.21	16.24	24.56	10.60	13,291.65

waterway ships in Jiangsu Province, mainly depending on the type and total tonnage distribution of ships in the research area.

In terms of emission contributions from various operating conditions, normal navigation emissions > lock entry and exit emissions > port entry and exit berthing emissions. For the ship's main engine, the order of emission proportions for each operating condition is: normal navigation emissions > lock entry and exit emissions > port entry and exit berthing emissions. The main reasons for this are: (1) The time a ship spends

Table 4.22 Proportion of main pollutant emissions from different types of ships

Ship type	Percentage of emissions (%)						
	PM_{10}	$PM_{2.5}$	NO_x	SO_2	CO	HC	CO_2
Dry cargo ships	80.07	80.07	80.06	79.91	80.03	79.97	79.94
Chemical tankers	3.24	3.24	3.32	3.30	3.32	3.33	3.31
Tug	14.26	14.27	14.05	14.12	13.98	13.85	14.10
Tanker	1.07	1.07	1.16	1.24	1.24	1.43	1.23
Container ship	0.36	0.36	0.38	0.39	0.39	0.39	0.39
Other ships	1.00	1.00	1.04	1.04	1.04	1.04	1.04
Total	100.00	100.00	100.00	100.00	100.00	100.00	100.00

Table 4.23 Proportion of main pollutant emissions from ships of different tonnages

Ship tonnage distribution		Percentage of emissions (%)						
		PM_{10}	$PM_{2.5}$	NO_x	SO_2	CO	HC	CO_2
First	> 1600 t	0.36	0.36	0.33	0.34	0.35	0.35	0.34
Second-class	600–1600 t	14.12	14.12	13.62	13.69	13.98	14.07	13.69
Third class	200–600 t	64.77	64.76	65.55	65.34	65.15	65.01	65.37
Fourth-class	50–200 t	18.71	18.72	18.43	18.52	18.43	18.53	18.50
Fifth class	< 50 t	2.04	2.05	2.06	2.11	2.08	2.04	2.10
Total		100.00	100.00	100.00	100.00	100.00	100.00	100.00

Table 4.24 Comparison of pollutant area ratio emissions between ports and waterways

Contaminant		PM_{10}	$PM_{2.5}$	NO_x	SO_2	CO	HC	CO_2
Area	Area (km^2)	1.92						
	Port area specific emissions (t/km^2)	37.13	32.69	153.76	8.46	12.79	5.52	6922.73
Waterway	Area (km^2)	92.45						
	Area ratio emissions (t/km^2)	15.66	13.77	170.89	8.03	10.96	4.97	6802.79

navigating in the waterway is longer than the time spent entering and exiting locks and ports, which is the main reason why the proportion of emissions from normal navigation conditions is the largest; (2) Ships navigating in the Dongdu Port area include not only those arriving at ports along the route but also those passing through. The total number of ship trips is much larger than the number of ships arriving at the port. Therefore, under similar operating times, the emission of atmospheric pollutants from ships entering and exiting locks is greater than that from ships entering and exiting ports and berthing. For the ship's auxiliary engine, the order of emission proportions for each operating condition is: normal navigation emissions > berthing emissions >

lock entry and exit emissions > berthing navigation emissions. This is mainly due to the long duration of normal navigation and berthing, and the short duration of lock entry and exit, and berthing navigation. The ship's main engine is the main source of ship atmospheric pollutant emissions, with the contribution rate of each pollutant being over 96%, resulting in the characteristics of the ship's total emissions in terms of operating conditions being consistent with the ship's main engine.

4.3 Prediction of Port and Ship Atmospheric Pollutant Emissions

4.3.1 Overview of Prediction Methods

(1) Selection of prediction model

The choice of prediction methods is worth further discussion, as existing prediction methods are very diverse, each with its own advantages and disadvantages. The multivariate linear regression prediction method requires establishing a correlation between independent and dependent variables, then establishing a prediction model to predict the target. This model requires a certain data foundation and involves a large amount of calculation, which can easily increase the instability of the prediction results, leading to distortion of the prediction results. The BP neural network prediction model has similar drawbacks to the multivariate linear regression prediction model. It requires the collection of a large amount of sample data to predict the target, the calculation process is complex, and when the sample data is insufficient, the prediction results obtained also have a large deviation (Ready 2008). The time series autoregressive model is based on the statistical data of its own variables in the past, forming its own time series variables, but the accuracy of this prediction model will be affected by its own time series variables. If the data in the time series is easily affected by external factors, the accuracy of this prediction model will also be greatly reduced. Compared with the previous types of prediction methods, the grey prediction model is still very applicable to sequences with less sample data. The number of sample data is small, but it shows a clear trend. When predicting such sample sequences, the accuracy of the results obtained by the grey prediction model is relatively high (Du et al. 2019). In 1982, Deng Julong established the grey prediction model, mainly for the prediction of grey systems, to solve the trend problems of future development in certain fields. The grey system is composed of two parts, one is the data information part that can be directly obtained, and the other is the data information part that cannot be determined or is unknown (Yang et al. 2013). All prediction models are obtained from the known part to the unknown part. The grey prediction model is the same. According to the known discrete data, a new and regular time series is regenerated through accumulation or subtraction, and then based on the new time series, the mathematical model required for the research problem is established, and finally the prediction value is calculated. MATLAB software has powerful matrix operation functions, so this article uses MATLAB software to solve the algorithm problem of the grey prediction GM(1,1) model. not only the program is concise, the algorithm is accurate, and the prediction accuracy has been proven to be high (Cai 2013).

(2) Steps to build the grey prediction GM(1,1) model

① Level ratio test: Feasibility analysis of modelling

Assume that the discrete original sequence of ship air pollutant emissions in Qingdao is $X^{(0)} = \left(x^{(0)}(1), x^{(0)}(2), x^{(0)}(3), \ldots\ldots, x^{(0)}(n)\right)$. with n observation values; accumulate the original data sequence to generate a new sequence: $X^{(1)} = \left(x^{(1)}(1), x^{(1)}(2), x^{(1)}(3), \ldots\ldots, x^{(1)}(n)\right)$, $X^{(1)}(k) = \sum_{i=1}^{k} X^{(0)}(i), k = 1, 2, 3, \ldots, n$. First, the original sequence $X^{(0)}$ and the new sequence $X^{(1)}$ need to be tested for quasi-smoothness and quasi-exponential law respectively:

Quasi-smoothness test:

$$\rho(t) = \frac{X^{(0)}(t)}{X^{(0)}(t-1)} \tag{4.1}$$

When t < 3, if $\rho(t)$ is in the range of $\rho(t) < 0.5$, it satisfies the quasi-smoothness test;

Quasi-exponential law test:

$$\delta^{(t)} = \frac{X^{(1)}(t)}{X^{(1)}(t-1)} \tag{4.2}$$

When $t > 3$ is in the range of $1 < \delta^{(1)}(t) < 1.5$, it satisfies the quasi-exponential law test, it satisfies the quasi-exponential law test. If it passes both of the above tests, the grey prediction model can be used for prediction.

② Construction of GM(1,1) Model

Based on the original sequence $X^{(0)}$ and the newly generated cumulative sequence $X^{(1)}$, the original form of the GM(1,1) model can be represented as:

$$x^{(0)}(k) + \alpha x^{(0)}(k) = \mu \tag{4.3}$$

where α is the development grey number, and μ is the endogenous control grey number;

The whitening equation corresponding to the GM(1,1) model, also known as the shadow equation, is:

$$\frac{dX^{(1)}}{dt} + \alpha X^{(1)} = \mu \tag{4.4}$$

The solution corresponding to the above whitening equation is:

$$X^{(1)}(t) = \left[X^{(1)}(1) - \frac{\mu}{\alpha}\right]e^{-at} + \frac{\mu}{\alpha} \tag{4.5}$$

Equation 2–(9), also known as the time response function, is the predicted value of the new sequence $X^{(1)}$;

Based on the original predicted value, the cumulative or cumulative reduction and other changes can be made, and the time response sequence of the GM(1,1) model 2-(7) can be obtained. Finally, the predicted simulation value of the original sequence $X^{(0)}$ can be calculated based on the time response sequence.

$$\hat{x}^{(0)}(k+1) = \hat{x}^{(1)}(k+1) - \hat{x}^{(1)}(k) = (1 - e^{\alpha})e^{-\alpha k}, k = 1, 2, 3, ..., n \tag{4.6}$$

(2) Calculation Principle of Grey Prediction GM(1,1) Model The following is the detailed calculation process of the GM(1,1) model: Eq. (4.9) satisfies the initial condition: when $t = t_0$, The solution of $X^{(1)} = X^{(1)}_{(t_0)}$ is:

$$X^{(1)}_t = \left[X^{(1)}_{(t_0)} - \frac{\mu}{\alpha}\right]e^{\alpha(t-t_0)} + \frac{\mu}{\alpha} \tag{4.7}$$

For the discrete values of equal interval sampling (note $t_0 = 1$), it is:

$$X^{(1)}_{(k+1)} = \left[X^{(1)}_{(1)} - \frac{\mu}{\alpha}\right]e^{-\alpha k} + \frac{\mu}{\alpha} \tag{4.8}$$

Estimate the constants α and μ through the least squares method. Because $X^{(1)}_{(1)}$ is used as the initial value, $X^{(1)}_{(2)}, X^{(1)}_{(3)}, \ldots\ldots, X^{(1)}_{(n)}$ is substituted into the differential equation:

$$\begin{aligned} X^{(0)}_{(2)} + \alpha X^{(1)}_{(2)} &= \mu \\ X^{(0)}_{(3)} + \alpha X^{(1)}_{(3)} &= \mu \\ &\cdots \\ X^{(0)}_{(n-1)} + \alpha X^{(1)}_{(n-1)} &= \mu \\ X^{(0)}_{(n)} + \alpha X^{(1)}_{(n)} &= \mu \end{aligned} \tag{4.9}$$

where:

$$\begin{aligned} X^{(0)}_{(2)} &= \left[-X^{(1)}_{(2)}, 1\right]\begin{bmatrix}\alpha \\ \mu\end{bmatrix} \\ X^{(0)}_{(3)} &= \left[-X^{(1)}_{(3)}, 1\right]\begin{bmatrix}\alpha \\ \mu\end{bmatrix} \\ &\cdots \\ X^{(0)}_{(n)} &= \left[-X^{(1)}_{(n)}, 1\right]\begin{bmatrix}\alpha \\ \mu\end{bmatrix} \end{aligned} \tag{4.10}$$

Since $\frac{\Delta X^{(1)}}{\Delta t}$ involves the values of two moments of the cumulative column, therefore $X^{(1)}_{(i)}$. It is more reasonable to replace it with the average of the two moments before and after, that is, replace $X^{(1)}_{(i)}$ with: $\frac{1}{2}\left[X^{(1)}_{(i)} + X^{(1)}_{(i-1)}\right]$, $i = 1, 2, 3, ..., n$.

From this, we can conclude:

$$\begin{bmatrix} X^0_{(2)} \\ X^0_{(3)} \\ \cdots \\ X^0_{(n)} \end{bmatrix} = \begin{bmatrix} -\frac{1}{2}\left[X^{(1)}_{(2)} + X^{(1)}_{(1)}\right] 1 \\ -\frac{1}{2}\left[X^{(1)}_{(3)} + X^{(1)}_{(2)}\right] 1 \\ \cdots \\ -\frac{1}{2}\left[X^{(1)}_{(n-1)} + X^{(1)}_{(n-1)}\right] 1 \\ -\frac{1}{2}\left[X^{(1)}_{(n)} + X^{(1)}_{(n-1)}\right] 1 \end{bmatrix} \begin{bmatrix} \alpha \\ \mu \end{bmatrix} \tag{4.11}$$

$$Y_n = \begin{bmatrix} X^{(0)}_{(2)} \\ X^{(0)}_{(3)} \\ \cdots \\ X^{(0)}_{(n)} \end{bmatrix}, B = \begin{bmatrix} -\frac{1}{2}\left[X^{(1)}_{(2)} + X^{(1)}_{(1)}\right] 1 \\ -\frac{1}{2}\left[X^{(1)}_{(3)} + X^{(1)}_{(2)}\right] 1 \\ \cdots \\ -\frac{1}{2}\left[X^{(1)}_{(n-1)} + X^{(1)}_{(n-1)}\right] 1 \\ -\frac{1}{2}\left[X^{(1)}_{(n)} + X^{(1)}_{(n-1)}\right] 1 \end{bmatrix} \tag{4.12}$$

$$U = \begin{bmatrix} \alpha \\ \mu \end{bmatrix}, Y = BU \tag{4.13}$$

The least squares estimation is:

$$\hat{U} = \begin{bmatrix} \hat{\alpha} \\ \hat{\mu} \end{bmatrix} = (B^T B)^{-1} B^T Y \tag{4.14}$$

Substitute the estimated values $\hat{\alpha}$ and $\hat{\mu}$ to get the time response equation:

$$\hat{X}^{(1)}_{(k+1)} = \left[X^{(1)}_{(1)} - \frac{\mu}{\alpha}\right] e^{-\hat{\alpha}k} + \frac{\hat{\mu}}{\hat{\alpha}} \tag{4.15}$$

According to the principle of the grey prediction method, $-\alpha$ mainly controls the scale of system development, reflecting the predicted development trend, known as the development coefficient; μ reflects the relationship of data changes, known as the grey action quantity, where:

When $-\alpha < 0.3$, the GM(1,1) model can be used for medium and long-term forecasting;

When $0.3 < -\alpha \leq 0.5$, the GM(1,1) model is suitable for short-term forecasting, but not for medium and long-term forecasting;

When $0.5 < -\alpha \leq 0.8$, the GM(1,1) model is not good for short-term forecasting;

When $0.8 < -\alpha \leq 1$, the GM(1,1) model should use residual correction;
When $-\alpha > 1$, the GM(1,1) model should not be used.

③ Markov Model

According to the standard of the accuracy test table of the grey GM(1,1) model, the accuracy level of the established model can be determined. Models with lower accuracy levels can be corrected by the Markov model for their prediction results. This method has been widely used, with the specific steps as follows:

i. Divide the state interval

Based on the error range and sample quantity obtained from the grey GM(1,1) model, it is divided into n state intervals, and the interval range can be represented as $E_i = [e_{1i}, e_{2i}]$, $(i = 1, 2, 3, ..., n)$. The more state intervals are divided, the closer the revised prediction result is to the original value. Usually, the most suitable number of state intervals is 3–5.

ii. Establish the state transition probability matrix

In the process of event development, the probability of an event from a state E_i at a certain moment to a state E_j at the next moment is called the state transition probability, that is, $P(E_i \to E_j) = P\left(\frac{E_j}{E_i = P_{ij}}\right)$. Therefore, the state transition probability matrix is constructed according to the state transition probability:

$$P = \begin{bmatrix} P_{11} & P_{12} & ... & P_{1n} \\ P_{21} & P_{22} & ... & P_{2n} \\ ... & ... & ... & ... \\ P_{n1} & P_{n2} & ... & P_{nn} \end{bmatrix} \tag{4.16}$$

where,

$$\begin{cases} 0 \leq P_{ij} \leq 1, (i, j = 1, 2, ..., n) \\ \sum_{j=1}^{n} P_{ij} = 1, (i = 1, 2, ..., n) \\ P^{(m)} = P^m \end{cases} \tag{4.17}$$

iii. Revision of Predicted Values

Through the state transition probability matrix, the state of the predicted event E_i can be obtained. Then, based on the predicted value $\hat{x}(k)$ obtained from the grey GM(1,1) model, and using the interval $E_i = [e_{1i}, e_{2i}]$ where the predicted event is located, the predicted value of the Markov model can be obtained through the following formula:

$$\hat{Y}(k) = \hat{X}^{(0)}(k) * [1 + 0.5(e_{1i} + e_{2i})] \tag{4.18}$$

4.3.2 Case Analysis

Based on the data of NOx, SO_2, CO, PM_{10}, and VOCs atmospheric pollutant emissions from the Qingdao Port ship emission inventory from 2009 to 2021, the preliminary data processing process is carried out, the corresponding grey prediction model is established, and the accuracy of the prediction model is tested. The VOCs prediction model with low prediction accuracy is corrected, and its prediction accuracy is optimized through the Markov model. Finally, the emission of atmospheric pollutants from ships in Qingdao Port from 2022 to 2032 is predicted (Navrud and Ready 2007).

(1) Preliminary Data Verification

As mentioned earlier, before using the grey prediction model—GM(1,1) model, the original sequence $X^{(0)}$ and the newly generated cumulative sequence $X^{(1)}$ need to be tested for quasi-smoothness and quasi-exponential law respectively. The data from 2009 to 2021 is used for modeling and predicting the emission of atmospheric pollutants from 2022 to 2032. This paper involves NOx, SO_2, CO, PM_{10}, and VOCs, five different atmospheric pollutants, so we test them separately.

① NOx Emission Data Verification

From Table 4.25, the original data sequence of NOx emissions is $X_{NO_x}^{(0)}$,

$$X_{NO_x}^{(0)} = (12159.81,\ 14163.18,\ 16485.89,\ 18263.05,\ 19339.38,\ 21470.07,\ 21761.19,\ 22660.27,\ 24715.05,\ 25694.69,\ 26675.44,\ 27415.61,\ 27313.30).$$

The newly generated cumulative sequence is $X_{NO_x}^{(1)}$,

$$X_{NO_x}^{(0)} = (12159.81,\ 26322.99,\ 4280888,\ 61071.93,\ 80411.31,\ 101881.38,\ 123642.57,\ 146302.84,\ 171017.89,\ 196712.58,\ 223388.02,\ 250803.63,\ 278116.93).$$

The above sequences are tested, and the results are shown in the following Tables 4.26 and 4.27.

② SO_2 Emission Data Verification

From Table 4.25, the original data sequence of SO_2 emissions is $X_{SO_2}^{(0)}$

$$X_{SO_2}^{(0)} = (288416,\ 3350.36,\ 3894.23,\ 4304.49,\ 4560.05,\ 5064.52,\ 5097.57,\ 5280.57,\ 5751.41,\ 5977.89,\ 6202.80,\ 637012,\ 6345.73).$$

The newly generated cumulative sequence is $X_{SO_2}^{(1)}$,

Table 4.25 Emission inventory of atmospheric pollutants from ships in Qingdao port from 2009 to 2021

Year	Passenger throughput	Cargo throughput	Container throughput	NO_x	SO_2	CO	PM_{10}	VOC_s
2009	972	18,727	630.7	12,159	2884	1513	319	112
2010	999	22,438	770.2	14,163	3350	1734	366	120
2011	1080	26,507	946.2	16,485	3894	2000	422	135
2012	1055	30,029	1002.4	18,263	4304	2185	462	135
2013	1145	31,668	1026.2	19,339	4560	2320	491	144
2014	1302	35,012	1201.2	21,470	5064	2583	546	165
2015	791	37,971	1302.0	21,761	5097	2504	532	123
2016	414	41,465	1450.3	22,660	5280	2519	537	95
2017	333	45,782	1552.2	24,715	5751	2722	581	92
2018	324	47,701	1658.4	25,694	5977	2826	603	95
2019	288	49,749	1743.6	26,675	6202	2923	624	95
2020	225	51,463	1805.0	27,415	6370	2989	639	92
2021	215	51,314	1830.9	27,313	6345	2976	636	92

Table 4.26 Quasi-Smoothness test of original data sequence of NOx emissions

t	1	2	3	4	5	6	7	8	9	10	11	12	13
$\rho(t)$	0	0	0.626	0.427	0.317	0.267	0.214	0.183	0.169	0.150	0.136	0.123	0.109

Table 4.27 Quasi-Exponential law test of new sequence of NOx emissions

t	1	2	3	4	5	6	7	8	9	10	11	12	13
$\delta^{(1)}(t)$	0	0	1.626	1.427	1.317	1.267	1.214	1.183	1.169	1.150	1.136	1.123	1.109

$$X_{SO_2}^{(1)} = (2884.16, 6234.52, 10128.75, 14433.24, 18993.29, 24057.81, 29155.38, 34435.95, 40187.36, 46165.25, 52368.05, 58738.17, 65083.9).$$

The above sequences were tested, and the results are shown in the following Tables 4.28 and 4.29.

Table 4.28 SO_2 emission original data sequence quasi-smoothness test

t	1	2	3	4	5	6	7	8	9	10	11	12	13
$\rho(t)$	0	0	0.626	0.425	0.316	0.267	0.212	0.181	0.167	0.149	0.134	0.122	0.108

Table 4.29 SO_2 emission new sequence quasi-exponential law test

t	1	2	3	4	5	6	7	8	9	10	11	12	13
$\delta^{(1)}(t)$	0	0	1.626	1.425	1.316	1.267	1.212	1.181	1.167	1.149	1.134	1.122	1.108

③ CO Emission Data Test

From Table 4.25, the original data sequence of CO emissions is $X_{CO}^{(0)}$

$$X_{CO}^{(0)} = (1513.33, 1734.05, 2000.63, 2185.91, 2320.72, 2583.03, 2504.47, 2519.93, 2722.97, 2826.13, 2923.61, 2989.48, 2976.35).$$

The new sequence generated by accumulation is $X_{CO}^{(1)}$,

$$X_{CO}^{(1)} = (1513.33, 3247.38, 5248.01, 7433.92, 9754.64, 12337.67, 14842.14, 17362.07, 20085.04, 22911.17, 25834.78, 28824.26, 31800.61).$$

The above sequences were tested, and the results are shown in the following Table 4.30 and 4.31.

④ PM_{10} Emission Data Test

From Table 4.25, the original data sequence of PM 10 emissions is $X_{PM_{10}}^{(0)}$:

$$X_{PM_{10}}^{(0)} = (319.01, 366.16, 422.84, 462.68, 491.08, 546.44, 532.38, 537.74, 581.69, 603.84, 624.92, 639.38, 636.62).$$

The new sequence generated by accumulation is $X_{PM_{10}}^{(1)}$:

Table 4.30 CO emission original data sequence quasi-smoothness test

t	1	2	3	4	5	6	7	8	9	10	11	12	13
$\rho(t)$	0	0	0.616	0.417	0.312	0.265	0.203	0.170	0.157	0.141	0.128	0.116	0.103

Table 4.31 CO emission new sequence quasi-exponential law test

t	1	2	3	4	5	6	7	8	9	10	11	12	13
$\delta^{(1)}(t)$	0	0	1.616	1.417	1.312	1.265	1.203	1.170	1.157	1.141	1.128	1.116	1.103

$$X_{PM_{10}}^{(0)} = (319.01,685.17, 1108.01,1570.69, 2061.77,2608.21,$$
$$4260.02,4863.86, 5488.78,6128.16, 6764.78).3140.59,3678.33,$$

The above sequences were tested, and the results are shown in the following Tables 4.32 and 4.33:

⑤ VOC $_S$ Emission Data Test

From Table 4.25, the original data sequence of VOC S emissions is $X_{VOC_S}^{(0)}$:

$$X_{VOC_S}^{(0)} = (112.71,120.72, 135.05,135.05, 144.10,165.23, 123.27,$$
$$95.27,92.06, 95.50,95.66, 92.45,92.59).$$

The new sequence generated by accumulation is $X_{VOC_S}^{(1)}$:

$$X_{VOC_S}^{(1)} = (112.71,233.43, 368.48,503.53, 647.63,812.86, 936.13,1031.4, 1123.46,$$
$$1218.96, 1314.62, 1407.07,1499.66).$$

The above sequences were tested, and the results are shown in the following Tables 4.34 and 4.35:

Table 4.32 PM $_{10}$ emission original data sequence Quasi-Smoothness test

t	1	2	3	4	5	6	7	8	9	10	11	12	13
$\rho(t)$	0	0	0.692	0.407	0.319	0.261	0.208	0.179	0.147	0.146	0.118	0.146	0.112

Table 4.33 PM $_{10}$ emission new sequence quasi-exponential law test

t	1	2	3	4	5	6	7	8	9	10	11	12	13
$\delta^{(1)}(t)$	0	0	1.692	1.407	1.319	1.261	1.208	1.179	1.147	1.146	1.118	1.146	1.112

Table 4.34 VOCs emission original data sequence quasi-smoothness test

t	1	2	3	4	5	6	7	8	9	10	11	12	13
$\rho(t)$	0	0	0.692	0.407	0.319	0.261	0.208	0.179	0.147	0.146	0.118	0.146	0.112

Table 4.35 VOCs Emission new sequence quasi-exponential law test

t	1	2	3	4	5	6	7	8	9	10	11	12	13
$\delta^{(1)}(t)$	0	0	1.692	1.407	1.319	1.261	1.208	1.179	1.147	1.146	1.118	1.146	1.112

As pointed out above, when $t > 3$, if $\rho(t) < 0.5$, it satisfies the quasi-smoothness test; when $t > 3$, if $1 < \delta^{(1)}(t) < 1.5$, it satisfies the quasi-exponential law test. If it passes both of the above tests, the grey prediction model can be used for prediction. After testing the five different types of atmospheric pollutants NOx, SO_2, CO, PM_{10}, and VOCS, we found that all five types of atmospheric pollutants passed these two tests and met the modeling requirements. Therefore, the GM(1,1) model can be used to predict the emission of atmospheric pollutants.

(2) Establishment of the GM(1,1) model for ship atmospheric pollutant emission-sPreliminary Data Verification

① Establishment of the GM(1,1) model for NOx emissions

Based on the original data series $X_{NO_x}^{(0)}$ and the new series formed by accumulation $X_{NO_x}^{(1)}$, the parameter column [image] is estimated by the least squares method to obtain the following data: $\hat{U} = [\hat{\alpha}, \hat{\mu}]^T$, $\hat{U} = [\hat{\alpha}, \hat{\mu}]^T = (B^T B)^{-1} B^T Y = (-0.053, 15278.211)^T$, so this model can be used for medium and long-term prediction. From this, the equation of the NOx emission prediction model can be established: The time response equation of the whitening equation corresponding to the GM(1,1) model is $\hat{X}_{NO_x}^{(1)}(k+1) = 302400.0 \times e^{0.053t} - 290244.0$, according to the formula, the simulated value of the new series $X_{NO_x}^{(1)}$ can be calculated. According to the formula, the time response equation of the GM(1,1) model can be obtained: $\hat{X}_{NO_x}^{(0)}(k+1) = 15506.5889 \times e^{0.053t}$, and the simulated prediction value corresponding to the original series $X_{NO_x}^{(0)}$ can be calculated for the corresponding years.

② Establishment of the GM(1,1) model for SO_2 emissions

Based on the original data series $X_{SO_2}^{(0)}$ and the new series formed by accumulation $X_{SO_2}^{(1)}$, the parameter column $\hat{U} = [\hat{\alpha}, \hat{\mu}]^T$ is estimated by the least squares method to obtain the following data: $\hat{U} = [\hat{\alpha}, \hat{\mu}]^T = (B^T B)^{-1} B^T Y = (-0.051, 3618.357)^T$, $-\alpha = 0.051 < 0.3$, so this model can be used for medium and long-term prediction.

From this, the equation of the SO_2 emission prediction model can be established: The time response equation of the whitening equation corresponding to the GM(1,1) model is$\hat{X}_{SO_2}^{(1)}(k+1) = 73959.0 \times e^{0.051t} - 71075.0$, according to the formula, the simulated value of the new series $X_{SO_2}^{(1)}$ can be calculated. According to the formula, the time response equation of the GM(1,1) model can be obtained: $\hat{X}_{SO_2}^{(0)}(k+1) = 3670.9517 \times e^{0.051t}$, and the simulated prediction value corresponding to the original series $X_{NO_x}^{(0)}$ can be calculated for the corresponding years.

③ Establishment of the GM(1,1) model for CO emissions

Based on the original data series $X_{CO}^{(0)}$ and the new series formed by accumulation $X_{SO_2}^{(1)}$, the parameter column $\hat{U} = [\hat{\alpha}, \hat{\mu}]^T$ is estimated by the least squares method to obtain the following data: $\hat{U} = [\hat{\alpha}, \hat{\mu}]^T = (B^T B)^{-1} B^T Y = (-0.041, 1889.245)^T$,

$-\alpha = 0.041 < 0.3$, so this model can be used for medium and long-term prediction. The following data was estimated using the least squares method: $\hat{X}_{CO}^{(1)}(k+1) = 47288.0 \times e^{0.041t} - 45775.0$, thus, this model can be used for medium and long-term forecasting. From this, the equation for the CO emission prediction model can be established: The time response equation of the whitening equation corresponding to the GM(1,1) model is: $\hat{X}_{CO}^{(1)}(k+1) = 47288.0 \times e^{0.041t} - 45775.0$, according to the formula, the new sequence $X_{CO}^{(1)}$ can be calculated. According to the formula, the time response equation of the GM(1,1) model can be obtained: $\hat{X}_{CO}^{(0)}(k+1) = 1911.9760 \times e^{0.041t}$, and the simulated prediction value corresponding to the original sequence $X_{CO}^{(0)}$ can be calculated.

④ Establishment of PM_{10} emission GM(1,1) model

Based on the original data sequence $X_{PM_{10}}^{(0)}$ and the new sequence formed by accumulation $X_{PM_{10}}^{(1)}$, the parameter column $\hat{U} = [\hat{\alpha}, \hat{\mu}]^T$ was estimated using the least squares method to obtain the following data: $\hat{U} = [\hat{\alpha}, \hat{\mu}]^T = (B^T B)^{-1} B^T Y = (-0.043, 398.387)^T$, $-\alpha = 0.043 < 0.3$, thus, this model can be used for medium and long-term forecasting. From this, the equation for the PM_{10} emission prediction model can be established: The time response equation of the whitening equation corresponding to the GM(1,1) model is: $\hat{X}_{PM_{10}}^{(1)}(k+1) = 9682.3 \times e^{0.043t} - 9363.3$, according to the formula, the new sequence $X_{PM_{10}}^{(1)}$ can be calculated. According to the formula, the time response equation of the GM(1,1) model can be obtained: $\hat{X}_{PM_{10}}^{(0)}(k+1) = 403.3196 \times e^{0.043t}$, and the simulated prediction value corresponding to the original sequence $X_{PM_{10}}^{(0)}$ can be calculated.

⑤ Establishment of VOCS emission GM(1,1) model Based on the original data sequence $X_{VOC_S}^{(0)}$ and the new sequence formed by accumulation $X_{VOC_S}^{(1)}$, the parameter column $\hat{U} = [\hat{\alpha}, \hat{\mu}]^T$ was estimated using the least squares method to obtain the following data: $\hat{U} = [\hat{\alpha}, \hat{\mu}]^T = (B^T B)^{-1} B^T Y = (-0.042, 152.326)^T$, $-\alpha = 0.042 < 0.3$, thus, this model can be used for medium and long-term forecasting. From this, the equation for the PM_{10} emission prediction model can be established: The time response equation of the whitening equation corresponding to the GM(1,1) model is: $\hat{X}_{VOC_S}^{(1)}(k+1) = 3593.9 - 3481.2 \times e^{0.042t}$, according to the formula, the new sequence $X_{VOC_S}^{(1)}$ can be calculated. According to the formula, the time response equation of the GM(1,1) model can be obtained: $\hat{X}_{VOC_S}^{(0)}(k+1) = 150.72 \times e^{0.042t}$, and the simulated prediction value corresponding to the original sequence $X_{VOC_S}^{(0)}$ can be calculated. Simulated prediction values for the corresponding years.

(3) Accuracy test of the grey prediction GM(1,1) model

Based on the time response equation derived from the GM(1,1) model, we can calculate the simulated emission amounts of five different types of atmospheric pollutants from 2009 to 2021. By using the existing data and the simulated data calculated from the model, we can test the established model.

① Emission GM(1,1) model test

Through the MATLAB program, we can derive the time response equation of the GM(1,1) model. According to the response equation, we can obtain the simulated data corresponding to the original data, and compare and analyze the original data and simulated data of the emissions. The accuracy of the model is mainly analyzed by calculating the residuals and relative errors The analysis results are as follows (Table 4.36).

From the above table, it can be seen that the absolute values of the relative errors $\Phi(i)$ are generally less than 0.05, indicating that this model can be called a residual qualified model; the average relative error $\overline{\Phi}(i) = \frac{1}{13}\sum_{i=1}^{13}\Phi(i) = 0.03666$ shows that the prediction accuracy of the model is relatively high and can be used for medium and long-term forecasting. According to formula (4.9), the mean square deviation ratio is calculated, and the mean square deviation ratio test is carried out $C = 0.136$. According to formula (4.10), the small error probability P test is carried out $P = 1$. Because $C = 0.136 < 0.35, P = 1 > 0.95$,the prediction model accuracy of the emissions is excellent at the first level.

② SO_2 emission GM(1,1) model test

Through the MATLAB program, we can derive the time response equation of the GM(1,1) model. According to the response equation, we can obtain the simulated data corresponding to the original data, and compare and analyze the original data and simulated data of SO_2 emissions. The accuracy of the model is mainly analyzed by calculating the residuals and relative errors. The analysis results are as follows (Table 4.37).

Table 4.36 Analysis of the NOx emission prediction model test calculation for 2009–2021

Year	Actual data $x_{NOx}^{(0)}$	Simulated data $\hat{x}_{NOx}^{(0)}$	Residuals $\Delta^{(0)}(i)$	Relative error $\Phi(i)$
2009	12,159.81	–	–	–
2010	14,163.18	16,344.72	– 2181.54	– 0.1540
2011	16,485.89	17,228.16	742.27	0.0450
2012	18,263.05	18,159.34	103.71	0.0057
2013	19,339.38	19,140.85	198.53	0.0103
2014	21,470.07	20,175.42	1294.65	0.0603
2015	21,761.19	21,265.90	495.29	0.0228
2016	22,660.27	22,415.33	244.94	0.0108
2017	24,715.05	23,626.88	1088.17	0.0440
2018	25,694.69	24,903.91	790.78	0.0308
2019	26,675.44	26,249.97	425.47	0.0159
2020	27,415.61	27,668.79	– 253.18	– 0.0092
2021	27,313.3	29,164.29	– 1850.99	– 0.0678

Table 4.37 Analysis of the SO_2 emission prediction model test calculation for 2009–2021

Year	Actual data $x_{NOx}^{(0)}$	Simulated data $\hat{x}_{NOx}^{(0)}$	Residuals $\Delta^{(0)}(i)$	Relative error $\Phi(i)$
2009	2884.16	–	–	–
2010	3350.36	3862.68	– 512.32	– 0.1529
2011	3894.23	4064.41	– 170.18	– 0.0437
2012	4304.49	4276.69	27.80	0.0065
2013	4560.05	4500.05	60.00	0.0132
2014	5064.52	4735.07	329.45	0.0651
2015	5097.57	4982.37	115.20	0.0226
2016	5280.57	5242.59	37.98	0.0072
2017	5751.41	5516.39	235.02	0.0409
2018	5977.89	5804.50	173.39	0.0290
2019	6202.8	6107.65	95.15	0.0153
2020	6370.12	6426.64	– 56.52	– 0.0089
2021	6345.73	6762.28	– 416.55	– 0.0656

From the above table, it can be seen that the absolute values of the relative errors $\Phi(i)$ are generally less than 0.05, indicating that this model can be called a residual qualified model; the average relative error $\overline{\Phi}(i) = \frac{1}{13}\sum_{i=1}^{13}\Phi(i) = 0.03622$ shows that the prediction accuracy of the model is relatively high and can be used for medium and long-term forecasting. According to formula (4.9), the mean square deviation ratio is calculated, and the mean square deviation ratio test is carried out $C = 0.140$. According to formula (4.10), the small error probability P test is carried out $P = 1$. Because $C = 0.140 < 0.35, P = 1 > 0.95$,the prediction model accuracy of the emissions is excellent at the first level.

③ CO emission GM(1,1) model test

The time response equation of the GM(1,1) model is obtained through the MATLAB program. According to the response equation, the simulated data corresponding to the original data can be obtained. The original data and simulated data of CO emissions are compared and analyzed, mainly through the calculation of residuals and relative errors to analyze the accuracy of the model. The analysis results are as follows (Table 4.38).

From the above table, it can be seen that the absolute value of the relative error $\Phi(i)$ is generally less than 0.05, indicating that this model can be called a residual qualified model. The average relative error $\overline{\Phi}(i) = \frac{1}{13}\sum_{i=1}^{13}\Phi(i) = 0.03582$ shows that the prediction accuracy of the model is high and can be used for medium and long-term forecasting. The mean square deviation ratio is calculated according to formula (4.9), and the mean square deviation ratio test is carried out $C = 0.173$. The small error probability P test $P = 1$ is carried out according to formula (4.10). Because $C = 0.173 < 0.35, P = 1 > 0.95$,the prediction model accuracy is excellent.

Table 4.38 Analysis of the CO emission forecast model verification ca culation for 2009–2021

Year	Actual data $x_{NOx}^{(0)}$	Simulated data $\hat{x}_{NOx}^{(0)}$	Residuals $\Delta^{(0)}(i)$	Relative error $\Phi(i)$
2009	1513.33	–	–	
2010	1734.05	1992.54	– 258.49	– 0.1491
2011	2000.63	2076.50	– 75.87	– 0.0379
2012	2185.91	2163.99	21.92	0.0100
2013	2320.72	2255.17	65.55	0.0282
2014	2583.03	2350.20	232.83	0.0901
2015	2504.47	2449.23	55.24	0.0221
2016	2519.93	2552.43	– 32.50	– 0.0129
2017	2722.97	2659.98	62.99	0.0231
2018	2826.13	2772.06	54.07	0.0191
2019	2923.61	2888.86	34.75	0.0119
2020	2989.48	3010.59	– 21.11	– 0.0071
2021	2976.35	3137.44	– 161.09	– 0.0541

④ PM_{10} Emission GM(1,1) Model Verification

The time response equation of the GM(1,1) model is obtained through the MATLAB program. According to the response equation, the simulated data corresponding to the original data can be obtained. The original data and simulated data of PM_{10} emissions are compared and analyzed, mainly through the calculation of residuals and relative errors to analyze the accuracy of the model. The analysis results are as follows (Table 4.39).

From the above table, it can be seen that the absolute value of the relative error $\Phi(i)$ is generally less than 0.05, indicating that this model can be called a residual qualified model. The average relative error $\overline{\Phi}(i) = \frac{1}{13}\sum_{i=1}^{13}\Phi(i) = 0.03572$ shows that the prediction accuracy of the model is high and can be used for medium and long-term forecasting. The mean square deviation ratio is calculated according to formula (4.9), and the mean square deviation ratio test is carried out $C = 0.167$. The small error probability P test $P = 1$ is carried out according to formula (4.10). Because $C = 0.167 < 0.35$, $P = 1 > 0.95$,the prediction model accuracy is excellent.

⑤ VOCs Emission GM(1,1) Model Verification

The time response equation of the GM(1,1) model is obtained through the MATLAB program. According to the response equation, the simulated data corresponding to the original data can be obtained. The original data and simulated data of VOCs emissions are compared and analyzed, mainly through the calculation of residuals and relative errors to analyze the accuracy of the model. The analysis results are as follows (Table 4.40):

Table 4.39 Analysis of the PM_{10} emission forecast model verification calculation for 2009–2021

Year	Actual data $x_{NOx}^{(0)}$	Simulated data $\hat{x}_{NOx}^{(0)}$	Residuals $\Delta^{(0)}(i)$	Relative error $\Phi(i)$
2009	319.01		–	–
2010	366.16	420.85	– 54.69	– 0.1494
2011	422.84	439.14	– 16.30	– 0.0386
2012	462.68	458.23	4.45	0.0096
2013	491.08	478.15	12.93	0.0263
2014	546.44	498.93	47.51	0.0869
2015	532.38	520.62	11.76	0.0221
2016	537.74	543.25	– 5.51	– 0.0102
2017	581.69	566.86	14.83	0.0255
2018	603.84	591.50	12.34	0.0204
2019	624.92	617.21	7.71	0.0123
2020	639.38	644.03	– 4.65	– 0.0073
2021	636.62	672.03	– 35.41	– 0.0556

Table 4.40 Analysis of the PM_{10} Emission Forecast Model Verification Calculation for 2009–2021

Year	Actual data $x_{NOx}^{(0)}$	Simulated data $\hat{x}_{NOx}^{(0)}$	Residuals $\Delta^{(0)}(i)$	relative error $\Phi(i)$
2009	112.71	–	–	–
2010	120.72	144.47	– 23.75	– 0.1967
2011	135.05	138.47	– 3.42	– 0.0253
2012	135.05	132.72	2.33	0.0172
2013	144.10	127.22	16.88	0.1172
2014	165.23	121.94	43.29	0.2620
2015	123.27	116.88	6.39	0.0519
2016	95.27	112.03	– 16.76	– 0.1759
2017	92.06	107.38	– 15.32	– 0.1664
2018	95.50	102.92	– 7.42	– 0.0777
2019	95.66	98.65	– 2.99	– 0.0313
2020	92.45	94.56	– 2.11	– 0.0228
2021	92.59	90.63	– 1.96	0.0211

From the above table, it can be seen that the relative error $\Phi(i)$ absolute values are basically less than 0.1, indicating that this model can be called a qualified residual model; the average relative error is $\overline{\Phi}(i) = \frac{1}{13}\sum_{i=1}^{13}\Phi(i) = 0.08965$, indicating that the prediction accuracy of the model is high and can be used for later medium and long-term forecasting; according to formula (4.9), the mean square error ratio is calculated, and the mean square error ratio test is carried out $C = 0.50$, according to formula (4.10), the small error probability P test is carried out: $P = 0.92$, because $C = 0.50 \leq 0.50$, so the prediction model accuracy of VOC_S is good at level two.

(4) Improvement of the accuracy of the grey GM(1,1) model

According to the mean square error ratio test C and the small error probability P test, referring to the accuracy test value, it can be concluded that the prediction model accuracy of NOx, SO_2, CO, and PM_{10} is excellent at level one, and the prediction model accuracy of VOCS is good at level two. Therefore, the prediction model accuracy of VOCS is improved according to the Markov model.

① Divide the state interval

According to the relative error value of the GM(1,1) model of VOCS, the emission prediction situation of VOCS is divided into the following five state intervals: $E_1(-0.1967, -0.1050)$, $E_2(-0.1050, -0.0132)$, $E_3(-0.0132, 0.0785)$, $E_4(0.0785, 0.1703)$, $E_5(0.1703,0.2620)$. The division results are as follows (Table 4.41):

② Establish the state transition probability matrix

In the 3 states starting from E_1 (transferring out), one is from E_1 to E_1, and two are from E_1 to E_2, which can be concluded $p_{11} = \frac{1}{3}$, $p_{12} = \frac{2}{3}$; in the 4 states starting from E_2, two are from E_2 to E_2, and two are from E_2 to E_3, which can be concluded $p_{22} = \frac{2}{4}$, $p_{23} = \frac{2}{4}$; in the 3 states starting from E_3, two are from E_3 to E_1. Of them, one is from E_3 to E_4, and we can derive $p_{31} = \frac{2}{3}$, $p_{34} = \frac{1}{3}$; in one state starting from E_4, one is from E_4 to E_5, and we can derive $p_{45} = 1$; in one state starting from E_5, one is from E_5 to E_3, and we can derive $p_{53} = 1$. The established state transition probability matrix is as follows:

$$P = \begin{bmatrix} \frac{1}{3} & \frac{2}{3} & 0 & 0 & 0 \\ 0 & \frac{2}{4} & \frac{2}{4} & 0 & 0 \\ \frac{2}{3} & 0 & 0 & \frac{1}{3} & 0 \\ 0 & 0 & 0 & 0 & 1 \\ 0 & 0 & 1 & 0 & 0 \end{bmatrix}$$

③ The revised prediction value

The predicted emission of VOCs from 2009 to 2021 is revised. The grey prediction for 2006 is 144.47, and its state is E_1. The predicted value after Markov model correction is $\hat{Y}_{(2006)} = 144.47 * [1 + 0.5 * (-0.1967 - 0.1050)] = 122.6767$. Similarly, the

Table 4.41 State division table of VOCS emissions from 2009 to 2021

Year	2005	2006	2007	2008	2009	2010	2011	2012	2013	2014	2015	2016	2017
state	E3	E1	E2	E3	E4	E5	E3	E1	E1	E2	E2	E2	E3

grey Markov prediction values for 2007–2017 can be calculated and compared with the grey prediction model values. The results are shown in Table 4.17.

④ Accuracy test

The accuracy test of the GM(1,1) prediction model for VOCs is good at the second level, where the absolute value of the average relative error is $\overline{\Phi}(i) = \frac{1}{13}\sum_{i=1}^{13}\Phi(i) = 0.08965$, the mean square error ratio test C = 0.50, and the small error probability P test: $P = 0.92$; The average relative error after correction by the Markov model, the mean square error ratio test $C = 0.50$, and the small error probability P test: $P = 1$. According to Table 2.1, the accuracy of the model after correction by the Markov model becomes excellent at the first level (Table 4.42).

The predicted emission of atmospheric pollutants from ships in Qingdao Port from 2022 to 2032 is as follows (Table 4.43).

(5) Management implications

① Focus the governance and regulation on the emissions of NOx, SO_2, and PM_{10}, especially the ship emissions of PM_{10}. The emission level of NOx is already high, and controlling it requires the application of technical research, either denitrification during the combustion of fuel oil or after combustion. To reduce the emission of SO_2, it is necessary to strictly control the sulfur content in fuel oil, reducing sulfur emissions from the source. The emission of PM_{10} particulates is relatively low, but its negative externality cost factor is the highest, indicating its difficulty in governance and its ability to damage the environment. Moreover, the emission of PM_{10} shows an increasing trend year by year, making it a

Table 4.42 Comparison of prediction results of two models

Year	Actual data $x_{NOx}^{(0)}$	Simulated data $\hat{x}_{NOx}^{(0)}$	Residuals $\Delta^{(0)}(i)$	Relative error $\Phi(i)$	Year	Actual data $x_{NOx}^{(0)}$	Simulated data $\hat{x}_{NOx}^{(0)}$
2009	112.71	–	–	–	–	–	–
2010	120.72	144.47	– 23.75	– 0.1967	122.6767	1.956701	0.016209
2011	135.05	138.47	– 3.42	– 0.0253	130.2864	– 4.76358	– 0.03527
2012	135.05	132.72	2.33	0.0172	137.0533	2.003308	0.014834
2013	144.10	127.22	16.88	0.1172	143.0462	– 1.05383	– 0.00731
2014	165.23	121.94	43.29	0.2620	148.2973	– 16.9327	– 0.10248
2015	123.27	116.88	6.39	0.0519	120.6961	– 2.57387	– 0.02088
2016	95.27	112.03	– 16.76	– 0.1759	95.1303	– 0.13973	– 0.00147
2017	92.06	107.38	– 15.32	– 0.1664	91.1817	– 0.87827	– 0.00954
2018	95.50	102.92	– 7.42	– 0.0777	96.8374	1.337428	0.014004
2019	95.66	98.65	– 2.99	– 0.0313	92.8198	– 2.84022	– 0.02969
2020	92.45	94.56	– 2.11	– 0.0228	88.9715	– 3.4785	– 0.03763
2021	92.59	90.63	– 1.96	0.0211	93.5891	0.99907	0.01079

Table 4.43 Predicted emission of atmospheric pollutants from ships in Qingdao Port from 2022 to 2032

Year	NO_x/t	SO_2/t	CO/t	PM_{10}/t	VOCs/t
2009	34,153.49	7878.11	3550.98	763.52	82.42
2010	35,999.49	8289.56	3700.61	796.71	64.96
2011	37,945.27	8722.5	3856.54	831.34	68.99
2012	39,996.22	9178.06	4019.04	867.47	72.57
2013	42,158.02	9657.4	4188.38	905.18	57.2
2014	44,436.66	10,161.78	4364.86	944.52	60.75
2015	46,838.47	10,692.5	4548.78	985.58	58.23
2016	49,370.09	11,250.95	4740.45	1028.42	55.82
2017	52,038.55	11,838.55	4940.19	1073.12	53.5
2018	54,851.24	12,456.85	5148.35	1119.76	51.28
2019	57,815.96	13,107.43	5365.29	1168.43	49.15

top priority for future environmental governance. The generation of particulates mainly comes from the incomplete combustion of fuel oil in ship engines, so it is necessary to use scientific technology to modify the engine device to allow the fuel oil to burn fully. For unavoidable pollutant emissions, follow-up emission treatment measures should be taken to ensure that they meet emission standards before being discharged.

② While reducing ship pollution emissions, regulatory measures should be taken for other fuel-powered equipment in the port area to improve the environmental quality of the port area. The ship emissions in the Qingdao Port area have already had a negative impact on the air quality of the entire city of Qingdao, and the share rate has a continuous upward trend. Therefore, reducing the ship emissions in Qingdao Port will be key to improving the air quality of Qingdao city. Reducing pollution emissions in the area should not be limited to ship emissions. There are a large number of machinery powered by fuel oil in the port area. While taking certain regulatory measures, some equipment can be directly replaced with clean energy sources such as electricity.

③ Develop a shore power system in the port area, setting the corresponding power supply frequency according to the ship's own needs. Ships entering the port area need to keep their auxiliary engines working to maintain production and living needs, which will continuously emit atmospheric pollutants. To improve this situation, a new power source needs to be provided for the ships. The port shore power system can solve this problem by using land power to supply the main shipboard systems. It is an emerging technology with great development prospects. In addition, China's power frequency is 50 Hz, and the United States' is 60 Hz. To deal with this situation, shore power systems with different power supply frequencies can be set according to the specific needs of the ship itself.

The use of shore power systems can greatly reduce the atmospheric pollution emissions of ships in the port area.

④ Levy some taxes based on the type of ship, engine type, fuel quality, and emission treatment capacity, etc. The amount of tax is directly proportional to the ship's emissions, to protect and encourage green ships and curb or even drive away "gray" ships. A special control fund can be established based on the tax, to upgrade and modify ships as needed, achieving pollution treatment before discharge. In addition, the fuel cost part of the cruise ticket price can be flexibly priced based on the above factors, allowing passengers to share some of the negative externality costs generated by ship emissions.

⑤ Strengthen the environmental awareness and social responsibility of shipping companies, and adopt appropriate subsidies and other incentive measures, especially for ship manufacturing companies. Encourage shipping companies to actively participate in industry emission reduction, to enhance their reputation, and they can also gain corresponding benefits through emission rights trading. For ship manufacturing companies committed to energy conservation and emission reduction, the government can provide certain subsidies.

References

Cai L (2013) Improved grey Markov model and its prediction of the total volume of national postal and telecommunications services. Nanjing Univ Posts Telecommun 1–42

Chen D, Wang X, Nelson P et al (2017) Ship emission inventory and its impact on the $PM_{2.5}$ air pollution in Qingdao Port North China. Atmos Environ 166:351–361

Du B, Zhu P, Liang M et al (2019) Prediction of container throughput in Shenzhen Port based on grey Markov model. J Zhejiang Ocean Univ (Natural Sci Ed) 2:180–187

Feng J, Zhang Y, Li S, Mao J, Patton AP, Zhou Y, Ma W, Liu C, Kan H, Huang C, An J, Li L, Shen Y, Fu Q, Wang X, Liu J, Wang S, Ding D, Cheng J, Ge W, Zhu H, Walker K (2019) Atmos Chem Phys 19(9):6167–6183

Gu J, Wang W, Peng Y et al (2017) Research on the inventory of atmospheric pollutant emissions from ships berthed at port based on STEAM. J Saf Environ 5:1963–1968

Liang Y, Liao R, Yan M et al (2016) Accounting for ship atmospheric pollutant emissions in Shenzhen Port. Environ Sci Guide 164(02):31–35

Navrud S, Ready R (2007) Lessons learned for environmental value transfer. In: Environmental value transfer: issues and methods

Peng C, Qiao B (2014) Policy measures and practices to control ship atmospheric pollutant emissions. Water Transport Manage 2:1–5

Ready R (2008) Environmental value transfer: issues and methods. Eur Rev Agric Econ 35(2):290–259

Song S (2014) Ship emissions inventory, social cost and eco-efficiency in Shanghai Yangshan port. Atmos Environ 82:288–297

Tan J, Song Y, Ge Y et al (2014) Inventory of ocean-going ship emissions in Dalian sea area. Environ Sci Res 12:1426–1431

Wan L, He L, Huang X (2013) Research progress on ship atmospheric pollution emissions. Environ Sci Technol 05:57–62

Wang T, Song EK, Lin M et al (2007) Research on particulate capture and forced regeneration characteristics of fuel catalyst particulate trap. J Intern Combust Engines 6:527–531

Xu W, Yin C, Xu X et al (2019) Inventory and characteristics of atmospheric pollutant emissions from inland river ships in Jiangsu Province. Environ Sci 40(06):105–116

Yang X, Teng F, Wang G (2013) Incorporating environmental co-benefits into climate policies: a regional study of the cement industry in China. Appl Energy 112:1446–1453

Ye H, Xu Y, Xiao Z (2001) Research on diesel vehicle exhaust particulate after treatment. Environ Sci Res 4:54–56

Yin P, Huang Z, Zheng D et al (2017) Inventory and spatiotemporal distribution characteristics of ship emissions in Ningbo-Zhoushan Port. China Environ Sci 37(1):27–37

Chapter 5
Research on the Carbon Footprint Calculation Model of Regional Port Clusters

Ports are the strategic fulcrums and important hubs of China's "Belt and Road" initiative. In fact, ports mainly rely on the consumption of petrochemical energy for production operations, which makes them major carbon emitters. Statistical data also shows: the carbon emissions from ports and maritime shipping activities exceed 2.7% of the global total each year. Events such as the Durban Conference in 2011 and the EU Maritime Carbon Tax in 2013 have forced China's port industry, which has the highest throughput in the world, to accelerate its path to low-carbon development. Currently, the problems of uncontrollable greenhouse gas emissions and low energy utilization efficiency in China's port industry have not been effectively solved, making it difficult to keep up with the pace of low-carbon construction in developed countries' ports. Therefore, accelerating the construction of low-carbon ports is not only the core issue of green port construction, but also a practical issue for the transformation of the port industry (World Ports Climate Initiative 2008).

5.1 Research on the Driving Factors of Low-Carbon Ports from the Perspective of Energy Consumption

Accelerating the construction of low-carbon ports requires a lot of basic work to be done thoroughly and in detail. Among them, the driving factors of port carbon footprint are one of the most basic tasks, which play a very important role in clarifying and improving the direction and specific strategies to reduce port carbon emissions. In fact, although the current port and shipping academia has conducted detailed research on port carbon footprint calculation, construction paths, etc., it is still in the qualitative stage as a whole. On the other hand, the port industry has also taken measures to reduce carbon emissions such as using shore power and updating loading and unloading equipment, but there is still a need for in-depth research to dig deeper for effective measures. Therefore, this chapter intends to study the calculation of the

B. Lu, *The Sustainable Development of Port Group*,
https://doi.org/10.1007/978-981-97-2378-2_5

carbon footprint of port clusters and its driving factors, in order to provide a reference for China to build first-class green ports.

5.1.1 Structure of Port Carbon Footprint Driving Factors

From the review and sorting of existing literature on carbon footprint influencing factors, they can be roughly divided into internal and external factors.

(1) Internal Factors

The internal factors contributing to the formation of a port's carbon footprint mainly include technology, management, and structure. Technological factors include the level of ship design, process equipment and operational level, port infrastructure, etc. For example, Li et al. (2011) have analyzed the factors of port infrastructure such as gantry cranes that hinder the development of low-carbon ports in China. Liu and Ge (2018) used queuing theory to study the problem of optimizing the layout of container terminal cranes to minimize CO_2 emissions. Yu and others analyzed the carbon efficiency allocation of electric tire gantry cranes at container terminals under uncertainty. Tang et al. (2019) pointed out that the use of the same bay synchronous loading and unloading operation scheme can ensure the efficiency of loading and unloading and effectively reduce the carbon emissions of trucks in the port. Xu and Ma (2013) proposed that China should promote the development of low-carbon ports by setting low-carbon emission standards, adjusting energy consumption structure, developing clean energy, and introducing low-carbon technologies. Zhang Yamin pointed out that the factors affecting port carbon emissions include port planning and design, port management, loading and unloading equipment, loading and unloading processes and auxiliary production facilities, the technical level of staff operations, energy-saving awareness, etc. Kuang Haibo and Niu Wenyuan constructed a theoretical model of multi-period investment optimization decision-making for container ports under constraints such as port ecological carrying capacity. Peng et al. (2023) conducted a simulation study on the carbon reduction strategy of container port terminal operations under four scenarios: reducing channel speed, reducing berth auxiliary time, using shore power and alternative fuels, and improving the efficiency of port equipment. Tsai et al. (2018) focused on analyzing the nine emission reduction strategies and three management actions for the main greenhouse gases and air pollutants in Taichung Port. As for structural factors, they include the energy consumption structure of the port. Although it has been widely studied at the national level or in other high-energy-consuming industries, the research on the structural factors of the port's carbon footprint based on energy consumption has not yet received high attention.

(2) External Factors

Overall, the external factors influencing the carbon footprint of ports include location, industry, and policy. Location factors include geographical location, economic potential, and regional functions, etc. For example, Jiang and Zhen (2012) believe that the construction of low-carbon ports needs to strengthen the management of landlord ports and the dislocation development between ports. Industrial factors include the type, scale, and structure of industries near the port. For example, Jiang Guannan studied the relationship between the structure of the industrial cluster near the port and the development of the low-carbon port. Shen Yufang and others used the theory of coordinated development to conduct an empirical analysis of the low-carbon development status and coordination status of the industrial group, city group, and port group in the Yangtze River Delta region. They believe that the Yangtze River Delta has a lot of space in promoting the coordination of the three groups and proposed measures to promote the coordinated low-carbon development of the industrial group, city group, and port group in the Yangtze River Delta region. Policy factors include economic, energy, and environmental protection policies. Similar to the structural factors in the internal factors, the academic community has not yet conducted specialized research (Bailey and Solomon 2004).

5.1.2 Port Carbon Footprint Measurement and Driving Factor Decomposition Model

(1) The Thought Process of Port Carbon Footprint Measurement and Driving Factor Analysis

Following the thread of "raising questions → analyzing problems → solving problems", this chapter conducts research on the calculation and driving factors of port carbon footprint. The following three steps are set:

① Construct a port carbon footprint calculation model based on energy consumption. According to the different types of energy consumed by the port, multiplied by the corresponding carbon emission factors, the corresponding total carbon footprint is calculated. To increase the comparability of carbon footprints, the cargo throughput produced by the port is converted into a unit cargo throughput carbon footprint. The basic process of carbon footprint calculation is: first determine the energy consumption of the source of the port carbon footprint, then determine the carbon footprint of various energy consumption at the port, the third step is to determine the total carbon footprint of the port, and finally determine the unit cargo throughput carbon footprint of the port.

② Construct a port carbon footprint driving factor analysis model based on LMDI. Decompose the driving factors of the port carbon footprint from the perspective of energy consumption, and deeply analyze the impact of its energy consumption structure and energy consumption efficiency.

③ Construct a model of the evolution of port carbon footprint and energy-saving emission reduction fund input. Obtain the co-evolution relationship between the port's energy-saving emission reduction fund input and the unit cargo throughput carbon footprint, to provide decision-making reference for better energy-saving emission reduction fund investment in key areas of low-carbon port construction.

Unlike the existing port carbon footprint calculation perspective, this chapter calculates the port carbon footprint and analyzes the driving factors from the perspective of port energy consumption, mainly for two considerations: one is that the energy consumption within a certain period is easy to count. Although the current data on the energy consumption of the main equipment and main links of port production is difficult to systematically obtain, it can be estimated by summarizing the daily purchase volume of diesel, fuel oil, and electricity by port companies. The second is that it can objectively analyze the impact of the energy consumption structure and energy consumption efficiency on the port carbon footprint.

In addition, this chapter only considers the carbon footprint produced by energy consumption in the port production process when calculating the port carbon footprint, and does not consider the carbon footprint produced by ships docking at the port, infrastructure construction activities, etc. Specifically, the sources of port carbon footprint include the carbon footprint produced by energy consumption in the loading and unloading, unloading and transportation process of port production, involving mainly diesel, gasoline, electricity, coal, natural gas, etc. According to the different types of energy, the carbon footprint produced by energy consumption is divided into direct carbon footprint and indirect carbon footprint. The direct carbon footprint is the carbon footprint produced by terminal energy consumption (such as diesel, gasoline, coal, natural gas, etc.), and the indirect carbon footprint is the carbon footprint produced by electricity consumption. This chapter considers electricity as one type of energy. Here, the research is mainly conducted from the perspective of carbon emissions from the consumption of diesel, gasoline, electricity, coal, natural gas, and other energy sources by the port.

The idea of port carbon footprint calculation and driving factor analysis based on energy consumption is shown in Fig. 5.1.

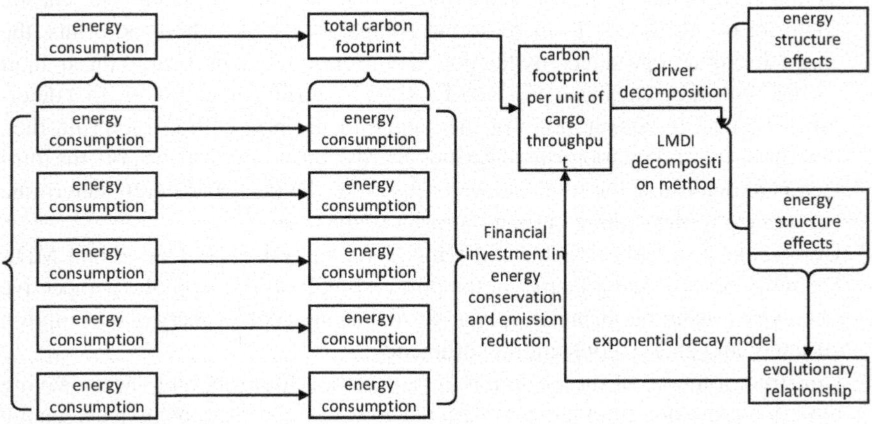

Fig. 5.1 Research idea of port carbon footprint calculation and driving factor analysis

(2) Port Carbon Footprint Calculation Model from the Perspective of Energy Consumption

The port's carbon footprint mainly comes from the consumption of various energies in its production and operation process. Looking at the energy consumption of key links in the port, it is mainly concentrated in key links such as loading and unloading, handling, and warehousing. Among them, port loading and unloading operations are the most critical link, and the energy consumption and carbon emissions account for nearly 80% of the total energy consumption.

Therefore, based on the consumption of major energy sources such as diesel, fuel oil, electricity, and coal in the port, the equation for calculating the port's carbon footprint for the calculating the port's carbon footprint for the t year ($t = 0, 1, 2, \ldots, T$) can be expressed as:

$$C_t = \sum_i C_{it} \tag{5.1}$$

where, C_t is the total carbon footprint of the port in the t year; C_{it} is the carbon footprint of the t year's i type of energy. In Eq. (5.1), the carbon footprint of the t year's i type of energy C_{it} calculation equation is:

$$C_{it} = E_{it} F_{it} \tag{5.2}$$

where, E_{it} is the consumption of the t year's i type of energy, F_{it} is the carbon footprint emission factor of the t year's i type of energy, that is, the carbon footprint produced per unit consumption of the t year's i type of energy

(3) Decomposition of Port Carbon Footprint Influencing Factors

Currently, there are mainly two methods for analyzing the influencing factors of carbon footprint: Structural Decomposition Analysis (SDA) and Index Decomposition Analysis (IDA). Among them, SDA is a relatively static analysis method based on input–output tables and their data. IDA is a more dynamic analysis method that expands the differential of each explanatory variable, with the reporting period or base period index value of other explanatory variables as weights (Villalba and Gemechu 2011). The above IDA is based on the Kaya identity, decomposing the target variable into the product of multiple factor variables. IDA can be further divided into methods based on Divisia, Laspeyres, etc. Each of these models has its own characteristics and uses.

This chapter adopts the IDA method based on Divisia (LMDI) to construct the decomposition model of port carbon footprint influencing factors. The reasons are: first, the decomposition of port carbon footprint influencing factors in this chapter uses the total direct consumption data of different types of energy, and LMDI can effectively avoid the residual item situation in the Laspeyres decomposition process. Second, there are fewer influencing factors of port carbon footprint in this chapter, and the data series period is shorter, while LMDI is suitable for decomposition with fewer factors and less data, and is suitable for comparing time series data, avoiding the shortcomings of SDA that require high-quality, more data analysis from the input–output perspective (Peng 2012). The relationship between the total port carbon footprint and various decomposition influencing factors is as follows:

$$C_t = \sum_i C_{it} = \sum_i \frac{C_{it}}{E_{it}} \times \frac{E_{it}}{C_t} \times \frac{E_t}{B_t} \times B_t \tag{5.3}$$

where, C_t is the port's Annual total carbon footprint; C_{it} is the carbon footprint of the i type of energy in the t year; E_t is the total energy consumption of the port in the t year; E_{it} s the consumption of the i type of energy in the t year of the port; B_t is the cargo throughput of the port in the t year.

Definition: Energy structure factor $S_{it} = E_{it}/E_t$, the share of the i type of energy in the port's energy consumption in the t year; Energy efficiency factor, $I_t = E_t/B_t$, the energy consumption of the port's unit cargo throughput in the t year. Therefore, the carbon footprint of the port's unit cargo throughput in the t year can be expressed as:

$$A_t = \frac{C_t}{B_t} = \sum_i F_{it} S_{it} I_t \tag{5.4}$$

where, A_t is the carbon footprint of the port's unit cargo throughput in the t year; F_{it} is the carbon emission intensity of the port's energy in the t year; S_{it} is the energy structure of the port in the t year I_t; is the energy efficiency factor of the port in the t year.

Equation (5.4) shows that the change in the carbon footprint of the port's unit cargo throughput in the t year is caused by A_t the changes in the energy carbon emission intensity, energy structure, and energy efficiency factors of that year.

Therefore, the change in the carbon footprint of the port's unit cargo throughput in the $t = 0$ period relative to the base period can be expressed as:

$$\Delta A_t = A_t - A_0 = \sum_{it} F_{it} S_{it} I_t - \sum_{it} F_{i0} S_{i0} I_0 = \Delta A_{Ft} + \Delta A_{St} + \Delta A_{It} + \Delta A_{rsdt} \tag{5.5}$$

$$D_t = \frac{A_t}{A_0} = D_{Ft} D_{St} D_{It} D_{rsdt} \tag{5.6}$$

where, ΔA_{Ft}, D_{Ft} is the energy carbon emission intensity factor of the port in the t year; ΔA_{St}, D_{St} is the energy structure of the port in the t year; ΔA_{It}, D_{It} is the energy efficiency factor of the port in the t year; ΔA_{rsdt}, D_{rsdt} is the port to decompose the balance for the t year.

In Eq. (5.5), ΔA_{Ft}, ΔA_{St}, ΔA_{It} represent the contribution of the change of various factors in the t year of the port to the change of the carbon footprint of the port per unit cargo throughput. In Eq. (5.6), D_{Ft}, D_{St}, D_{It} represent the contribution rate of the change of various factors in the t year of the port to the change of the carbon footprint of the port per unit cargo throughput.

LMDI decomposition of Eq. (5.6) is performed, and the decomposition result is as follows:

$$\Delta A_{Ft} = \sum_i W_{it} \ln(\frac{F_{it}}{F_{i0}})$$
$$\Delta A_{St} = \sum_i W_{it} \ln(\frac{S_{it}}{S_{i0}})$$
$$\Delta A_{It} = \sum_i W_{it} \ln(\frac{I_{it}}{I_{i0}}) \tag{5.7}$$

where:

$$W_{it} = \frac{A_{it} - A_{i0}}{In(A_{it}/A_{i0})} \tag{5.8}$$

Hence the result:

$$\Delta A_{rsdt} = \Delta A_t - (\Delta A_{Ft} + \Delta A_{St} + \Delta A_{It}) = \Delta A_t - A_0 - \sum_i W_{it} \ln \frac{A_{it}}{A_{i0}} = 0 \tag{5.9}$$

Taking the logarithm on both sides of Eq. (5.6), we can get:

$$\ln D_t = \ln D_{F_t} + \ln D_{S_t} + \ln D_{I_t} + \ln D_{rsdt} \tag{5.10}$$

Compare Eqs. (5.5) and (5.10), and let each item be proportional accordingly, there are:

$$\frac{\ln D_t}{\Delta A_t} = \frac{\ln D_{Ft}}{\Delta A_{Ft}} = \frac{\ln D_{St}}{\Delta A_{St}} = \frac{\ln D_{It}}{\Delta A_{It}} = \frac{\ln D_{rsdt}}{\Delta A_{rsdt}} \tag{5.11}$$

Separately:

$$\frac{\ln D_t}{\Delta A_t} = \frac{\ln A_{Ft} - \ln A_0}{A_{Ft} - A_0} = W_t \tag{5.12}$$

The contribution rate of the change of each factor to the change of carbon footprint per unit cargo throughput of the port in the t year can be obtained:

Based on the LMDI analysis model of port carbon footprint driving factors, the influencing factors of port carbon footprint change are investigated from a higher level, which improves the analysis and depth of carbon footprint driving factors, deepens the explanation of the energy consumption sources of port carbon footprint, and takes detailed measures to reduce port carbon emissions with more guidance and pertinence.

$$\begin{aligned} D_{Ft} &= \exp(W_t \Delta A_{Ft}) \\ D_{St} &= \exp(W_t \Delta A_{St}) \\ D_{It} &= \exp(W_t \Delta A_{It}) \\ D_{rsdt} &= 1 \end{aligned} \tag{5.13}$$

(4) Analysis of the Relationship between the Carbon Footprint Per Unit of Port Cargo Throughput and the Evolution of Energy-saving and Emission-reduction Fund Input.

In addition to being directly related to energy consumption, the port carbon footprint also has a co-evolution effect with the input of emission reduction funds. Therefore, this chapter will also examine the evolutionary relationship between the carbon footprint per unit of port cargo throughput and the input of emission reduction funds. The co-evolution effect of carbon footprint emission intensity and energy-saving and emission-reduction fund input has three characteristics: one is negative correlation. Generally speaking, as the input of emission reduction funds increases, the intensity of carbon footprint emissions will correspondingly decrease. The second is temporality. Energy-saving and emission-reduction fund input includes equipment investment, R&D investment, behavior investment, etc. Among them, equipment investment has a quick effect in the short term, while R&D investment, behavior investment, etc. will have a slowly releasing effect on the intensity of carbon footprint emissions, thus causing a lag effect on the carbon footprint per unit of cargo throughput. The third is the rigidity of emission reduction. Due to the impossibility of all port loading and unloading equipment being updated to new energy equipment in the short term, it will cause the carbon footprint per unit of port cargo throughput to have a lower ideal level for a longer period of time. As the port carbon emission reduction governance deepens, the carbon footprint per unit of cargo throughput gradually approaches this ideal level (World Ports Initiative 2010). Therefore, this chapter constructs the following exponential decay model to analyze the co-evolution relationship between the carbon footprint per unit of cargo throughput A_t and the input of energy-saving and emission-reduction funds X_t:

$$A_t = \alpha \exp^{-\sum_{j=0}^{k} (\beta_j X_{t-j})} \tag{5.14}$$

where, parameter α is the constant to be estimated, β_j is the lagged parameter to be estimated in the j year, and k is the lagged term. The meaning of Eq. (5.14) is: A_t the carbon footprint per unit of cargo throughput in the t year is affected by the cumulative effect of energy-saving and emission-reduction fund input in the previous j years. Specifically, A_t the carbon footprint per unit of cargo throughput in the t

year is affected by X_t the energy-saving and emission-reduction fund input in the $t, t-1, \ldots, t-j, t-k$ year, and the earlier the year of carbon emission reduction fund input, the smaller the impact, and there is an exponential decay relationship.

It should be noted that the sources of funds for energy conservation and emission reduction in ports mainly include self-raised funds from port enterprises, special fund subsidies from the Ministry of Transport for energy conservation and emission reduction equipment updates and new energy technology research and development, and local government special support funds for energy conservation and emission reduction. The investment in energy conservation and emission reduction in ports can be obtained by summing up these related items. In fact, in the practice of energy conservation and emission reduction in our country's ports, these special funds also include those used for the control of emissions of other greenhouse gases such as sulfides, but the proportion has always been very low. This is different from the IMO's "Sulphur Limit Order" in 2020, which led to a surge in investment in sulphur emission reduction in ships. The energy conservation and emission reduction faced by ports is still more focused on carbon emission reduction investment. Therefore, this chapter assumes that the recent investment in energy conservation and emission reduction in ports is all used for carbon emission control.

After logarithmizing, we have:

$$\ln A_t = \ln \alpha - \sum_{j=0}^{k} (\beta_j X_{t-j}) \quad (5.15)$$

With the help of Eq. (5.15), the fitting model can solve the impact of the energy conservation and emission reduction investment factor, which cannot be included in the LMDI-based port carbon footprint driving factor analysis model, on the carbon footprint of the port unit cargo throughput.

5.1.3 Case Study

In July 2012, the Shanghai Municipal People's Government issued the "Implementation Opinions on Carrying out Carbon Emission Trading Pilot Work". The pilot was carried out from 2013 to 2015, and the key emission enterprises with CO2 emissions of 10,000 tons or more in any year from 2010 to 2011 in the non-industrial sectors such as aviation, ports, airports, railways, commerce, hotels, and finance within the administrative region of Shanghai were implemented with carbon emission trading pilot. That year, Shanghai International Port (Group) Co., Ltd. (hereinafter referred to as: SIPG, stock code 600,018) was included in the first batch of pilot units. Therefore, this chapter conducts an in-depth analysis of the carbon footprint of SIPG.

(1) Data Collection

The analysis of the carbon footprint of SIPG from 2011 to 2021 requires data in three aspects:

① Emission factors, mainly referring to the CO2 emission factors of various types of energy consumed by SIPG, see Tables 5.1 and 5.2. SIPG is located in the East China region, so the power carbon footprint emission factor in Table 5.1 is taken from the annual regional power grid baseline emission factor data in China. The standard coal conversion coefficient is collected from Baidu Literature. Since there is no authoritative department in China to publish unified carbon emission factor data for direct energy, this chapter still cites the default data of carbon emission factors for direct energy in the "IPCC Carbon Emission Calculation Guide (2006)".

② Port energy consumption. The types of energy consumed by SIPG are mainly diesel, fuel oil, and electricity, of which diesel and fuel oil are direct energy consumption, and electricity is indirect energy consumption. The energy consumption data of SIPG from 2011 to 2021 is shown in Table 5.3.

③ Other port data. The port cargo throughput and energy-saving emission reduction special funds mainly come from the "Sustainable Development Report" and

Table 5.1 Baseline carbon emission factor of East China regional power grid

Vintage	EF_{grid}, OM, y (tons CO_2/kWh)	EF_{grid}, OM, y (tons CO_2/kWh)
2011	0.8046	0.4923
2012	0.8086	0.5483
2013	0.8112	0.5945
2014	0.8095	0.6861
2015	0.8100	0.7125
2016	0.8244	0.6889
2017	0.8367	0.6622
2018	0.8592	0.6789
2019	0.8825	0.6826
2020	0.9540	0.8236

Note OM in the table is the weighted average of the marginal emission factor of electricity; BM is the weighted average of the marginal emission factor of capacity

Table 5.2 Standard coal conversion coefficient and carbon emission factor of energy

Type of energy	Discount factor for standard coal	Carbon emission factor
Diesel fuel	1.4571	0.5921
Fuel oil	1.4286	0.6185
Electricity (kWh)	0.1229	See Table 5.1

Note The carbon emission factor comes from the "IPCC Carbon Emission Calculation Guide (2006)"

Table 5.3 Original energy consumption data of SIPG from 2011 to 2021 (*Unit* tons, ten thousand kilowatt-hours)

Type of energy	Diesel fuel	Fuel oil	Electricity
2011	128,585	51,262	27,853
2012	109,233	53,368	27,468
2013	123,852	53,608	30,542
2014	130,139	55,692	34,495
2015	127,066	55,628	36,085
2016	122,260	57,760	35,961
2017	120,324	70,955	35,682
2018	110,763	65,965	38,732
2019	102,549	63,687	39,320
2020	94,507	66,879	40,621
2021	88,873	74,100	41,022

Note The data comes from the SIPG's annual sustainable development reports from 2011 to 2021

"Shanghai Port Group Financial Report" published by the Shanghai Port Group over the years. The data for these two factors can be found in Table 5.4.

(2) Carbon Footprint Calculation of Shanghai Port Group

Using the data related to Eqs. (5.1), (5.2) and Tables 5.1, 5.2 and 5.3, the carbon footprint generated by the energy consumption of the Shanghai Port Group from 2011 to 2021 is calculated. The specific process is as follows: ① Calculation of the

Table 5.4 Original data of port throughput and energy-saving emission reduction funds of Shanghai Port Group from 2011 to 2021 (Unit: ten thousand tons, ten thousand yuan)

Vintage	Port cargo throughput	Revenue from energy saving and emission reduction funds
2011	36,900	18,000
2012	36,500	33,700
2013	42,800	69,446
2014	48,400	69,446
2015	50,900	75,705
2016	54,300	81,105
2017	53,900	84,686
2018	51,300	88,730
2019	51,400	96,481
2020	56,100	105,880
2021	56,100	17,000

Note The investment in energy-saving and emission-reduction funds is the annual cumulative number. The data of energy-saving and emission-reduction funds each year comes from the annual sustainable development reports and annual disclosure reports of the Shanghai Port Group from 2011 to 2021. Some of the annual energy-saving and emission-reduction fund data comes from the total amount of emission reduction project funds involved in government subsidies in the annual disclosure reports carbon footprint of port electricity energy. Since the weighted average value OM of the marginal emission factor of electricity is calculated from the total carbon footprint generated by the total net power generation fuel consumption of all power plants in the power system, and BM is calculated from the total carbon footprint generated by the total fuel consumption of the newly installed capacity of all power plants in the power system, this chapter chooses the weighted average value OM of the marginal emission factor of electricity in Table 5.1 as the electricity carbon footprint emission factor. ② Calculation of the carbon footprint of direct energy at the port. Diesel and fuel oil are calculated by multiplying the consumption in Table 5.3 by the corresponding carbon emission factor in Table 5.2. The detailed results of the carbon footprint of the Shanghai Port Group from 2011 to 2021 can be found in Table 5.5.

The results show: Over the past 11 years, the total carbon footprint of the Shanghai Port Group's energy consumption has shown a slow growth trend, rising from 373,600 tons in 2011 to 428,500 tons in 2021, with an average annual growth rate of only 1.47%. The rate of change is quite large, with the carbon footprint decreasing by 8.96% in 2012 compared to the previous year, while maintaining a positive growth trend from 2013 to 2015, with growth rates of 8.47%, 8.63%, and 1.59% respectively. In 2016, there was a slight negative growth of 1.9%, an increase of 4.11% in 2021 compared to the previous year, a decrease in growth rate to around -0.6% in 2019, and an increase of 1.03% in 2021 compared to the previous year. Among them, the diesel carbon footprint decreased from 76,100 tons in 2011 to 52,600 tons in 2020, a cumulative decrease of 30.88%, with an average annual decrease of 3.09 percentage points, making it the only energy source with a decreasing carbon footprint in the Shanghai Port Group. The carbon footprint of fuel oil increased from 31,700 tons in 2011 to 45,900 tons in 2021, a cumulative increase of 44.55%, with an average annual increase of 4.46 percentage points. The carbon footprint generated by electricity

Table 5.5 Carbon footprint and total amount of three types of energy consumption of Shanghai Port Group from 2011 to 2021 (Unit: tons, tons/ten thousand tons)

Vintage	Diesel fuel	Fuel oil	Electricity	Figure	Carbon footprint per unit of throughput
2011	76,135.18	31,705.55	265,717.62	373,558.35	10.1235
2012	64,676.86	33,008.11	242,405.10	340,090.07	9.3175
2013	7332.77	33,156.55	262,416.86	368,906.18	8.6193
2014	77,055.30	35,064.00	288,619.67	400,738.97	8.2797
2015	75,235.78	34,405.92	297,484.74	407,126.44	7.9986
2016	72,390.15	35,724.56	291,284.10	399,398.81	7.3554
2017	71,243.84	43,885.67	28,845.79	403,975.30	7.4949
2018	65,582.77	40,799.35	314,193.98	418,051.19	8.1984
2019	60,719.26	39,390.41	317,941.52	420,576.11	8.1333
2020	55,957.59	41,364.66	326,836.57	4,241,558.82	7.5608
2021	52,621.70	45,830.85	330,063.01	428,515.82	7.6384

consumption increased significantly from 265,700 tons in 2011 to 330,100 tons in 2021, a cumulative increase of 24.22%, with an average annual increase of 2.42 percentage points.

Figure 5.2 shows the proportion of carbon footprints from three types of energy consumption, drawn according to Table 5.5. As can be seen from Fig. 5.2, the proportion of electricity carbon footprint in the carbon footprint of Shanghai Port Group has consistently maintained a high level, with an 11-year average proportion reaching 73.45%, and the proportion showing an upward trend, rising from 71.13% in 2008 to a peak of 77.06% in 2017, then slightly dropping to 77.02% in 2021. The significant increase in electricity consumption has led to a significant increase of 2.31 percentage points in the proportion of the electricity carbon footprint of Shanghai Port Group. The proportion of fuel oil carbon footprint was 8.49% in 2008 and 10.07% in 2021, an increase of 2.21 percentage points. However, the proportion of diesel carbon footprint shows a trend opposite to that of electricity carbon footprint, that is, the proportion is continuously decreasing, and the cumulative decrease is basically equal to the cumulative increase in the proportion of carbon footprints of electricity and fuel oil. The total carbon footprint of Shanghai Port Group is increasing year by year, mainly due to the annual increase in electricity and fuel oil energy consumption, and electricity energy consumption is the main source of port carbon footprint; the main reason for the change in carbon footprint growth rate is that the growth of electricity energy consumption is faster, far exceeding direct energy consumption, and the growth rate is faster.

(3) Analysis of Driving Factors of Carbon Footprint Per Unit of Cargo Throughput

Since the energy carbon emission intensity (Fit) is fixed, so $\Delta AF = 0, DF = 1$. Therefore, the factors affecting the carbon emissions per unit of cargo throughput of Shanghai Port Group are mainly energy structure factors (Sit) and energy efficiency

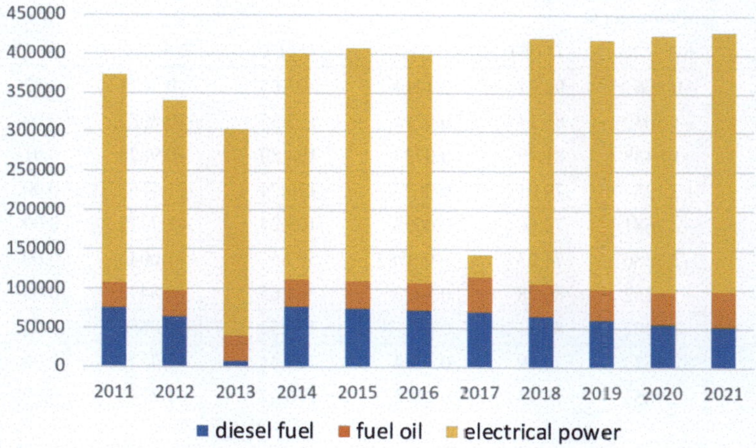

Fig. 5.2 Structure of carbon footprint from three types of energy consumption by Shanghai port group

factors (It). According to Eqs. (5.7) and (5.13), and taking 2011 as the base year, the effects of energy structure and energy efficiency on the carbon footprint per unit of cargo throughput of Shanghai Port Group are shown in Table 5.6.

As shown in Table 5.6, the energy structure has a weak negative driving effect on the reduction of carbon footprint per unit of cargo throughput of Shanghai Port Group. However, energy efficiency has a significant positive driving effect on the carbon footprint per unit of cargo throughput.

In terms of energy structure effect, Table 5.6 shows that from 2012 to 2021, ΔA_S is slightly greater than 0 in all years except 2014, and D_S is also over 100% in all years except 2014 when it was 58.85%. As can be seen from Tables 5.2 and 5.3, the actual carbon emission coefficient of indirect energy from electricity in China is still relatively high (mainly due to thermal power generation, which requires a large amount of direct energy such as coal, coupled with conversion efficiency issues, resulting in a high actual carbon emission coefficient of electricity in China). Shanghai Port Group has made great efforts in recent years to adopt measures such as "oil to electricity", leading to a significant increase in electricity consumption. This indicates that the current adjustment of energy structure in China has not yet played a significant role in reducing the carbon footprint of ports.

In terms of energy efficiency effect, Table 5.6 shows that from 2012 to 2021, ΔAI are all negative, with the maximum contribution value in 2012 reaching −0.2671, DI. except for 2012, when it was 8.82%, the carbon footprint contribution rate in other years was less than 0.1%. This fully demonstrates that the significant reduction in the carbon footprint per unit of cargo throughput of Shanghai Port Group in recent years mainly comes from the improvement of energy efficiency.

Table 5.6 Effects of energy structure and energy efficiency on carbon footprint per unit of cargo throughput of Shanghai port group from 2011 to 2021

Vintage	Carbon footprint per unit of throughput		Energy structure		Energy efficiency	
	ΔA	D (%)	ΔA_S	D_S (%)	ΔA_t	D_t (%)
2012	−0.806	92.04	0.1214	301.65	−0.2671	8.82
2013	−1.5042	85.14	0.0231	123.35	−0.808	0.06
2014	−1.8438	81.79	0.0733	194.80	−0.9828	0.01
2015	−2.125	79.01	0.0623	176.24	−1.176	0.00
2016	−2.7681	72.66	0.0098	109.27	−1.7475	0.00
2017	−2.6286	74.03	−0.0583	58.85	−1.6046	0.00
2018	−1.9252	80.98	0.1423	364.65	−0.8472	0.05
2019	−1.9902	80.34	0.05	157.53	−0.8856	0.03
2020	−2.5628	74.69	0.1304	327.41	−1.4575	0.00
2021	−2.4851	75.45	0.0622	176.07	−1.3746	0.00

(4) The Relationship between Carbon Footprint and Energy-saving and Emission-Reduction Fund Investment

The evolution trend between the carbon footprint per unit of cargo throughput and the investment in energy-saving and emission-reduction funds at the port is shown in Fig. 5.3. In Fig. 5.3, there is a "scissors difference" between the carbon footprint per unit of cargo throughput and the investment in energy-saving and emission-reduction funds at the port. As the investment in energy-saving and emission-reduction funds at the port continues to increase, the carbon footprint per unit of cargo throughput is generally declining. Using the data of carbon footprint per unit of cargo throughput and energy-saving and emission-reduction fund investment in Tables 5.4 and 5.5, the correlation coefficient is −0.6198, showing a negative linear correlation. This indicates that the investment in energy-saving and emission-reduction funds at the port has significantly reduced carbon emissions.

Using Eq. (5.15), with the carbon footprint per unit of cargo throughput as the dependent variable and the investment in energy-saving and emission-reduction funds as the independent variable for regression. By comparing the adjusted R^2 of different lag items k, a better fitting equation was obtained when the lag item was 1 year. Its adjusted R^2 is 0.683, the main parameters are $\alpha = 2.246$, $\beta_0 = -3.230E-7$, $\beta_1 = -1.977E-6$. Therefore, the co-evolution relationship model can be written as:

$$\ln A_t = \ln 2.246 + 3.23E - 7X_t + 1.977E - 6X_{t-1} \tag{5.16}$$

Figure 5.3 is the evolution fitting situation between the carbon footprint per unit of cargo throughput and the energy-saving and emission-reduction fund investment

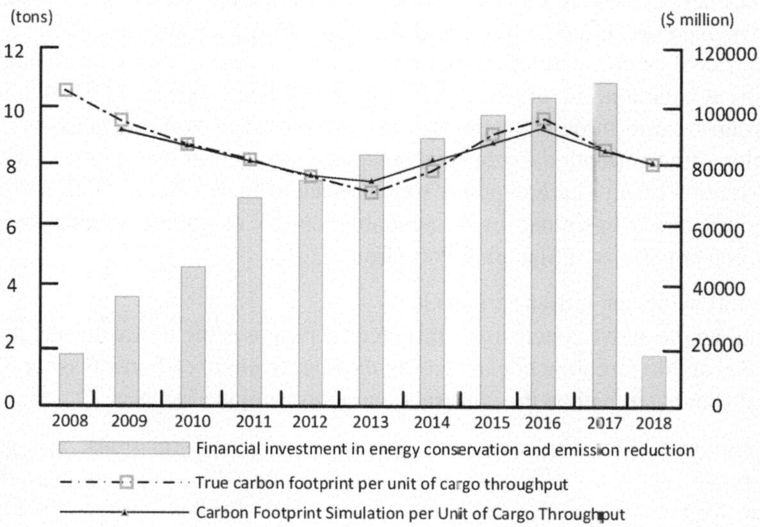

Fig. 5.3 Evolution fitting situation between carbon footprint per unit of cargo throughput and energy-saving and emission-reduction fund investment of Shanghai Port group

of Shanghai Port Group. It can be seen that the effect of Shanghai Port Group's investment in energy-saving and emission-reduction funds on reducing the carbon footprint per unit of cargo throughput is quite significant. This shows that the port's increased investment in energy-saving and emission-reduction funds, and the adoption of advanced technology and management to reduce carbon emissions, can significantly reduce the carbon footprint per unit of cargo throughput.

(5) Main Views and Suggestions

The main views are as follows:

A. Since 2011, affected by the annual increase in electricity and fuel oil energy consumption, the total carbon footprint of Shanghai Port Group's energy consumption has shown a slow growth trend overall, and electricity energy consumption is the main source of Shanghai Port Group's carbon footprint (accounting for more than 70%). The rapid growth of electricity energy consumption has led to a faster growth rate of Shanghai Port Group's carbon footprint.
B. In the past 11 years, the inhibitory effect on the carbon footprint per unit of cargo throughput of Shanghai Port Group mainly comes from the improvement of energy efficiency, and the adjustment of energy structure has little impact on the carbon footprint per unit of cargo throughput.
C. In the past 10 years, the evolution relationship between the carbon footprint per unit of cargo throughput and the investment in energy-saving and emission-reduction funds of Shanghai Port Group has shown a "scissors difference" direction year by year. The investment in energy-saving and emission-reduction funds has a significant effect on reducing the carbon footprint per unit of cargo throughput.
D. Since 2011, the role of energy structure in reducing the carbon footprint of Shanghai Port Group has remained weak, and China's power still mainly comes from coal, with no fundamental changes in the energy structure. Under the current situation, the effect of reducing the carbon footprint of Shanghai Port Group's cargo throughput through the promotion of "oil-to-electricity" technology transformation is not very obvious. However, in the long run, with the revolution of zero-carbon power sources such as hydropower, wind power, and nuclear power in China, it will inevitably lead to a significant reduction in the carbon emissions of Shanghai Port Group.

The following suggestions are made:

Based on the above conclusions, this chapter proposes the following suggestions for Shanghai Port Group: while increasing the investment in carbon emission control funds, it should strengthen the construction in three targeted areas:

A. Continue to increase equipment upgrades and transformations, and greatly improve energy use efficiency. Focus on promoting the equipment upgrade and transformation in the loading and unloading link, further optimize the loading and unloading process and equipment selection design, replace old equipment with high energy consumption and low efficiency such as shore cranes, tire-type container gantry cranes, and tractors, accelerate the "oil-to-electricity" technology transformation of port area power supply, and adopt energy feedback technology in large quantities to improve energy utilization efficiency.

B. Continue to optimize production processes and management, and promote a further reduction in carbon footprint intensity. By optimizing the layout of the port area and the dock, scientifically coordinating port scientific production scheduling, further improving key processes such as "loading and unloading → handling → warehousing" from the perspective of emission reduction, improving the efficiency of cargo and container loading and unloading operations, reducing the empty driving rate of trucks, etc. At the same time, in comparison with energy-saving and emission-reduction standards, learn from the construction experience of international green ports such as Singapore, New York, London, and Long Beach, systematically sort out weak links in production management, and strengthen the effect of management emission reduction.

C. Continue to strengthen carbon emission reduction technology innovation, and strive to increase the proportion of clean energy. Under the current situation where it is difficult to adjust and optimize China's energy structure in the short term, Shanghai Port Group can fully utilize the policy support opportunities for new energy technology innovation, adapt to local conditions, and explore the use of solar energy, tidal energy, wind energy, etc. in the port area in conjunction with new energy-related technology companies, and increase the proportion of its own clean energy.

5.2 Construction of a Low-Carbon Port Formation Mechanism Fitting Model

Based on Gamma Distribution Data shows: Currently, the greenhouse gas emissions from the global port shipping industry account for 2.6% of the global total. As a major emitter of greenhouse gases, the port industry faces tremendous pressure for energy conservation, emission reduction, and green growth under the current national implementation of carbon reduction strategies. In fact, the formation of a low-carbon port depends on: on the one hand, the optimization of energy consumption structure and the iterative upgrade of carbon reduction technology. On the other hand, the port's internal carbon reduction construction: through technological progress, such as eliminating high-energy-consuming loading and unloading equipment, using shore power facilities, etc. Through optimized management, such as optimizing loading and unloading processes, improving docking efficiency, etc. Through scale operation, such as port business growth, port group integration, etc. (Martiinez et al. 2019) However, in the process of various ports across the country taking measures to promote carbon reduction, there are prominent problems of high investment but poor carbon reduction effects. One of the fundamental reasons is that the mechanism of low-carbon port formation is not clear. If the mechanism of low-carbon port formation is not understood and grasped for a long time, on the one hand, it may lead to a large deviation in the formulation of port industry carbon reduction related policies and measures by the transportation management department; on the other hand, it may lead to some ports not having enough carbon reduction measures and the effect needs to be improved (Kwon et al. 2019). Therefore, the mechanism of low-carbon port formation needs to be analyzed in depth.

5.2.1 Fitting Model Without Influencing Factors

The evolution of the low-carbon formation mechanism is simulated with the Gamma function, which is as follows:

$$d_t = N\frac{1}{\beta^{\alpha}\Gamma(\alpha)}t^{\alpha-1}e^{-t/\beta} \tag{5.17}$$

where, $\Gamma(\alpha) = \int_0^{\infty} t^{\alpha-1}e^{-t}dt$, α is a proxy evaluation parameter

Let:

$$\eta = N\frac{1}{\beta^{\alpha}\Gamma(\alpha)e^{-1/\beta}} \tag{5.18}$$

$$\gamma = (\alpha - 1)\beta \tag{5.19}$$

Then Eq. (5.17) can be written as:

$$d_t = \eta t^{(\gamma/\beta)}e^{(1-t)/\beta} \tag{5.20}$$

where: N, γ and β are the total, maximum and decay rate of carbon emissions per unit of cargo throughput during this period; η is the carbon emission per unit of cargo throughput in the first year.

Logarithmic transformation is performed on Eq. (5.19), resulting in:

$$\begin{aligned} y_t = \ln(d_t) &= \ln(\eta t^{(\gamma/\beta)}e^{(1-t)/\beta}) + \varepsilon_t \\ &= \ln(\eta) + (\gamma/\beta)\ln(t) + (1-t)/\beta + \varepsilon_t \\ &= \ln(\eta) + \lambda\ln(t) + \theta(1-t) + \varepsilon_t \end{aligned} \tag{5.21}$$

where $\lambda = \gamma/\beta$, $\theta = 1/\beta$, ε_t is a residual.

5.2.2 Fitting Model with Influencing Factors

To deeply analyze the driving factors of the low-carbon port formation mechanism, a low-carbon formation mechanism analysis model with influencing factors is constructed. In Eq. (5.21), the $\ln(\eta)$ term can be replaced by a function of specific influencing factors of the low-carbon formation mechanism, such as port scale, technical effect, low-carbon investment, etc. Generally, the linear function of these influencing factors is adopted, and its expression is:

$$\ln(\eta) = f(X) = c + \sum b_j \ln(x_j) \tag{5.22}$$

where, c is a constant term, X is the vector of influencing factors of carbon emissions per unit of port cargo throughput, x_j is the component of the j influencing factor, b_j is the parameter to be estimated for each influencing factor.

Combining Eqs. (5.21) and (5.22), we get the influencing factor analysis model of the low-carbon formation mechanism, as follows:

$$y_t = \ln(\eta) + \lambda \ln(t) + \theta(1 - t) + \varepsilon_t = c + \sum b_j \ln(x_j) + \lambda \ln(t) + \theta(1 - t) + \varepsilon_t \tag{5.23}$$

It should be pointed out that the model does not include indicators to measure policy effects and management effects, because there are no quantifiable measures for policy effects and management effects. At the same time, policy effects are more often indirectly promoting carbon reduction through policy support for technological innovation and management optimization. Therefore, we do not consider it here.

5.2.3 Case Study

This chapter selects Rizhao Port as the research object to analyze the mechanism of low-carbon formation in ports. The reasons are as follows: First, Rizhao Port ranked 7th in the national coastal ports in terms of cargo throughput in 2021, and it is a typical large carbon-emitting port in China. It was identified as one of the first batch of national green port thematic pilot ports by the Ministry of Transport in 2014. Second, the carbon emission-related data of Rizhao Port is relatively easy to obtain. After consulting a large number of databases and yearbooks, and consulting related port entrepreneurs, it was found that there is a lack of direct and indirect data on carbon emissions from ports in China. However, we indirectly obtained the energy consumption data of Rizhao Port.

(1) Data Collection and Conversion Calculation of Carbon Emissions

This chapter collects the comprehensive unit consumption of production energy of Rizhao Port from 1991 to 2021, and indirectly estimates carbon emissions. The data sources are: first, the data from 1991 to 2005 comes from literature; second, the data from 2006 to 2021 comes from Rizhao Port (Shanghai Stock Exchange listing code: 600,017) 2017–2021 "Corporate Social Responsibility Report". In addition, the cargo throughput of Rizhao Port in the corresponding years and the energy consumption of China's unit GDP were collected, as shown in Table 5.7.

To convert the comprehensive unit consumption of production energy (ten thousand tons of throughput/ton of standard coal) into carbon emissions, it is necessary to obtain the carbon emission coefficient of standard coal.

Let dt be the carbon emission value of the port unit cargo throughput in the t year, at be the comprehensive unit consumption of port production energy in the t year, Ce be the CO_2 emission coefficient, equal to 2.457 tons CO_2/ton of standard coal (National Development and Reform Commission Energy Research Institute standard), B_t be the port cargo throughput in the t year. Then, the conversion equation for the carbon emission of the port unit cargo throughput is:

$$d_t = a_t \times C_e \tag{5.24}$$

Total port carbon emissions:

$$D_t = B_t \times d_t \tag{5.25}$$

Using Eqs. (5.24) and (5.25), combined with the data in Table 5.7, the carbon emission value and total carbon emissions of the unit cargo throughput of Rizhao Port can be calculated. See Table 5.8 for details.

(2) Analysis of the Fitting Results of the Formation Mechanism

① Formation mechanism without influencing factors

Using Eq. (5.21) and the data in Table 5.8, the fitting results are shown in Table 5.9.

Table 5.7 Rizhao port carbon emission related indicators and original data

Targets	Cargo throughput (tons)	Combined production energy unit consumption (tons of standard coal/ton of throughput)	Energy consumption per unit of GDP (tons of standard coal/ billion dollars)
1991	425	22.50	7.19
1992	650	20.00	6.18
1993	840	16.00	5.70
1994	925	13.00	5.27
...	...	...	...
2019	33,700	3.92	0.62
2020	35,062	3.68	0.59
2021	36,000	3.61	0.54

Table 5.8 Carbon emission value and total carbon emissions of Rizhao port unit cargo throughput

Targets	Standard coal (tons)	Total carbon emissions (tons of C02)	Carbon emissions per unit of cargo throughput (tons of CO2 per million tons of throughput)
1991	9563	23,495	55.28
1992	13,000	31,941	49.14
1993	13,440	33,022	39.31
1994	12,025	29,545	31.94
…	…	…	…
2019	131,946	324,192	9.62
2020	129,179	317,394	9.05
2021	1,299,883	319,367	8.87

Table 5.9 Estimated values of fitting parameters of the formation mechanism without influencing factors

Parameter	Totally	Step1	Step2	Step3
$\ln(\eta)$	3.955	3.969	2.852	2.499
	(0.000)	(0.000)	(0.000)	(0.000)
λ	−0.150	−0.192	−0.096	−0.022
	(0.008)	(0.153)	(0.242)	(0.286)
θ	0.043	0.033	0.025	0.040
	(0.000)	(0.141)	(0.320)	(0.001)
R^2	0.968	0.854	0.955	0.995

Note The confidence interval is 95%

Therefore, the simulation equation of the low-carbon formation mechanism of Rizhao Port without influencing factors is:

$$d_t = 52.196t^{-0.15}e^{0.043(1-t)} \tag{5.26}$$

$$d_t = \begin{cases} 52.932t^{-0.192}e^{0.033(1-t)}, \ Step1 \\ 17.322t^{-0.196}e^{0.025(1-t)}, \ Step2 \\ 12.170t^{-0.022}e^{0.040(1-t)}, \ Step3 \end{cases} \tag{5.27}$$

Looking at Table 5.9 and Fig. 5.4, the low-carbon evolution fitting effect of Rizhao Port in all stages and three stages is good.

② Mechanism of formation with influencing factors

Using Eq. (5.24), combined with the data from Tables 5.7 and 5.8, the calculation results are shown in Table 5.10.

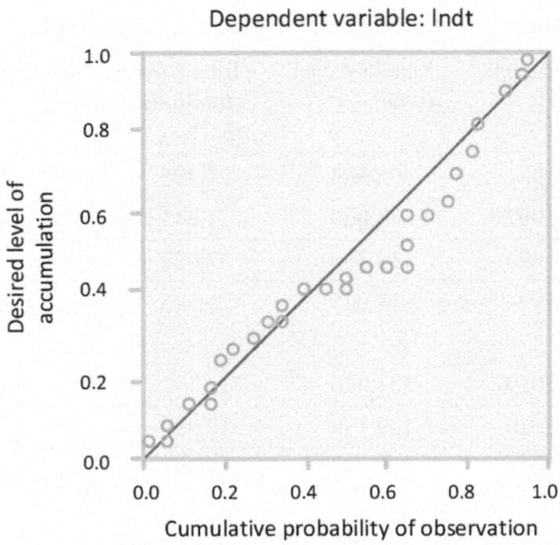

Fig. 5.4 Standard P-P plot of standardized residuals of fitting mechanism without influencing factors

Table 5.10 Estimated parameters of the fitting mechanism with influencing factors

Parameter	Totally	Step1	Step2	Step3
c	4.919	8.749	4.339	−0.653
	(0.000)	(0.001)	(0.100)	(0.754)
λ	−0.356	−0.048	−0.041	−0.119
	(0.000)	(0.796)	(0.811)	(0.114)
θ	0.072	0.044	−0.003	0.090
	(0.001)	(0.397)	(0.984)	(0.040)
b_1	0.028	−0.624	−0.179	0.302
	(0.719)	(0.117)	(0.448)	(0.202)
b_2	−0.530	−0.460	0.011	−0.891
	(0.001)	(0.149)	(0.988)	(0.148)
R^2	0.983	0.957	0.971	0.998

Note The confidence level is 95%

Similarly, the simulation equation for the low-carbon formation mechanism of Rizhao Port with influencing factors is:

$$d_t = 136.866x_1^{0.028}x_2^{-0.53}t^{-0.356}e^{0.072(1-t)} \tag{5.28}$$

$$d_t = \begin{cases} 6304.381x_1^{-0.624}x_2^{-0.46}t^{-0.048}e^{0.044(1-t)}, & Step1 \\ 76.631x_1^{-0.179}x_2^{0.011}t^{-0.041}e^{-0.003(1-t)}, & Step2 \\ 0.52x_1^{0.302}x_2^{-0.891}t^{-0.119}e^{0.09(1-t)}, & Step3 \end{cases} \tag{5.29}$$

Although the full-stage fitting coefficient b_1 is not significant, the overall fitting effect is good. The fitting effects of the three stages are all good.

Through the Gamma model simulation analysis, some characteristics and rules of the low-carbon evolution of Rizhao Port are revealed: First, in terms of the fitting of the low-carbon formation mechanism of Rizhao Port, the full-stage fitting effect of the Gamma simulation model of the formation mechanism with and without influencing factors is very ideal. The fitting degree of the formation mechanism model with influencing factors is better than that without influencing factors. Second, in terms of the influencing factors of low-carbon formation in Rizhao Port. As technology and energy efficiency continue to improve, the carbon emission intensity of Rizhao Port continues to decrease. As the scale of port throughput increases, the carbon emissions per unit of cargo throughput at the port show a slight decrease, but it is not significant. The decay rate of carbon emissions per unit of cargo throughput in Rizhao Port gradually decreases with time migration. Third, in terms of explaining the low-carbon formation mechanism of Rizhao Port. The formation mechanism of a low-carbon port in Rizhao Port is a process of promoting port decarbonization through policy support, optimization of port energy consumption structure, innovation and upgrading of low-carbon technology, optimization of management system, and mutual cooperation. From a historical perspective, the formation of a low-carbon port is a gradual process from spontaneous, to exploration, and then to strengthening carbon emission reduction construction. From the perspective of the formation path, it has gone through three processes: scale effect → scale effect, energy effect, technology effect → policy effect, technology effect, management effect. From the perspective of the reasons for formation, in the process of decarbonization of Rizhao Port, the contribution of scale factors is getting lower and lower, and the contribution of optimizing energy consumption structure and upgrading carbon emission reduction technology is getting larger and larger (Fig. 5.5).

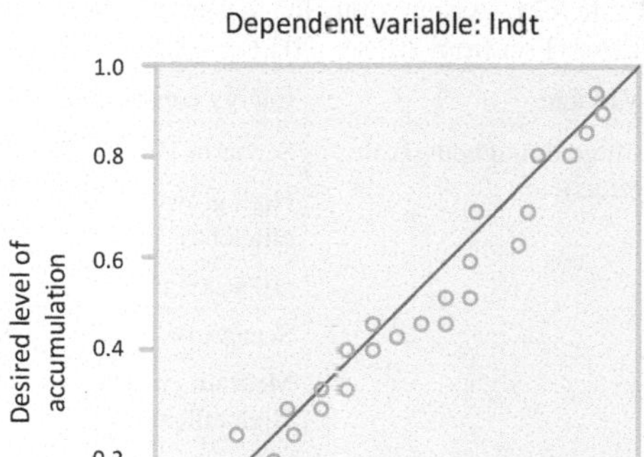

Fig. 5.5 Standard P-P plot of standardized residuals of fitting mechanism with influencing factors

(3) Analysis of Low-carbon Evolution Trend

Next, we will analyze the trend of the carbon emission per unit of cargo throughput index of Rizhao Port from 2022 to 2030.

The predicted values obtained from the Gamma simulation model of the low-carbon formation mechanism without influencing factors are shown in the second column of Table 5.12.

The low-carbon formation mechanism Gamma simulation model involving two variables is used for prediction through scenario analysis. For the annual growth rate of cargo throughput at Rizhao Port from 2022 to 2030, it is difficult for China's port business to maintain a high growth rate before 2030. In view of this, combined with the literature, the annual increase in cargo throughput at Rizhao Port from 2022 to 2030 is set to high growth of 10%, medium growth of 5%, and low growth of 0%. According to the 2030 emission reduction agreement reached in 2014, the annual reduction in China's GDP energy consumption per unit from 2022 to 2030 is set to high efficiency of 8%, medium efficiency of 5%, and low efficiency of 2%. A total of 9 combination scenarios are detailed in Table 5.11. Combining Table 5.11 and Eq. (5.12), the predicted values of carbon emissions per unit of cargo throughput at Rizhao Port from 2022 to 2030 under various scenarios are obtained, as detailed in columns 3 to 11 of Table 5.12. From Table 5.12, it can be seen that Scenario 9 has the smallest predicted value of carbon emissions per unit of cargo throughput, with a predicted value of only 3.43 in 2030, a decrease of 61.34% from 2021. During the period from 2018 to 2030, regardless of the scenario, the decarbonization of Rizhao Port is showing a slow downward trend, indicating that decarbonization is becoming more and more difficult. This also means that the effects of Rizhao Port's previous carbon reduction measures are weakening or even ineffective, and more reliance on energy effects, technical effects, and management effects is needed. In

Table 5.11 Assumptions for the prediction of carbon emissions per unit of cargo throughput at Rizhao Port from 2018 to 2030

Variable	Energy consumption per unit of GDP (technology and energy effects)		
Cargo throughput (scale effect)	Scenario 1	Scenario 2	Scenario 3
	High growth + High efficiency	High growth + Medium efficiency	High growth + Low efficiency
	(10%, 8%)	(10%, 5%)	(10%, 2%)
	Scenario 4	Scenario 5	Scenario 6
	Medium growth + High efficiency	Medium growth + Medium efficiency	Medium growth + Low efficiency
	(5%, 8%)	(5%, 5%)	(5%, 2%)
	Scenario 7	Scenario 8	Scenario 9
	Low growth + High efficiency	Low growth + Low efficiency	Low growth + Low efficiency
	(0%, 8%)	(0%, 5%)	(0%, 2%)

fact, with the transformation and upgrading of China's economy, the adjustment of Rizhao Port's cargo structure, which was originally dominated by bulk raw materials, will result in its throughput scale not showing the high growth trend of the past. In addition, the optimization of China's energy structure and technological upgrades will significantly improve carbon reduction efficiency. Therefore, in this process, Rizhao Port is likely to be in Scenario 9.

Overall, for Rizhao Port's low-carbon construction to truly achieve the effect of Scenario 9, one is to focus on improving technology and energy effects, and continue to strengthen technological transformation and optimization of energy structure. The second is to focus on improving management effects, and continue to promote process innovation. The third is to focus on improving cooperation effects, and strengthen cooperation with international major ports in carbon emissions.

This chapter takes Rizhao Port as an example, establishes a Gamma-based fitting model without influencing factors and with influencing factors, and reveals the mechanism of low-carbon port formation. According to the mathematical analysis results of the low-carbon formation mechanism of Rizhao Port, as the technology and energy effects improve, the carbon emission intensity correspondingly decreases; as the scale of port throughput increases, the carbon emission intensity decreases slightly; the decay speed of carbon emission intensity significantly decreases with time migration. The scenario simulation analysis results of the low-carbon evolution trend of Rizhao Port from 2022 to 2030 show that the value of carbon emissions per unit of cargo throughput is the smallest under the scenario of low growth + high efficiency (0%, 2%).

The implications of this case are as follows: First, the construction of low-carbon ports should gradually shift the focus to improving technology and energy effects, and continuously strengthen port carbon reduction technology transformation and energy structure optimization to achieve continuous reduction of carbon emission intensity. Second, the construction of low-carbon ports should strengthen the improvement of management effects, especially continue to promote port business process innovation

Table 5.12 Predicted values of carbon emissions per unit of cargo throughput at Rizhao Port from 2022 to 2030

Vintage	No impact factor	Includes influencing factors								
		Scenario 1	2	3	4	5	6	7	8	9
2022	6.77	7.47	6.62	6.10	7.16	6.94	6.05	7.11	6.53	6.02
2023	6.46	7.21	6.29	5.69	6.91	6.24	5.65	6.85	6.19	5.60
2024	6.16	6.72	5.97	5.32	6.66	5.91	5.27	6.60	5.86	5.22
2025	5.88	6.50	5.67	4.97	6.43	5.61	4.92	6.36	5.55	4.86
2026	5.61	6.28	5.39	4.64	6.20	5.32	4.59	6.13	5.26	4.53
2027	5.35	6.07	5.12	4.34	5.99	5.05	4.29	5.91	4.98	4.23
2028	5.11	5.87	4.87	4.06	5.78	4.80	4.00	5.70	4.73	3.94
2029	4.88	5.67	4.63	3.80	5.59	4.55	3.74	5.50	4.48	3.68
2030	4.66	5.49	4.40	3.55	5.40	4.33	3.49	5.30	4.25	3.43

and optimization. Finally, cooperation should be strengthened, and the intensity of cooperation in carbon emission technology and management with international low-carbon major ports such as Singapore and Hamburg should be strengthened.

References

Bailey D, Solomon G (2004) Pollution Prevention at ports: clearing the air. Environ Impact Assessment Rev 24(7/8):749–774

Jiang C, Zhen H (2012) Input-output multiplier model of port economic contribution. China Navigation 35(04):100–103+118

Joseph B, Po-Hsing T (2012) Estimating the environmental costs of port related emissions: the case of Kaohsiung. Transport Res Part D-Transport and Environ 17(1):35–38

Kwon Y, Lim H, Lim Y, Lee H (2019) Implication of activity—based vessel emission to improve regional air inventory in a port area. Atmos Environ 203:262–270

Li J, Liu X, Jiang B (2011) An exploratory study on low-carbon ports development strategy in China. The Asian J Ship Ping and Logist 27(1):91–111

Liu D, Ge YE (2018) Modeling assignment of quay cranes using queueing theory for minimizing CO_2 emission at a container terminal. Transport Res Part D 61(Part A):140–151

Madan BR, Shinya H (2012) Assessment of intermodal transport corridors: cases from North-East and Central Asia. Res Transp Bus Manag 5:27–37

Martínez-Moya J, Vazquez-Paja B, Maldonado JAG (2019) Energy efficiency and CO_2 emissions of port container terminal equipment: evidence from the port of Valencia. Energy Policy 131:312–319

Pang CS (2012) Port carbon emission accounting methods—an example of the 2010 carbon footprint report of Jurong Port in Singapore. Port Econ 7:5–9

Peng D, Song H, Guannan F et al (2023) Optimization path of metro commercial passageway based on computational analysis. Sustainability 15(14):11140–11140

Tang G, Qin M, Zhao X et al (2019) Influence of container truck scheduling mode on carbon emission in container port area. Water Transport Eng 6:46–51

Tsai YT, Liang CJ, Huang KH, Hung KH, Liang JJ (2018) Self—management of greenhouse gas and air pollutant emissions in Taichung Port. Transp Res Part D: Transp Environ 63:576–587

Villalba G, Gemechu ED (2011) Estimating GHG emissions of marine ports-the case of Barcelona. Energy Policy 39(3):1363–1368

World Ports Climate Initiative (2008) Carbon foot printing guidance document. http://wpci.Iaphworldports.org/carbon-footprinting/index

Xu S, Ma Y (2013) Research on the construction standards and development countermeasures of low-carbon ports. China Port 6:6–8

Yu DY, Li D, Sha M et al (2019) Carbon-efficient deployment of electric rubber-tyred gantry cranes in container terminals with workload uncertainty. Eur J Oper Res 275(2):552–569

Chapter 6
Evaluation of Regional Port Environmental Carrying Capacity Based on System Dynamics

6.1 Research on the Indicator System of Regional Port Environmental Carrying Capacity

Environmental carrying capacity refers to the support capacity of socioeconomic development resources and the environment for the population size and economic scale of a specific region within a certain level of the scope of socioeconomic development and specific regions and population. Similar to the concept of "support" in physics, environmental carrying capacity refers to the support of resources and environmental conditions for population, society, and economic development. It has a large scale and a clear direction, and technological conditions and socioeconomic development are both important factors affecting it. At the same time, the environmental carrying capacity has a certain range, which mainly depends on the ability of five types of resource support, environmental transportation capacity, the degree of social civilization, the efficiency of economic development, and the level of progress in technological development. Among them, the first two factors directly affect the environmental carrying capacity, and the other three factors potentially affect the development of regional resources and environmental carrying capacity. On the other hand, environmental carrying capacity includes the support of the socioeconomic system under resource environmental pressure. At the same time, it can also serve as the judgment standard for the relationship between the two, and then determine the transportation status of environmental resources in the planning area. When the environmental carrying capacity of the planning area is within the bearing range, the pressure of the socioeconomic system must be less than the pressure of the resource environment system. Conversely, if the environmental carrying capacity of the planning area is overloaded, the pressure of the socioeconomic system must be greater than the pressure of the resource environment system. The environmental carrying capacity of the port refers to the potential ability of the port ecosystem to maintain its own health and stable development, and the ability to withstand various human socioeconomic activities within a certain period and range (Zhang et al. 2008).

B. Lu, *The Sustainable Development of Port Group*,
https://doi.org/10.1007/978-981-97-2378-2_6

6.1.1 Principles for Establishing Indicator System

The selection of indicators and the establishment of an evaluation indicator system are the first steps that need to be completed in the evaluation process, and it is also a crucial step. The same applies to the evaluation of port environmental carrying capacity. Reasonable and scientific selection of evaluation indicators will have a significant impact on the credibility of the evaluation results (Ooba et al. 2015). This book mainly follows the following related guidelines, and combines the relevant definitions and connotations of port environmental carrying capacity to select evaluation indicators.

(1) System comprehensiveness

The factors affecting the port's environmental carrying capacity are complex and diverse, so evaluating the port's environmental carrying capacity is a systematic work process, and it is necessary to select comprehensive and multi perspective indicators that reflect the actual level and development stage of port environmental carrying capacity. These indicators cannot be simply listed, they should comprehensively consider the relevant influencing factors of the port's environmental carrying capacity, and follow the principle of system comprehensiveness to form the evaluation indicator system of the port's environmental carrying capacity.

(2) Scientific

The evaluation indicator system obtained by combining theory and practice can abstractly describe the objective reality. But every evaluation indicator system will involve multiple factors, and the port's environmental carrying capacity is the same. When designing an evaluation indicator system, before converting influencing factors from an abstract form to specific quantified evaluation indicators, it is necessary to follow scientific and standard principles. The established indicator system should not only ensure its completeness, but also have a clear sense of hierarchy.

(3) Specificity

The evaluation indicators of port environmental carrying capacity need to have strong specificity, which is different from other traditional evaluations, and such evaluation indicators can fully reflect the characteristics of port environmental carrying capacity, ensuring the scientific nature and the effect of the evaluation.

(4) Operability

The operability of evaluation indicators is a principle that must be strictly adhered to when selecting and establishing an evaluation indicator system. The established indicator system not only requires an appropriate size, but also needs to reflect the relationship between the evaluation indicators and the objectives. It is important to avoid having too many or too few levels in the evaluation indicator system. The former can easily lead to cross-issues due to over-detailed problems, while the latter cannot comprehensively reflect the level of port environmental carrying capacity. In addition, the availability of data should also be considered to ensure that the evaluation indicators have strong operability.

(5) Combination of qualitative and quantitative

The environmental carrying capacity of the port involves many influencing factors, so the evaluation indicator system established for port environmental carrying capacity is also a complex and comprehensive system. The indicators included in the port environmental carrying capacity evaluation indicator system include both quantifiable indicator factors and qualitative indicator factors that cannot be quantified. The combination of the two can compensate for the shortcomings of both sides in the evaluation process. The information conveyed by the indicators has both breadth and depth, and its evaluation effect is far greater than that of using them separately. Therefore, the establishment of the evaluation indicator system should follow the principle of combining quantitative and qualitative.

(6) Stability and development

As the economy, society, and life will change after a period of time, the composition and quantity of the evaluation indicator system should remain relatively stable, and should also change accordingly with the changes in the objective environment, reflecting the strong applicability of the indicator system.

(7) Unity

In order to reflect comparability when evaluating port environmental carrying capacity, differences between evaluation indicator units should be eliminated during the evaluation process.

(8) Combination of absolute indicators and relative indicators

From a statistical perspective, the evaluation indicators for port environmental carrying capacity should combine relative and absolute indicators, including not only factors reflecting total amount and scale, but also factors reflecting speed, ratio, structure and so on.

6.1.2 Construction of Indicator System Framework

Ecological carrying capacity has become an important indicator reflecting the sustainable development capacity of the ecosystem, therefore, the establishment of the indicator system is crucial to the study of ecosystem carrying capacity (Bendewald 2013). Not only does the state of the internal environment of the ecosystem (atmospheric environment, water environment, noise environment, etc.) and natural resources (energy, water resources, land resources, shoreline resources, etc.) directly affect the carrying capacity of the ecosystem, but also human activities indirectly represented by social and economic conditions also affect the sustainable development capacity of the ecosystem (Wang 2014). Existing studies generally divide ecological carrying capacity indicators into three aspects: ecosystem status, resource environment, and human activities (Guo et al. 2017). This book, based on the principles of scientificity, comprehensiveness, conciseness, operability, and hierarchy, combined with the system dynamics model of port ecological carrying capacity, selects general indicators from three aspects: environmental pollution absorption capacity, resource supply capacity, and human support capacity. Through multicollinearity analysis, we construct a comprehensive evaluation indicator system for port ecological carrying capacity, including four levels: goal layer, sub-goal layer, criterion layer, and indicator layer, with a total of 22 indicators. To eliminate the impact of dimension and magnitude of the original data, each indicator is dimensionless processed by the ratio of the current value to the ideal state value. The ideal state reference values at different times are determined according to national standards or industry regulations at each development stage, and the weights of each indicator are calculated using principal component analysis.

6.1.3 Hierarchical Analysis of Indicator System

This book, based on the characteristics of the natural-economic-social composite ecosystem of ports, uses the ecological carrying capacity of ports as the evaluation target. It starts from three aspects: resource supply capacity, environmental pollution absorption capacity, and human support capacity. Using the target hierarchy method, a multi-level progressive indicator system is constructed. Among them, the measurement indicators of resource supply capacity are mainly selected from four aspects: energy, water resources, land resources, and shoreline resources, to reflect the characteristics of port resource utilization. The environmental pollution absorption capacity mainly unfolds from four aspects: atmospheric environment, water environment, solid waste, and noise environment, and fully considers the main pollution sources of port production. Human support capacity mainly considers social economic progress, management and construction level, and technological progress, focusing on human support for pollution emission control, resource utilization optimization, comprehensive management and technical input, and ecological construction (Fig. 6.1).

6.1.4 Construction Method of the Indicator System Hierarchy

(1) Multi-objective model optimization method

The multi-objective model optimization method has its specific thinking. Its idea is to adopt a decomposition and coordination approach of a large system. This system can be decomposed into many branch systems. These branch systems have many ways of operation, and they can run in coordination or operate separately. There are also core models in the multi-objective model, called the master control model. There is a certain relationship between each branch system, which can be extracted in the

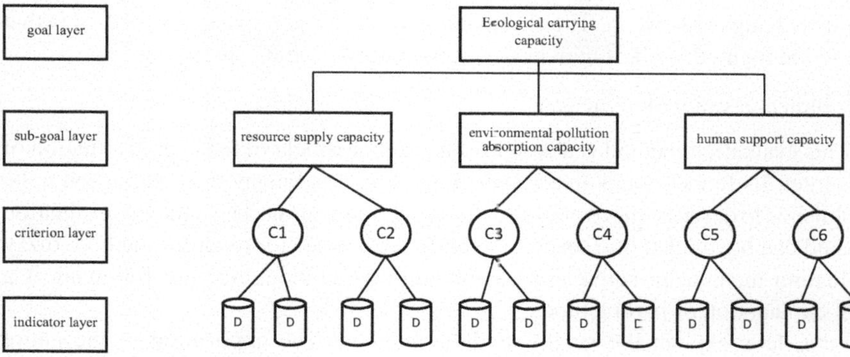

Fig. 6.1 Ecological carrying capacity indicator hierarchy system

core model. There are many variables in this system, and there are many inevitable connections between the variables. Using these connections, the relationships within the entire system can be analyzed and judged as a whole. Models can also be established using each branch system. These branch system models also have their specific functions. They can be used to analyze the state of local systems in the entire system. Some scholars have already used this method to conduct some analyses on carrying capacity. The most representative ones are scholars like Ran Shenghong. Their analysis object is Beihai City. They finally calculated the index of environmental carrying capacity and gave feasible opinions and suggestions on the environmental situation of Beihai City (Ran et al. 1998). In addition, scholars like Jiang Xiaohui also used this method to analyze the carrying status of the environment (Jiang et al. 2001). This method is a quantitative research method for carrying capacity, but the downside is that the amount of data required by this method is very large, and the solution of the model is not easy.

(2) System dynamics

The origin of the system dynamics method is at the Massachusetts Institute of Technology in the United States, and it was established in 1956. Initially, it was a discipline studying information feedback systems, and later developed into a quantitative research for carrying capacity. It regards the research target as a unified whole, and the interior of the whole is divided into different modules. There is a relationship between these modules. In this method, the first-order differential equation in mathematics is also used. The relationship between the modules is reflected through this equation. When we use this method to study carrying capacity, we can choose the most suitable development plan from several different environmental development plans set in advance. There are scholars at home and abroad who use the system dynamics method to conduct carrying capacity research, such as: British scholars, whose research methods have been widely recognized internationally (Castellani 2012), and Chinese scholars like Zhang Qi, who have also conducted a series of analysis and research and established a port ecological carrying capacity dynamic evaluation model based on system simulation, which also obtained relatively good results (Zhang et al. 2017). The shortcoming of the system dynamics method is that due to the method itself, it may lead to some unreasonable conclusions.

(3) Indicator evaluation method

This evaluation method is a comprehensive assessment of the overall situation of the target. Its foundation is mathematical methods, and many indicators need to be established to describe the overall situation in its application. The indicator evaluation method can be divided into several methods, such as vector modulus method, fuzzy evaluation method, principal component analysis method, etc. The following is a brief explanation of part methods.

First, let's explain the vector modulus method. The application of the entire method is carried out in a dimensional space. In order to describe the overall environmental conditions, indicators are established, and the mathematical concept of vector is used. A vector is a quantity that has both magnitude and direction. This vector will change with the changes in human economic activities, both in size and direction. When using this method, for economic environments with different development methods, their carrying conditions are also different. In this multi-dimensional space, the modulus of the vector is calculated. The sizes of these moduli are different, reflecting the size of the environmental carrying capacity under different development methods. The disadvantage of this method is that because this method involves establishing an indicator system, but the importance of each indicator in the indicator system is different, we require determining the weight, and the determination of the weight in this method is not very objective, leading to inaccurate conclusions.

The fuzzy comprehensive evaluation method is a comprehensive evaluation method based on fuzzy mathematics. This comprehensive evaluation method transforms qualitative evaluation into quantitative evaluation according to the membership theory of fuzzy mathematics, that is, it uses fuzzy mathematics to make a comprehensive evaluation of things or objects restricted by multiple factors (Zhang et al. 2009). However, due to the model itself, the fuzzy comprehensive evaluation method has many shortcomings, and there is a serious loss of information in the actual calculation process, which greatly increases the possibility of incorrect conclusions.

(4) Matter-element analysis method

The matter-element analysis method mainly studies the laws and methods to solve contradictory problems. It is a marginal science intersecting system science, thinking science, and mathematics. It is also a cross-disciplinary subject widely used and run through in natural sciences and social sciences. The matter-element analysis method calculates the correlation between various factors and quality levels, and then summarizes them through weights to obtain the correlation between the entire evaluation plan and the evaluation level. The evaluation plan is judged to be at which level by judging which level the evaluation plan is most associated with. Its application technology is the matter-element transformation method.

Through the above analysis of some methods of carrying capacity research, it can be seen that the indicator evaluation method has achieved certain results in the research of urban ecological carrying capacity. Its advantages are that it considers more comprehensive factors and is more flexible in application. It is suitable for situations where there are many levels of evaluation indicators, but its defects and shortcomings are that it requires a lot of data, and the evaluation process is relatively complex and large. The system dynamics method is useful for predicting the future comprehensive carrying capacity of the urban environment, but the disadvantage is that it cannot judge the current carrying state, cannot determine whether it is reasonable or unreasonable, and its specific practical significance is very limited. Among the quantitative methods of carrying capacity research, there is another method, which is the multi-objective model optimization method. Although this method is relatively novel and has opened up a new path for carrying capacity research, the conditions for using this method are quite strict. An important point is to check a large amount of data, which is quite difficult. Even if researchers have the conditions to obtain a large amount of data, they may not necessarily get the desired conclusion, because there is also the problem of model solving, which is very difficult. Therefore, in this book's research, the system dynamics model construction method was chosen for indicator evaluation analysis.

6.1.5 Analysis of Factors Affecting the Environmental Carrying Capacity of Port Areas

The factors affecting the environmental carrying capacity of ports include two major aspects: the ecological environment system and the socioeconomic system. After analysis, we select the following main influencing factors:

(1) Natural conditions of the port

The environmental carrying capacity of a port is largely limited by its natural conditions. Therefore, when considering evaluation indicators, the natural conditions related to the port must be taken into account. The development of ports is constrained by its natural conditions. If the impact of natural conditions is ignored, the environmental carrying capacity of the port will become an empty talk. Natural conditions are the prerequisite for the environmental carrying capacity of a port, and are its foundation and essence. And the pollution carrying capacity of the marine environment where the port is located should considers the impact of natural conditions. Ports are areas where some marine organisms grow and other organisms and microbes survive. The quantity, quality, and utilization rate of forest land in these areas are key factors in the environmental carrying capacity of regional ports. In this regard, several specific influencing factors are mainly considered: the climatic conditions of the region where the port is located, the navigation conditions of the port itself, and the local hydrogeological conditions.

(2) Port hardware and software conditions

The hardware and software conditions of a port also have a significant impact on the environmental carrying capacity of the port. The hardware and software conditions and natural conditions of the port are considered together as the internal influencing factors of the port. Both are essential influencing factors of the environmental carrying capacity of the port. To some extent, they determine the environmental capacity of the port and the size of a port's operating capacity. For example, the level of infrastructure, management, and technology of the port itself. Among them, the technological level of the port has both positive and negative impacts on the environmental carrying capacity. Technological progress first meets the demand for large-scale use of port environmental resources, and then makes the development of alternative resources, the conservation of port resources, and the reduction of pollution emissions from production activities possible, thereby alleviating the contradiction between the supply and demand of port environmental resources. Technological progress has multiple effects on improving the environmental carrying capacity of the port. The discovery and use of new materials and energy have reduced the pressure of economic development on the material resources of the port. Finally, technological progress has improved the utilization rate of resources consumed during cargo transportation, thereby reducing emissions from underutilized resources. Pollution treatment technology has also reduced the range of pollutant diffusion, reducing the amount of pollutants that need to be purified and absorbed by the sea.

(3) The traffic conditions of surrounding and hinterland

The construction of the port itself is a change in local traffic conditions. Whether the traffic conditions around the port are convenient to some extent determines its operating profits, and it determines whether the goods transported from the port can be quickly delivered to the destination. The port is an individual that cannot exists independently of the socioeconomic context, so when considering the environmental carrying capacity of the port, the traffic conditions in its hinterland are also very important factors, and currently, countries around the world are discussing the issue of sustainable development of transportation. The traffic conditions of the port also have a great impact on the lives of local residents, thereby having a certain effect on the population of the port. In this regard, the following factors should be considered: hinterland road traffic, water traffic, international routes, pipeline conditions, etc.

(4) Socioeconomic conditions

Ports cannot exist independently of the socioeconomic context. The purpose of people establishing ports is partly to facilitate people's lives and strengthen material exchanges, and on the other hand, to obtain certain benefits. When considering its socioeconomic conditions, the main considerations should be the population in the hinterland, the industrial base in the hinterland, foreign trade in the hinterland, and consistency with national policies. Among them, the population is a very complex factor. A smaller population is surely conducive to the protection of the ecological environment of the port, but it is not conducive to the port's activities and normal operation of the port. However, an overly dense population will have a great impact on the ecological environment of the port, thereby affecting regional economic development.

(5) Energy resource conditions

The production, use, and maintenance processes in the port area will consume various resources. In addition, various transportation tools and facilities serving the hinterland related to the port will also consume resources in their construction, operation, and maintenance. The main natural resources used for the transportation system include: land resources, energy resources, and mineral resources. The level of resources to some extent determines the development potential of the port, so a port lacking resources does not have much potential for development.

(6) Level of Environmental Pollution

The corresponding environmental quality standards of the port, local and foreign pollution sources including the pollution carrying capacity of the marine environment where the port is located, the domestic sewage discharged by local residents. The domestic garbage, solid waste, etc., resulted in these conditions will all affect the environmental carrying capacity of the port. When considering these influencing factors, we should consider the impact of the port's normal operation on the surrounding ecological environment, such as the pollution of the atmosphere, noise, and water.

6.1.6 Index System Construction Process and Index Screening

Referring to the theories of ecological carrying capacity and compound ecosystem, the ecological carrying capacity of the port in this book refers to the supply capacity and pollution absorption capacity of the system within the resilience limit of the ecosystem in the water and land areas of the port, and the social and economic scale and population scale it can support (Zhang 2016). The ecological carrying capacity of the port can be described from the sustainable supply capacity of resources, the environmental pollution absorption capacity, and the human support function. This book, based on the characteristics of the port's natural-economic-social compound ecosystem, uses the ecological carrying capacity of the port as the evaluation target, and constructs a multi-level hierarchical index system using the target layering method, starting from the resource supply capacity, environmental pollution absorption capacity, and human support capacity. Among them, the resource supply capacity measurement indicators mainly select indicators reflecting the port's resource utilization characteristics from four aspects: energy, water resources, land resources, and shoreline resources. The environmental pollution absorption capacity mainly expends from four aspects: atmospheric environment, water environment, solid waste, and noise environment, and fully considers the main pollution sources of port production. The human support capacity mainly considers social and economic progress, management and construction level and technological progress, focusing on human support for pollution emission control, resource utilization optimization, comprehensive management and technology investment, and ecological construction.

In the process of index screening, following the basic principles of scientificity, pertinence, conciseness, operability, and comprehensiveness, starting from the connotation of ecological carrying capacity, we consider the characteristics of port ecological carrying capacity and existing sustainable development indicators, various planning indicators and environmental, resource, social and economic assessment indicators, etc., and as much as possible docking with the output parameters of the system dynamics model. Based on the above principles, preliminary screening of indicators is carried out to obtain a general index system. Then, multicollinearity analysis is used to eliminate the errors caused by multicollinearity between variables, so as to obtain the final evaluation index system of port ecological carrying capacity.

Based on the above index hierarchy system and index screening principles, this book establishes an evaluation index system of port ecological carrying capacity with the ecological carrying capacity of the port as the evaluation target, including three sub-objective layers of resource supply capacity, environmental pollution absorption capacity, and human support capacity, 11 criteria layers including atmospheric environment, water environment, solid waste, noise environment, energy, water resources, land resources, shoreline resources, social and economic progress, management and construction level, technological progress, and 22 indicators (Fig. 6.2).

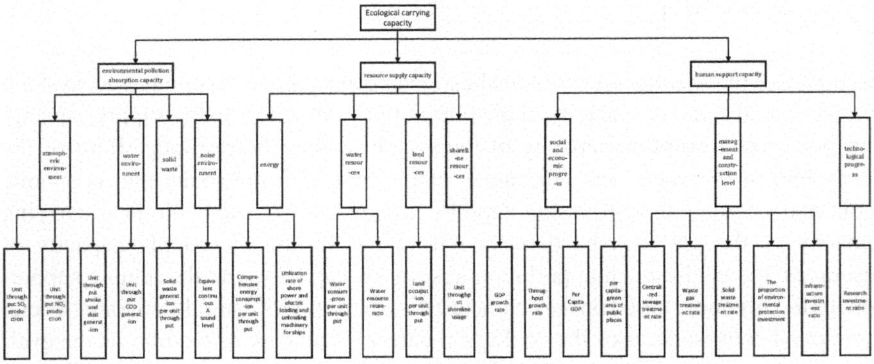

Fig. 6.2 Evaluation index system of port ecological carrying capacity

6.2 Construction of System Dynamics Model of Port Area Environmental Carrying Capacity

6.2.1 Analysis of Port Ecological Environment System

The analysis of the port ecological system is the foundation for simulating the behavior of the port ecological system. The port ecological system is located at the intersection of the urban land ecological system and the marine ecological system, with superior resources and environmental conditions, and is closely related to human social and economic development. At present, there is very little research on the port ecological system, and there is no universally recognized research result on the definition, boundaries, and formation of the port ecological system. Therefore, it is necessary to conduct theoretical research on the basic attributes of the port ecological system before carrying out simulations of port ecological system behavior and evaluations of ecological carrying capacity.

(1) Definition of Port Ecosystem

The ecosystem refers to a biological functional unit formed by continuous material and energy exchange between organisms and their non-living environment (physical environment) within a certain area. Any normally functioning ecosystem is constantly undergoing material cycling and energy exchange with the external environment, such as obtaining solar energy and nutrients from the external environment, and discharging heat and metabolites to the outside world. Therefore, the behavior of the ecosystem is often influenced by the external environment, and itself is a semi-open dynamic system. At the same time, ecosystems have the ability to self-regulate. When subjected to external forces or human interference, to a certain extent, ecosystems can maintain a relatively balanced state through feedback mechanisms, so ecosystems also belong to a feedback system. Ecosystems are divided into natural ecosystems and artificial ecosystems. The latter are relatively complex, and they are human-dominated ecosystems with few species of animals and plants. Human activities have a significant impact on natural ecosystems, and artificial ecosystems are composite ecosystems of natural ecosystems and human socioeconomic systems.

Ports are generally built on coasts, river mouths, or inland rivers, located at the junction of land and water. Ports are hubs of water and land transportation, mainly providing logistics services, information services, commercial and industrial value-added services. The production and operation process of ports does not generate matter and energy, but constantly obtains matter and energy from the external environment, and discharges a large amount of pollutants to the external environment, such as oily sewage, ballast water, domestic sewage, atmospheric pollutants released by port loading and unloading machinery and ships in port, dust, etc. Ports interact and influence each other with the surrounding ecological environment, forming a semi-open, dynamic ecological system, namely the port ecosystem. The port ecosystem is located at the intersection of the two major ecosystems of urban land and ocean, and is part of the coastal ecosystem. It is influenced by both the urban and ocean ecosystems. On the one hand, the port ecosystem has rich resources, high biodiversity, and rapid gradient changes. On the other hand, the port ecosystem is frequently disturbed by the city and the ocean, and has a high ecological vulnerability. The port boundary is determined by the overall port planning, distinguishing the water and land areas of the port from its peripheral areas, which is convenient for effective management of the port. The spatial scale of the port is relatively small. According to the "Harbor Overall Design Code (JTS165-2013)", the average land depth of the container trunk terminal is 800–1200 m. Therefore, the boundary of the port ecosystem in the narrow sense refers to the port boundary. The definition of the coastal zone range is: the inner boundary of the coastal zone is usually near 10 km on the land side of the coastline, and the outer boundary extends to near the 15 m isobath on the sea side. Considering that the port production and operation have clear requirements for the water depth of the port channel and the water depth in front of the wharf, the current sixth-generation container ships and 10,000 TEU ships have a draft of at least 14 m, requiring the water depth of the channel and the water depth in front of the wharf to reach more than 15 m, and the 300,000-ton bulk carrier can reach a full load draft of 23 m, and there is a trend of gradual increase, which will inevitably lead to an increase in port water depth. Drawing on the research results of predecessors, considering that the port ecosystem and the surrounding coastal zone frequently exchange material and energy, and have a large mutual influence, as well as the increase in port water depth brought about by the large-scale ships, the boundary of the port ecosystem in the broad sense is defined as the area boundary formed by advancing 10 km to the land side of the coastline and advancing to the 25 m isobath on the sea side.

(2) Characteristics of Port Ecosystem

Ports are located in the water-land interaction zone. In addition to the characteristics of the two major ecosystems, the port ecosystem also has unique characteristics, mainly manifested in the following aspects:

High biodiversity. Ports are located in the transition zone between water and land. Compared with adjacent ecosystems, the community structure is more complex. This is not only the habitat of many aquatic and terrestrial organisms, but also some edge species or endemic species that can adapt to changing environments. The species are rich and the gradient changes are high.

High openness. Ports are regional transportation hubs, goods distribution centers, logistics processing centers, and information service centers. They exchange materials and energy frequently, and economic and social activities are closely related. A large number of ships, vehicles, goods, personnel, etc. flow in and out every day, and external activities are closely related. The ecosystem is highly open.

High productivity. With the development of the service industry and the advancement of information technology, ports not only provide basic services such as cargo loading and unloading, temporary storage, transshipment, etc., but also add processing, packaging, distribution, information processing and other logistics value-added services, attracting finance, insurance, law, information and other service industries to gather in ports, making ports play an increasingly important role in resource allocation, showing high productivity characteristics.

Ecological vulnerability. Ports are located at the ecological intersection of urban ecosystems and marine ecosystems. Their unique regional location makes port ecosystems more sensitive to external changes. Coupled with the high intensity of port development, a large amount of pollutants and waste are output to the surrounding environment during construction and operation. At the same time, emergencies such as fires, explosions, oil spills, and chemical hazard leaks occur frequently, causing the port's ecosystem's resistance to disturbances to gradually deteriorate, significantly highlighting its ecological vulnerability.

6.2.2 Analysis of the Structure of the Port Group's Ecological Environment System

The port ecosystem is a natural-economic-social composite ecosystem dominated by human activities. The various elements within this system interact and influence each other, forming a complex system. Resources, environment, and socio-economy are three sub-level elements that promote the development of the composite ecosystem through synergistic action. As an open complex mega-system, the port ecosystem's factors influencing coordinated development are very complex, but the mutual influence and interaction between each subsystem within the system are the intrinsic reasons. Therefore, it is necessary to deeply explore the internal coordinated development mechanism of the system and discuss the evolution process of system coordinated development before establishing a system simulation model.

The port resource subsystem provides energy, water, land, shoreline, and other resources for port production activities, serving as the material basis for the entire ecosystem. The port environment subsystem provides space for human activities and port production, accommodates pollution from production and life, and carries resources, serving as the spatial support for the entire ecosystem. The port socioeconomic subsystem obtains production elements from the resource and environment subsystems, realizes the function of material reproduction while consuming resources and emitting environmental pollutants. In addition, the port socioeconomic subsystem provides material and financial support for the improvement and enhancement of the resource and environment subsystems.

Overall, the development of the port socioeconomic subsystem has both conflicts and coordination with other subsystems: the development of the port socioeconomic subsystem will increase resource consumption and occupation, reducing resource stocks. While, it also drives technological progress and non-productive investment, promoting resource utilization and the development of renewable resources, increasing resource stocks; the development of the port socioeconomic subsystem will increase pollution and emissions, reducing environmental quality, while it also

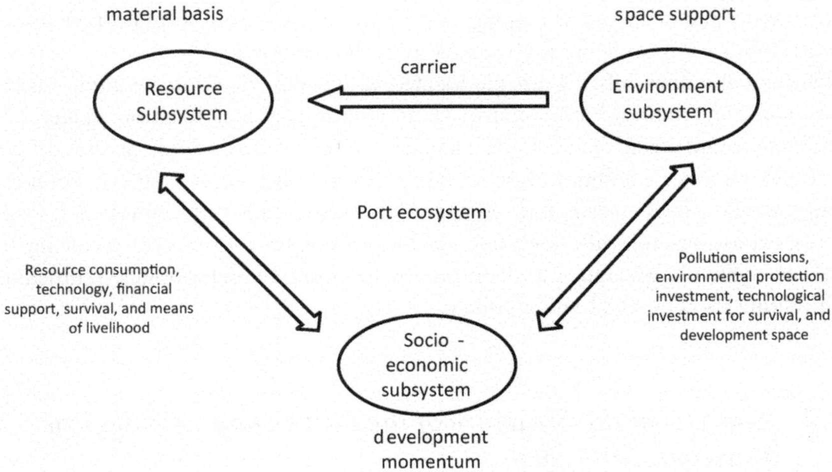

Fig. 6.3 Conceptual model of port ecosystem

increases environmental protection investment and the level of environmental remediation technology, enhancing the environment's pollution absorption capacity. The relationship between the resource subsystem and the environment subsystem is that the environment is the carrier of resources, and the quality of the environment will affect the level of resource stocks (such as forest resources) and quality (such as water resources). In summary, the port socioeconomic, resource, and environment subsystems interact with each other and promote sustainable development of the system through synergistic action (Fig. 6.3).

The synergistic action within the port ecosystem is realized through the mutual connections, interactions, and coordination between each subsystem and the feedback mechanism within the subsystem. The specific manifestations of the synergistic behavior between each subsystem within the port ecosystem are:

(1) The output value created by the port will drive regional economic development, and the growth of regional economic demand and shipping development will increase the region's economic extroversion, further expanding the demand for foreign trade, thereby increasing port throughput and driving port production;
(2) Social production in ports will inevitably lead to the consumption of resources such as energy and water, and the occupation of resources such as land and shoreline. Insufficient resource supply will restrict port development and regional economic growth;
(3) Port production will cause water pollution, air pollution, noise pollution, etc., to the surrounding environment. Severe environmental pollution will in turn restrict port and regional development.
(4) With the development of ports and regional economies, the level of resource utilization technology and renewable resource research and development has improved, the rate of resource utilization has increased, the stock of available

resources has increased, and the resource crisis hindering port production has been alleviated;

(5) With the development of ports and regional economies, environmental protection investment has increased, the level of environmental remediation technology has improved, environmental pollution has been managed and improved, and the contradiction between port development and environmental pollution has been coordinated.

Based on the analysis of the characteristics of the port's natural-economic-social composite ecosystem, we select the main variables representing the characteristics of each subsystem to reflect the important factors within the system, and determine the causal feedback relationships between the variables.

1. The socioeconomic subsystem

The socioeconomic subsystem is mainly reflected through port throughput, employment population, consumption, regional GDP, tax revenue, fixed asset investment, green GDP, trade volume, port income, port construction investment, environmental protection investment, resource consumption economic loss cost, environmental pollution economic loss cost, etc. Among them, port throughput, employment population, tax revenue, fixed asset investment, regional GDP, and trade volume are state variables, showing the accumulation of socioeconomic elements over time. Green GDP, environmental protection investment, resource consumption economic loss cost, environmental pollution economic loss cost, etc. are auxiliary variables, serving as interfaces with other subsystems, reflecting the impact of the socioeconomic subsystem on resources and environmental subsystems, and the feedback of resource consumption and environmental pollution on the socioeconomic subsystem.

On the one hand, the increase in port throughput not only can increase port income, but also stimulate employment in port-related industries, stimulate consumption, all of which will promote the growth of regional GDP, thereby driving tax revenue, increasing regional fixed asset investment. And the increase in fixed asset investment further drives the increase in port construction investment and the expansion of port facility resources, promoting the increase in dock shoreline resource load, thereby driving the development of port throughput. At the same time, the growth of fixed asset investment will further stimulate consumption, forming a virtuous cycle. In addition, the increase in port income will drive port construction investment, and the scale of port facility resources will expand accordingly, thereby driving the load of dock shoreline resources, and promoting port production.

On the other hand, the increase in port throughput will promote the growth of regional GDP through the direct and indirect contributions of the port to the regional economy (driving the development of port-related industries, stimulating consumption), driving the increase in trade volume, and the increase in trade volume will generate more port demand, promote port production, increase port throughput, forming a positive feedback loop (Fig. 6.4).

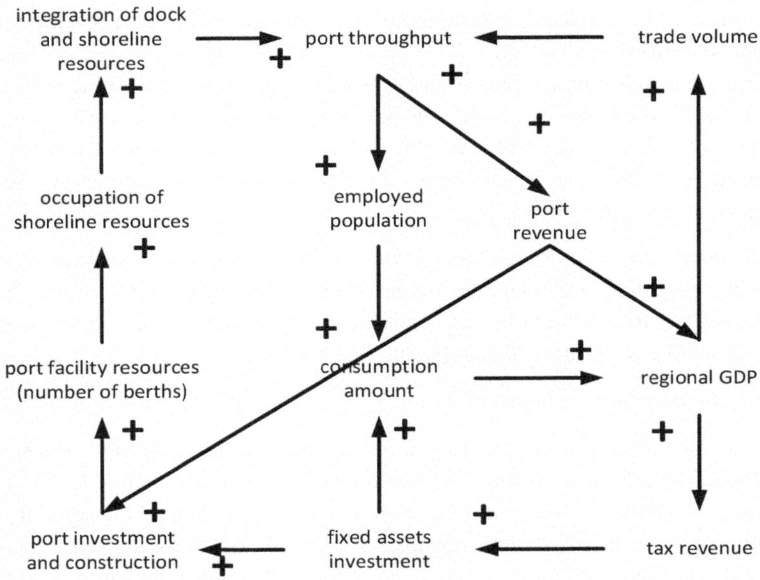

Fig. 6.4 Causal feedback loop of the port socioeconomic subsystem

2. The resource subsystem.

According to the utilization characteristics of port resources and energy, we select the main variables such as port facility resources (number of berths), land resource occupancy, shoreline resource occupancy, energy consumption, water resource consumption, unit throughput land occupancy, unit throughput shoreline occupancy, etc. Among them, port facility resources (number of berths) are state variables, reflecting the accumulation of dock berths over time, and unit throughput land occupancy, unit throughput shoreline occupancy, etc. serve as auxiliary variable interfaces.

The causal feedback loop of the port resource subsystem is built on the basis of the port socioeconomic subsystem feedback loop. On the one hand, the increase in port throughput will lead to the consumption of energy and water resources, increasing the cost of economic losses due to resource consumption, restricting the growth of green GDP, and thus limiting the increase in trade volume and port throughput. This is a negative feedback loop. On the other hand, the increase in port throughput will promote the growth of regional GDP, thereby driving the increase in government tax revenue, fixed asset investment, and port construction investment (or the increase in port throughput will drive the increase in port revenue, and port construction investment will increase accordingly), the scale of port facility resources will expand accordingly, the area of land occupied by the port and the length of the coastline will increase, the cost of economic losses due to resource consumption will increase,

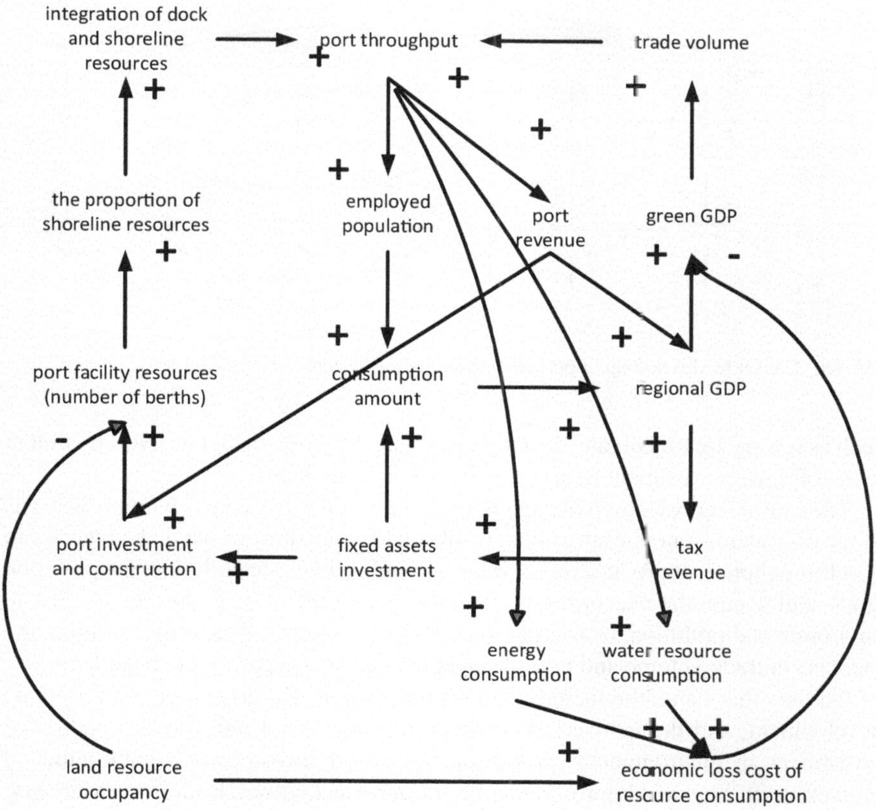

Fig. 6.5 Causal feedback loop of port resource subsystem

restricting the growth of green GDP, and thus limiting the increase in trade volume and port throughput. This is another negative feedback loop (Fig. 6.5).

3. The environmental subsystem.

Port production will cause water pollution, air pollution, and solid waste pollution in the surrounding environment. Considering the main sources of pollution in the port ecological environment, we select COD as the measurement index for water pollution, dust, SO_2, and NO_2 as the measurement indices for air pollution, and solid waste as the measurement index for solid waste pollution. The port environmental subsystem can be reflected by the environmental level (pollution stock), environmental pressure (pollution generation), and environmental resistance (pollution treatment). The pollution stock characterizing the environmental level (COD stock, dust stock, SO_2 stock, NO_2 stock, solid waste stock) is a state variable, the pollution generation characterizing environmental pressure and the pollution treatment characterizing environmental resistance are rate variables, and other variables

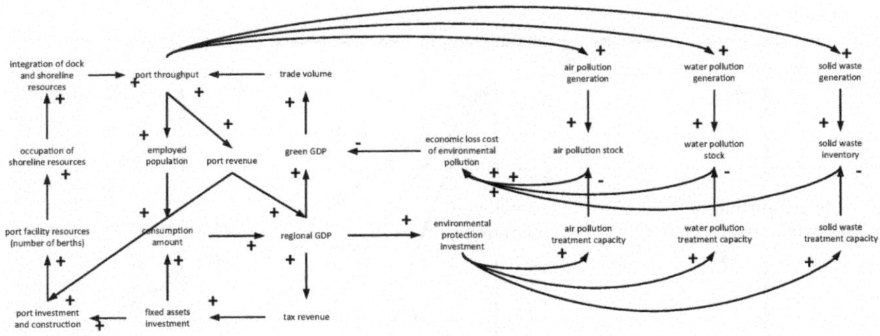

Fig. 6.6 Causal feedback loop of port environmental subsystem

such as sewage treatment rate, dust treatment rate, SO_2 treatment rate, NO_2 treatment rate, solid waste treatment rate, etc. are auxiliary variables.

The causal feedback loop of the port environmental subsystem is built on the basis of the port socioeconomic subsystem feedback loop. On the one hand, the increase in port throughput will produce more water, air, and solid waste pollution, the pollution stock will accumulate accordingly, increasing the cost of economic losses due to environmental pollution, restricting the growth of green GDP, and thus limiting the increase in trade volume and port throughput. This is a negative feedback loop.

On the other hand, the increase in port throughput will drive regional economic development, and the increase in regional economic total will promote increased investment in environmental protection, increased investment in environmental protection facilities and improved pollution control technology, leading to an increase in pollution treatment, thereby alleviating the increase in pollution stock, the cost of economic losses due to environmental pollution will decrease accordingly, the restrictive effect on the growth of green GDP will decrease accordingly, thereby driving the increase in trade volume and port throughput. This is a positive feedback loop (Fig. 6.6).

Port production is the link connecting the port resource, environment, and socioeconomic subsystems. Therefore, we use port throughput, which reflects port production and operation activities, as the interface to combine the three subsystems, integrating the above sub-modules as shown in Fig. 6.7.

6.2.3 Explanation of Main Parameters of Environmental Carrying Capacity Model

1. Model parameter input

For most constant parameters, we determine them by methods such as arithmetic mean and regression based on survey data and statistical materials, such as the impact coefficient of throughput on employment, the impact coefficient of port construction

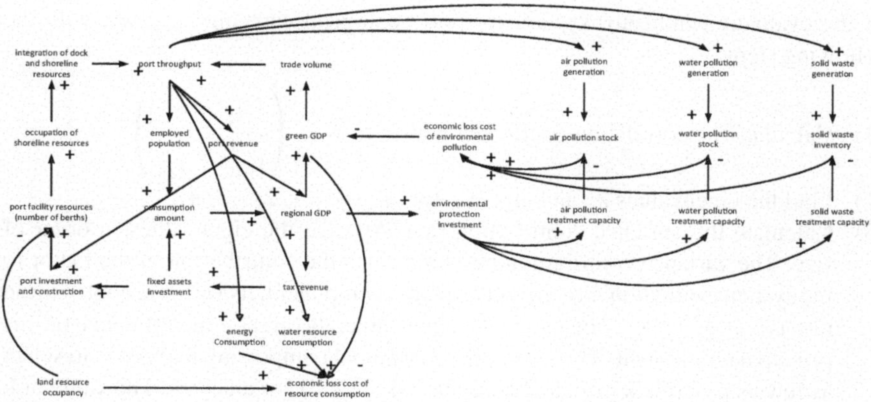

Fig. 6.7 Main causal feedback loop of port ecosystem

investment on port facility resources (number of berths), the impact coefficient of port facility resources (number of berths) on shoreline resource occupancy, the impact coefficient of port facility resources (number of berths) on land resource occupancy, etc.

For situations where some variables have a nonlinear relationship, we use table functions for definition. The model defines table functions such as unit throughput comprehensive energy consumption, unit throughput water consumption, unit throughput SO_2 production, unit throughput COD production, and the impact of trade volume on port throughput.

In addition, some important relationships between variables in the model are referenced from international or similar development level regions, such as the relationship between per capita GDP and education investment ratio, research investment ratio, infrastructure investment ratio, environmental protection investment weight, per capita green space area, etc. These relationships are then adjusted based on historical data from the research area before being applied to specific parameter calculations.

2. Determination of Evaluation Indicator Weights

The objective weighting method is a method to determine weights based on the objective environment and the degree of connection or information provided by each indicator. Its judgment results do not depend on human subjective judgment and are more objective and scientific. This study uses the principal component analysis method in the objective weighting method to determine weights.

The principal component analysis method mainly uses factor analysis to determine the size of the eigenvalues corresponding to each indicator value's contribution to variance. Generally speaking, the larger the information load of the indicator value on the original data, the larger the weight of the indicator. This study uses the principal component analysis function of statistical analysis software to determine the weight of the evaluation indicator system for port ecological carrying capacity, with the following steps:

(1) Calculate the correlation coefficient matrix R. $R = \begin{pmatrix} r_{11} & \cdots & r_{1n} \\ \cdots & \cdots & \cdots \\ r_{n1} & \cdots & r_{nn} \end{pmatrix}$.
(2) Find the eigenvalues λ_g and eigenvectors $L_g (g = 1, 2, \ldots, n)$.
(3) Calculate the variance contribution rate. Arrange the eigenvalues in order of size. The variance contribution rate represents the contribution of the factor to the system evaluation. For the gth principal component, its variance contribution rate is $\lambda_g / \sum_{g=1}^{n} \lambda_g$. The larger the eigenvalue, the greater the influence of this principal component. The principle of principal component analysis is to select as few as possible k principal components ($k \leq n$) for analysis. The value of k is determined by the cumulative variance contribution rate $\lambda_g / \sum_{g=1}^{n} \lambda_g \geq 85\%$ and the eigenvalue $\lambda_g \geq 1$.
(4) Principal component transformation; for each eigenvalue, there is a corresponding eigenvector $L_g = (L_{g1}, L_{g2}, \ldots, L_{gn})$. Then the principal component can be expressed as $F_g = L_{g1} R_1^* + L_{g2} R_2^* + \ldots + L_{gn} R_n^*$ ($g = 1, 2, \ldots, n$; R^* is the result of data averaging), and the subscript g represents the gth principal component.
(5) The weight of each indicator equals the normalized value of the weighted average of the contribution matrix $L_k = (L_1, L_2, \ldots, L_n)$, with the variance contribution rate of each principal component as the weight.

The weight of the evaluation indicators is calculated according to the weight determination method, specifically using factor analysis to obtain the eigenvalues, variance contribution rates, and component matrix of each principal component. The weight of each indicator equals the normalized value of the weighted average of the contribution matrix, with the variance contribution rate of each principal component as the weight. The weights of each indicator are shown in Table 6.1.

6.3 Case Analysis

Taking a certain port area as an example, we investigate and statistically analyze the port throughput, number of berths, employment population, port income, port construction investment and other socioeconomic operation indicators U, and the change rules of resource environment measurement indicators such as unit throughput comprehensive energy consumption, unit throughput NO_2 generation, unit throughput SO_2 generation, unit throughput dust generation, unit throughput COD generation, etc. We input these into the simulation model, apply the composite evaluation model of port ecological carrying capacity, analyze the current status of the ecological carrying capacity of the port area, identify the main influencing factors through parameter sensitivity analysis, design simulation schemes, and predict the evolution trend of the ecological carrying capacity of the port area.

Table 6.1 Weight of evaluation indicators for port ecological carrying capacity

Target layer	Sub target layer	Criterion layer	Indicator layer	Weight
Port ecological carrying capacity (P)	Environmental pollution capacity (A)	Atmospheric environment (A1)	SO_2 production per unit throughput (A11)	0.041
			NO_2 production per unit throughput (A12)	0.043
			Unit throughput smoke and dust generation (A13)	0.030
		Water environment (A2)	Unit throughput COD generation (A21)	0.073
		Solid waste (A3)	Solid waste generation per unit throughput (A31)	0.017
		Noise environment (A4)	Equivalent continuous A-sound level (A41)	0.020
	Resource supply capacity (B)	Energy (B1)	Comprehensive energy consumption per unit throughput (B11)	0.084
			Utilization rate of shore power and electric loading and unloading machinery for ships (B12)	0.031
		Water resource (B2)	Water consumption per unit throughput (B21)	0.025
			Water resource reuse ratio (B22)	0.022
		Land resource (B3)	Land occupation per unit throughput (B31)	0.058
		Shoreline resources (B4)	Unit throughput shoreline usage (B41)	0.064
	Human support capability (C)	Socio-economic progress (C1)	GDP growth rate (C11)	0.032
			Throughput growth rate (C12)	0.030
			Per Capita GDP (C13)	0.050
			Per capita green area of public places (C14)	0.029
		Management and construction level (C2)	Centralized sewage treatment rate (C21)	0.062
			Waste gas treatment rate (C22)	0.048
			Solid waste treatment rate (C23)	0.021
			The proportion of environmental protection investment (C24)	0.082
			Infrastructure investment ratio (C25)	0.044
		Technological advances (C3)	Research investment ratio (C31)	0.094

6.3.1 *Current Status Analysis of Ecological Carrying Capacity*

After inputting the model parameters and calculating the indicator weights, we take a certain port area as an example and use the established composite evaluation model to analyze the current status of the ecological carrying capacity of the port area, that is, to analyze and evaluate the ecological carrying capacity of the target layer of the port area from 2013 to 2021 and the carrying capacity of the three sub-target layers (environmental pollution absorption capacity, resource supply capacity, human support capacity).

1. Analysis of the Carrying Capacity of the Target Layer

Overall, the ecological carrying capacity of the port area from 2013 to 2021 ranged from 1.99 to 3.62, always in an overloaded state. However, as time went on, the curve of the ecological carrying capacity showed a decreasing trend year by year, indicating that the ecological carrying capacity of the port area was gradually improving, and the overloaded state was gradually easing. It dropped from 3.62 in 2013 to 1.99 in 2021, with an average annual decrease of 7.2%, of which the decrease in 2014 was the largest, with a decrease of 10.3%. Overall, the curve is slowing down, and although the ecological carrying capacity has improved, it is still in an overloaded state in the short term (Table 6.2).

2. Analysis of the Carrying Capacity of the Sub-Target Layer

Based on previous analysis of the port ecosystem, the port ecosystem is a composite ecosystem with multiple factors interacting. Therefore, this section evaluates the carrying capacity of the three sub-target layers and their criterion layers based on the overall evaluation of the ecological carrying capacity of the port area, in order to find the main reasons for the change in the ecological carrying capacity of the port area.

Table 6.2 Current status analysis of the ecological carrying capacity of the port area

Time	Ecological carrying capacity	Increase (%)
2013	3.62	–
2014	3.25	– 10.28
2015	3.00	– 7.59
2016	2.77	– 7.69
2017	2.55	– 7.93
2018	2.35	– 7.82
2019	2.23	– 5.32
2020	2.04	– 8.40
2021	1.99	– 2.57
Average annual growth rate (%)		– 7.22%

According to the data on the load-bearing conditions of the target layers in the port area, from 2013 to 2021, all three target layers were in an overloaded state, with human support capacity being the most overloaded, followed by resource supply capacity, and the overload of environmental pollution absorption capacity was relatively less. The load-bearing curves of human support capacity, resource supply capacity, and environmental pollution absorption capacity all showed a downward trend year by year. Among them, the resource supply capacity load-bearing curve had the largest decrease, with an average annual decrease of 7.38%, indicating that the improvement of resource supply capacity load-bearing conditions from 2013 to 2021 was the largest, followed by environmental pollution absorption capacity. The human support capacity had the smallest decrease in the load-bearing curve, with an average annual decrease of 7.16%, indicating that the development of human support capacity has been slow in the past nine years, becoming the main reason for restricting the improvement of the ecological load-bearing conditions in the port area. Overall, the load-bearing conditions of the three target layers in the port area are showing a trend of easing, but they will still maintain an overloaded state in the short term, especially the human support capacity needs to be further improved. While accelerating social and economic development, the management and construction level of the port area should also be enriched, and technical input should be increased (Table 6.3).

(1) Analysis of the load-bearing conditions of environmental pollution absorption capacity

As can be seen from Table 6.4, the load-bearing conditions of the environmental pollution absorption capacity of the port area were overloaded from 2013 to 2021,

Table 6.3 Analysis of the current situation of the load-bearing conditions of the target layers in the port area

Time	Environmental pollution capacity		Resource supply capacity		Human support capability	
	Carrying condition	Increase (%)	Carrying condition	Increase (%)	Carrying condition	Increase (%)
2013	3.34	–	3.48	–	3.32	–
2014	2.95	– 11.54	3.09	– 11.07	3.46	– 9.47
2015	2.52	– 14.54	2.96	– 4.19	3.22	– 6.97
2016	2.36	– 6.60	2.72	– 8.20	2.97	– 7.75
2017	2.18	– 7.49	2.28	– 16.02	2.84	– 4.37
2018	2.03	– 6.79	2.18	– 4.60	2.57	– 9.33
2019	1.96	– 3.44	2.14	– 1.75	2.38	– 7.38
2020	1.86	– 5.14	1.96	– 8.24	2.16	– 9.51
2021	1.83	– 1.46	1.88	– 4.14	2.11	– 2.20
Annual growth rate (%)		– 7.21		– 7.38		– 7.16

but the degree of overload decreased year by year, from 3.34 in 2013 to 1.83 in 2021, with an average annual decrease of 7.21%. Among them, the decrease in 2015 was the largest, reaching 14.54%. Overall, the overloaded state of environmental pollution absorption capacity is gradually easing, but the speed of easing is slowing down, and the later development is weak.

According to the analysis table of the current situation of environmental pollution absorption capacity, the overload degree of water environment load-bearing conditions in environmental pollution absorption capacity is the largest, followed by the atmospheric environment, and the overload degree of solid waste and noise environment is relatively small. The load-bearing conditions of solid waste changed from overload to full load in 2021, and the load-bearing conditions of the noise environment changed from overload to full load in 2020. The load-bearing curves of water environment, atmospheric environment, and solid waste show a downward trend year by year, and the load-bearing conditions are gradually improving. Among them, the improvement of solid waste load-bearing conditions is the fastest, from 2.51 to 1.08, with an average annual decrease of 10.0%, approaching full load from overload, followed by water environment, with an average annual decrease of 7.51%, and atmospheric environment, with an average annual decrease of 7.01%. The load-bearing conditions of the noise environment have always been between 1.09 and 1.18, with little inter-annual change, and are slowly developing towards a full load state. Overall, the overload of water environment and atmospheric environment load-bearing conditions in the port area is more and the development is slow, which has become the main reason for restricting the development of environmental pollution absorption capacity.

Table 6.4 Analysis of the current situation of the load-bearing conditions of environmental pollution absorption capacity in the port area

Time	Environmental pollution carrying capacity			
	Water environment	Atmospheric environment	Solid waste	Noise environment
2013	3.35	3.85	2.51	1.18
2014	2.93	3.43	2.22	1.18
2015	2.36	3.08	2.01	1.16
2016	2.31	2.74	1.89	1.15
2017	2.08	2.65	1.33	1.15
2018	2.02	2.35	1.25	1.15
2019	2.00	2.22	1.18	1.11
2020	1.94	2.03	1.13	1.09
2021	1.87	2.06	1.08	1.09
Annual growth rate (%)	− 7.01	− 7.51	− 10.0	− 0.90

(2) Analysis of the load-bearing conditions of resource supply capacity

As can be seen from Table 6.5, the resource supply capacity of the port area was consistently overloaded from 2013 to 2021, but the situation improved year by year, decreasing from 3.48 in 2013 to 1.88 in 2021, with an average annual reduction of 7.38%. The largest decrease occurred in 2017, reaching 16.02%. Overall, the resource supply capacity curve shows a fluctuating downward trend, and the overloaded state is gradually easing. According to the current analysis table of the port area's resource supply capacity, the energy overload is the greatest, followed by shoreline resources, land resources, and water resources. The carrying capacity of each criterion layer is gradually improving, with shoreline resources and land resources decreasing the fastest, from 3.69 and 3.45 in 2013 to 1.65 and 1.54 in 2021, respectively, with an average annual reduction of 10.94%. This indicates that the development of shoreline resources and land resources is rapid, gradually approaching full load status. The decrease in water resource carrying capacity is relatively slow, with an average annual reduction of 6.39%. The energy carrying capacity curve decreases the slowest, with an average annual reduction of 5.35%. Therefore, the port area's energy carrying capacity is the most overloaded and improves slowly, which is the main reason restricting the development of resource supply capacity, followed by the overload of shoreline resources and land resources.

(3) Analysis of Human Support Capacity

As can be seen from Table 6.6, the human support capacity of the port area was consistently overloaded from 2013 to 2021, but the situation improved year by year, decreasing from 3.82 in 2013 to 2.11 in 2021, with an average annual reduction of 7.16%. The largest decrease occurred in 2020, reaching 9.51%. Overall, the human support capacity curve shows a yearly downward trend, and the overloaded state is gradually easing.

Table 6.5 Current analysis of port area resource supply capacity

Time	Resource supply capacity carrying capacity			
	Energy	Water resource	Land resource	Shoreline resources
2013	3.80	2.11	3.45	3.69
2014	3.40	1.94	3.04	3.25
2015	3.42	1.81	2.75	2.94
2016	3.07	1.72	2.59	2.76
2017	2.88	1.46	1.80	1.92
2018	2.78	1.39	1.67	1.79
2019	2.81	1.34	1.54	1.65
2020	2.53	1.29	1.46	1.56
2021	2.45	1.25	1.37	1.46
Annual growth rate (%)	– 5.35	– 6.39	– 10.94	– 10.94

Table 6.6 Current analysis of port area human support capacity

Time	Human support capacity carrying capacity		
	Socioeconomic progress	Management and construction level	Technological advances
2013	2.49	3.94	4.97
2014	2.42	3.59	4.33
2015	2.33	3.41	3.77
2016	2.31	3.14	3.34
2017	2.14	3.07	3.10
2018	2.03	2.74	2.83
2019	1.86	2.55	2.60
2020	1.72	2.26	2.45
2021	1.63	2.24	2.36
Annual growth rate (%)	– 5.17	– 6.80	– 8.88

According to the data analysis of the carrying capacity of each criterion layer of human support capacity, the overload of technological progress is the greatest, followed by management and construction level, and the overload of socioeconomic progress is relatively less. The carrying capacity curves of technological progress, management and construction level, and socioeconomic progress show a yearly downward trend. Among them, technological progress develops the fastest, decreasing from 4.97 in 2013 to 2.36 in 2021, with an average annual reduction of 8.88%. This indicates that although the port area is lagging in terms of technological progress, research and technology support have developed rapidly in the past nine years. The carrying capacity curve of management and construction level fluctuates downward, with an average annual reduction of 6.80%. The carrying capacity curve of socioeconomic progress changes relatively little and develops steadily. Overall, the relative backwardness of technological progress and management and construction level in the port area is the bottleneck restricting the development of human support capacity. It is necessary to gradually increase environmental protection and technology investment in the port area, strengthen infrastructure construction, and improve management level.

6.3.2 Dynamic Prediction of Ecological Carrying Capacity

1. Prediction Scheme Design

In order to understand the development trend of the ecological carrying capacity of the port area, a dynamic prediction is made. According to the ecological carrying capacity of the port area and its main influencing factors, combined with the actual situation of the region and related planning, two prediction schemes are set up when predicting the future development trend of the port area's ecological carrying capacity: the natural development scheme and the comprehensive control scheme.

(1) Natural Development Scheme (Scheme One)

The natural development scheme refers to advancing according to the existing development trend of the port area. The specific parameter settings are predicted based on the curve regression model established according to the historical data of each parameter. The prediction equations of some parameters are as follows:

Research investment ratio: $y(t) = 2.830E - 6\Delta t^3 - 1.611E - 4\Delta t^2 + 0.00301\Delta t + 0.00863$

Unit throughput energy consumption: $y(t) = -1.137LN(\Delta t) + 7.714$

Per capita green space area: $y(t) = 0.00170\Delta t^3 - 0.978\Delta t^2 + 1.859\Delta t + 12.591$

Exhaust gas treatment rate: $y(t) = -1.343E - 4\Delta t^2 + 0.0360\Delta t - 0.0826$

In the formula, $y(t)$ represents the parameter value of year t, Δt represents the time difference between the forecast year and the starting year.

(2) Comprehensive regulation plan (Plan Two)

The comprehensive regulation plan is to adjust based on the existing development trend, set the regulation parameter values for the main factors limiting the development of the port area's ecological carrying capacity, and carry out policy regulation on the system to achieve the purpose of improving the ecological carrying capacity of the port area (Table 6.7).

According to the current analysis results of the ecological carrying capacity of the port area, the main problems facing the ecological carrying capacity of the port area are the lagging development of human support capacity, serious environmental pollution, and excessive resource consumption. Specifically, the port area's technological progress and management and construction levels are relatively backward, water environment and atmospheric environment pollution exceed standards, and energy consumption overload is serious are the main constraints on the ecological carrying capacity of the port area. Therefore, the regulation plan parameters should be set from these aspects. Combining the main influencing factors of the ecological carrying capacity of the port area identified in the parameter sensitivity analysis, the simulation regulation parameters are selected as the proportion of environmental protection investment, unit throughput comprehensive energy consumption, centralized sewage treatment rate, research investment ratio, unit throughput dust generation, unit throughput water consumption, unit throughput S generation, unit throughput NO_2 generation, unit throughput COD generation, GDP growth rate, and other parameters are set consistent with the natural development plan. The GDP growth rate, centralized sewage treatment rate, etc. are mainly determined based

Table 6.7 Main parameter settings under the two plans

Time	Research investment ratio		Unit throughput COD generation		Unit throughput SO_2 production		Comprehensive energy consumption per unit throughput	
	Plan 1	Plan 2	Plan 1	Plan 2	Plan 1	Plan 2	Plan 1	Plan 2
2022	0.0259	0.0254	0.00197	0.00176	0.00759	0.00666	5.285	5.065
2023	0.0262	0.0261	0.00173	0.00147	0.00747	0.00608	5.047	4.731
2024	0.0264	0.0279	0.00157	0.00111	0.00739	0.00569	4.879	4.508
2025	0.0265	0.0288	0.00143	0.00106	0.00733	0.00541	4.748	4.342
2026	0.0267	0.0313	0.00131	0.00092	0.00727	0.00519	4.642	4.211
2027	0.0268	0.0336	0.00121	0.00080	0.00723	0.00501	4.552	4.103
2028	0.0269	0.0356	0.00112	0.00079	0.00719	0.00487	4.474	4.012
2029	0.0269	0.0375	0.00108	0.00076	0.00716	0.00474	4.405	3.934
2030	0.0270	0.0393	0.00102	0.00071	0.00713	0.00462	4.343	3.865
2031	0.0271	0.0411	0.00097	0.00066	0.00710	0.00453	4.287	3.803
2032	0.0271	0.0417	0.00092	0.00062	0.00708	0.00444	4.236	3.748
2033	0.0272	0.0423	0.00088	0.00056	0.00706	0.00436	4.190	3.698
2034	0.0272	0.0428	0.00084	0.00051	0.00704	0.00428	4.146	3.652
2035	0.0273	0.0433	0.00081	0.00046	0.00702	0.00422	4.106	3.610
2036	0.0273	0.0438	0.00077	0.00043	0.00700	0.00416	4.068	3.571
2037	0.0274	0.0443	0.00074	0.00039	0.00698	0.00410	4.033	3.535
2038	0.0274	0.0447	0.00073	0.00035	0.00697	0.00405	3.999	3.501

on regional development planning, and the proportion of environmental protection investment, research investment ratio, etc. refer to the corresponding indicator levels in developed countries internationally.

2. Forecast analysis of ecological carrying capacity under different plans

Based on the two forecast plans, the composite evaluation model is used to dynamically forecast and analyze the ecological carrying capacity of the port area from 2022 to 2038, and compare the changing trends of the ecological carrying capacity of the port area under the two plans.

(1) Forecast of the target layer carrying capacity

Overall, under both scenarios, the ecological carrying capacity of the port area from 2022 to 2038 shows a downward trend, with the ecological carrying capacity showing signs of improvement. The difference is that in the natural development scenario, the decline in the ecological carrying capacity is smaller, with an average annual decrease of only 86%, the improvement of the ecological carrying capacity is slow, reaching 1.700 in 2038, still in an overloaded state. In the comprehensive control scenario, the decline in the ecological carrying capacity is larger, with an average annual decrease of 3.17%, the development of the ecological carrying capacity is faster, reaching 1.150 in 2038, close to the full load state, the ecological carrying capacity has been significantly improved. Comparing the two scenarios, it can be seen that the carrying capacity of the comprehensive control scenario in the same year is better than that of the natural development scenario, and the distance between the two plans is getting further and further, indicating that the improvement effect of the ecological carrying capacity under the comprehensive control scenario is very obvious, and the improvement efficiency of the ecological carrying capacity of the comprehensive control scenario in 2038 reaches 32.35% (Table 6.8).

(2) Forecast of Sub-objective Layer Carrying Capacity

From the forecast analysis of the sub-objective layer carrying capacity in the port area under the two scenarios, it can be seen that from 2022 to 2038, the improvement of the carrying capacity of the environmental pollution absorption, resource supply, and human support in the natural development scenario is slow, with average annual decreases of 1.01%, 0.81%, and 0.83% respectively. Under the comprehensive control scenario, the development of the carrying capacity of the environmental pollution absorption, resource supply, and human support in the port area is faster, with average annual decreases of 3.14%, 3.04%, and 3.24% respectively. After optimizing and adjusting the parameters in the comprehensive control scenario, the sub-objective

Table 6.8 Forecast analysis of ecological carrying capacity in the port area under two scenarios

Time	Ecological carrying capacity		Increase (%)	
	Plan 1	Plan 2	Plan 1	Plan 2
2022	1.952	1.926	–	–
2023	1.923	1.811	– 1.49	– 5.97
2024	1.889	1.705	– 1.77	– 5.85
2025	1.867	1.629	– 1.16	– 5.04
2026	1.847	1.555	– 1.07	– 3.95
2027	1.831	1.493	– 0.87	– 3.99
2028	1.808	1.430	– 1.26	– 4.22
2029	1.793	1.387	– 0.83	– 3.01
2030	1.770	1.330	– 1.28	– 4.11
2031	1.758	1.286	– 0.68	– 3.31
2032	1.740	1.256	– 1.02	– 2.33
2033	1.726	1.228	– 0.80	– 2.23
2034	1.720	1.212	– 0.35	– 1.30
2035	1.713	1.191	– 0.41	– 1.73
2036	1.708	1.172	– 0.29	– 1.60
2037	1.704	1.163	– 0.23	– 0.77
2038	1.700	1.150	– 0.23	– 1.12
Annual growth rate (%)			– 0.86	– 3.17

layer carrying capacity gradually approaches the full load state. The carrying capacity of the environmental pollution absorption changes from an overloaded state to a full load state in 2033, reaching 1.008 in 2038, an improvement of 34.80% compared to the natural development scenario. The carrying capacity of resource supply reaches 1.105 in 2038, close to the full load state, an improvement of 31.80% compared to the natural development scenario. The carrying capacity of human support reaches 1.233 in 2038, in an overloaded state, an improvement of 31.84% compared to the natural development scenario. Overall, the three sub-objective layer carrying capacities in the comprehensive control scenario have been significantly improved, and the control effect is obvious (Table 6.9).

(1). Forecast of Environmental Pollution Absorption Carrying Capacity (Table 6.10)

According to the predictive analysis of the environmental pollution absorption capacity under two scenarios, the changes in the water and atmospheric environment carrying conditions are significant from 2022 to 2038, with slight improvements

Table 6.9 Forecast Analysis of Sub-objective Layer Carrying Capacity in the Port Area under Two Scenarios

Time	Environmental pollution capacity		Resource supply capacity		Human support capability	
	Plan 1	Plan 2	Plan 1	Plan 2	Plan 1	Plan 2
2022	1.820	1.680	1.846	1.810	2.066	2.088
2023	1.772	1.536	1.832	1.668	2.037	1.997
2024	1.739	1.433	1.806	1.565	1.999	1.887
2025	1.715	1.372	1.788	1.492	1.974	1.784
2026	1.692	1.313	1.760	1.426	1.960	1.720
2027	1.670	1.283	1.743	1.388	1.947	1.634
2028	1.653	1.238	1.712	1.346	1.926	1.554
2029	1.638	1.212	1.709	1.302	1.905	1.504
2030	1.630	1.177	1.683	1.248	1.876	1.438
2031	1.615	1.133	1.678	1.223	1.863	1.383
2032	1.599	1.107	1.667	1.200	1.840	1.347
2033	1.582	1.087	1.662	1.180	1.822	1.312
2034	1.569	1.064	1.657	1.161	1.818	1.300
2035	1.563	1.047	1.638	1.146	1.817	1.275
2036	1.558	1.032	1.629	1.132	1.815	1.251
2037	1.552	1.024	1.621	1.119	1.812	1.245
2038	1.546	1.008	1.620	1.105	1.809	1.233
Annual growth rate (%)	– 1.01	– 3.14	– 0.81	– 3.04	– 0.83	– 3.24

Table 6.10 Forecast Analysis of Environmental Pollution Absorption Carrying Capacity in the Port Area under Two Scenarios

Time	Water environment		Atmospheric environment		Solid waste		Noise environment	
	Plan 1	Plan 2	Plan 1	Plan 2	Plan 1	Plan 2	Plan 1	Plan 2
2022	1.840	1.646	2.074	1.952	1.072	1.163	1.068	1.057
2023	1.795	1.527	2.012	1.733	1.071	1.139	1.053	1.036
2024	1.764	1.426	1.963	1.583	1.070	1.123	1.042	1.021
2025	1.740	1.367	1.932	1.513	1.069	1.114	1.034	1.009
2026	1.721	1.315	1.899	1.423	1.068	1.113	1.028	0.999
2027	1.705	1.283	1.862	1.386	1.067	1.112	1.022	0.991
2028	1.692	1.238	1.836	1.325	1.066	1.112	1.017	0.984
2029	1.683	1.203	1.807	1.304	1.065	1.111	1.013	0.978
2030	1.682	1.164	1.786	1.264	1.064	1.100	1.009	0.972
2031	1.673	1.125	1.758	1.197	1.063	1.088	1.003	0.967
2032	1.664	1.099	1.728	1.163	1.062	1.076	1.000	0.963
2033	1.656	1.087	1.691	1.123	1.061	1.071	0.998	0.958
2034	1.649	1.050	1.665	1.115	1.060	1.060	0.995	0.954
2035	1.642	1.020	1.660	1.112	1.059	1.051	0.993	0.951
2036	1.635	0.994	1.654	1.110	1.058	1.037	0.991	0.947
2037	1.630	0.983	1.647	1.102	1.058	1.031	0.989	0.944
2038	1.624	0.956	1.640	1.0.99	1.057	1.022	0.986	0.941
Annual growth rate (%)	− 0.78	− 3.34	− 1.46	− 3.53	− 0.09	− 0.30	− 0.48	− 0.72

in solid waste and noise environment. Under the natural development scenario, the annual average reduction rates of water environment, atmospheric environment, solid waste, and noise environment carrying conditions are 78%, 1.46%, 0.09%, and 0.48% respectively, with slow improvements. Under the comprehensive control scenario, the annual average reduction rates are 3.34%, 3.53%, 0.80%, and 0.72% respectively, with faster development. Under the comprehensive control scenario, the carrying conditions of each criterion layer of environmental pollution absorption capacity gradually develop from overload to full load. Among them, the water environment carrying condition changes from overload to full load in 2032, reaching 0.956 in 2038, an improvement of 41.23% compared to the natural development scenario. The atmospheric environment carrying condition transitions to full load in 2038, reaching 1.099, an improvement of 33.00% compared to the natural development scenario. The solid waste carrying condition changes to full load in 2030, reaching 1.022 in 2038, an improvement of 3.31% compared to the natural development scenario. The noise environment remains at full load with slight improvements, reaching 0.941 in 2038, an improvement of 4.85% compared to the natural development scenario. It can be seen that optimizing the main influencing factors restricting the development of environmental pollution absorption capacity can effectively improve the carrying conditions and promote the transition to positive development.

(2). Prediction of Resource Supply Capacity Carrying Conditions (Table 6.11)

From the predictive analysis of the port resource supply capacity carrying conditions under the two scenarios, it can be seen that from 2022 to 2038, the port energy, shoreline resources, land resources, and water resources carrying curves under the natural development scenario change smoothly, with annual average reduction rates of 0.90%, 0.40%, 0.71%, and 0.99% respectively, and slow improvements in carrying conditions. Under the comprehensive control scenario, the development of energy and water resources carrying conditions is faster, with annual average reduction rates reaching 3.50% and 3.00% respectively. The development speed of shoreline resources and land resources carrying conditions is moderate, with annual average reduction rates of 1.86% and 1.99% respectively. Under the comprehensive control scenario, the energy carrying condition in the resource supply capacity gradually develops from severe overload to slight overload, reaching 1.351 in 2038, an improvement of 35.36% compared to the natural development scenario, but it is still the

Table 6.11 Prediction analysis of port resource supply capacity carrying conditions under two scenarios

Time	Energy		Shoreline resources		Land resource		Water resource	
	Plan 1	Plan 2	Plan 1	Plan 2	Plan 1	Plan 2	Plan 1	Plan 2
2022	2.417	2.389	1.434	1.329	1.319	1.259	1.165	1.219
2023	2.411	2.169	1.417	1.257	1.292	1.195	1.125	1.181
2024	2.377	2.021	1.406	1.186	1.273	1.139	1.099	1.137
2025	2.353	1.901	1.397	1.172	1.258	1.114	1.081	1.096
2026	2.308	1.801	1.389	1.143	1.246	1.086	1.066	1.058
2027	2.284	1.747	1.383	1.130	1.236	1.061	1.055	1.024
2028	2.231	1.683	1.378	1.110	1.228	1.047	1.045	0.991
2029	2.230	1.623	1.373	1.082	1.220	1.022	1.037	0.961
2030	2.186	1.532	1.369	1.066	1.213	1.005	1.030	0.932
2031	2.179	1.499	1.365	1.052	1.207	0.990	1.024	0.905
2032	2.164	1.470	1.361	1.040	1.202	0.977	1.018	0.880
2033	2.157	1.443	1.358	1.028	1.197	0.964	1.013	0.855
2034	2.151	1.419	1.355	1.018	1.192	0.952	1.009	0.832
2035	2.118	1.401	1.352	1.009	1.188	0.941	1.005	0.810
2036	2.104	1.385	1.350	1.000	1.184	0.931	1.001	0.789
2037	2.091	1.369	1.347	0.991	1.180	0.922	0.997	0.769
2038	2.090	1.351	1.345	0.984	1.177	0.913	0.994	0.749
Annual growth rate (%)	− 0.90	− 3.50	− 0.40	− 1.86	− 0.71	− 1.99	− 0.99	− 3.00

biggest factor restricting the improvement of resource supply capacity. The shoreline resource carrying condition transitions from overload to full load in 2021, reaching 0.984 in 2038, an improvement of 26.84% compared to the natural development scenario. The land resource carrying condition changes to full load in 2026, reaching 0.913 in 2038, an improvement of 22.43% compared to the natural development scenario. The water resource carrying condition transitions to full load in 2025, and then develops into a bearable condition in 2032, reaching 0.749 in 2038, an improvement of 24.65% compared to the natural development scenario. Therefore, it can be seen that the resource supply capacity under the comprehensive control scenario has been significantly improved, with shoreline resources, land resources, and water resources gradually entering positive development, and the energy carrying condition needs to be improved.

(3). Prediction of Human Support Capacity Carrying Conditions (Table 6.12)

From the data on the human support capacity of the port area under the two plans, it is known that the changes in the carrying capacity of technological progress and socioeconomic progress under the natural development plan from 2022 to 2038 are very small, with an average annual decrease of 0.36% and 0.49% respectively. The

Table 6.12 Prediction analysis of port human support capacity carrying conditions under two scenarios

Time	Technological advances		Management and construction level		Socioeconomic progress	
	Plan 1	Plan 2	Plan 1	Plan 2	Plan 1	Plan 2
2022	2.318	2.362	2.186	2.221	1.614	1.582
2023	2.293	2.255	2.150	2.123	1.595	1.520
2024	2.275	2.153	2.095	1.975	1.578	1.491
2025	2.262	2.012	2.059	1.860	1.568	1.450
2026	2.251	1.914	2.041	1.798	1.560	1.407
2027	2.242	1.787	2.025	1.699	1.549	1.388
2028	2.234	1.684	1.994	1.603	1.539	1.362
2029	2.227	1.598	1.914	1.555	1.536	1.335
2030	2.221	1.535	1.894	1.464	1.523	1.325
2031	2.216	1.461	1.856	1.392	1.514	1.313
2032	2.211	1.439	1.827	1.341	1.509	1.294
2033	2.206	1.419	1.823	1.299	1.502	1.263
2034	2.202	1.401	1.822	1.294	1.499	1.242
2035	2.198	1.384	1.821	1.258	1.498	1.228
2036	2.195	1.369	1.820	1.231	1.497	1.204
2037	2.191	1.356	1.818	1.232	1.495	1.191
2038	2.188	1.343	1.814	1.224	1.492	1.170
Annual growth rate (%)	– 0.36	– 3.47	– 1.16	– 3.66	– 0.49	– 1.87

carrying capacity has slightly improved and there is still a large room for improvement. The changes in the carrying capacity of management and construction level are relatively large, with an average annual decrease of 1.16%. Under the comprehensive control plan, the carrying capacity of technological progress, management and construction level, and socioeconomic progress have all significantly improved, with an average annual decrease of 3.47%, 3.66%, and 1.87% respectively. Under the comprehensive control plan, the human support capacity of the port area gradually changes from severe overload to near full load. The carrying capacity of technological progress has developed from 2.362 in 2022 to 1.342 in 2038, improving by 38.62% compared to the natural development plan in 2038. The carrying capacity of management and construction level has developed from 2.221 in 2022 to 1.224 in 2038, improving by 0.53% compared to the natural development plan in 2038. The carrying capacity of socioeconomic progress has developed from 1.582 in 2022 to 1.170 in 2038, improving by 21.58% compared to the natural development plan in 2038. Overall, the comprehensive control plan has a very obvious effect on improving human support capacity. With the progress of technology, the improvement of management and construction level, and socioeconomic progress, human support capacity will play a huge role in improving the ecological carrying capacity of the port area.

References

Bendewald M, Zhai ZQ (2013) Using carrying capacity as a baseline for building sustainability assessment. Habitat Int 37(SI):22–32

Castellani V, Sala S (2012) Ecological footprint and life cycle assessment in the sustainability assessment of tourism activities. Ecol Ind 16:135–147

Guo ZJ, Zhang JF, Song XQ et al (2017) Evolution of port ecological carrying capacity under multi-mode development. J Saf Environ 358–364

Jiang XH, Huang Q, Hui YH et al (2001) Study on water environment carrying capacity in Guanzhong area, Shaanxi. J Environ Sci X26

Ooba M, Hayashi K, Fujii M et al (2015) A long-term assessment of ecological-economic sustainability of woody biomass production in Japan. J Clean Prod 88:318–325

Ran SH, Xue JY, Wang HD (1998) Application of regional environmental carrying capacity in the study of urban sustainable development in Beihai City. China Environ Sci X26

Wang R (2014) Study on the evaluation of port environmental carrying capacity of Tianjin Port. Ocean University of China, Qingdao

Zhang YD, Cui KJ, Peng ST (2008) Preliminary exploration of the concept of port environmental carrying capacity and its influencing factors. Waterway Port 29(5):372–376

Zhang SK, Lu ZA (2009) Study on the fuzzy evaluation method of port environmental resource ecology based on AHP. Waterway Eng 80–82

Zhang JF (2016) Study on the composite evaluation model of port ecological carrying capacity. Dalian University of Technology, Dalian

Zhang Q, Zhang JF, Wang WY (2017) Dynamic evaluation model of port ecological carrying capacity based on system simulation. J Dalian Maritime Univ 43(01):91–100

Chapter 7
Comprehensive Evaluation of Regional Port Group and Environmental Coordinated Development

Port group are an important infrastructure and strategic resource for economic and social development. In the era of low-carbon economy, the development of green ports has become an important area for sustainable development of global transportation. How to enhance the service capacity of ports and achieve green and sustainable development has strategic significance for every port (Liu 2017; Lee 2016). In the coordinated development of regional port group and the environment, scientific evaluation and policy guidance are key (Yu 2004; Kim 2017). This section proposes to construct a green port development evaluation index system based on the DPSIR model, and quantitatively analyze the impact of each index on green ports.

7.1 Selection of Port Environmental Impact Evaluation Method

In recent years, with the continuous infiltration of relevant knowledge from other fields around multi-index comprehensive evaluation, the methods of multi-index comprehensive evaluation have been continuously enriched, and research in this area has been deepening. At present, dozens of comprehensive evaluation methods have been proposed at home and abroad, but they can generally be divided into two categories: subjective weighting evaluation methods and objective weighting evaluation methods. The former mostly adopts qualitative methods, and the weights are obtained by experts based on experience, such as the Analytic Hierarchy Process, Fuzzy Comprehensive Evaluation Method, etc. (Guo 2008; Deng 2012); the latter determines the weights based on the correlation between indicators or the coefficient of variation of each indicator, such as the Grey Relational Analysis Method, TOPSIS Method, etc. (Zhu 2019).

B. Lu, *The Sustainable Development of Port Group*,
https://doi.org/10.1007/978-981-97-2378-2_7

7.1.1 Entropy Method

Entropy is a measure used in probability theory to determine the uncertainty of information. Suppose there are n objects to be evaluated and m evaluation indicators, forming the original index data matrix $X = \left(x_{\text{ij}}\right)_{\text{nxm}}$. For a certain indicator X_j, the larger the gap in the indicator value X_{ij}, the greater the role it plays in the comprehensive evaluation. If all the values of an indicator are equal, then this indicator plays almost no role in the comprehensive evaluation. Given a series of schemes and attributes, the entropy method can determine the objective weight value of each attribute.

In information theory, information entropy $H(x) = -\sum P(x_i)\ln P(x_i)$ reflects the degree of disorder in the system. The less information entropy, the greater the degree of disorder in the system; the more information entropy, the smaller the degree of disorder in the system. The greater the degree of variation in the value of an indicator, the more information the indicator provides, and the greater the weight of the indicator. Conversely, the smaller the degree of variation in the value of an indicator, the less information the indicator provides, and the smaller the weight of the indicator. Therefore, the weights of each indicator can be calculated using the tool of information entropy according to the degree of variation of each indicator, providing a basis for multi-index comprehensive evaluation.

The steps of the entropy method are as follows:

(1) Data standardization processing

The ideal value for a positive indicator is $\max x_j$, and the ideal value for a negative indicator is $\min x_j$.

The proximity of the positive indicator is:

$$X_{\text{ij}}^{-} = \frac{x_{ij}}{\max x_j} \tag{7.1}$$

The proximity of the negative indicator is:

$$X_{\text{ij}}^{-} = \frac{\max x_j}{x_{\text{ij}}} \tag{7.2}$$

Since some data still have negative values after dimensionless processing, in order to avoid meaningless logarithms when calculating entropy weights, the data needs to be processed. The processing methods include the efficiency coefficient method and the standardization method, and here we use the standardization method. We first shift the data.

$$X_{\text{ij}}^{\bullet} = X_{\text{ij}}^{-} + 1 \tag{7.3}$$

Calculate the proportion of the indicator value of the jth sample under the ith indicator P_{ij}.

Define its standardized value as P_{ij}:

$$p_{ij} = \frac{X^{\bullet}_{\mathrm{ij}}}{\sum_{i=1}^{n} X^{\bullet}_{\mathrm{ij}}} \tag{7.4}$$

The standardization matrix of the data is $p = \{p_{ij}\}$.

(2) Calculate the entropy e and information utility value d of the j th indicator.

$$e_j = -k \sum_{i=1}^{n} p_{ij} \ln p_{ij} \tag{7.5}$$

$$d_j = 1 - e_j \tag{7.6}$$

In the formula, the constant k is related to the number of samples n in the system. For a completely disordered system, that is, when information is evenly distributed, the order is zero, the entropy is the largest, $e_j = 1$, $p_{\mathrm{ij}} = \frac{1}{n}$. At this time,

$$e_j = \frac{1}{\ln n \sum p_{ij} \ln p_{ij}} \tag{7.7}$$

(3) Define the weight w_j (entropy weight) of the j th indicator.

$$w_j = \frac{d_j}{\sum_{i=1}^{n} d_j} = \frac{1 - e_j}{n - \sum_{i=1}^{n} e_j} \tag{7.8}$$

The weight of several indicators is determined by the information utility value of the indicator. The greater the information utility value of the indicator, the greater its importance in evaluation, and the greater the weight.

(4) Calculate the comprehensive score of the evaluated sample in n.

$$S_i = \sum_{j=1}^{m} w_j p_{ij} \tag{7.9}$$

S_i is the comprehensive score of the i th evaluated sample.

7.1.2 Principal Component Analysis Method

Principal Component Analysis (PCA), also known as principal component analysis, was first introduced by American statistician Pearson in 1901 in his theoretical research in biology. In 1993, Hotelling applied this idea to psychological research and further developed it. In 1947, Karhunen independently studied it again in the form of probability theory, and subsequently, Loe've further expanded and perfected this theory. PCA is a statistical method that starts from multi-index analysis, uses statistical analysis principles and methods to extract a few unrelated comprehensive indicators while maintaining the large amount of information provided by the original indicators. In multivariate analysis, in order to collect information as completely as possible, many indicators are often measured for each sample to avoid missing important information. However, many indicators reflected in the form of variables may have a strong correlation, then the information may overlap, and the problem becomes more complex. Therefore, a few unrelated comprehensive variables are needed to reflect most of the information provided by the original variables. From a mathematical point of view, this is the idea of dimension reduction, transforming multiple indicators into a few comprehensive indicators (Ma 2007; Wan 2007).

The specific calculation steps of the principal component analysis method are as follows:

(1) Preprocess the original data

First, the "trendization" of indicators, that is, the conversion of reverse indicators into positive indicators, so that each indicator has comparable directionality. Secondly, the "standardization" of indicators, to eliminate the difference in dimension and order of magnitude between relative indicators and absolute indicators. The original value of the i th indicator of the j h sample is represented by x_{ij}.

The ideal value of the positive indicator is $\max x_j$, and the ideal value of the negative indicator is $\min x_j$.

The proximity of the positive indicator is:

$$X_{\mathrm{ij}}^{-} = \frac{x_{ij}}{\max x_j} \tag{7.10}$$

The proximity of the negative indicator is:

$$X_{\mathrm{ij}}^{-} = \frac{\max x_j}{x_{\mathrm{ij}}} \tag{7.11}$$

X_{ij} represents the ith indicator of the jth sample, $\max x_j$ and $\min x_j$ represent the maximum and minimum values of the jth indicator value respectively.

The Z-score method is used for standardization processing. The main purpose of using this method is to increase the difference between data and facilitate evaluation. The formula is as follows:

$$x_{ij}^{*} = \frac{x_{ij} - \overline{x_i}}{\sigma_i} \tag{7.12}$$

$$\overline{x_i} = \frac{\sum_{i=1}^{n} x_{ij}}{n} \tag{7.13}$$

$$\sigma_i = \sqrt{\frac{\sum_{i=1}^{n}\left(x_{ij} - \overline{x_i}\right)^2}{n-1}} \tag{7.14}$$

$\overline{x_i}$ and σ_i are the sample mean and standard deviation of the j th indicator respectively.

(2) Find eigenvalues and eigenvectors

Use the processed sample data matrix $X^* = \left(x_{ij}^*\right)$. Calculate its correlation coefficient, then find out the eigenvalues, and finally obtain the corresponding eigenvectors. The corresponding calculation steps are as follows:

$$R = \frac{1}{n}(X^*),\ X^* = \begin{pmatrix} r_{11} & \ldots & r_{1m} \\ \ldots & \ldots & \ldots \\ r_{m1} & \ldots & r_{mm} \end{pmatrix} \tag{7.15}$$

According to the equation $|R - \lambda_j E| = 0$, we can obtain R's m eigenvalues $\lambda_j (j = 1, 2, \ldots, m)$. And the corresponding eigenvectors U_j. $U_j = \left(U_{1j}, U_{2j}, \ldots, U_{mj}\right) (j = 1, 2, \ldots, m)$. The extracted components are denoted as $Y_j = X_j^* U_j$, that is, $y_j = x_{k1}^* u_{1j} + x_{k2}^* u_{2j} + \ldots + x_{km}^* u_{mj} (k = 1, 2, \ldots, n;\ j = 1, 2, \ldots, m)$. And calculate its variance contribution rate $v_k = \frac{\lambda_k}{m}$.

(3) Determine the number of principal components

Generally speaking, the first few principal components with a cumulative variance contribution rate exceeding contain most of the information, and the other principal components behind can be discarded.

(4) Determine the weights of each principal component

Calculate the score of the evaluated sample, and use the variance contribution rate of each principal component as the weight of the principal component to calculate the comprehensive score.

Advantages of principal component analysis:

(1) In practical problems, the study of multiple indicators (variables) is often encountered. However, in most cases, there is a certain correlation between different indicators. The principal component analysis method is based on the characteristic that there is a certain correlation in the evaluation indicators, and uses fewer indicators to replace the original more indicators, and makes these fewer indicators reflect the information of the original indicators as much as possible. It fundamentally solves the problem of information overlap between indicators, and greatly simplifies the indicator structure of the original indicator system. Therefore, it is the most widely used and effective method in social and economic statistics.

(2) In the principal component analysis method, the weights of each comprehensive factor are not artificially determined, but are determined according to the contribution rate of the comprehensive factor. This overcomes the defect of artificially determining the weight in some evaluation methods, making the comprehensive evaluation result unique and objectively reasonable.

Disadvantages of principal component analysis:

(1) The calculation process of the principal component analysis method is relatively cumbersome, and the requirements for the sample size are relatively large.
(2) The principal component analysis method is based on sample indicators for comprehensive evaluation, so the result of the evaluation is related to the scale of the sample size.
(3) The principal component analysis method assumes that the relationship between indicators is linear. But in practical applications, if the relationship between indicators is not linear, it may lead to bias in the evaluation results.

7.1.3 Hierarchical Analysis Method

The Analytic Hierarchy Process (AHP) is a systematic, hierarchical analysis method combining qualitative and quantitative aspects. It was proposed in the mid-1970s by Saaty, a renowned operations researcher and professor in the Department of Mathematics at the University of Pittsburgh, USA. This method quantifies the experience of decision-makers and is particularly suitable for situations with complex goal structures and lack of data. It is a simple, flexible, and practical multi-criteria decision-making method that has been applied to decision-making problems in various industries since its inception.

The basic principle of the Analytic Hierarchy Process is to decompose the various indicators in a complex problem into several ordered levels by defining their interrelationships. Each level's elements have roughly equal status, and each level has a certain connection with the previous and next levels. The hierarchical structure model generally includes the goal level, criterion level, and scheme level. In the hierarchical model, the importance of each level is reflected quantitatively based on judgments of certain objective facts. This is done by determining the relative importance of the elements in each level through pairwise comparison judgments and expressing them quantitatively to establish a judgment matrix (Tang 2007; Chen 2008). Then, the relative importance weights of each indicator in the judgment matrix of each level are calculated using mathematical methods. Finally, the importance weights of all indicators relative to the goal are obtained by combining the relative importance weights of each level within the hierarchical structure.

Advantages of the Analytic Hierarchy Process:

(1) In decision-making with limited goals, many problems requiring decisions have both qualitative and quantitative factors. Therefore, the decision-making process requires the organic combination of qualitative and quantitative analysis to avoid

disconnection between the two. The Analytic Hierarchy Process is a good scientific decision-making method that organically combines qualitative and quantitative analysis. It quantifies qualitative issues judged by people based on subjective experience through pairwise comparison scale values, effectively absorbing the results of qualitative analysis and leveraging the advantages of quantitative analysis. It includes both subjective logical judgments and analyses and relies on objective precise calculations and deductions, making the decision-making process highly organized and scientific. It can handle many practical problems that traditional optimization techniques cannot tackle, and its application range is quite wide.

(2) The Analytic Hierarchy Process analyzes and solves problems by viewing them as a system and making decisions based on the study of the relationships between the various components of the system and the environment in which the system is located. Many systems have a progressive hierarchical structure. For complex decision-making problems, the most effective way of thinking is the system way. The Analytic Hierarchy Process reflects the decision-making characteristics of such systems. It decomposes the problem to be decided into several levels, with the top level being the overall goal of the decision-making system. Based on the analysis of the dominant relationships of the factors affecting the overall goal of the system, the criterion level and sub-criterion level are established. Then, through pairwise comparison judgments, the ranking weights of each scheme relative to the overall goal of the decision-making system are calculated. The entire process reflects the system thinking mode of decomposition, judgment, and integration, and fully embodies the dialectical system thinking principle.

Disadvantages of the Analytic Hierarchy Process:

(1) Although the Analytic Hierarchy Process considers and integrates various qualitative and quantitative information in the evaluation process, it still cannot escape the randomness in the evaluation process and the subjectivity and uncertainty of the evaluation experts, as well as the fuzziness in understanding. For example, even the same evaluation expert may often make inconsistent subjective judgments on the same evaluation object at different times and in different environments. This inevitably makes the evaluation process highly subjective and arbitrary, thereby reducing the credibility of the results.

(2) Judgment matrices are prone to severe inconsistencies. When there are many elements at the same level, in addition to making the above problem more prominent, it can also easily cause decision-makers to make contradictory and confusing judgments, resulting in severe inconsistencies in the judgment matrix. For example, element i is slightly more important than j, and element j is slightly more important than k. According to the scale stipulated by AHP, there are $a_{ij} = 3$, $a_{jk} = 3$. According to the measurement of the AHP consistency matrix, there is $a_{ik} = a_{ij}a_{jk} = 9$. The meaning of AHP scale 9 is extremely important, which means that element i is extremely important compared to element k. Obviously, this judgment is not in line with common sense.

7.1.4 Other Methods

(1) TOPSIS Evaluation Method

TOPSIS (Technique for Order Preference by Similarity to Ideal Solution) was first proposed in 1981, and later scholars transformed the concept of TOPSIS for application to multi-objective decision-making problems in planning. The TOPSIS evaluation method is a common scientific method in multi-objective decision analysis of finite schemes.

The basic principle of the TOPSIS evaluation method: In the normalized original matrix, find the best and worst schemes among the finite schemes (represented by the best vector and the worst column vector), and then calculate the distance between the evaluation object and the best and worst schemes, obtain the relative closeness of the evaluation object to the best scheme, and use this as the basis for evaluating the merits. Its basic model is:

$$C_i = D_i^- / \left(D_i^+ + D_i^-\right)$$

where D_i^- is the distance between the evaluation scheme and the worst scheme. D_i^+ is the distance between the evaluation scheme and the best scheme. C_i is the relative closeness of the sample point to the best sample point. When $C_i \to 1$, the evaluation scheme is closer to the best scheme.

Advantages of the TOPSIS evaluation method:

① The TOPSIS method has no strict restrictions on data distribution, sample size, and number of indicators. The mathematical calculation is not complicated. It is suitable for small sample data and large systems with multiple samples. The evaluation object can be spatial or temporal. Its application range is wide and it has intuitive geometric meaning.
② It makes full use of the original data, and the loss of information is relatively small.

Disadvantages of the TOPSIS evaluation method:

① The weight $w_j(1, 2 \ldots j)$ is predetermined, and its value is usually subjective, so it has a certain arbitrariness.
② The so-called "optimal point" and "worst point" are generally selected from the dimensionless data matrix. However, when the evaluation environment and its own conditions change, the index value will also change accordingly. This may cause the "optimal point" and "worst point" to change, thereby changing the order of the rankings, which leads to the evaluation results not being unique.
3. This method also cannot solve the problem of repeated evaluation information caused by the correlation between evaluation indicators.

(2) Grey Relational Analysis Method

In 1982, Professor Deng Julong of Huazhong University of Science and Technology first proposed the concept of grey systems and established grey system theory.

Since then, grey system theory has been deeply studied and widely applied in many areas. Grey Relational Analysis (abbreviated as GRA) is one of the main applications of grey system theory. It is a method for whitening processing and making predictions or decisions using the potential information from existing data in situations with few data and unclear situations.

The basic principle of grey relational analysis: Grey relational analysis believes that the closer the geometric shapes of several statistical series curves are, that is, the more parallel the curves are, the closer their trends are, and the greater their correlation. Therefore, the objects can be compared and ranked based on the correlation between each scheme and the optimal scheme. This method first calculates the correlation matrix of each scheme with the ideal scheme composed of the best indicators, obtains the correlation from the correlation matrix, and then sorts and analyzes according to the size of the correlation, and draws conclusions.

Advantages of grey relational analysis:

① The calculation of the grey relational degree comprehensive evaluation method is simple, easy to understand, and the data does not need to be normalized, and can be directly calculated with the original data.
② The grey relational method does not require a large number of samples, nor does it require classic distribution rules, as long as there are representative small samples.

Disadvantages of grey relational analysis:

① There are many factors related to the grey relational degree, such as the reference sequence, comparison sequence, normalization method, resolution coefficient, etc. As long as these values are different, the grey relational degree will not be unique.
② The correlation degree obtained by the commonly used grey relational quantitative model is always positive, which cannot fully reflect the relationship between things, because there can be both positive and negative correlations between things. Moreover, the shapes of the time series curves with negative correlations are vastly different. If the commonly used correlation model is still used, incorrect conclusions will inevitably be drawn.
③ The theoretical basis for establishing various grey correlation degree quantification models is currently very narrow. It is inappropriate to determine the degree of correlation between factors solely from the perspective of comparing curve shapes. It can even be said that judging the degree of correlation between factors based on the similarity of curve shapes is incorrect. Things in nature are universally connected and interact with each other, and these universal connections and interactions constitute the movement and development of things. The development trends of interrelated factors do not always go in parallel directions; they can intersect and even develop in opposite directions. Obviously, completely linearly related sequences are not just parallel sequences, as long as their degree of correlation is equal. In general, the current "normative" criterion is not comprehensive or accurate and should be revised.

4. This method cannot solve the problem of repeated evaluation information caused by the correlation between evaluation indicators, so the choice of indicators has a significant impact on the evaluation results.

In summary, there are many mathematical methods that can be used for comprehensive evaluation, but each method focuses on different aspects of the problem. Given the different methods chosen, it may lead to different evaluation results. Therefore, when conducting a multi-objective comprehensive evaluation, one should analyze specific problems, choose the appropriate evaluation method based on the characteristics of the evaluated object itself, and adhere to the principles of objectivity, operability, and effectiveness.

7.2 Evaluation Model for Coordinated Development of Port Groups

The DPSIR (Driving force-Pressure-State-Impact-Response) model was proposed by the OECD (Organization for Economic Cooperation and Development) in 1993 and adopted by the European Environment Agency. It gradually evolved from the PSR and DSR models, ultimately becoming the DPSIR model, which complements and improves the previous two models. The original PSR model emphasized the logical relationship analysis of the cause-result-countermeasure of the problem. This framework has a wide range of applications and is currently mainly used for regional watershed ecological safety evaluation, health evaluation, vulnerability evaluation, and sustainable development evaluation (Cao 2005; Liu 2012). Although the PRS model is a clear conceptual model representing the causal chain in the system, the model cannot grasp the structure of the system and the decision-making process, and the choice of indicators is subjective. The PSR model provides a way of thinking for people to conduct ecological safety evaluations, guiding people to construct indicator systems, but it cannot provide specific methods to solve problems. The Driving-State-Response (DSR) model was initially developed in the 1996 OCED and UN environmental policy reports, replacing the pressure factors in the PSR model with driving factors. This model emphasizes the causes of environmental problems, changes in environmental quality or state, and choices and responses to changes. It has many environmental indicator factors, but it is difficult to find the root cause indicators of environmental problems, and some indicators are even harder to quantify. Finally, the European Environment Agency added “Driving force” and “Impact” indicators to the P-S-R basis to form the D-P-S-I-R evaluation system. The DPSIR model expands the PSR model to five aspects. The DPSIR model has a clear advantage in representing the direction of relationships between various factors in complex systems: for example, in ecological safety evaluations, it reflects the causal relationships between the economy, environment, and resources. The DPSIR model has a wide range of uses and can be used for ecological safety evaluations, risk evaluations, sustainability evaluations, etc., at different scales. This model not only inherits the advantages of the PSR model but also makes up for its shortcomings, and therefore is widely used by many scholars (Liu 2017).

The DPSIR model is widely used internationally as an evaluation index system model for green sustainable development. The DPSIR model analyzes issues from various aspects of things, and has comprehensive and flexible advantages in system integration, which helps in the formulation and revision of environmental protection plans, thereby better achieving the goals of green sustainable development. As a concept model of the evaluation index system widely used in the environmental system, the DPSIR model looks at the interaction between humans and the environmental system from the perspective of system analysis. It divides the evaluation indicators characterizing a natural system into five types: driving force, pressure, state, impact, and response, each of which is divided into several indicators.

In the DPSIR conceptual model, Driving Force represents the initial cause of a logical relationship of an event, that is, the potential cause of environmental changes. Pressure represents the direct cause of an event, that is, the impact of human survival activities on the living environment. State represents the state of the ecological safety system that bears human activities. Impact refers to the changes in the state of the ecological safety system before and after human activities. Response represents the measures taken to restore the initial state of the ecological safety system and maintain normal human life. The development of society and economy (driving force) will exert pressure on the environment. Thus, the state of the environment will change. This will lead to impacts on the ecological safety system, human health, and society. This impact will generate a social response that has a feedback effect on the driving force, state, or impact through various behaviors and measures. The structural relationship of the model is shown in Fig. 7.1.

The model can be widely used thanks to its two features: first, it is based on an indicator system established for policy goals that reflect environmental management issues; second, it clearly shows the causal relationships of various things with a clear framework structure, providing a theoretical basis for policy makers.

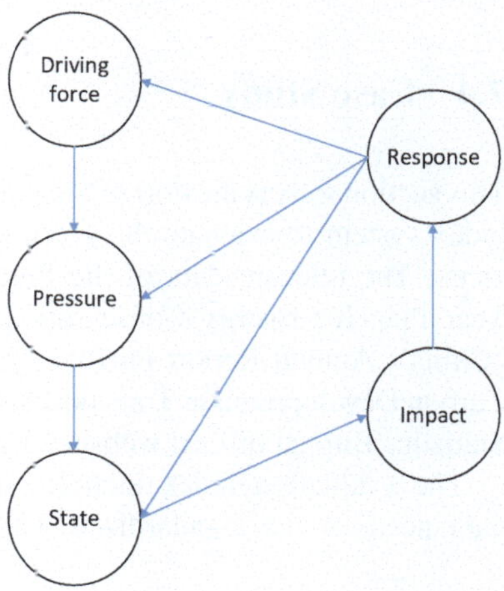

Fig. 7.1 DPSIR model relationship diagram

7.3 Establishment of the Indicator System for the Coordinated

Development of the Port Group Environment There are many methods to determine the weight of evaluation indicators, including statistical analysis, hierarchical analysis, and fuzzy clustering analysis. Among them, the hierarchical analysis method is the most widely used due to its simplicity, clear organization, and easy acceptance by the public. Based on these characteristics, this article uses the hierarchical analysis method to determine the weight of the evaluation indicators. The specific steps are as follows:

(1) Establish the hierarchical structure of the evaluation system: The evaluation system is divided into three levels. The first level is the ultimate goal; the second level is the five types of indicators of the DPSIR model; the third level is the specific evaluation indicators for evaluating the green development of the port. This section analyzes the conditions for building a green port based on the current situation of green port construction at home and abroad, summarizes the influencing factors of green port construction from four aspects: ecological civilization, resource utilization system, port energy-saving technology and environment, and economic development, and proposes 17 specific indicators for the evaluation of green port development based on these influencing factors, and refines the indicators to specific performance aspects. Finally, green port planning is carried out under the effect of the evaluation index system.
(2) Construct the judgment matrix of the evaluation system: Use the expert scoring method to determine the weight of each indicator, and use the Saaty scale method to judge the importance between indicators, and establish the judgment matrix.
(3) Determine the hierarchical weight value: Use the method of MATLAB programming to obtain the weight of each indicator, and check the consistency test results to judge the rationality of the weight. Through the above steps, the target layer judgment matrix is calculated to obtain the weights of each indicator as follows:

7.4 Case Study

This section selects the Port of Shanghai as the evaluation object, using the evaluation index system to evaluate the green development of the Port of Shanghai in recent years. The relevant data of the Port of Shanghai comes from the "Twelfth Five-Year Plan for Energy Conservation and Emission Reduction in Transportation", "China's Annual Report on Energy Conservation, Emission Reduction and Low-Carbon Development in Transportation", "Shanghai Statistical Yearbook", Shanghai Statistics Bureau official website, etc.

The evaluation index includes many aspects. For ease of measurement, the data needs to be standardized. Quantitative treatment of qualitative indicators, according to the expert's evaluation of qualitativindicators, combined with the current development status of green ports, the scores obtained are standardized.

The original data of the sample is denoted as X_i, and the result obtained after standardization is denoted as Y_i, $Y_i = (i = 1, 2, 3, \ldots, n)$. Where n is the average value of the variables, S is the standard deviation of n variables. For ease of evaluation, the calculation results are processed $= 100 + 10Y_i$.

According to the standardized data, 100 is selected as the benchmark value for evaluation, and the deviation of the evaluation index from the benchmark value is discussed. The larger the standard value of the evaluation index is greater than the benchmark value, the better the green port development; on the contrary, the larger the standard value of the evaluation index is less than the benchmark value, the worse the green port development.

According to the weight of the evaluation index obtained in Table 7.1, the standardized value is processed to obtain the situation of green port development in Shanghai Port from 2018 to 2021 Table 7.3.

As can be seen from Table 7.4, the green development of Shanghai Port has been on the rise from 2018 to 2021. The green development of Shanghai Port was good in 2018, and it entered a slow state in 2019 and 2020, and entered a rapid development stage in 2021.

From the weight of each index, it can be known that the pressure index has the largest weight, followed by the response index, which shows that the pressure index and the response index have a greater impact on the green development of the port. Among the pressure indicators, the indicators with the largest weight are the carbon dioxide emissions per unit throughput and the comprehensive energy consumption per unit throughput, reflecting that the key to the development of green ports is to reduce the carbon dioxide emissions per unit throughput and the comprehensive energy consumption per unit throughput. Among the response indicators, attention should be paid to the perfection of the port environmental supervision system and the promotion of green concepts among employees.

Next, we will analyze from five indicators and give countermeasure suggestions:

(1) Pressure index

From Table 7.2, we can see that among the criteria, the pressure index has the highest weight, accounting for 0.3945, which has the greatest impact on the development of green ports. Among the pressure indicators, the indicators that have the greatest impact on the development of green ports are the carbon dioxide emissions per unit throughput and the comprehensive energy consumption per unit throughput, which together account for 2/3 of the weight of the pressure indicators. To reduce the comprehensive energy consumption per unit throughput, it is necessary to reduce carbon dioxide emissions and enhance the ability to handle carbon dioxide. The Port of Shanghai has achieved significant achievements in the treatment of wastewater and solid waste, with emission compliance rates reaching 100%. Therefore,

Table 7.1 Green port evaluation index system

Target layer	Criterion layer	Index layer	Data type
Evaluation index system for green port development	Drving force B1	Annual port throughput (C1)	Quantify
		Back-land per capita GDP (C2)	Quantify
		Growth rate of port traffic (C3)	Quantify
	Pressure B2	Throughput per unit of CO_2 emissions (C4)	Quantify
		Comprehensive energy consumption per unit throughput (C5)	Quantify
		Sewage discharge reaches the standard efficiency (C6)	Quantify
		Waste gas emission standard efficiency (C7)	Quantify
		Solid waste recycling and utilization rate (C8)	Quantify
	State B3	Green coverage rate in the port area (C9)	Quantify
		Average noise value in the port area (C10)	Quantify
		Air quality conditions in the port area (C11)	Qualitative
	Impact B4	The proportion of clean energy use (C12)	Quantify
		Energy saving rate of wharf RTG "oil to electricity" (C13)	Quantify
		Port EDI usage (C14)	Qualitative
	Response B5	The improvement of the environmental regulatory system (C15)	Qualitative
		The establishment of the corresponding green port institutions (C16)	Qualitative
		Staff green publicity degree (C17)	Qualitative

the key to reducing comprehensive energy consumption per unit throughput is to reduce carbon dioxide emissions, which requires accelerating the development of port energy-saving technologies, increasing financial investment, introducing professional technical talents, and providing convenient conditions for the development of energy-saving technologies. Increasing the use of clean energy, replacing traditional fossil fuels with clean energy such as natural gas and electricity, accelerating the progress of RTG "oil-to-electricity" conversion, and strengthening electronic data exchange between various port departments. Learn and borrow advanced technologies from abroad, combine with the conditions of their own ports, and develop green ports with their own characteristics.

Table 7.2 Weight of green port evaluation index system

Criterion layer	Criterion layer weight	Index layer	Index layer weight
Drving force	0.1237	C1	0.0169
		C2	0.0295
		C3	0.0773
Pressure	0.3945	C4	0.1311
		C5	0.1311
		C6	0.0328
		C7	0.0519
		C8	0.0476
State	0.1237	C9	0.0309
		C10	0.0309
		C11	0.0619
Impact	0.1237	C12	0.0247
		C13	0.0495
		C14	0.0495
Response	0.2343	C15	0.0469
		C15	0.1406
		C17	0.0469

Table 7.3 Standardized data of green development evaluation index of Shanghai Port from 2018 to 2021

Evaluating indicator	2018	2019	2020	2021
C1	112.69	112.98	105.77	106.06
C2	111.68	103.99	104.33	111.36
C3	102.29	113.17	106.85	108.61
C4	112.08	103.01	103.62	111.47
C5	109.44	105.66	101.89	101.89
C6	113.22	101.72	105.17	109.77
C7	113.08	101.19	103.56	110.70
C8	107.99	107.99	103.29	112.69
C9	112.47	104.08	108.16	108.16
C10	107.07	107.07	100	114.14
C11	110.55	105.25	102.63	115.76
C12	113.75	101.05	107.40	107.40
C13	106.89	106.89	100.53	114.31
C14	105.92	101.48	105.18	113.32
C15	113.34	103.08	103.08	107.18
C16	108.25	104.13	100	114.44
C17	108.30	101.38	107.84	112.45

Table 7.4 Situation of green port development in Shanghai Port from 2018 to 2021

Year	2018	2019	2020	2021
Evaluation	109.76	105.17	103.66	112.28

(2) Response Indicators

Among the criteria, the weight of the response indicators is 0.2343, ranking second. It can be seen that response indicators are also very important for the development of green ports. Among the response indicators, the establishment of green port corresponding institutions occupies the largest proportion, reaching 0.1406. Therefore, strengthening the establishment of green port-related institutions is also an urgent problem for ports. Ports need to continuously improve green port management methods, carry out comprehensive environmental education and training for employees, and conduct regular assessments to improve the environmental awareness and capabilities of all port personnel. At the same time, strengthen the regulatory mechanism, improve the work of regulatory departments and personnel, formulate more detailed environmental evaluation systems and strictly implement them.

(3) Driving Force Indicators

Driving force indicators, status indicators, and impact indicators have the same weight in the evaluation system and have the same impact on green ports. The indicator with the highest weight in the driving force impact indicators is the port throughput growth rate. The Port of Shanghai is the second largest port in the world in terms of throughput, but in recent years, the throughput has declined due to the global economic downturn. It is necessary to continuously attract new sources of goods, expand the hinterland radiation range; make full use of existing transportation lines, and achieve resource allocation optimization.

(4) Status Indicators

The indicator with the highest weight among the status indicators is the air quality in the port area, which also involves the port's exhaust gas treatment compliance rate, the greening coverage rate in the port area, and other factors. Ports should continue to improve the air quality in the port area, reduce cost input while ensuring the waste treatment compliance rate. Ensure the greening coverage area in port planning and construction, strengthen real-time environmental monitoring in the port area, adjust policies in time, and ensure the coordinated development of port development and the ecological environment.

(5) Impact Indicators

The most influential indicator among the impact indicators is the energy saving rate of the dock RTG "oil-to-electricity" conversion. At present, the Port of Shanghai has achieved certain achievements in the dock RTG "oil-to-electricity" conversion, with an average energy saving rate of 30% or more, and the overall technical level has reached the world's advanced level. To achieve higher levels of green development goals, it is necessary to further accelerate the construction of RTG "oil-to-electricity", increase the use of clean energy such as electricity, and reduce waste generation.

The rapid development of ports has boosted economic benefits, but it has also brought about serious environmental pollution and other issues. In the future, the construction and development of our country's ports should change the traditional port operation mode, and achieve the goal of win–win environmental and economic benefits through the development and construction of green ports. In this regard, our country'ss ports should continuously improve the evaluation index system of green ports, adjust and optimize the planning, design, and operation goals of ports according to the evaluation results, organically combine port development with environmental protection, and lay the foundation for the sustainable development of ports.

References

Cao H (2005) A brief comment on the DPSIR model. Environ Sci Technol

Deng X, Li J, Zeng H, et al. (2012) A nalysis and application of weight calculation method of hierarchical analysis method. Res Practice and Understanding of Mathem 42(07)

Guo J, Zhang Z, Sun Q (2008) Research and application of analytic hierarchy process. China Safety Sci J 05

Hang C, Yuewei W (2008) Construction of evaluation index system for Port-city interaction relationship and analysis of Dalian. Port Econ 11:46–48

Kim S, Chiang B (2017) The role of sustainability practices in international port operations: an analysis of moderation effect. J Korea Trade 21(2):125–144

Lee J, Youl K, Hyunmi J (2016) A study on the sustainability of ports: the case of SuPorts and PPRISM. J Korean Navigation and Port Res 40(6):413–420

Liu C, Wang X, Jiang D (2017) Evaluation of low-carbon green development of oil terminal based on DPSIR model. J Shanghai Maritime Univer 38(01):62–67

Liu C, Ju J (2017) Research on the development evaluation of green ports. Port Economy 08

Liu C, Liu J, Liu N et al. (2012) Application of DPSIR model in ecological port group evaluation. J Shanghai Maritime Univer

Ma W (2007) Comprehensive evaluation of China's index funds based on principal component analysis and entropy method. Central South University, Changsha

Tang X, Xue P (2007) Application of hierarchical analysis method in port development condition evaluation. China Sci Technol Inform 01:114–115

Wan Z, Zhang W, Ti Z (2007) Research on comparative trend of port logistics development through principal component analysis—taking Guangzhou Port as an example. Water Transport Eng 08:21–27

Yu X, Fu D (2004) A review of multi-index comprehensive evaluation methods. Statistics and Decision 11

Zhu J (2019) Research on the competitiveness of Ningbo Zhoushan port based on entropy weight and TOPSIS method. Zhejiang Ocean University

References

Chapter 8
Strategies for Coordinated Environmental Governance of Port Groups Based on Green Technology

To address the environmental pollution problems faced by ports, most ports internationally now require ships to use shore power after docking. This not only reduces the emission of pollutants from the auxiliary engine's fuel power generation on the ship, but also effectively reduces noise pollution. In addition, for ship owners, using shore power also has certain economic benefits. Reasonable shore power prices can also reduce fuel consumption and reduce the operating costs of ships.

8.1 Economic Analysis of Ship Shore Power Technology

8.1.1 Shore Power Technology and Its Current Application

Cold Ironing is when a ship stops using its own auxiliary engine for power generation during its stay at the port, and instead uses the port's shore power supply for the production and living electricity needed during the docking period (such as communication, lighting, etc.). According to related statistics from the IMO, the emissions of NOX and SOX from global shipping activities account for about 15% and 13% of global anthropogenic emissions respectively. These pollutants can affect areas up to 400 km away through the climate (Zhao et al. 2021; Huang et al. 2022).

Although most of such emissions occur in maritime emissions, the most intensive part of shipping is in the port area. Relevant data shows that the auxiliary engine power generation after the ship docks can cause serious pollution in the vicinity of the port. However, if shore power is used after the ship docks, the emission reduction rates of NOX and SOX can reach 97% and 96% respectively (Song 2022).

In recent years, with the increasing emphasis on energy conservation, emission reduction, and environmental protection, many port management departments internationally have stipulated that ships must use shore power when docking. In February 2019, the Ministry of Transport issued the "Notice on Further Jointly Promoting the

B. Lu, *The Sustainable Development of Port Group*,
https://doi.org/10.1007/978-981-97-2378-2_8

Use of Shore Power by Ships at Ports (2019)", which focuses on solving prominent problems in the promotion of shore power, including unifying shore power standards and promoting the standardized construction of shore power, among other tasks (Kanellos 2019; Fang et al. 2023). In December of the same year, the Ministry of Transport issued the "Port and Ship Shore Power Management Measures", indicating that China's shore power has gradually transitioned from the construction stage to the operation and use stage (Wang 2018, 2013).

Currently, the ship's connection to the shore power system is generally composed of three parts.

(1) Port power supply system: This enables electrical energy to be supplied from the onshore high-voltage substation to the connection point near the ship. Here, it is necessary to complete the transformation and frequency conversion of the voltage level, and the non-stop power switching function with the ship's power receiving system.
(2) Cable connection equipment: This includes the cables and equipment connecting the onshore connection point and the ship's power receiving device. It must be quickly connected and can be installed on the port, ship, or barge.
(3) Ship power receiving system: This involves the fixed installation of power receiving equipment on the ship, which mainly includes on-board transformers, cable winches, and other electrical equipment.

The port power grid in China is generally 10kV/50Hz, while the voltage level and frequency of ships vary depending on their type. This requires the port dock to be equipped with a transformer and frequency converter to convert the shore power source, making it suitable for ship power supply. At the same time, in order to meet the power needs of the ship after docking, the capacity of the shore power must be correctly selected, which should be determined based on the calculation results of the ship's power load after docking (Li 2010).

8.1.2 Cost–Benefit Model of Ship Using Shore Power

In order to specifically analyze the economic benefits of ships using shore power, it is necessary to establish a cost–benefit model for ships using shore power, and analyze the economic benefits before and after ships use shore power.

(1) Ship cost model:

$$C_{\text{ship}} = B_{\text{gk}} + C_{\text{sb}} \cdot \left(1 - \beta_{\text{gov}}\right) \tag{8.1}$$

In the formula: B_{gk} represents the total cost of ships using shore power; C_{sb} represents the investment renovation cost of onboard power equipment, including onboard transformers, cables, etc.; β_{gov} represents the government subsidy rate.

$$\begin{aligned} B_{\mathrm{gk}} &= P_{\mathrm{i}}^{ship} \cdot T \cdot P_{tot} \\ &= P_{\mathrm{i}}^{ship} \cdot T \cdot (\mathrm{p}_{sf} + p_{ef}) \end{aligned} \tag{8.2}$$

$$\begin{cases} C_{\mathrm{sb}} = CFR \cdot \mathrm{p}_k^{gz\_Per} \cdot P_k^{ship} \\ CFR = \frac{r(1+r)^{life}}{(1+r)^{life}-1} \end{cases} \tag{8.3}$$

In the formula: P_{tot} represents the total cost per unit of shore power used by ships, including the shore-based electricity price p_{ef} and the service fee per unit of power p_{sf}; $p_k^{gz\_Per}$ represents the cost of ship power transformation per unit of power (yuan/kW); P_k^{ship} represents the power of k type of ship; CFR represents the investment recovery factor, which can convert the one-time investment cost of equipment into annual expenditure, r is the basic discount rate. $life$ represents the average life of the equipment.

(2) Ship revenue model:

$$B_{\mathrm{ship}} = C_{\mathrm{rl}} + C_{\mathrm{pw}} \tag{8.4}$$

In the formula: B_{ship} represents the cost reduction of the ship not using auxiliary engine power generation, which is considered as the revenue of the ship using shore power. C_{rl} is the cost of the ship originally using fuel. C_{pw} is the pollution discharge fee of ship fuel pollution emission, its calculation formula can be expressed as follows:

$$\begin{cases} C_{\mathrm{rl}} = P_{\mathrm{total}} \cdot T \cdot E_1 \cdot p_{rl}/1000000 \\ C_{pw} = p_{dl} \sum_{i=1}^{n} P_k^{\mathrm{ship}} \cdot T \cdot F_i/1000/E_{dl\_i} \end{cases} \tag{8.5}$$

In the formula: E_1 is the fuel consumption per unit of electricity (g/kWh); p_{rl} is the unit fuel price (yuan/t); p_{dl} is the unit pollution discharge fee of pollution equivalent (yuan/equivalent); F_i and E_{dl_i} are the emission factor (g/kWh) and pollution equivalent value (kg) of the i type of pollutant, respectively.

(3) Ship cost-benefit model:

$$F_{\mathrm{ship}} = B_{\mathrm{ship}} - C_{\mathrm{ship}} \tag{8.6}$$

8.1.3 Case Analysis

Based on the corresponding transformation costs for ship power, we now assume the power and per kilowatt transformation cost of three types of ships are as follows: for bulk carriers, power is 400 kW and the cost is1530 yuan/kW; for cruise ships, power is 800 kW and the cost is 800 yuan/kW; for container ships, power is 1200 kW and the cost is 550 yuan/kW.

Other related parameter settings are as follows: government subsidy rate β_{gov} is 30%, fuel price p_{rl} is 9900 yuan/ton, discount rate i is 8%. The equivalent value of ship fuel pollutants E_{dl_i} and emission factors F_i are as shown in Table 8.1. The pollutants produced by the use of auxiliary engines for ship power generation include: CO_2, NO_x, Volatile Organic Compounds, etc.

(1) The relationship between the minimum port time and shore power price

For a fixed shore power price, when the ship is divided into three types: bulk carriers, cruise ships, and container ships, consider the port time of different ships when the cost-effectiveness is exactly zero, that is, the minimum port time for the ship.

Figure 8.1 shows the relationship between the shore power price p_{tot} and the minimum berthing time of different types of ships. At this time, the shore power price F_{ship} is increased from 1.6 yuan/kWh to 2.4 yuan/kWh, and then the ship's cost-effectiveness is zero to find out the critical berthing time of the ship, that is, the minimum berthing time required to ensure the shi"s income is positive. It can be seen from the figure:

1) There is a zero point in the relationship between the minimum berthing time and the shore power price. The zero point at this time is a critical value. The berthing time is not allowed to have a negative value, that is, the electricity price after the zero point is not in line with reality. It can be calculated that the shore power price must be less than 2.177 yuan/kWh to ensure that the minimum berthing time of the ship is positive. When the shore power price is within the normal range (i.e., less than 2.177 yuan/kWh), regardless of the type of ship, as the shore power price rises, the minimum berthing time of this type of ship also rises. This is because the shore power price reflects the electricity cost of the ship, which is reflected in the cost part of the ship's cost-effectiveness function. To offset this part of the cost, it is necessary to increase the berthing time to increase the ship's income. Although the electricity cost also increases at this time, the overall cost-effectiveness function is increasing.

Table 8.1 Equivalent value and emission factor of fuel pollutants

Fuel oil pollutants of ship auxiliary engines	Pollution equivalent value (kg)	Emission factor (g/kw*h)
SO_X	0.46	0.95
NO_X	0.95	11.80
VOC	0.05	0.53
CO	1.68	16.7
General dust PM_{10}	4	0.30
CO_2	5000	698

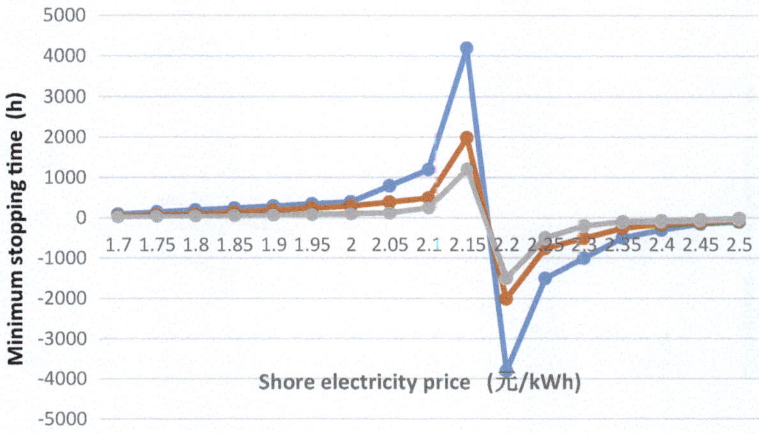

Fig. 8.1 Relationship between shore power price and minimum berthing time

2) Bulk carriers have the longest minimum docking time, followed by cruise ships, and the shortest is container ships. From the cost–benefit function of the ship, it can be seen that under the critical condition where the cost–benefit function of the ship is zero, the power term of the ship is eliminated, and the factors affecting the cost–benefit of the ship are only the renovation cost of unit power. Therefore, the size of the renovation cost of different ship unit power determines the order of their corresponding minimum docking time. The unit power renovation cost of bulk carriers is the highest, followed by cruise ships, and finally container ships.

(2) Relationship between docking time and ship cost–benefit Through the analysis of the previous section, we can derive the shore power price corresponding to the critical docking time of the ship. Now, assuming that the shore power price is fixed, we consider the relationship between the cost–benefit of different types of ships and the docking time. Among them, the shore-based service fee is 1.25 yuan/kWh, and the shore-based electricity price is 0.9 yuan/kWh (the shore power price is 2.15 yuan/kWh, which is in line with the previous analysis, that is, less than 2.177 yuan/kWh); the docking time increases from 0 to 4000 h.

The simulation results are shown in Fig. 8.2: When the shore power price is fixed, the relationship curve between the docking time of the three types of ships and the cost–benefit of this type of ship. It can be seen from the figure

1) When the type of ship is certain, as the annual docking time of the ship increases, the ship's income continues to increase. This is because as the docking time increases, the saved fuel costs and the environmental benefits obtained will gradually exceed the renovation costs of the shore power equipment, shore-based service fees, and shore-based electricity fees, and the ship begins to gain benefits.

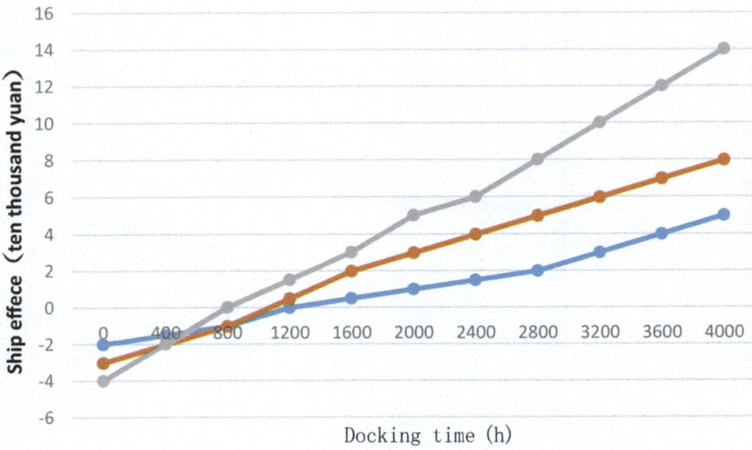

Fig. 8.2 Relationship curve between docking time and ship cost–benefit

2) When the type of ship is different, as the power of the ship increases, although the unit power renovation cost of the ship is decreasing, the total renovation cost is also increasing. Therefore, when the docking time is short, the excessive renovation cost makes the cost–benefit curve of the container ship at the bottom. However, because the power of large ships is the largest, once the docking time becomes longer, the benefits obtained by the ship will increase rapidly, and the saved fuel costs and environmental benefits obtained are far greater than the renovation costs of shore power equipment, shore-based service fees, and shore-based electricity fees. Therefore, the slope of the cost–benefit curve of the container ship is the largest, followed by the cruise ship, and finally the bulk carrier.

(1) The impact of peak and valley electricity prices on ship cost–benefit

In this section, for the ship cost–benefit model, the impact of the peak and valley effect of the shore-based electricity price is considered, and the docking time of the ship is also divided into peak, flat, and valley periods. The ship docks in these three periods, and at the same time, the three different types of ships, bulk carriers, cruise ships, and container ships, are considered to find out the relationship curve between peak and valley electricity prices and ship cost–benefit.

For the ship cost–benefit model, the cost of the ship using shore power B_{gk} is:

$$B_{\mathrm{gk}} = P_{\mathrm{k}}^{\mathrm{ship}} \cdot \left[T_{\mathrm{f}} \cdot p_f + T_p \cdot p_p + T_g \cdot p_g\right] + P_k^{ship} \cdot T \cdot p_{sf} \tag{8.7}$$

T_f, T_p, T_g corresponds to the berthing time of ships during peak periods, normal periods, and off-peak periods; p_f, p_p, p_g corresponds to shore-based electricity prices are shown in the images.

The shore-based electricity prices and the division of peak and off-peak periods charged by the power grid are as follows (Fig. 8.3):

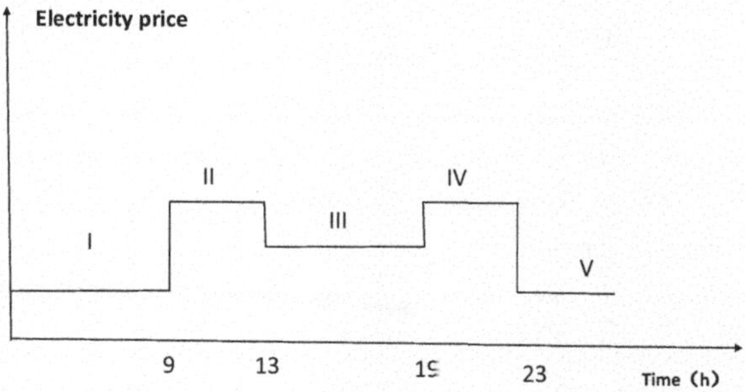

Fig. 8.3 Current peak and off-peak electricity prices in a certain province

Peak period: 9 to 12 o'clock, 19 to 22 o'clock, shore-based electricity price 1.4585 yuan/kWh; Normal period: 13 to 19 o'clock, base electricity price 0.8751 yuan/kWh; Off-peak period: 23 o'clock to 8 o'clock the next day, shore-based electricity price 0.3917 yuan/kWh. Now consider multiple peak and off-peak electricity prices, as shown in Table 8.2. When considering peak and off-peak electricity prices, the peak and off-peak price spread ratio is generally used as an important indicator. The peak and off-peak price spread ratio refers to the difference between the peak electricity price and the normal electricity price divided by the difference between the normal electricity price and the off-peak electricity price, that is:

$$\beta = (p_f - p_p)/(p_p - p_g) \tag{8.8}$$

The shore-based service fee is fixed at 1.25 yuan/kWh, and other data are the same as in the first section. Here we set the berthing time to 3000 h. For the division of peak and off-peak periods, we consider two scenarios:

Scenario one: The peak period accounts for 60% of the berthing time, the normal period accounts for 30% of the berthing time, and the off-peak period accounts for 10% of the berthing time;

Scenario two: The peak period accounts for 10% of the berthing time, the normal period accounts for 30% of the berthing time, and the off-peak period accounts for 60% of the berthing time;

The cost-effectiveness of ships under two different peak and off-peak period division scenarios corresponding to four different peak and off-peak electricity prices is shown in Fig. 8.4.

As can be seen from the figure:

Table 8.2 Shore-based electricity prices

	Peak	Flat	Valley	Opening ratio β
Electricity price I	1.4485	0.8651	0.3917	1.207
Electricity price II	1.4235	0.8501	0.3867	1.210
Electricity price III	1.4135	0.8441	0.3847	1.213
Electricity price IV	1.3985	0.8351	0.3817	1.216

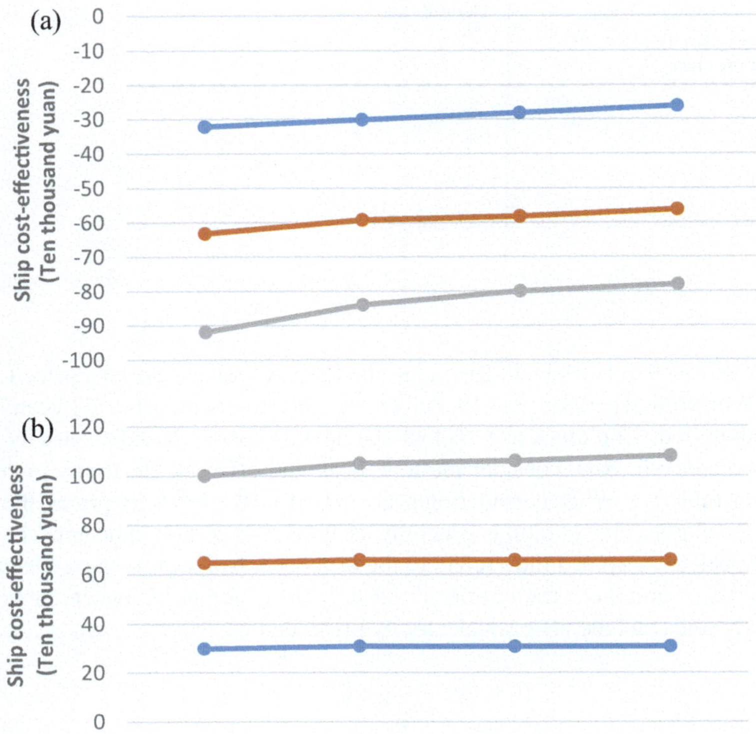

Fig. 8.4 Peak and off-peak price spread ratio and ship cost-effectiveness curve: **a** Scenario one **b** Scenario two

1) Regarding the peak-valley spread ratio: From Scenario One, most of the time when ships are docked is during peak periods, when electricity prices are relatively high. Therefore, regardless of the type of ship, its cost-effectiveness is negative, meaning the ship is operating at a loss during this time. From Scenario Two, most of the time when ships are docked is during valley periods. Compared to the previous scenario, the average electricity price at this time is relatively low. Therefore, for all three types of ships, their cost-effectiveness is positive, meaning the ships are operating at a profit. From the comparison of these two scenarios, it is clear that for each peak-valley spread ratio, the docking time of the ships needs to be reasonably arranged. Only when the docking times during peak, normal, and valley periods are balanced can all ships have positive cost-effectiveness and be profitable.
2) Regarding different peak-valley spread ratios: Regardless of the type of ship, as the peak-valley spread ratio continues to increase, the ship's profits are also continuously increasing. In Scenario One, because ships mainly use peak period electricity prices, the ships are operating at a loss, and container ships, with their high power and relatively expensive average electricity prices, suffer the most

severe losses. In Scenario Two, because ships mainly use valley period electricity prices, the ships are profitable. At this time, as the power of the ship increases, the cost-effectiveness of the ship also increases, i.e., the cost-effectiveness of bulk carriers is the lowest, cruise ships are next, and container ships can achieve the highest cost-effectiveness.

8.2 Modeling of Multi-port Integrated Energy Systems

In actual port planning and operation, due to the different natural environments, geographical locations, development levels, and functional positioning of different ship docks, large ports are often divided into multiple port areas. Therefore, due to the objective laws of resource conditions and production schedules, the load size and timing of different port areas are often different (Tai et al. 2022). For example, the load of the cruise ship dock area is often higher during the day and lower at night, while the load of the bulk carrier dock area may be just the opposite. For the same port area, when the electrical load is high, the heat/cold load may not necessarily be at a high level, i.e., the peak and valley periods of various loads do not match (Yin 2019; Zhang and Song 2017). Therefore, if the energy systems of each port area are still planned and operated separately, there will inevitably be problems such as low equipment utilization and high total planning costs. Therefore, breaking the existing model of separate planning and independent operation of the integrated port energy system (IPES) in multiple areas, and achieving coordinated planning and operation of multiple port areas, is a problem that needs to be solved urgently in the current IPES (Wang 2014; Hary 2010).

This section proposes a coordinated planning model for multi-port integrated energy systems considering Energy Interconnection (EI). First, a simplified EI network model including network investment costs, interconnection models, and transmission constraints is established. Then, a mixed integer nonlinear programming model that considers EI multi-area IPES coordinated optimization is constructed, and it is transformed into a 0–1 mixed integer linear programming problem through linearization. Finally, taking a port in northern China as a simulation object, the interaction of heat and cold energy in the integrated energy systems of each port area and the changes in the transmission volume of the interconnected power grid are discussed in detail, and the impact of changes in key port parameters on the coordinated planning of multiple port areas is analyzed for sensitivity.

8.2.1 Architecture and Planning Process of Multi-port Integrated Energy Systems

(1) Multi-port energy system architecture

Each port area is connected to the natural gas network and the superior energy market through the port power distribution network. The IPES system architecture within each port area is similar to the internal architecture of a single port area, and is connected to the internal network of the energy local area network of the energy-using unit through the multi-energy flow port energy hub (energy hub, EH). The port areas are interconnected through the interconnected power grid to achieve interconnection and mutual aid between multiple EHs.

(2) Planning Process

Considering the actual situation of the multi-port area energy system, the planning process is as follows:

Step 1: Collect basic data related to the planning of each port area, such as multi-energy load data, etc.;

Step 2: According to the geographical location of the port area, load type, and resource distribution, divide the port area and select the site for EH through field investigation;

Step 3: Establish a multi-port area IPES collaborative optimization planning model that includes an interconnected power grid, and solve the model by inputting multi-energy load data, EH equipment parameters, and power line parameters from each area;

Step 4: Select EH equipment and power lines based on optimization results.

Among them, steps 1 and 2 are preparatory work, and step 4 is the actual application of the optimization planning results. Therefore, this section focuses on the research of step 3 to establish a multi-port area IPES collaborative planning model that includes an interconnected power grid.

8.2.2 Interconnected Power Grid Modeling Between Port Areas

(1) Interconnected Power Grid Investment Model

$$C_{\text{inv}}^{Line} = \sum_{j} CFR^{Line} L_{i,j} \omega_{line}^{cap} \left(\overline{P}_{i-j}^{line} \right) \tag{8.9}$$

In the formula: CFR^{Line} is line investment recovery factor; The length $L_{i,j}$ of the interconnection line between EH_i and EH_j; The investment cost ω_{line}^{cap} of the unit line, which is related to the transmission capacity $\overline{P}_{i-j}^{line}$ of the line.

(2) Interconnected Power Grid Transmission Model

The energy transmission unit can realize the interconnection between the port area EHs, effectively improving the economy and reliability of the system. The expression of the actual delivered electric power is:

$$\begin{cases} P_{i,t}^{EI} = \sum_{j} \left(P_{i,j,t}^{end} x_{i,j,t}^{Line} - P_{j,i,t}^{start} x_{j,i,t}^{Line} \right) \\ x_{i,j,t}^{Line} + x_{j,i,t}^{Line} \le 1 \end{cases} \tag{8.10}$$

In the formula: $P_{i,j}^{start}$ and $P_{i,j}^{end}$ respectively represent the electric power transmitted from the head EH_i end to EH_j at the moment t, and the actual delivered electric power from EH_j to EH_i; then in the multi-port area IPES, EH_i the total power of the energy interconnection actually received by $P_{i,t}^{EI}$; $x_{i,j,t}^{Line}$, $x_{j,i,t}^{Line} \in \{0, 1\}$ respectively indicate whether power is transmitted to EH_j at the moment t, and whether power is transmitted to EH_i at the moment EH_j. In the same line, power cannot be transmitted in both directions at the same time.

(3) Power transmission loss in interconnected power grid

$$P_{i,j,t}^{end} = P_{i,j,t}^{start} \left(1 - \delta L_{i,j}\right) \tag{8.11}$$

$L_{i,j}$ is the distance between port area i(EH_i) and port area j(EH_j), δ is the loss rate per kilometer (%/km) of the power line. This formula represents the relationship between the initial transmission of power and the actual delivered power.

8.2.3 IPES Collaborative Optimization Model Considering Demand Response and Energy Interconnection

The multi-port energy system is regarded as a whole, and an IPES collaborative optimization model considering demand response and energy interconnection is established. The specific objectives and constraints are as follows:

Similar to the single-port EH optimization configuration in Chap. 4, this chapter uses the equivalent annual value method to calculate the economy of multi-port IPES collaborative planning, and constructs the objective function with the minimum annual total planning cost:

$$\min C_{\text{tot}} = C_{inv}^{Line} + \sum_{i} \left(C_{inv}^{i} + C_{E}^{i} + C_{mat}^{i} + C_{IDR}^{i} + C_{cart-wind}^{i} \right) \tag{8.12}$$

In the formula: C_{tot} is the total annual planning cost of all port areas of the port, including the investment cost of the interconnected power grid between port areas C_{inv}^{Line}, the investment cost C_{inv}^{i} of each port area EH_i , energy cost C_{E}^{i}, equipment maintenance cost C^i_{mat}, IDR call cost C^i_{IDR}, and wind abandonment cost $C^i_{curt-wind}$. There are five costs in total.

1) Energy coupling model (power balance constraint)

The power balance state of the EH electric/thermal/cold energy source in each port area is expressed as follows. Although energy interconnection only changes the expression of power balance, due to the mutual coupling of multiple energies in IPES, the supply and demand relationship between other energies will also be affected accordingly.

Electric balance:

$$L_{i,t}^{ele} + L_{i,t}^{ship} + P_{i,t}^{PtG} = \alpha P_{i,t}^{ele} + \gamma \eta_{cchp}^{ele} H^{gas} V_{i,t}^{gas} + \beta P_{i,t}^{Wind} + P_{i,t}^{EI}, \forall t \in T \tag{8.13}$$

Heat balance:

$$L_{i,t}^{heat} = q_{cchp,i,t}^{heat} + q_{i,t}^{GB} = \gamma \eta_{cchp}^{heat} H^{gas} V_{i,t}^{gas} + (1-\gamma)\eta^{GB} H^{gas} V_{i,t}^{gas}, \forall t \in T \tag{8.14}$$

Cold balance:

$$L_{i,t}^{cool} = q_{cchp,i,t}^{cool} + q_{i,t}^{AC} = \gamma \eta_{cchp}^{cool} H^{gas} V_{i,t}^{gas} + \left((1-\alpha) P_{i,t}^{ele} + (1-\beta) P_{i,t}^{Wind}\right)\eta^{AC}, \forall t \in T \tag{8.15}$$

Combining the coupling device models in Chap. 3, the multi-energy power balance is represented in the form of an EH coupling matrix, namely:

$$\begin{bmatrix} L_{i,t}^{ele} + L_{i,t}^{ship} + P_{i,t}^{PtG} \\ L_{i,t}^{heat} \\ L_{i,t}^{cool} \end{bmatrix} = \begin{bmatrix} \alpha & \gamma \eta_{cchp}^{ele} H^{gas} & \beta & 1 \\ 0 & \left(\gamma \eta_{cchp}^{heat} + (1-\gamma)\eta_{GB}\right) \cdot H^{gas} & 0 & 0 \\ (1-\alpha)\eta^{AC} & \gamma \eta_{cchp}^{cool} H^{gas} & (1-\beta)\eta^{AC} & 0 \end{bmatrix} \cdot \begin{bmatrix} P_{i,t}^{ele} \\ V_{i,t}^{gas} \\ P_{i,t}^{Wind} \\ P_{i,t}^{EI} \end{bmatrix} \tag{8.16}$$

2) Line energy transmission capacity constraint

$$0 \le P_{i,j,t}^{start} \le \overline{P}_{i-j}^{line} \tag{8.17}$$

In the formula, The maximum transmissible capacity of the interconnected grid, this formula indicates that the transmission power between EHs should not exceed the maximum transmission power of the line.

3) Equipment selection constraint

$$\sum_{\omega \in \varphi^D} \chi^D \le 1, \quad D \in \{CCHP, GB, \text{PtG}, GS\} \tag{8.18}$$

Assume that there is only one EH in each port area, and at most one new one can be selected for each type of equipment in EH.

4) Other constraints

In addition, it includes equipment capacity constraints, output upper and lower limit constraints, energy storage constraints, and IDR constraints.

The model proposed in this section is a mixed integer nonlinear programming model (MINLP). The nonlinear terms originate from the product of binary variables and continuous variables in formula (8.10), which will increase the solution time and difficulty of the model. When solving such problems, two approaches are generally considered. One is to use heuristic algorithms, such as commonly used genetic algorithms, particle swarm algorithms, etc. However, these algorithms have certain inherent limitations, the solution efficiency is low, and even if various improved algorithms are used, the global optimality of the results cannot be guaranteed. The other is to transform the nonlinear model into an equivalent linear model through mathematical transformation, and then use a commercial solver to solve it. But this method also has obvious disadvantages, that is, some nonlinear models are difficult to transform, and even there are situations where they cannot be transformed. In this case, the previous method or nonlinear solver must be used to solve it.

In order to improve the solution efficiency, this section transforms the MINLP problem, linearizes the nonlinear terms in the model, makes it an MILP problem, and then uses the commercial solver CPLEX to solve it. The specific conversion method is the linearization method of binary variables multiplied by continuous variables, and the "Big M method" is used to transform it into an MILP model. The general method is as follows: suppose $x \in \{0, 1\}$ is binary variable, y is a continuous variable, and Z is the product of x and y:

$$Z = x \cdot y \tag{8.19}$$

Then, introduce the upper limit value M of y, then the above equation can be converted into the following set of inequalities:

$$Z \le y + (1 - x) \cdot M \tag{8.20}$$

$$-Z \le y - (1 - x) \cdot M \tag{8.21}$$

$$Z \le x \cdot M \tag{8.22}$$

After the nonlinear terms in formula (8.10) are converted by the above method, this model is converted into an MILP problem, and the CPLEX commercial solver can be used to solve this model by calling the YALMIP toolbox in MATLAB.

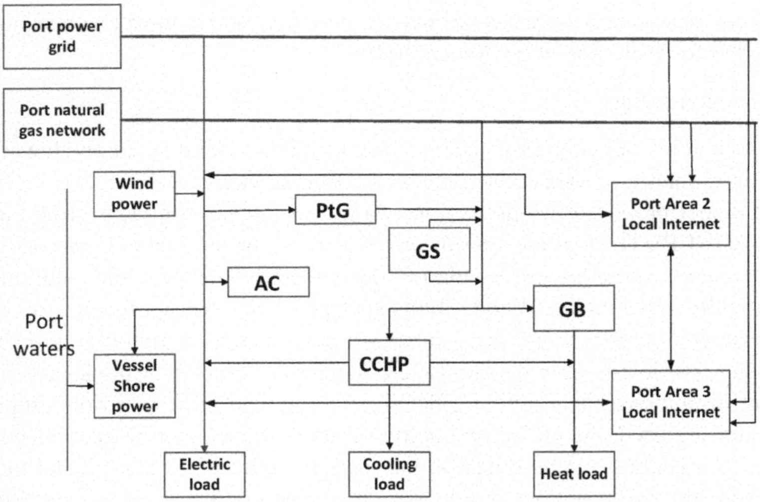

Fig. 8.5 Basic architecture diagram of multi-port IPES

8.2.4 Case Analysis

This section selects a large port in northern China as the research object. According to the geographical location and energy supply positioning, the port can be divided into three port areas. In addition to having common multi-energy loads such as port operations and commercial tourism, each port area has a ship dock with specific working conditions, including a bulk cargo dock with a construction area of 25 km^2 (Port Area 1), a cruise dock with an area of 34 km^2 (Port Area 2), and a container dock with an area of 41 km^2 (Port Area 3). It is assumed that the port's energy system can be regarded as a multi-port area IPES composed of multiple EHs, and its energy transmission path is similar to that shown in Fig. 8.5.

1) Due to the different geographical locations and functional positioning of each port area, the new energy output and multi-energy consumption of each port area are different. The wind power output, multi-energy load, and the predicted load of shore power used by bulk cargo ships, cruise ships, and container ships in different seasons in each port area are shown in Fig. 8.6.

2) The loss of the interconnection line between EHs is 0.03%/km. According to the cost and capacity of typical models of power lines, the linear relationship between unit length price and capacity can be expressed as:

$$\omega_{line}^{\text{cap}} = 0.405\overline{P}_{i-j}^{line} + 49.19 \tag{8.19}$$

where, $\omega_{line}^{\text{cap}}$ is the price per unit length of the power line, $\overline{P}_{i-j}^{line}$ is the rated capacity of the power line.

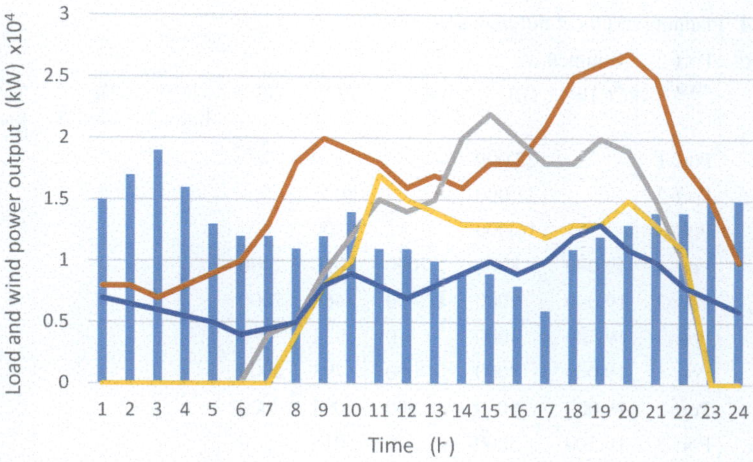

Fig. 8.6 Typical daily load and wind power curve of each port area

3) Scenario setting: The multi-port area IPES is optimized for the following 5 scenarios, as shown in Table 8.3:

Scenario A: Traditional port energy system separate supply mode;

Scenario B: Port integrated energy system collaborative supply mode based on EH;

Scenario C: Port integrated energy system collaborative supply mode considering integrated demand response (IDR);

Scenario D: Port integrated energy system collaborative supply mode considering energy interconnection (EI);

Scenario E: Port integrated energy system collaborative supply mode considering both energy interconnection (EI) and integrated demand response (IDR).

(1) Comparative analysis of multi-port area IPES optimization results

The EH optimization configuration and annual planning cost results of each port area are shown in Tables 8.4 and 8.5.

Table 8.3 Scenario setting

Scenario	Traditional distribution	Integrated energy methods	Taking into account IDR	Multi-port coordination
A	√	–	–	–
B	–	√	–	–
C	–	–	√	–
D	–	–	–	√
E	–	√	√	√

Table 8.4 Planning results of different scenarios

Scenario	Port area	Volume/kw							
		CCHP	GB	PtG	AC	GS	Tie line1-2	Tie line1-3	Tie line2-3
A	Port-1	–	22,000	–	5350	–	–	–	–
	Port-2	–	21,000	–	8025	–			
	Port-3	–	16,000	–	8500	–			
B	Port-1	19,000	8000	7000	1050	2000	–	–	–
	Port-2	19,000	9000	12,500	3468	7000			
	Port-3	19,500	3000	0	3924	0			
C	Port-1	19,000	7000	7000	793	2000	–	–	–
	Port-2	19,000	8000	12,500	3093	7000			
	Port-3	19,500	3000	0	3018	0			
D	Port-1	19,500	8000	0	1050	0	0	5692	18,353
	Port-2	19,500	8000	0	3449	0			
	Port-3	19,500	13,000	7000	3924	0			
E	Port-1	19,000	7000	0	0	0	4294	7830	16,794
	Port-2	19,500	7000	0	2978	0			
	Port-3	19,000	11,000	0	3318	0			

Table 8.5 Various costs of different scenarios (in hundred thousand yuan)

Scenario	C_{inv}^{line}	C_{inv}	C_E	C_{mat}	C_{DR}	$C_{curt-wind}$	C_{tot}
A	–	64.32	5008.34	29.34	–	238.90	5340.90
B	–	293.65	3537.93	113.86	–	8.85	3954.29
C	–	290.60	3198.91	110.76	239.59	4.98	3844.83
D	5.34	296.16	3230.30	105.80	–	0.00	3632.31
E	3.28	286.72	2946.54	103.80	221.65	0.00	3558.99

1) Comparison of Scenarios A, B, and C

The comparison between Scenarios A, B, and C mainly explains that the multi-port areas adopt traditional individual energy system planning methods, IPES After planning methods, including IDR, are taken into account in the IPES planning, the differences in the operating costs, wind abandonment costs, and EHs optimal configuration of multi-port planning under different scenarios are analyzed. From the perspective of wind abandonment cost, the existence of conversions such as power-to-gas in scenarios B and C has improved the utilization rate of wind power, thereby greatly reducing the penalty cost of wind abandonment. If the wind abandonment costs in scenarios B and C are compared, it can be seen that IDR has a certain role in promoting the absorption of wind power in multi-ports. In addition to considering the cost of wind abandonment, other optimization results are essentially similar to the research content of Chap. 4, so they will not be repeated here. The following focuses on the comparison of scenarios D and E (i.e., multi-port collaboration) with the above scenarios.

2) Comparison of Scenario D and Scenario B

From Tables 8.4 and 8.5, it can be seen that the comprehensive energy planning method considering EI in Scenario D has reduced the redundant configuration of PtG and GS in Port 1 and Port 2, optimizing the configuration of multi-port EHs. At the same time, although Scenario D has increased the investment cost of power lines, its proportion of the total cost is only 0.15%, and the investment and operating costs have been greatly reduced, resulting in a total cost reduction of 8.14%. In addition, the wind abandonment cost in this scenario is zero, meaning all wind power in each port has been fully utilized or converted, demonstrating the significant advantage of EI in promoting cross-port wind power absorption.

3) Comparison of Scenario E and Scenario B

In Scenario E, IDR and EI are considered simultaneously for multi-port collaborative planning. Compared with Scenario B, the total cost has been reduced by 9.99%. From the perspective of investment cost and energy consumption, the cost reduction is more significant. In addition, the optimization results show that no PtG and GS equipment has been installed in each port, and the wind power output of each port has been completely absorbed.

4) Comprehensive Comparison of Optimization Results of Each Scenario

Through the mutual aid of energy interconnection between ports, the peak-shifting and peak-adjusting benefits between different ports can be better utilized, and the supply cost and EH equipment installation capacity can be reduced. Compared with traditional energy supply solutions, the IPES supply method based on EH (Scenario B) can greatly reduce the total planning cost (Scenario A). After considering IDR (Scenario C) and EI (Scenario D) separately, the total cost of IPES can be further reduced, while promoting the absorption of renewable energy. However, the effect of EI is better than IDR. In addition, if IDR and EI are considered simultaneously (Scenario E), the effects of the two can be superimposed, making the multi-port IPES planning more economical. Moreover, from Table 5.3, it can be seen that the line investment cost accounts for a very small proportion of the total cost in either Scenario D or Scenario E, which also explains from another perspective why EI can greatly reduce the planning operating cost of IPES.

(2) Analysis of Multi-Port IPES Operating Conditions

From 1:00 to 8:00, the output of Port 1 and Port 2 is abundant, but their daytime load is relatively low. In order to meet the higher electrical load demand in Port 3, the excess power is injected from EH1 and EH2 into the interconnected network and transmitted to EH3. At the same time, when EI still cannot meet the electrical load demand of Port 3, the remaining part will be supplied by purchasing electricity directly from the port distribution network.

From 9:00 to 22:00, the CCHP in each port EHs is nearly full, and IDR will offset part of the power demand. On the one hand, the excess power in EH1 and EH2 will be converted to cooling power through AC to meet the cooling load demand, on the other hand, it will be transmitted to EH3 through the interconnected power grid, showing the coupling and complementarity between various energies and the coordination and mutual aid between multiple EHs. From 23:00 to 24:00, the electricity price is at a low level, CCHP will be shut down, and the load demand will be met by wind power, grid power purchase, IDR. The needs are met collectively. Meanwhile, due to the reduction of load during the previous peak load period, a large amount of rebound load appears during this period.

Each port area EH's cooling load demand is provided by CCHP and AC. From 1:00 to 7:00, port areas 1 and 3 have no cooling load demand. During this period, the electricity price is lower, and the AC in EH2 serves as the main cooling power device. At 8:00, since the AC capacity in port area 1 is 0, its cooling load is met by CCHP, while port areas 2 and 3 use AC cooling. From 9:00 to 22:00, the port electricity price and cooling demand of each port area increase simultaneously, so CCHP is used to provide most of the cooling power, and AC is used as a backup cooling source when CCHP cannot fully meet the cooling demand. At the same time, due to the adjustability of the cooling load, IDR effectively reduces the peak demand for cooling load, achieves energy span transfer, and thus reduces the investment and operating costs of equipment.

The heat load demand in each port area EH is provided by CCHP and GB. From 1:00 to 8:00, most of the heat load demand in each port area is met by the GB in EH3. Among them, in port area 3 from 2:00 to 4:00, part of the heat load is supplied by CCHP, because CCHP generates electricity and heat at the same time, which has better economic benefits. From 9:00 to 22:00, CCHP provides most of the heat energy, and if it cannot meet the heat demand, GB serves as a backup heating source. Similarly, the heat load participates in IDR, playing a role in peak shaving and valley filling.

In summary, EI has achieved the coordinated scheduling of multi-port energy systems. On the one hand, through EHs' unified scheduling of equipment in each area, EI achieves optimal cooperation among multiple ports; on the other hand, EI cooperates with EHs to couple independent multi-energy loads in different ports, utilizing the complementarity of different load patterns, achieving interconnection and mutual aid among multiple ports and multiple energies, and further improving the economy of the overall IPES planning operation.

(3) Comparative analysis of wind power absorption capacity in multiple ports and multiple scenarios

1) Wind power absorption situation under different scenarios

To further illustrate the impact of IDR and EI on cross-port wind power absorption, after magnifying the wind power penetration rate to 1.5 times, the wind power utilization rate in each port area is analyzed under comprehensive energy supply scenarios B, C, and D, taking a typical summer day as an example, as shown in Fig. 8.7.

In port area 3, the hourly wind power utilization rate in each scenario has reached 100%, which is due to the comprehensive energy planning method adopted in each scenario. On the one hand, port area 3 has a large demand for multi-energy loads,

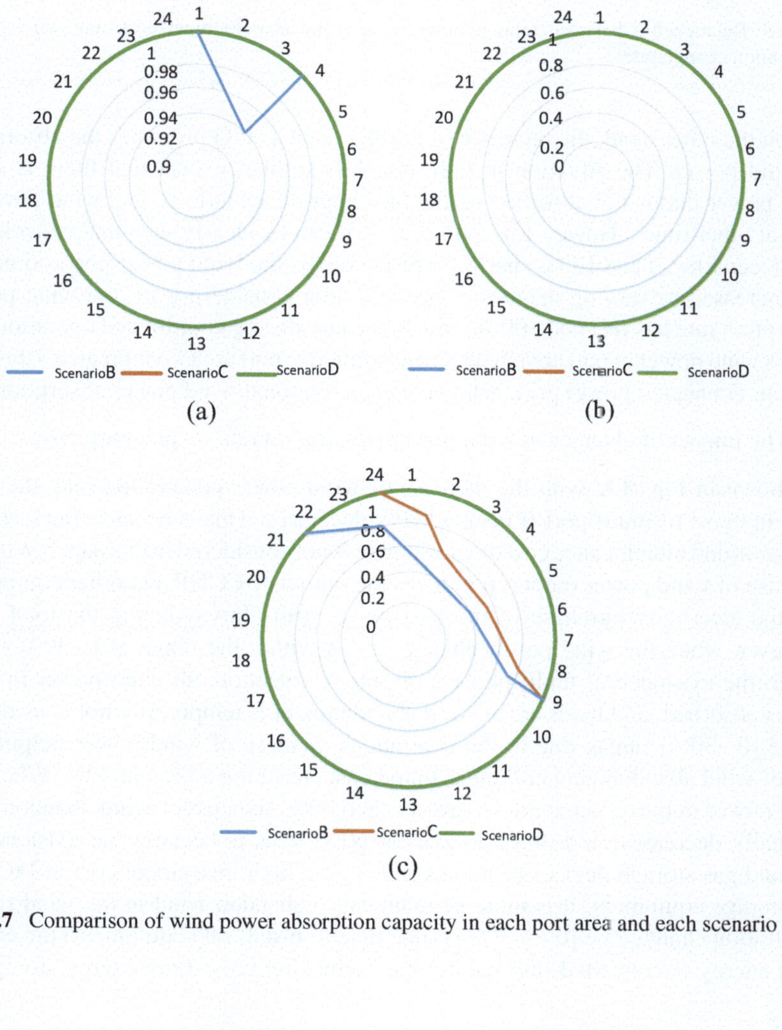

Fig. 8.7 Comparison of wind power absorption capacity in each port area and each scenario

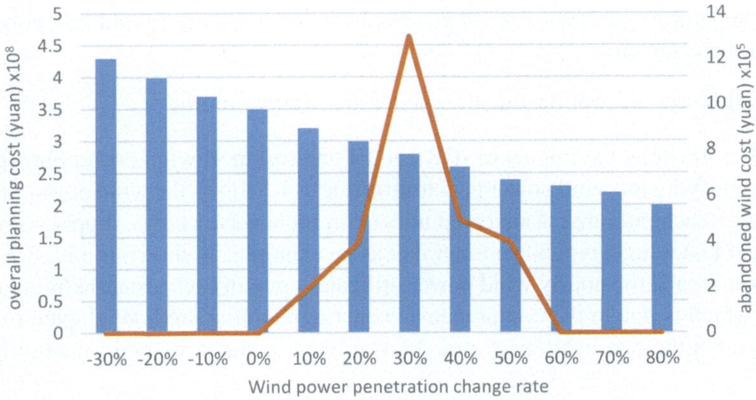

Fig. 8.8 Relationship between total planning cost, wind abandonment cost, and wind power penetration change rate

and on the other hand, the presence of devices such as PtG promotes the absorption of wind power. The situation in port area 1 is similar, except that there is some wind power that is not absorbed in the third hour of scenario B, and wind power is used at other times. However, in port area 2, it can be clearly seen that considering IDR (scenario C) and EI (scenario D) respectively, the wind power absorption rate has increased to varying degrees, especially after considering EI, the wind power absorption rate has reached 100%. This is because during coordinated operation, the excess wind power in port area 2 can be transmitted to port area 1 or port area 3 through the interconnected power grid, achieving cross-regional wind power absorption.

2) The impact of changes in wind power penetration rate on planning costs

As shown in Fig. 8.8, with the increase of wind power penetration rate, the total planning cost of multi-port IPES gradually decreases. This is because the installed operation and maintenance cost of wind power is not considered in this paper. With the increase of wind power output, it reduces the output of CCHP and other equipment and the electricity purchase of the port power grid, thus reducing the total cost. However, when the wind power change rate is within the range of [−30%−0%], due to the existence of multi-port energy interconnection, all wind power in each port is absorbed, and the issue of wind abandonment is temporarily not considered. In the [0−30%] range, due to the continuous increase of wind power output, the cost of wind abandonment continues to increase, reaching a peak at 30%. When the wind power output change rate is greater than 30%, the cost of wind abandonment gradually decreases, and drops to zero at 60%. This is because the existence of PtG and gas storage devices promotes (due to the high investment cost of PtG and gas storage equipment, it is more economical to abandon wind in the wind power penetration change rate [0%−30%] range than to install PtG equipment) the excess wind energy is converted into natural gas, achieving cross-time energy storage or utilization, thereby reducing the energy cost of natural gas, and further reducing the total planning cost of multi-port IPES.

(4) Analysis of the impact of different parameter changes on IPES configuration results

To further analyze the impact of different parameter changes on IPES configuration results, this section studies the changes in CCHP capacity and annual total planning cost in each EH when port energy prices and ship shore power usage behavior characteristics change respectively.

1) Energy price changes

The prices of natural gas/electricity in the port energy market often change, so it is necessary to analyze the impact of changes in natural gas/electricity prices in IPES optimization planning.

As shown in Figs. 8.9 and 8.10, the capacity of CCHP increases with the rise in electricity prices and decreases with the rise in natural gas prices [90%–110%]. However, due to the high investment cost of CCHP, these changes are not significant. When the natural gas price rises from 50 to 70%, the total cost changes the most (about 16%). At the same time, from the line chart in the figure, it can be seen that when the electricity price and gas price increase at the same rate, the total cost is more sensitive to the change in gas price. This is mainly because after considering the coupling and coordination between energy systems, natural gas has a high penetration rate in IPES, so the impact of gas price on total planning cost is higher than that of electricity price.

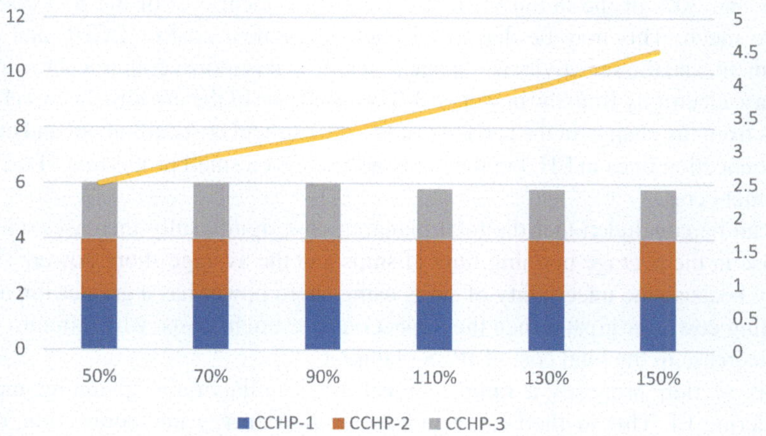

Fig. 8.9 Relationship between planned CCHP capacity and total planning cost in each port area and changes in natural gas prices

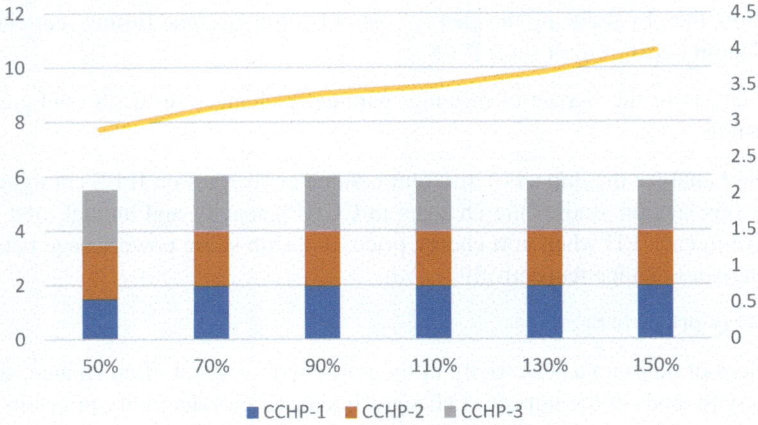

Fig. 8.10 Relationship between planned CCHP capacity and total planning cost in each port area and changes in electricity prices

2) Changes in key parameters of ship shore power

The behavior characteristics of ships using shore power have a large uncertainty, such as the length of port time and the size of shore power usage will affect the planning operation cost of the system. This section analyzes the impact of ship shore power usage on the planning cost of the IPES system by changing the mean values of these two parameters in the probability distribution function of ship shore power usage.

When the average port time and average shore power of ships change between −20% and 20% of the initial value, the total investment cost of the port does not change much. This may be due to the high investment cost of CCHP and other equipment, and the sensitivity to change is small, so it is more economical to directly purchase electricity from the power grid. The small part of the investment cost change comes from the change in the capacity of low-investment cost equipment and energy interconnection lines in EH, but they only account for a small proportion of the total investment cost.

It can be concluded that the total planning cost significantly increases with the increase in the average berthing time of ships and the average shore power. This is mainly because the uncertainty of ships using shore power has a greater impact on operating costs, far greater than the impact on investment costs, which in turn leads to an increase in the total cost of IPES planning.

This section proposes a multi-regional IPES collaborative planning method considering EI. This method can achieve inter-port energy interconnection, effectively solve problems such as mismatch of load peak and valley periods, staggered peak and valley of user cold and heat power loads, etc. Each port EH can coordinate output to avoid waste of unit capacity and achieve energy optimization scheduling from a macro-regional perspective. The conclusions of this chapter are as follows:

1) The case analysis shows that the comprehensive energy system planning method for multiple ports based on EI proposed in this chapter is feasible and effective. It can achieve multi-energy complementarity, alleviate the mismatch of load peak and valley periods in multiple ports, abandon new energy, improve energy utilization efficiency, and ultimately reduce the total planning cost of multiple ports by 9.99%.
2) By comparing EI and IDR, EI generates greater economic benefits than IDR; if both are considered in the model, their impact on reducing total costs can be superimposed, and the redundant configuration of PtG and GS equipment is reduced.
3) EI has realized the consumption of wind power across ports, breaking through the bottleneck of wind power consumption in a single port, and greatly improving the utilization rate of wind power. At the same time, as the penetration rate of wind power increases, the total planning cost of IPES gradually decreases, and due to the existence of PtG and GS, the cost of abandoning wind shows a process of first rising and then falling.
4) Sensitivity analysis shows that: if the energy prices in the market are changed, the CCHP capacity in multiple ports does not change much. At the same time, compared to changes in electricity prices, the total planning cost is more sensitive to changes in gas prices; in addition, the uncertainty of ships using shore power has a smaller impact on equipment investment costs, and a larger impact on operating costs. The increase in ship berthing time and shore power leads to an increase in the total planning cost of IPES.

References

Fang SZ, Zhao CH, Ding ZH et al (2023) Port integrated energy system for carbon neutrality (I): typical system structure and key issues. Proc Chinese Soc Electri Eng 43(1):114–135

Hary G, Ron VD (2010) A new method for assessing CO2 emissions from container terminals: a promising approach applied in Rotterdam. J Cleaner Prod 19(6)

Huang YW, Huang WT, Wei W et al (2022) Logistics-energy coordinated optimization scheduling method for large seaport integrated energy system. Proc Chinese Soc Electri Eng 42(17):6184–6196

Kanellos FD (2019) Multiagent-system-based operation scheduling of large Ports' power systems with emissions limitation. IEEE Syst J 13(2):1831–1840

Li Q (2010) Research on the indicator system of energy saving and emission reduction in Chinese ports. Dalian Maritime University

Song TI (2022) Research on port integrated energy system considering demand response. Nanjing, Southeast University

Tai NL, Wang XB, Huang WT et al (2022) Review of low-carbon technology for port integrated energy system. Power Syst Technol 46(10):3749–3764

Wang W (2018) Discussion on green port construction measures. China Water Transport (second Half Month) 18(09):123–124

Wang FL (2013) Evaluation and analysis of power quality and load operation characteristics of port power grid. Anhui University

Wang TS (2014) Research on the development of green ports in China. Dalian Maritime University

Yin L (2019) Practice and development thinking of smart port construction in China. Port Technology 8

Zhang JT, Song YJ (2017) Mathematical model and algorithm for the reefer mechanic scheduling problem at seaports. Discrete Dynamics in Nature and Society, pp 1–13

Zhao JX, Mi HN, Cheng HW et al (2021) Planning model and method for port integrated energy system considering shore power load elasticity. J Shanghai Jiaotong Univ (chin Ed) 55(12):1577–1585

Chapter 9
Port Cluster and Environmental Coordination Governance Strategy Based on Green Operation

Intermodal container transport has always been a mode of transport that our country strongly promotes. In 2020, the national port container rail-water combined transport volume was about 6.8 million TEU, an increase of 31.8% year-on-year. The China–Europe train ran a total of 12,400 trains, an increase of 50% year-on-year. In recent years, with the release of the national "dual carbon" target policy, intermodal container transport, a clean and efficient mode of transport, has become the main direction of transport.

9.1 Analysis of the Port Hinterland Container Intermodal Transport Network

Based on the characteristics of the actual port and hinterland container transport system, this section constructs a multi-level transport network that includes hinterland cities, inland ports, dry ports, and coastal ports, and involves road, rail, and waterway intermodal transport. See Fig. 9.1. The container flow direction of the transport network between the port and the hinterland usually includes: (a) The export goods of the hinterland cities are gathered to various coastal ports through this network; (b) The imported goods from the sea to the port are dispersed to various hinterland cities through this network.

9.1.1 Characteristics of the Port Hinterland Container Intermodal Transport Network

The port hinterland container intermodal transport network has the following characteristics in providing transport services:

B. Lu, *The Sustainable Development of Port Group*,
https://doi.org/10.1007/978-981-97-2378-2_9

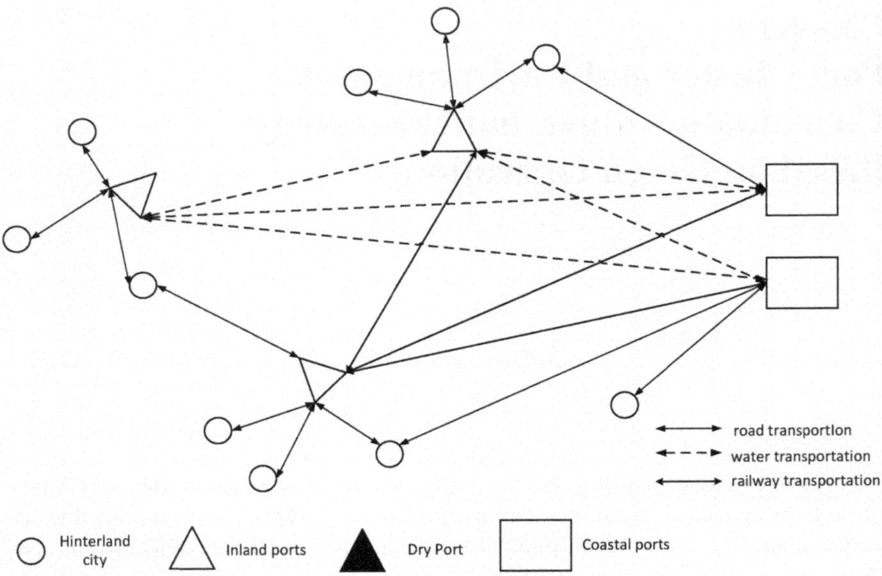

Fig. 9.1 Network diagram

(1) Inland port nodes and dry port nodes undertake the intermodal transfer function of inland goods, that is, the connection between different modes of transport can only be carried out at the intermodal transfer node; among them, there are container inland waterway transport routes between inland ports and coastal ports, and container railway transport trains between dry ports and coastal ports.
(2) This transport network also considers the goods transport channels between different intermodal nodes, that is, some different inland ports have opened waterway transport service routes, and some inland ports have railway port facilities and have opened railway transport trains with some inland dry ports, etc.
(3) Compared to inland cities, the demand for import and export of goods can be directly fulfilled through highway transportation routes with coastal ports on one hand, and on the other hand, it can be completed through nearby inland multimodal transit stations.
(4) An inland city can connect to multiple inland multimodal transit nodes, and there are limitations in container handling capabilities at river ports, dry ports, and coastal ports.

9.1.2 Modes of Goods Transportation Between Coastal Ports and Inland Cities

Figure 9.1 depicts the process of container goods transportation between coastal ports and inland cities through different modes of transportation such as highways, railways, waterways, etc. These modes of transportation can be summarized into the following three categories:

(1) Direct transportation between coastal ports and inland cities

When an inland city is close to a coastal port or there are no river ports or dry ports nearby, the demand for goods transportation generated by the city is often directly completed through highway transportation routes with coastal ports.

(2) One-time transit transportation via a river port or dry port

When there are river ports or dry ports near an inland city, the demand for container goods transportation generated by the city can choose to be completed through combined road-rail or road-water modes. It consists of a short-distance road haulage stage between the inland city and the nearby river port or dry port, and a long-distance river route transportation or container railway transportation stage between the river port or dry port and the coastal port.

This mode of transportation is often suitable for inland cities far from coastal ports. Compared with direct road transportation, this method allows the demand for inland container transportation to be completed in a more efficient, faster, and more economical way. This can also help attract more inland goods transportation demand to coastal ports.

(3) Two-time transit transportation via two different multimodal transit nodes

In the port hinterland transportation system, multiple transit transportation often exists in the transportation process between coastal ports and some inland cities further away. At this time, direct road transportation has shown high transportation costs, long transportation time, and low efficiency. Multiple transit transportation has achieved connectivity between different multimodal transit nodes, while also reducing transportation costs, improving efficiency, and helping to alleviate environmental pollution to some extent.

Taking the export direction as an example, the transportation demand generated by these distant inland cities, in addition to reaching the coastal ports through the above-mentioned combined road-rail or road-water one-time transit mode, may also first complete a consolidation transit at a nearby river port or dry port, then continue through river routes or railway transportation to reach the second multimodal transit node for the second consolidation of container goods, and finally reach the coastal port through the third stage of river routes or railway transportation. This mode of transportation ultimately presents as combined road-rail-water, road-water-water, road-rail-rail, and road-water-rail multimodal transportation. Moreover, in the port hinterland transportation system, considering that too many times of goods transit will reduce the efficiency of goods transportation and increase the cost of multiple loading and unloading transits (Saeedi et al. 2017), this chapter only considers one-time transit mode and two-time transit mode.

According to existing research on the optimization of multimodal transportation networks in inland transportation, most of them mainly target combined road-rail or road-water multimodal transportation modes (Bouchery et al. 2015), few studies have simultaneously considered the complex multimodal transportation modes among road, water, and rail, especially in inland areas where waterway and railway transportation systems coexist (Caris et al. 2014). For example, in the hinterland of the Yangtze River Economic Belt in our country, some cities' long-distance transportation to coastal ports, in addition to road-rail or road-water intermodal transportation, may also involve complex multimodal transportation modes such as road-rail-water, road-water-rail, road-rail-rail, and road-water-water. Therefore, the multimodal transportation network structure of the port hinterland described in Fig. 9.1 can better conform to the actual situation of the container transportation system in the port hinterland.

9.2 Considering the Impact Factors of Port Hinterland Container Transportation Network Modeling with Carbon Emissions

The research object of this chapter—the multimodal transportation network of port hinterland containers, is an important part of the whole container transportation chain. Its network rationality and service level directly affect the transportation efficiency of international container transportation in the inland stage. Therefore, based on the multimodal transportation network of port hinterland containers constructed in Sect. 9.1, combined with the "dual carbon" policy and the requirements of green development, this chapter proposes that the main factors affecting the optimization modeling of this network include: transportation cost, transportation time, carbon emissions, network transportation supply capacity, fluctuations in transportation demand of hinterland cities, carbon emission reduction policies and regulations, etc. (Song 2017).

9.2.1 Cost Factors

Container transportation between ports and hinterlands is mainly completed through direct transportation modes, one-time transfer modes, and two-time transfer modes. Its transportation cost includes the transportation cost on the route between each node and the transfer and storage cost at the multimodal transfer node. In addition to these, there is also the carbon tax that needs to be paid due to the carbon dioxide produced during transportation and transfer at the transfer node.

(1) Transportation cost on the route

Different transportation methods have different transportation characteristics. The transportation cost between each node is related to the transportation distance, unit transportation cost, and transportation volume of the selected transportation method, i.e., the cost of goods transportation = transportation distance × unit transportation cost × transportation volume.

(2) Transfer cost at the multimodal transfer node

The transfer cost at the transfer node refers to the operation cost incurred when the goods are converted between different transportation methods at this node. This part of the cost is mainly related to the container transfer volume at this transfer node and the unit operation cost of transferring between different transportation methods. That is, the cost of goods transfer = unit transfer cost × transportation volume. When goods are transferred multiple times, the shipper needs to pay multiple transfer fees, so the impact of transfer costs on the total logistics cost cannot be ignored.

(3) Storage cost at the multimodal transfer node

For the containers integrated into the multimodal transfer node, they may need to be temporarily stored in the inland river port yard or railway yard due to waiting for the waterway route or railway train that is dispatched at a fixed time, thus generating a certain storage cost. This part of the cost is closely related to the storage volume of containers and the unit storage cost.

(4) Carbon tax to be paid

Carbon tax refers to the tax levied on carbon dioxide emissions. It is for environmental protection For the purpose of slowing down global warming, it is hoped to reduce carbon dioxide emissions. Throughout the process of multimodal transport, goods will generate a certain amount of carbon dioxide during transportation in different modes of transport, as well as during loading, unloading, and transshipment at transfer nodes. The cost of this part is mainly related to the amount of carbon dioxide produced and the tax rate of unit carbon emissions.

9.2.2 *Time Factor*

The time of container transportation between the port and the hinterland includes the transportation time on the route between each node and the transshipment and storage time at the multimodal transport transfer node.

(1) Transportation time on the route

Different modes of transport, due to different speeds, result in vastly different times spent to complete transportation tasks. The transportation time of goods on the transportation route is closely related to the transportation distance and speed of the adopted mode of transport. Transportation time affects the service level of transportation, which in turn affects the shipper's choice of route.

(2) Transshipment time at the multimodal transport transfer node

The transshipment time at the transfer node refers to the time consumed when the goods are transferred between different modes of transport at this node. The length of this time is mainly related to the efficiency of container loading and unloading and operation at this transfer node. When goods are transshipped multiple times, the consumed transshipment time will also be more. Therefore, the impact of transshipment time cannot be ignored.

(3) Storage time at the multimodal transport transfer node

Similarly, for containers integrated into the multimodal transport transfer node, they may have a certain waiting period due to waiting for fixed-time shipping water routes or railway trains. During this period, container goods need to be stored in the inland river port yard or railway freight yard, so there is also the consumption of this part of the storage time during transshipment.

9.2.3 Carbon Emission Factor

Considering the "dual carbon" policy and green development requirements, one of the negative externalities of greenhouse effect caused by transportation activities—CO_2 emissions, is also an important consideration in the shipper's transportation decision. Different modes of transport have different carbon emission characteristics. The CO_2 emissions from container transportation between the port and the hinterland are mainly composed of CO_2 emissions generated during the transportation process on each segment of the route and CO_2 emissions generated during the transshipment and other logistics processes at the multimodal transport transfer node.

(1) Carbon emissions from transportation on the route

The size of transportation carbon emissions is related to the carbon emission factor of different modes of transport on this route, transportation distance, and freight volume. Among them, the estimation of the carbon emission factor of the mode of transport is closely related to various factors such as the transportation scale of different regions, transportation distance, adopted transportation tools, and the type and quantity of fuel used. Under the demand for low-carbon development, the impact of carbon emissions generated by transportation activities cannot be ignored.

(2) Carbon emissions from transshipment at the multimodal transport transfer node

The carbon emissions from transshipment at the transfer node refer to the operation emissions generated when the goods are transferred between different modes of transport at this node. This part of CO_2 emissions is mainly related to the container transshipment volume at this transfer node and the unit operation emission volume. When goods are transshipped multiple times, the emissions generated by transshipment will also increase.

9.2.4 Transport Supply Capacity of the Network

The supply capacity of the port hinterland container multimodal transport network mainly includes the supply capacity of the transport channel, the operation capacity of the multimodal transport transfer node, and the capacity limit of the coastal port. The specific analysis of these influencing factors is as follows:

(1) Supply capacity of the transport channel

The various modes of transportation connecting the hinterland cities with the inland multimodal transport hubs, the inland multimodal transport hubs with the coastal ports, and the hinterland cities with the coastal ports form the transport corridors. On the one hand, different modes of transportation have certain capacity limitations, such as the size of the capacity of container truck transportation, railway container train transportation, and container shipping routes, which are related to the scale of the transport company, the number and frequency of trains, the number and frequency of shipping routes, and even sudden situations caused by weather or accidents leading to road congestion or shipping route stoppages. On the other hand, in the aforementioned transport corridors, the number, size, and loading capacity of the transport tools used, including container trucks, railway container trains, and waterway container ships, will also affect the supply capacity of the transport corridors.

(2) Operational capacity of inland multimodal transport hubs

Inland multimodal transport hubs are responsible for the transshipment and distribution of inland container goods. The operational capacity of inland river ports and dry ports handling container transshipment is influenced by factors such as their type, construction scale, infrastructure conditions, and processing efficiency, which limit their container handling capacity within a certain range. (Wang 2016) In the hinterland container multimodal transport network, the operational capacity limitations of these hubs will subsequently affect the decision-making content of the transport network. For example, when the operational capacity of a certain hub tends to be saturated, the original optimal choice of transshipping a portion of the freight volume at this hub has to change the transport mode and choose other sub-optimal transport routes, thereby further changing the transport scheme of the entire hinterland container multimodal transport network.

(3) Coastal port conditions, shipping capacity, and operational capacity

The conditions of coastal ports include hardware conditions and soft environment. The former refers to the geographical location of the port, container berths, channels, container yards, loading and unloading equipment, etc., while the latter refers to the development positioning of the port, the support of the port for logistics, finance, law, and information industries, etc. Good conditions of the coastal port itself can attract more goods from the hinterland and further increase the throughput of the port. Similarly, the number of shipping routes, shipping capacity, and container operation capacity owned by the coastal port will also affect its attractiveness to hinterland goods.

9.2.5 *Fluctuation Factors of Transportation Demand in Hinterland Cities*

Due to the influence of various factors such as the economic development of the city, industrial layout, economic and legal policies related to container transportation, and the seasonal characteristics of goods generation, the generation of container transportation demand in hinterland cities has become fluctuating, and this fluctuation may be long-term. In the hinterland container multimodal transport network, the fluctuation of transport demand will also have a certain impact on the choice of multimodal transport routes in the network. For example, within a certain planning period, the fluctuation of city demand may lead to the need for multiple frequencies of design and planning for the hinterland transport network, making the network transport scheme results unstable for a period of time and losing its guiding significance for reality. Therefore, its network design needs to consider in advance the fluctuation of transport demand and its possible impact, to prevent the occurrence of repeated design and planning in the short term and the inability of transport mode capacity to keep up, affecting the choice of goods routes.

9.2.6 *Carbon Emission Policy and Regulatory Factors*

Some policies and regulations introduced by national or local governments for the transportation industry, such as the government's positioning on the development of inland multimodal transport infrastructure, regulations on the operation and management of coastal ports, technical upgrades of transportation tools, and policies and regulations on their energy consumption control, will directly or indirectly affect the planning and development direction of the hinterland container transport system of ports (Zhang et al. 2016). For example, in promoting emission reduction, national or local governments may take the following measures:

(1) Multimodal transport policy subsidies

Due to the multiple advantages of multimodal transport in improving transport efficiency, reducing energy consumption, and reducing carbon emissions compared to road transport, policymakers will increase policy support for multimodal transport. For example, policy subsidies for multimodal freight projects, financial policy subsidies for shippers or transport companies using multimodal transfer stations and multimodal transport services, etc. These measures can compensate for part of the cost of companies engaged in multimodal transport, encouraging them to actively carry out multimodal transport business.

The measures of multimodal transport policy subsidies not only increase the enthusiasm of shippers and transport companies to use multimodal transport, but also make a certain contribution to CO_2 emission reduction and environmental protection.

(2) Implementation of carbon emission reduction policies

The requirements of low-carbon economic development will promote the government to adopt some administrative management or economic policy means to control the emission of carbon dioxide, such as carbon tax, carbon emission trading, carbon emission quota, and mixed emission reduction means such as carbon tax-carbon emission quota, carbon emission trading-carbon emission quota.

The use of different carbon reduction policies will have different impacts on the design of the hinterland container multimodal transport network of ports; the implementation of the same carbon reduction policy, but different constraint intensities will also result in different transport network design results. Therefore, the design of the hinterland container multimodal transport network of ports needs to conduct a longitudinal comparative analysis of the network result changes under different policy implementations, and also needs to conduct a horizontal comparative analysis of the impact of different policy implementation levels on network results under the implementation of a single policy. Only in this way can we more comprehensively understand the changes in the results of the hinterland container multimodal transport network after the introduction of carbon reduction policies, and can we have a deeper understanding of the impact of considering carbon emission factors on this transport network.

In summary, in the hinterland container multimodal transport network of ports, in addition to considering the total cost of goods transport, total time, and low-carbon development requirements, the transport supply capacity of the network, the fluctuation of transport demand in hinterland cities, and carbon emission policies and regulations will also affect the transport decisions of shippers. These factors are also aspects that need to be considered.

9.3 Factors Influencing Low-Carbon Optimization Decision of Hinterland Container Transport Network

Low-carbon transport emphasizes taking various measures to reduce the CO_2 emissions of transport activities (Lu 2009). When the hinterland container multimodal transport network of ports faces the requirements and tasks of low-carbon development, the selection of multimodal transfer stations in the network, the selection of outbound ports, and the choice of single-mode transport or multimodal transport routes and network cargo flow schemes will be affected. The specific analysis is as follows:

9.3.1 *Impact on the Choice of Transport Mode and Route*

The CO_2 emissions from transport activities mainly come from the energy consumption of transport tools. Among several modes of transport, rail and pipeline transport produce the lowest carbon emissions and are the most environmentally friendly, while water, road, and air transport's CO_2 Emissions are relatively high. Therefore, under the demand for low-carbon development, railway transportation will become increasingly important in the hinterland container transportation system of ports. When facing the demand for environmentally friendly development, the choice of transportation methods and routes (direct transportation, one-time transfer transportation or two-time transfer transportation) by the cargo owners in the multimodal transport network of hinterland containers will no longer only consider the lowest total transportation cost or the shortest total transportation time, but also need to consider the least environmental impact.

For example, if the government implements policy tools such as carbon tax or carbon emission trading, in addition to the transportation cost for completing the cargo transportation, the cargo owner also needs to bear the additional external cost of carbon emissions. The increase in this external cost will force the cargo owner to change the road transportation method and choose a lower carbon transportation mode such as multimodal transportation. Moreover, the degree of this impact depends on how much external cost is generated. The external cost generated by road transportation is often larger because its CO_2 emissions are higher than those of waterway and railway transportation.

Secondly, if the multimodal transport network of hinterland containers faces a total limit on CO_2 emissions, that is, there is a constraint on the total emissions of the network, the choice of transportation routes by the cargo owners in the network will change due to the impact of carbon restrictions. The cargo owner needs to choose a transportation route with lower CO_2 emissions, complete the cargo transportation task without exceeding the emission limit, but this may increase the transportation cost. Therefore, in this case, there will be a conflict between emissions and cost objectives, and the cargo owner needs to balance between the two and choose a more compromise solution according to the actual situation.

9.3.2 The Impact on the Choice of Transfer Nodes in Multimodal Transportation

The multimodal transport network of hinterland containers constructed in this chapter includes inland waterway ports and inland dry ports at the same time on the transfer nodes of multimodal transportation, and considers one-time transfer and two-time transfer modes at the same time. Different transfer nodes and different transfer modes have resulted in differences in transportation costs and transportation emissions. Therefore, the requirements of low-carbon transportation development will not only affect the cargo owner's impact on the choice of transfer nodes in multimodal transportation, but also affect the cargo owner's choice of these two transfer modes.

As analyzed in the previous section, railway transportation will be increasingly advocated under the requirements of low-carbon development and plays an important role in emission reduction. Inland dry ports will also need to attract more attention and importance in providing rail-road transfer services. In the actual situation in our country, the proportion of railway freight in the hinterland transportation system of ports is still not high. With the increasing emphasis on environmental protection by the state, the investment in the construction of inland dry port infrastructure and the improvement of transfer operation capabilities and efficiency still need to be strongly supported.

9.3.3 The Impact on the Distribution of Cargo Flow in the Network

In the multimodal transport network of hinterland containers, under the capacity limit of transfer nodes and the capacity limit of transportation methods, the container cargo flow between hinterland cities and coastal ports will choose the most reasonable (usually the lowest cost), the second reasonable, the third reasonable and so on. However, under the requirements of low-carbon transportation, these cargo flow structures may change, because cargo owners are increasingly inclined to choose more low-carbon and environmentally friendly transportation modes, not just the lowest cost transportation plan. This will lead to an increase in the cargo flow on the transportation routes with carbon emission reduction advantages in the multimodal transport network of hinterland containers. Therefore, the requirements for the development of low-carbon transportation will also bring about changes in the final distribution of cargo flow in the transportation network.

Nevertheless, the extent to which low-carbon measures or requirements affect the distribution of cargo flow in the network also depends on the intensity of the implementation of low-carbon measures. It is possible that a small intensity of low-carbon measures could have an impact on the distribution of transport network flow, and it is also possible that only a sufficiently large intensity of low-carbon measures could cause changes in the distribution of transport network flow. These are issues worth exploring in depth in the multimodal transport network of hinterland container ports, and specific analyses need to be carried out according to actual conditions.

9.4 Analysis of Low-Carbon Network Optimization Issues in Multimodal Transport of Hinterland Container Ports

Inland containers not only generate logistics costs in transportation activities, which are economically referred to as "internal costs" or "private costs", but also produce carbon dioxide emissions due to fuel use, impacting the ecological environment. This impact is one manifestation of transport externalities.

The starting point of this section's research is to consider carbon dioxide emission factors. Therefore, this section will analyze the optimization issues of the multimodal transport network of hinterland container ports from three different low-carbon perspectives, as follows:

9.4.1 Optimization Issues Considering the Impact of Carbon Tax and Carbon Trading Policies

Levying a carbon tax is an economic means to internalize CO_2 emissions as a cost, and the size of this cost is directly related to the amount of carbon emissions from transportation activities (Zhou et al. 2012). The implementation of a carbon tax policy will increase the operating costs of emitters, forcing transport companies to choose lower-carbon transport modes, thus forming a constraint. In the optimization of the multimodal transport network of hinterland container ports, the implementation of the carbon tax constraint mechanism will affect the choice of transport modes and routes, transit nodes, and the choice of goods arriving at the port, thereby changing the decision optimization of the entire transport network. On the other hand, different levels of carbon tax constraints may also lead to different optimization results for the transport network.

The carbon emissions trading mechanism allows the purchase and sale of CO_2 emission rights, enabling emitters to gain additional income or incur additional transaction costs, thereby achieving control of carbon emissions. This method also internalizes the externalities of CO_2 emissions from transport activities as a cost, and its implementation will also affect the choice of transport modes and routes, transit nodes, and the choice of goods arriving at the port in the optimization decision of the multimodal transport network of hinterland container ports (Chen et al. 2017). Moreover, in this mechanism, the most important thing is how to set CO_2 emission quotas and analyze the impact of different carbon trading price levels on the optimization decision of the multimodal transport network of hinterland container ports, to find the appropriate network emission quota and carbon trading price, and promote the multimodal transport network of hinterland container ports to achieve both cost savings and emission reduction benefits.

Therefore, by introducing the perspectives of carbon tax and carbon trading, two carbon reduction policy tools, carbon emission externalities can be internalized as costs through different economic means, and this part of the cost is also referred to as "external cost". This type of optimization problem needs to construct the lowest optimization model of total social cost, which includes private costs and external costs, according to different carbon reduction policies, and focus on the impact of the introduction of external costs on the optimization of the multimodal transport network of hinterland container ports.

9.4.2 Optimization Issues Considering the Uncertainty of Carbon Quota Constraints

Carbon emission quota constraints are a means of directly limiting the total amount of carbon emissions, stipulating that they cannot exceed a certain amount. To control greenhouse gas emissions, the United Nations Framework Convention on Climate Change, the Kyoto Protocol, and the Paris Agreement were successively reached. They have become legally binding climate agreements internationally, and humanity is jointly undertaking obligations to address climate change and carrying out practical actions to reduce emissions. Under the framework of the Paris Agreement, China proposed that by 2030, the carbon dioxide emissions per unit of GDP will decrease by 60–65% compared to 2005, and decrease by 18% compared to 2015, taking a series of measures to effectively control the total carbon emissions. Many local governments in our country have also formulated requirements to meet the government's total carbon reduction requirements by setting the maximum carbon emissions in their region.

Currently, carbon emission quota constraints are mainly used in the research of national or regional macro carbon emission control. For example, the world allocates emission reduction tasks to various countries to reduce carbon dioxide emissions; our country further assigns emission reduction targets to various provinces and cities to set quotas for carbon emissions in various provincial and city regions. Setting an appropriate carbon emission quota according to the actual situation is very important. If the carbon emission quota set by the government is too high, this constraint may not have a significant effect on environmental improvement and emission reduction; but if the carbon quota is set too low, it may restrict the normal production and management activities of the emission subject and is not conducive to its development, and the cost paid for emission reduction is too high (Li et al. 2019). There is currently no universal calculation method for the allocation of carbon emission quotas. The proposed methods mainly include allocation according to the population of the country or region, allocation according to the land area, and allocation according to GDP, but the carbon emission situations of different industries vary greatly, and these methods are not suitable for setting carbon emission quotas in the transportation industry.

In the multimodal transport system of the port hinterland container, different modes of transport need to achieve certain emission reduction tasks; due to incomplete historical data or biased estimation methods, the setting of carbon emission quotas for each mode of transport may have incomplete data or biased judgment problems, which makes the carbon emission quota (i.e., the allowable CO2 emissions on each mode of transport) have fuzzy characteristics (Tsao et al. 2018). Therefore, although the optimization problem considering carbon quota constraints is also an optimization problem under the influence of carbon emission policies, it is different from the previous optimization problem focusing on economic means such as carbon tax and carbon trading policies, and is an optimization modeling perspective focusing on total carbon emission control. This type of optimization problem needs to set carbon emission quotas, especially the modeling and analysis of the fuzziness of carbon quotas for each mode of transport.

9.4.3 Dual-Objective Optimization Problem Considering Carbon Emission Targets and Demand Uncertainty

Different from the above two types of network optimization problems from the perspective of carbon policy impact, the analysis of CO_2 emissions (i.e., environmental goals) and cost (i.e., economic goals) dual-objective optimization modeling is the third type of optimization problem related to low-carbon port hinterland container multimodal transport network studied in this paper. This type of optimization problem directly considers carbon emission indicators as the goal, focusing on the analysis of the trade-off relationship between multiple goals (Yuan et al. 2020).

In multi-objective optimization problems, each sub-goal is usually contradictory and mutually influential. Decision-makers need to coordinate and compromise between different goals to make each sub-goal as optimal as possible. An effective way to solve multi-objective optimization problems is based on the concept of non-dominated solutions, Pareto Optimality, and the set of optimal solutions obtained is Pareto optimal solutions, and the surface formed by the optimal solutions in space is Pareto. In the frontier aspect, the solution obtained by this method is not unique, but a set or series of Pareto optimal solutions.

Therefore, the optimization problem of the intermodal container transportation network in the hinterland considering cost and emission dual-objective modeling focuses on treating carbon emissions as an independent optimization goal, rather than transforming it into cost through economic means; moreover, the trade-off relationship between economic goals and environmental goals is the key research content of this type of optimization problem.

References

Bouchery Y, Fransoo J, Cost (2015) Carbon emissions and modal shift in intermodal network design decisions. Int J Prod Econ 164:388–399

Caris A, Limbourg S, Macharis C et al (2014) Integration of inland waterway transport in the intermodal supply chain: a taxonomy of research challenges. J Transp Geogr 41:126–136

Chen et al. (2017) Supply chain decision optimization model based on fuzzy theory under carbon tax. Comput Integrat Manufact Syst 23(04):860–866

. Li et al. (2019) Optimization of green intermodal transportation path under mixed uncertainty. Transport Syst Eng Inform 19(04):13–19

Lu HP (2009) Ways to achieve urban green transportation. Urban Transport 7(06):23–27

Song et al. (2017) A review of research on integrated transportation network planning. World Sci Technol Res Developm 39(02):182–188

Saeedi H, Wiegmans B, Behdani B et al (2017) European intermodal freight transport network: market structure analysis. J Transp Geogr 60:141–154

Tsao Y, Thanh V, Lu J et al (2018) Designing sustainable supply chain networks under uncertain environments: fuzzy multi-objective programming. J Clean Prod 174 1550–1565

Wang X (2016) Stochastic resource allocation for containerized cargo transportation networks when capacities are uncertain. Transport Res Part e: Logist Transport Rev 93:334–357

Yuan et al. (2020) Research on robust optimization of fuzzy intermodal transportation path based on interval under low carbon policy. Indust Eng Managem 1–13

Zhang et al. (2016). Research on the design of mixed carbon reduction system. China Populat Resour Environ 26(12):39–45

Zhou et al. (2012) A literature review on the economics of carbon emissions and carbon reduction. Econ Rev (05):144–151

Chapter 10
Case Analysis of Environmental Coordinated Development of Domestic and Foreign Port Clusters

10.1 Case of Environmental Coordinated Development of Foreign Port Clusters

Ports are the hubs connecting water and land transportation, they are important nodes supporting the construction of China's "Belt and Road", and they are also important carriers for promoting the high-quality and rapid development of China's economy. General Secretary Xi Jinping has made important speeches on port industry issues many times. In January 2019, when inspecting Tianjin, General Secretary Xi Jinping proposed that to develop the economy and strengthen the country, transportation, especially maritime transportation, must be strengthened first. We must aim far and strive to build world-class smart ports and green ports to better serve the coordinated development of Beijing, Tianjin and Hebei and the construction of the "Belt and Road".

Since the reform and opening up, China's port industry has achieved remarkable achievements that have attracted worldwide attention. The number of shipping routes and service levels are among the top in the world, strongly supporting the rapid development of China's economy. However, at the same time, environmental issues related to ports have gradually emerged. Ports are key energy-consuming units, and the sulfur dioxide, nitrogen oxides, and particulates produced during port operations have become important sources of air pollutants in port cities. Under the "dual carbon" background, in response to the instructions of General Secretary Xi Jinping, actively building green ecological ports and strengthening pollution prevention and energy conservation in the port area have become a common consensus in the industry.

B. Lu, *The Sustainable Development of Port Group*,
https://doi.org/10.1007/978-981-97-2378-2_10

10.1.1 American Port Group Environmental Coordinated Development Case

In response to the global energy crisis and environmental degradation, many foreign ports have also contributed advanced experiences in the construction of green ports. For example, the Port of Los Angeles-Long Beach implemented the "San Pedro Bay Clean Air Action Plan, which formulated a series of economic subsidies for energy conversion of port ships, container trucks, loading and unloading equipment, etc.; The New York-New Jersey Port implemented the "Clean Air Measures and Port Air Management Plan", promoting channel dredging, equipment electrification, ship engine modification, and vehicle replacement, etc.

Located in southern California, the Port of Long Beach is an important deep-water container port in the United States, located at the hub leading to Asia. In 2005, the Port of Long Beach began to promote the construction of green ports on a large scale, proposing the Green Port Policy (GPP) to guide the sustainable development of the Port of Long Beach; In 2007, the Port of Long Beach implemented the "Clean Air Action Plan", taking measures to require ships to reduce their speed to effectively reduce fuel consumption and exhaust emissions, and use shore power equipment to reduce carbon emissions during ship berthing. Starting in 2008, the Long Beach Port Authority and the Los Angeles Port Authority cooperated to launch the famous "Clean Truck Program", aiming to gradually eliminate 16,000 heavily polluting trucks and reduce the total emissions of truck pollutants by more than 80% within 5 years (Zhang 2023). On August 23, 2021, the Port of Long Beach announced the completion of the world's first all-electric, zero-emission mega terminal, paving a new way for a more environmentally friendly freight business. The Port of Long Beach reflects the concept of green development in all stages of terminal design, development, and operation: construction waste recycling; active development of new "green" technologies; use of available environmentally friendly materials and supplies on the market; reducing port losses through waste, energy and water resource protection plans, encouraging the use of new energy such as solar, wind, and hydro power to replace traditional energy. As one of the advocates of green ports, the many measures taken by the Port of Long Beach in the construction of green ports have not only promoted the sustainable development of the Port of Long Beach, but also provided a reference for the construction of green ports in countries around the world.

Since implementing the Clean Air Action Plan with the Port of Long Beach in 2008, the Port of Los Angeles has been publicly recognized as a global leader in environmental management. The Clean Air Action Plan was updated in 2017, with the goal of reducing port greenhouse gas emissions by 40% from 1990 levels by 2030; by 2050, port greenhouse gas emissions will be reduced by 80% from 1990 levels. To this end, the Clean Air Action Plan proposes four major strategies: clean vehicle and equipment technology and fuel, freight infrastructure investment and planning, supply chain efficiency, and energy resource planning.

(1) Establish a pollutant emission inventory and create a green, low-carbon port. The Port of Los Angeles has developed a scientifically sound inventory of air

pollutant emissions, regularly publishes air quality reports and emission reduction assessment reports, and has developed individual plans for pollution sources such as ships, trucks, trains, port operation vessels, and cargo handling equipment. The main measures include: encouraging ships to use shore power, implementing ship speed reduction programs and green ship incentive programs, etc., to reduce the carbon emissions of ships; implementing clean truck programs, encouraging fleets to use zero-emission and near-zero-emission trucks through technology and rate measures; cooperating with railway operators and technology developers to develop zero-emission and near-zero-emission locomotive technologies; installing scrubbers on port operation vessels, or requiring the use of clean fuels for port operations; promoting the electrification of cargo handling equipment to reduce port carbon emissions.

(2) Combining standards and technology to improve the efficiency of the entire supply chain. Standards guide port terminals to save energy and reduce emissions, for example: implementing the Leading Energy and Environmental Design certification program, encouraging terminals to focus on sustainable environmental development, and achieving energy conservation and emission reduction; using the 80 performance indicators of the container terminal quality index evaluation system to provide a basis for improving terminal operating efficiency. In addition, digital information technology is used to improve the efficiency of the entire supply chain, for example: developing port information portal websites, connecting the data flow between cargo owners, shipping companies, customs, etc., improving the predictability and reliability of the supply chain; integrating port truck appointment systems, reducing the operation time for trucks entering the port area to 1 h.

(3) Extensively carry out cooperation, become a leader in port emission reduction, widely seek technical cooperation, initiate technology advancement programs between ports, regulatory agencies, and industry partners, provide funding for promising emission reduction technology research and development and demonstration applications, funding focuses include ship zero emissions, cargo handling equipment zero emissions, truck zero emissions, and freight efficiency improvement technologies, actively seek federal and state government funds, policy support, incorporate port emission reduction strategies into federal or state regulations, avoid cargo loss to other ports with lower environmental requirements. Carry out international cooperation with other stakeholders, cooperate with international port organizations such as the C40 Green Port Forum, the World Port Sustainable Development Program of the International Port Association, the Pacific Rim Port Clean Air Collaboration Organization, the World Port Climate Action Plan, etc., jointly respond to the global climate change crisis and share advanced technologies.

The Port of New York and New Jersey, located on the east coast of the United States and adjacent to the Atlantic Ocean, is primarily composed of the Port of New York and the Port of New Jersey. It spans 9.55 km north to south and 12.43 km east to west. The port complex has favorable natural conditions and good water depth.

The two ports are located in the Hudson River Basin, specifically in New York Bay and Newark Bay. Due to their geographical proximity and overlapping economic hinterlands, the ports, which belong to the states of New York and New Jersey respectively, have historically experienced conflicts of interest leading to clashes between the police forces of the two states. However, they gradually realized the harm caused by their opposition and the importance of resource integration. In 1921, the local governments where the two ports are located jointly decided to establish a joint organization similar to a port authority to manage the two ports. This organization has both governmental and public characteristics and is responsible for the unified management of 25 transportation facilities within a radius of 25 miles centered on the Statue of Liberty. The unique aspect of the cooperation model of the New York-New Jersey port complex is the joint establishment of an interstate port authority, which manages and plans the two ports across state lines. The main responsibilities of the New York-New Jersey Port Authority are reflected in the following aspects: (1) joint construction and maintenance of the two port docks; (2) unified construction and maintenance of public infrastructure in the two ports; (3) sharing of information systems between the two ports; (4) joint construction of a port security system; (5) formulation of port development plans. In 2017, the New York-New Jersey Port Authority proposed the "30-Year Major Port Plan," emphasizing the development of "community and industry." In the field of economic construction, it proposed maximizing economic density; in the field of infrastructure, it proposed meeting future trend changes in infrastructure construction; in the field of environmental protection, it proposed supporting environmental quality and reducing production impact; in terms of land use, it proposed optimizing land use and promoting functional diversification; in terms of community integration, it proposed becoming a strong employer and improving positive impact.

The New York-New Jersey port complex mainly carries out green port construction from three aspects: first, establishing a port environmental management system (EMS). International standard norms are introduced as guiding standards to assess the significant impact of various port operations on the environment, making it easy to find potential hazards and provide timely warnings and interventions. Second, improving the port logistics system. The construction of an efficient railway shunting system has greatly reduced the air pollution caused by truck queues entering the port area; the government's environmental protection department controls the fuel of transport tools such as trucks in the port area to ensure that the port's exhaust emissions meet the standards. Third, incentivizing ships to reduce emissions for a fee. A policy was once introduced to incentivize ocean-going fleets to use low-sulfur fuel, requiring all ocean-going ships docking at the New York-New Jersey port docks to participate in cooperation, strictly monitor port pollution facilities through the implementation of air quality improvement strategic plans, and promote the "green port" process.

10.1.2 Case Study of Environmental Coordinated Development of Japanese Port Group

The Tokyo Bay port group in Japan occupies an excellent geographical location. The two peninsulas of Miura and Boso form a bag-shaped bay, creating a superb port environment with deep water and small waves. The bag-shaped mouth is 8 km wide, and the bag-shaped length is 80 km. Along the two wings of Tokyo Bay, it extends 175 km end to end, with densely populated ports and factories, forming Japan's largest port industrial area and city group. This famous port group includes six major ports: Tokyo, Yokohama, Chiba, Kawasaki, Yokosuka, and Kimitsu.

The Tokyo Bay Green Port Cluster in Japan is an early large-scale port in Japan to put forward the concept of green development, which advocates a series of environmentally friendly construction to improve the port landscape. In terms of green space planning, Tokyo Port has implemented green planning measures through the Port Authority, carried out large-scale green space layout in port parks, and ensured the green and reasonable use of land. At the same time, in terms of port environmental construction, Tokyo Port pays great attention to the construction of coastline scenic areas and coastal landscapes, is committed to the restoration of beaches, and the greening construction of ports. Currently, Tokyo Port has completed the construction of green parks, and at the same time has begun to carry out land reclamation operations, and strengthen the construction of marine environment, with the greening construction and protection of near-sea landscape facilities such as marine parks, natural landscapes, and wildlife habitats as the focus of work, embarking on a sustainable green development path.

Ports in Japan attach great importance to green port logistics, and government agencies and the public monitor environmental protection vigorously, and each port submits and formulates environmental protection and emergency response plans every year. Each port actively adopts advanced and practical environmental protection prevention and control technology to solve the pollution problems involved in port logistics activities. For dust pollution during port logistics operations, two basic dust removal methods, dry and wet, are adopted to prevent and control advanced dust control methods. In the prevention and control of air pollution, the electrification of the port is realized. In terms of wastewater treatment technology, the port area has a collection of closed rainwater, production and living sewage catchment system, and all kinds of port wastewater can be used for recycling (mainly for sprinkling) or discharged in compliance with the standards after treatment at the treatment site. In terms of marine and river oil spill emergency response technology, remote sensing technology is applied in practice (Wang and Li 2023).

10.1.3 Case Study of Environmental Coordinated Development of Singapore Port Cluster

The Port of Singapore is located along the southern coast of Singapore Island, to the southeast of the Malacca Strait to the west, and to the north of the Singapore Strait to the south. It is the largest transshipment port in the Asia–Pacific region and one of the largest container ports in the world. Also known as Lion City, Star State or Star Island. The port controls the shipping route between the Pacific and Indian Oceans, and its strategic position is very important. It has been an international trade port since the thirteenth century and has now developed into a world-renowned transshipment port. The Port of Singapore is the national center of politics, economy, culture, and transportation.

The Port of Singapore, a leading global hub port and international maritime hub, has been certified five times under the Asia Pacific Green Port Award Scheme. The goal of the Port of Singapore is: by 2030, carbon emissions will be at least 60% lower than in 2005; by 2050, achieve zero carbon emissions. To this end, the Maritime and Port Authority of Singapore launched the Green Shipping Program in 2011, and in 2022 released the "Singapore Maritime Decarbonization Blueprint: Towards 2050", taking actions in seven major areas including port terminals, ships, ship fuel oil and infrastructure, classification societies, international organizations, R&D and talent training, and low-carbon awareness (Tang 2015).

(1) Embrace automation and digitization to build a green, low-carbon dock. The Port of Singapore uses cleaner energy and automation and digitization technologies to build a future low-carbon port. In addition to fully promoting the electrification of port equipment, requiring port auxiliary operation ships to gradually adopt clean energy, developing green buildings, expanding photovoltaic power generation and other common measures, it also actively takes the following measures: Implementing a digital port single window to shorten the operation time of ships and vehicles in the port to reduce exhaust emissions; using intelligent fleet systems to optimize vehicle routes, avoid sudden braking and excessive acceleration, thereby achieving eco-driving; using port smart grids and smart energy systems to monitor the energy use efficiency of port equipment, and choosing the optimal energy combination according to different power demands, thereby optimizing energy efficiency.

(2) Gather talents and technology projects to become a global low-carbon maritime R&D hub. The Maritime and Port Authority of Singapore has committed to providing $80 million in funding support for decarbonization R&D activities in the maritime industry, fostering about 20 technology projects and training over 100 researchers, scientists, and engineers within 5 years, and setting up a venture capital fund to provide financial support. In addition, Singapore's higher education institutions and research centers enrich the maritime innovation ecosystem by promoting cutting-edge R&D, for example: The Maritime Energy and Sustainable Development Center of Excellence at Nanyang Technological University conducts globally leading research on sustainable maritime

energy transformation; American Bureau of Shipping, DNV GL, and others have set up knowledge centers in Singapore to promote decarbonization in shipping. Industry participants of different identities carry out R&D cooperation in multiple fields such as electrification, sustainable energy, emission reduction measures, and future marine fuels.

(3) Build a green financing ecosystem and develop a green maritime financial center. Relying on more than 20 ship financing banks in Singapore and the Singapore Exchange, the Maritime and Port Authority of Singapore and the Monetary Authority of Singapore have taken a series of measures to attract shipping companies to choose Singapore as the preferred place for green financing: The Maritime and Port Authority of Singapore and the Singapore Exchange have formulated carbon emission accounting and reporting guidelines to standardize carbon emission accounting methods, thereby supporting shipping companies to obtain green financing; The Monetary Authority of Singapore has launched a green and sustainable development-related loan subsidy program to pay for the consulting fees incurred by shipping companies when applying for green loans; cooperate with technology R&D companies to establish a green shipping data ecosystem to help investors measure the carbon emission reduction capabilities of shipping companies; cooperate with banks to develop a carbon trading market, explore carbon trading in the maritime field, and build Singapore into a leading green maritime financial center in Asia and even the world through extensive cooperation.

(4) Explore the commercial feasibility of green shipping technology with industrialization thinking From the perspective of the entire industry chain, opinions from the Port of Singapore Authority and other port operators, research institutions such as the National University of Singapore, and some local consortiums are widely sought. Through pilot projects, the technical feasibility, operation, and commercial feasibility of new energy in port terminals, domestic port ships, and Singapore-registered container ships are tested, and national standards for shore power, port ships, etc. are formulated. Relying on the development foundation of Singapore's high-end shipping such as financial services, it is planned to establish the Singapore Maritime Financial Hub Port.

10.1.4 Case Study of Environmental Coordinated Development of Dutch Port Cluster

The Port of Rotterdam is located at the mouth of the Rhine and Meuse rivers, bordered by the North Sea to the west and tracing the Rhine and Danube rivers to the east, leading to the Black Sea. Known as the "Gateway to Europe," the port covers an area of about 100 km^2, with a total dock length of 42 km. The deepest part of the port is 22 m, accommodating super oil tankers of up to 545,000 tons. After World War II, with the revival of the European economy and the establishment of the common market, the Port of Rotterdam rapidly developed due to its advantageous geographical location. In 1961, its throughput exceeded that of the Port of New York (180 million tons), making it the world's largest port, a position it has maintained ever since. The Port of Rotterdam receives over 30,000 ships annually, with over 120,000 inland vessels heading to various European countries. The port houses the world's most advanced ECT container terminal, with an annual transport volume of 6.4 million standard containers, ranking fourth in the world. The Port of Rotterdam employs over 70,000 people, accounting for 1.4% of the national employment population. Its freight volume accounts for 78% of the country's total, with a total output value of 12 billion Dutch guilders, approximately 2.5% of the Netherlands' GDP. The most significant feature of the Port of Rotterdam's services is its integrated storage, transportation, and sales. Through bonded warehouses and distribution centers, it adds value to goods and then delivers them to destinations in the Netherlands and Europe via various transport routes such as roads, railways, rivers, air, and sea.

The Port of Rotterdam's port prospect plan for 2020 is based on the following six concepts: (1) A multifunctional and integrated port, providing ample space and facilities for loading, unloading, unpacking, processing, and transportation, as well as other businesses such as industry, logistics, shipping, and trade; (2) A sustainable and innovative port; (3) An intelligent port; (4) A fast and safe port; (5) An attractive port; (6) A clean and environmentally friendly port. Corresponding to these are the following five key tasks: (1) Constructing the "Maasvlakte 2" in the west (land reclamation from the North Sea), for containers, chemical industry, and other new processing industries. The "Maasvlakte 2" will become a high-standard sustainable development area with multimodal transport infrastructure; (2) Transforming the eastern port area into a mixed area (urban port) for port offices, residences, and work. After the completion of "Maasvlakte 2" in 2010, the overseas container operations will be moved to "Maasvlakte 2," making it possible to transform this area into a mixed port and urban area; (3) Making the most efficient use of the port area, establishing multi-purpose areas and innovative smart buildings, centralizing offices, and sharing facilities; (4) Addressing regional and national bottlenecks in infrastructure capacity and quality, especially the A15 highway, while making the most efficient use of existing facilities and encouraging the use of barges and railways; (5) Developing attractive residential areas on the north bank of the Maas River using creative environmental methods, further increasing industrial activities on the south bank, while each residential and activity area on the north bank has its specific traffic routes to the south bank.

As the largest port in Europe, the Port of Rotterdam joined the European Eco-Port Certification System in 2004, becoming a long-term member of the system and has passed the port environmental review certification of the system five times. The goal of the Port of Rotterdam is to reduce carbon dioxide emissions by approximately 55% by 2030 and to achieve carbon neutrality by 2050. To this end, the Port of Rotterdam Authority has developed a sustainable development strategy with efficiency and infrastructure, new energy systems, new raw material and fuel systems, and sustainable logistics chains as its four pillars. At the same time, the Port of Rotterdam, in conjunction with government agencies, business sectors, non-governmental organizations, and academia, has jointly developed a "three-step sustainable development" strategy. In terms of energy conservation and emission reduction, the Port of Rotterdam is gradually changing coal-fired power plants to gas-fired power plants, reducing carbon emissions in the refining sector (Lin et al. 2020).

(1) Aggregating innovative enterprises to develop a circular economy. The Port of Rotterdam Authority introduces innovative enterprises that are conducive to the development of the circular economy in the port industrial park and cooperates to develop new circular value chains. For example, the Porthos project plans to capture carbon dioxide emitted from port docks, store it in depleted natural gas fields in the North Sea, lay a large number of pipelines and cables, and use the residual heat of carbon dioxide to heat residential and commercial buildings near the port area; attracting recycling enterprises to gather near the Port of Rotterdam, guiding well-known enterprises such as Nestle and Shell to invest in the construction of biofuel factories, creating the largest biofuel industry cluster in Europe.
(2) Investing in hydrogen energy construction to create a European hydrogen hub. With the support of the Dutch National Hydrogen Energy Plan, the Port of Rotterdam Authority cooperates with public and private sectors to propose a hydrogen energy development roadmap, envisioning the Port of Rotterdam as an international hub and important energy port for hydrogen import, production, distribution, and use in Northwest Europe in the future, and has received government support. The Port of Rotterdam has designated 24 km^2 of port area to build the largest green hydrogen factory in Europe, and gathers enterprises that research and manufacture hydrogen fuel cells and hydrogen fuel trucks, laying out the entire industry chain of transportation, production, manufacturing, and application, thereby making the Port of Rotterdam a European hydrogen hub. The project plans to store 2.5 million tons of carbon dioxide each year. In July 2020, the Port of Rotterdam joined the Hydrogen Energy Council and is cooperating with various partners to achieve the production of green hydrogen, and introduce a large hydrogen network in the port complex, making the Port of Rotterdam an international hub for hydrogen production, import, application, and transportation to other countries in Northwest Europe, promoting the energy transformation of the Port of Rotterdam and achieving low-carbon green development.
(3) Protecting port ecology to achieve harmony with nature. The Port of Rotterdam Authority incorporates the development of nature and biodiversity into the port development vision for 2030, thereby protecting the unique ecosystem of the Port of Rotterdam. The relevant content includes: considering the balance between plants, animals, and human activities with nature as the design concept during the development and infrastructure construction of the port area; carrying out ecological management and monitoring in undeveloped areas of the port area to prevent species invasion; encouraging the construction of green roofs to provide shelter for local species.

10.1.5 Case Study of Environmental Coordinated Development of Australian Ports

Sydney Port, facing the Pacific Ocean to the east and the Parramatta River 20 km to the west, is surrounded by the most prosperous areas of Sydney on both sides. It is mainly composed of the Sydney Port District and the Botany Port District and is located in NSW (New South Wales, Australia. Located in the eastern part of New South Wales, Sydney Harbour is a state-owned port managed by the government. The ownership and operational rights are separated, with the government owning the port and the operators having the right to operate under the management of the port authority. Sydney Harbour is one of the earliest ports to adopt the concept of green development, implementing the "Green Port Guidelines" in seven areas: water quality, air quality, noise control, biodiversity, waste management, hazardous goods management, environmental education and training. Australia has established comprehensive environmental protection laws and regulations, which have had a positive constraining effect on Sydney Harbour. Under each environmental issue, the Sydney Port Company has set goals to reduce environmental impact, a set of evaluation standards, and proposed feasible measures that each organization needs to consider. Each measure is also evaluated based on its potential environmental benefits, ease of implementation, and overall return on investment. These guidelines use general definitions for these evaluations. The guidelines also determine the methods needed to achieve Green Star certification, which is a common rating system for the design, construction, and operation of buildings in Australia. The complete guidebook includes a checklist that must be submitted to the Sydney Port Company by any organization applying for a new development project or new activity. The checklist requires each applicant to explain whether each issue has been resolved, and how they plan to resolve it or why it has not been resolved. In terms of water quality, various port activities can cause port water pollution, such as the discharge of ship production/living wastewater, the discharge of land rainwater/wastewater, ship/shore oil spill accidents, etc. Sydney Harbour fully recognizes the threats these activities pose to the port water environment and has taken countermeasures. For ship production/living wastewater, Sydney Harbour has actively taken various measures to strengthen ship management. For example, leak-proof technology is used during the refueling process of ships; professionals are dispatched to supervise the handling of hazardous goods (oil, gas, and chemicals, etc.) on-site. For land rainwater/wastewater, Sydney Harbour has installed rainwater collection and treatment devices. The treated rainwater can meet Australian drinking water standards and is then used for garden irrigation and bathroom flushing, saving up to 45% of water. In 2003, Sydney Harbour installed three such devices in its Botany Bay area and later promoted them throughout the port. For sudden accidents such as ship/shore oil spills, Sydney Harbour has formed an advanced emergency team that holds at least three emergency drills each year. From 2007 to 2012, Sydney Harbour had very high environmental requirements and legally issued hundreds of environmental pollution fines, reporting more than 10 cases related to port pollution. Raising employees' environmental awareness is an important aspect of building a green port. In recent years, nearly 500 people in Sydney Harbour have participated in environmental professional training, with a total of more than 3000 h of study, covering a wide range, and basically every employee has participated in the training. After years of effort and active cooperation with the government and the community, the construction of a green port is not just an individual action of the port, but requires the participation of multiple parties including the government and the community. Sydney Harbour actively cooperates with the government, for example, in implementing relevant transportation regulations, quarantine regulations, hazardous goods management regulations, etc.

In addition, Sydney Harbour also actively cooperates with the community. For example, it funds community education, supports the construction of the Sydney Maritime Museum, etc. Sydney Harbour has been very successful in the construction of green ports and has become a model for other countries to learn from.

10.2 Case Study of Environmental Coordinated Development of Port Groups in China

Chinese ports are important hub nodes and strategic resources that connect dual cycles and serve the new development pattern. Like strings of glowing pearls, they are embedded along the long coastline and riverbanks, playing exemplary roles in utilizing the land, connecting the world, and pioneering the future.

In terms of green and low-carbon development of port clusters, Chinese ports are on par with ports in developed countries worldwide. Since the twenty-first century, especially since the 18th National Congress of the Communist Party of China, the green and low-carbon development of ports has continuously strengthened in aspects such as the transformation of development concepts, the perfection of policy systems, the formulation of technical standards, the application of technological innovation, and the demonstration and leadership of leading port enterprises, achieving positive results. As of May this year, 53 port enterprises (container and specialized bulk cargo terminals), represented by Yangshan Phase IV Container Terminal and Guoneng Huanghua Coal Terminal, have been awarded the title of "China Green Port" (Zhang 2018). Chinese ports are generally on par with ports in developed countries worldwide in terms of green and low-carbon development, and lead in some aspects, making a Chinese contribution to addressing global climate change with practical actions.

In terms of coordinated development of port clusters, it is based on the reasonable layout, division of labor, and functional positioning among internal ports. The good development status of a single port cannot guarantee a good development situation after port integration. The process of port integration needs to maximize the overall interests of the entire system. Port integration is not to eliminate competition between ports. On the contrary, competition and cooperation between ports are equally important. Competition is an effective way for the market economy to optimize resource allocation, a driving force to improve port services, and a way for superior enterprises to expand the market. While strengthening cooperation between ports, it is necessary to maintain a fair and reasonable competition mechanism between ports, and strengthen cooperation between ports based on competition. Strengthening cooperation between ports can share information resources, jointly handle environmental and safety issues, and each port can maximize regional overall benefits by assisting each other according to their competitive advantages.

10.2.1 Bohai Bay Port Cluster Environmental Coordinated Development Case

Considering natural element endowments, several large seaports have been built in the three provinces and one city around the Bohai Bay, playing an important role as shipping hubs. As we all know, the Bohai Sea is an inland sea of China, a semi-closed sea with poor hydrodynamics. It is estimated that the shortest circulation period of the entire Bohai Sea water is 40 years. Under the "dual carbon" background, the construction of green ports bears a heavy responsibility.

The following will take Tianjin Port, Huanghua Port, and Caofeidian Port in the Bohai Bay port cluster as examples to explore the new direction of port green and low-carbon construction.

1. Tianjin Port

On October 17, 2021, the C-section intelligent container terminal in the Beijiang Port Area of Tianjin Port, which was built in 21 months, officially went into operation. This is the world's first "smart zero-carbon" terminal, providing a model for the intelligent upgrade and low-carbon development of world ports in a new mode.

Since 2019, Tianjin Port has gradually overcome the automation upgrade of the entire yard rail bridge, the scaled operation of unmanned electric tractor fleets, and the full-process automation upgrade of traditional container terminals, exploring the Chinese solution for traditional port automation construction. The C-section intelligent container terminal is a 200,000 ton container terminal, which can meet the operation of the world's largest container ships, with a designed annual throughput of 2.5 million TEUs (Fig. 10.1).

This dock connects key dock equipment such as yard cranes and shore cranes through the pioneering "Intelligent Horizontal Transport System", achieving real-time interaction of all production element information. Based on AI technology, it automatically derives the optimal loading and unloading plan and commands each device, improving efficiency by about 20% compared to traditional docks.

Tianjin Port actively promotes green transportation and increases the development and construction of green energy. The successfully grid-connected intelligent green energy system of the C-section dock in the Beijiang Port Area is the first "wind-light-storage-load integration" intelligent green energy project in China's ports. It has achieved 100% self-supply of green electricity and zero carbon emissions throughout the process. Two 4.5 MW wind turbines and a photovoltaic system with a total

Fig. 10.1 Intelligent container terminal of C-section in Beijiang Port Area of Tianjin Port

installed capacity of 1.43 MW operate on the grid, creating a green electricity supply system for the C-section dock, saving about 7340 tons of standard coal each year and reducing carbon dioxide emissions by over 20,000 tons.

Not only that, in recent years, Tianjin Port has actively adjusted its transportation structure, promoted the green transportation mode of "full load in, full load out" for ore and coal, and built a "road to railway + bulk to container" dual demonstration port. As an important coal unloading port in northern China, the coal dock of Tianjin Port now realizes coal railway port transportation, greatly reducing exhaust emissions from transport vehicles and dust pollution.

The clean energy horizontal transport fleet composed of electric intelligent horizontal transport robots, unmanned electric tractors, electric tractors, and hydrogen fuel cell tractors has been put into production and operation in Tianjin Port. Compared with fuel tractors of the same capacity, each machine reduces fuel consumption by 50 kg per hundred kilometers and reduces carbon emissions by 155 kg. The fleet reduces fuel consumption by 279 tons and carbon emissions by 865 tons in one month, achieving zero carbon emissions throughout the loading and unloading process at the C-section dock in the Beijiang Port Area. During the "Fourteenth Five-Year Plan" period, Tianjin Port will also vigorously promote the construction of zero-carbon port areas and zero-carbon ports, increase the development and construction of green energy, and focus on the construction of breakwater centralized wind power and distributed wind power and photovoltaic power generation systems in the port area, with an estimated increase in green energy installed capacity of nearly 500 MW.

In terms of coordinated development: As the maritime gateway to Beijing-Tianjin-Hebei and the three northern regions, Tianjin Port is the nearest seaport to Xiong'an New Area and an important node of the "Belt and Road". Tianjin Port places its development in the overall situation of coordinated development of Beijing-Tianjin-Hebei, fully enhances its radiation driving ability, and helps the high-quality development of the inland hinterland economy. Based on the advantage of being an important node of the "Belt and Road", Tianjin Port currently has increased its container routes with ports in countries along the "Belt and Road" from more than 30 in 2019 to more than 50, trading with more than 800 ports in over 200 countries and regions, of which trade goods with ports along the "Belt and Road" account for more than 60%. With the support of port units, Tianjin Port strives to optimize the customs clearance process, vigorously promote the construction of a single window for port container business and the Tianjin "Customs Port Collection and Distribution Port Intelligence Platform". Currently, the shortest time for Tianjin Port to pick up imported containers is only 1.5 h, and exported goods can be loaded and exported as soon as they arrive at the port, effectively improving operational efficiency and reducing logistics costs for import and export enterprises.

2. Huanghua Port

In August 1986, Huanghua Port was built and put into operation, mainly exporting commodities such as bituminous coal, petroleum coke, and coke, and importing goods including iron ore, coking coal, zinc ore, manganese ore, bituminous coal, and seawater desalination equipment. Due to the complex dust generation mechanism, multiple and dispersed dust generation links in the coal port, coupled with many industry pollution control difficulties such as water sprinkling restrictions in the northern winter, there was a lot of coal dust and wastewater at that time. Decades have passed, and the people of Huanghua Port have reclaimed land from the sea, dug sand to build the port, replaced planting soil, raised the ground, controlled alkali return, and selected salt-tolerant plants… After arduous struggles, tremendous changes have taken place here. This traditional coal port, once covered in dust on sunny days and mud on rainy days, has transformed into a garden-style intelligent port.

On the dome of the west coast of Bohai Bay, the sea breeze is blowing in the coal port area of Huanghua Port in Cangzhou, Hebei. Coal transport trains from northern Shanxi arrive at the port one after another, and the long carriages are towed to the first stop of the port: the car dumper room. The huge "O"-shaped rotor of the four-flip car dumper opens its arms, flips 4 carriages at a time, and can flip the carriage and the track as a whole about 160° in 20 s. As the coal pours down into the underground bunker, fine water mist sprays out from both sides of the car dumper, quickly suppressing the rising coal dust. In just a few seconds, 320 tons of fine coal are unloaded, and the outside of the work area remains as clean as before.

"Once the carriage flips, the coal dust flies into the sky." In the past, the car dumper room was a major polluter at the coal port. Now, the application of new technology has wrapped the coal dust that should have been flying in the air with micron-sized fine water mist, effectively suppressing the generation of pollution. There are 4 large car dumpers in the room, each unloading about 8000 tons of coal per hour on average, and more than 100 million tons per year, keeping the car dumper room clean at all times.

As a major coal port, dust pollution is a fundamental problem hindering the development of the port. How to solve this problem? Huanghua Port has its own way: relying on intelligence, it has built a full-process dust suppression system.

On the basis of laying a firm foundation for the basic operation process of the port, Huanghua Port has pushed the port in the direction of intelligence by building the port's big data platform, online business hall, intelligent production platform and other informatization projects, which has effectively improved the quality and efficiency of port loading and unloading and injected new vitality into the construction of the comprehensive big port of Huanghua Port.

Huanghua Port takes adherence to green port construction as the key direction of port transformation and upgrading, strengthens port pollution prevention and control, and solidly pushes forward the prevention and control of port and ship pollution. It implements clean production and improves the cleanliness level of bulk cargo operation; implements clean and low-carbon energy use system, and promotes the use of clean energy in port operation machinery and transportation vehicles; promotes the transformation of shore power facilities of constructed wharves, and synchronizes the design and construction of shore-based power supply facilities of new wharf projects to improve the efficiency of shore power use; and improves the convergence and collaboration of the collection, reception, transfer and disposal of pollutants from ships between ships, ports and cities. Recently, all 19 berths of Huanghua Port coal port area which have been put into operation have completed the installation of shore power, marking that the port area has completed the pilot task of the Ministry of Transportation and Communications in advance, and has taken the lead in realizing the full coverage of the comprehensive layout of high-voltage and low-voltage shore power of the wharf in China. Huanghua Port continuously increases investment in software and hardware, establishes and improves environmental protection mechanisms, and actively creates a "green port". The port has realized dust suppression in the whole process of coal loading and unloading through environmental protection projects such as yard windbreak network, ballast water recycling, dry mist dust removal and water sprinkling renovation of overturning machine, and has established an ecological governance system covering the whole port area by applying a variety of means to manage coal-containing sewage.

In terms of synergistic development: Hebei Province has put forward the strategic plan of developing towards the sea and building strength towards the sea, and has set the goal of "accelerating the construction of a coastal economic powerhouse" for Cangzhou City. In order to achieve greater results in coastal economic development, Cangzhou City promotes the integrated development of port, industry and city, taking port to bring production, promoting city with production, port-city integration, industry-city co-development, and promotes the high-quality integrated development of port, industry and city, accelerates the transformation and upgrading of Huanghua Port, builds a modernized and comprehensive port, and strives to build a model city with coastal characteristics.

Huanghua Port accelerates the construction of modern comprehensive service port and international trade port, opens up a convenient channel for Xiong'an New Area to go out to the sea, and pushes the port's transportation function to transform into a hub port for two-way radiation, multimodal transportation integration and regional cooperative development on sea and land. Deepen the docking with Shanghai Port and Ningbo Port, strive to open up more direct container and foreign trade routes, improve the port function and transportation system, and implement major transportation projects such as the Shihheng Cangang Intercity Railway and Quangang and Handang. Especially after the completion of the Huanghua port collection and transportation system project, it will realize the Canggang Railway and Shuo Huang Railway, Hand Huang Railway connecting through, and together they will form an efficient and low-cost logistics corridor for coal, iron ore, bauxite, non-ferrous ores and other bulk bulk cargoes to the north of Shandong, south of Hebei, Shanxi, north of Shanxi, Inner Mongolia, etc., and realize the port cargoes' "public to railway" and "bulk to collection". "Bulk to collect", strengthen the sea-railway intermodal transportation, improve port functions, and become a powerful support to promote the transformation and upgrading of ports.

Once there is a breakthrough, the energy of science and technology innovation will burst out. Belt machine belt washing device, stacking machine boom sprinkling technology, coal powder cake making process, site cleaning automation …… a series of scientific and technological environmental protection achievements such as spring and endless, and ultimately realize the port drive regional economic green low-carbon development, and scientific and technological innovation to form a positive virtuous cycle.

3. Caofeidian Port

Caofeidian Port, as a key port in China's "Northern Coal Transportation to the South", undertakes the important task of maintaining national energy supply. Every day, a large amount of coal, iron ore, LNG and other bulk commodities "ashore" here, making it an important energy and raw materials port in the north of China.

The site of Caofeidian Port Area is a new industrial base created by sand-blowing and reclamation, which has changed the living environment of marine fish to a certain extent. Therefore, Huaneng Caofeidian Port Co., Ltd. has launched a comprehensive fishery ecological restoration and stocking program, actively docking with local fishery authorities to select economic species suitable for the aquatic environment of Caofeidian waters. Through strict bidding, the company selects high-quality seedling suppliers, adopts artificial propagation, and carries out offshore stocking before closing the sea every year to reduce man-made fishing, which effectively ensures the survival rate of the seedling. At the same time, relevant departments are invited to strengthen the supervision of stocking, both to ensure the quantity and quality of stocking, and to prevent the invasion of foreign organisms and genetic pollution, so as to ensure that the stocking meets the requirements of environmental protection and to improve the effect of stocking.

Not only to restore marine ecology, but also to manage the shoreline environment. In order to turn the busy quay shoreline into an oasis, Huaneng Caofeidian Port Co., Ltd. has leveled the land, improved the soil quality, and planted saline-resistant vegetation on a large scale. Through such measures, Huaneng Caofeidian Port not only achieves energy saving and emission reduction, creates a green and intelligent port, but also realizes production efficiency and service enhancement.

In Caofeidian Port of Guotou, with the full linkage operation of key projects of production intelligence such as starting unmanned, production management system and intelligent scheduling system, the advanced production technology has really brought into play the comprehensive performance including environmental protection. Among them, in the construction of the intelligent terminal, the intelligent monitoring and perception system can monitor data such as dust, wind speed, wind direction, temperature and humidity, cargo status, etc. in the harbor area, so as to grasp the environmental data in real time, strengthen the all-weather climate monitoring and provide decision-making support for the environmental protection of the harbor area and the continuous production in bad weather. Meanwhile, the intelligent eco-operation platform, based on the concept of "integrated" management and control, combines the water content measurement with the dust removal system, adjusts the strategy of water sprinkling and dust removal in real time, associates the environmental protection equipment with the operation status of the production equipment, and carries out the closed-loop management of the environmental protection equipment based on the information on environment, coal quality, and production, which realizes centralized and intelligent management of environmental protection equipment of the whole company under the complex working conditions, and improves the environmental protection of the port and the production of goods. It can realize the centralized intelligent management of environmental protection equipment of the whole company under complex working conditions and enhance the port's environmental protection response capability.

Not only that, in Huaneng Caofeidian Port Co., Ltd, the world's largest coal terminal unloading capacity of the overturning machine supporting the use of advanced dry mist dust suppression system, according to the characteristics of the coal and moisture content, precise sprinkler dust suppression, receiving and unloading of 10,000 tons of trains in just one hour to complete, and does not cause any dust pollution to the environment. At the same time, the belt conveyor is synchronized with the dry mist dust suppression system, which combines the flow rate of the belt scales and the coal dust characteristics to reasonably spray the coal loaded on the belt, realizing no dust and pollution in the belt transfer link, and no exceeding of the water content of the incoming coal. The yard adopts advanced multi-level intelligent dust suppression system, together with the fully enclosed dust net, constituting a multi-dimensional dust management system, realizing multi-point sprinkling, accurate spraying, timely and effective dust suppression. The first shore power project of Bohai Rim Coal Terminal, which is constructed and put into operation by adopting the national standard technology, realizes zero fuel consumption, zero emission and zero noise of the ships docking in port, which can reduce the pollutant emission of the ships during the berthing period and improve the environmental quality of the port, and has great social benefits.

10.2.2 Case of Coordinated Environmental Development of the Yangtze River Delta Port Group

In recent years, the Yangtze River Delta port cluster has been adhering to the requirements of the "Green Port Construction Action", integrating green concepts throughout the entire process of port planning, design, construction, maintenance, operation, and management. With a priority on ecology and green development, it has been promoting the greening of the golden waterway. Efforts have been made to strengthen regional joint prevention and control, implementing multiple strategies in port facility construction, shore power, comprehensive dust control, clean energy, and new energy promotion. This has optimized energy consumption structure, saved and recycled resources, strengthened port pollution prevention, promoted ecological restoration and landscape construction, innovated green transportation organization methods, and improved green port energy-saving and environmental protection management capabilities. Further measures have been implemented to control ship emissions, accelerate the promotion and application of shore power facilities, promote the application of LNG-powered inland vessels, increase the use of clean energy for non-road mobile machinery in the port area, and comprehensively implement the standardized reception and disposal of pollutants from ports and ships. They are actively responding to new requirements in the field of international shipping and port environmental protection.

The coordinated development of the Yangtze River Delta port cluster is a necessary measure to respond to new environmental situations. At the national level, the integration of the Yangtze River Delta has been elevated to a national strategy, bringing new development opportunities for the Yangtze River Delta port cluster, and also putting forward new and higher requirements. Specifically, the coordinated development of the Yangtze River Delta port cluster should be based on the national strategic height. At the regional level, with the deepening of regional development integration, cluster-style port development has become the main development trend. Specifically, the coordinated development of port clusters has become an important trend in the development of shipping in many countries; port clusters and city clusters mutually rely on and promote each other; the coordinated development of the Yangtze River Delta port cluster has become the key to building a world-class city cluster in the Yangtze River Delta. At the port level, with the advancement of the information technology revolution and the development of network informatization, the development of the port itself presents a new trend. Specifically, the world's shipping vessels are becoming larger, requiring constantly improving port water depth conditions; shipping is showing a trend of standardization and intelligent development; convenience and low-carbon have become the new trend of global shipping development.

Taking the Port of Shanghai as an example, to alleviate the contradiction between environmental protection and port development and achieve sustainable port development, the Shanghai Port Group took the lead in conducting research on green port construction planning in China in early 2005, incorporating green and low-carbon awareness and concepts into the overall strategy of port development. In 2013, it officially launched the creation of a green port, and through the implementation of a series of energy-saving and emission-reduction measures at the port, the Port of Shanghai has achieved good development in the creation of a green port. In recent years, the measures implemented by the Port of Shanghai in the development process of creating a green port include: environmental management system, green port development planning, application of energy-saving and emission-reduction technologies, and automated terminal construction.

In terms of energy-saving and emission-reduction technologies, the fourth phase of Yangshan automated terminal applied advanced technologies such as remote control bridge cranes, fully automatic rail cranes, all-electric AGVs, intelligent dispatching systems, second-generation port ship shore-based power supply, energy-saving new light sources, and solar auxiliary heating in its construction. The application of advanced technologies has given the fourth phase of Yangshan terminal more prominent advantages in energy saving, emission reduction, and environmental protection compared to traditional container terminals, and has laid a solid foundation for the construction of zero-emission green terminals.

Furthermore, the Port of Shanghai continues to update its diesel-powered container trucks, phase out yellow-label vehicles, carry out LED lighting energy-saving renovations, develop hybrid tugboats, and implement a series of energy-saving and emission-reduction measures such as technical renovations of gas-electric hybrid RTGs and oil-electric hybrid RTGs. This has led to the continuous updating and transformation of old port equipment, and the promotion and application of green equipment and green technology in the port. In 2020, the proportion of green power RTGs in the Port of Shanghai reached 87%, and the proportion of main production equipment using clean energy reached an industry-leading level.

In terms of management, Shanghai Port Group, as the operator of the public terminals of the Port of Shanghai, promotes the development of the energy management system through the establishment of regulations and scientific management, and incorporates environmental management into the daily business management process. In terms of energy management, Shanghai Port Group includes energy consumption in the annual budget target, and has a strict energy management assessment mechanism. It has established a budget leadership team and a working group to regularly evaluate the budget execution situation to ensure the achievement of budget goals. In recent years, it has continuously strengthened the centralized control and management of oil products, realized real-time control of main loading and unloading equipment, effectively guaranteed the quality of port oil products and controlled energy use. At the same time, professional training for port staff has further improved the professional level of the energy management team. These measures have promoted the coordinated development of Shanghai Port's operations, production, and resource environment, and have had a significant impact on the construction of green ports.

10.2.3 Case Study of Environmental Coordinated Development of the Pearl River Delta Port Cluster

The Pearl River Delta port cluster is an important hub of the comprehensive transportation network system in Guangdong. The port cluster has basically formed a port network system with Shenzhen and Guangzhou ports as the mainline ports, Shantou, Zhuhai, Huizhou, Dongguan, Zhongshan, Yangjiang, Maoming, etc. as branch ports, and many small terminals on the Pearl River system as feeder ports. The port cluster, with its geographical advantage of being adjacent to Hong Kong and Macao and the solid foundation of world-class manufacturing bases, has made a huge contribution to the economic development of Guangdong and the country through the developed Pearl River water system and other transportation networks such as rail and air.

Ports such as Shenzhen and Guangzhou have become leaders in the construction of green ports. Guided by the scientific development concept, Shenzhen Port has vigorously promoted port energy conservation and emission reduction to adapt to port transformation and upgrading and international and domestic environmental protection requirements. It uses the number of container throughput as an economic indicator for assessing port operations, and the species and number of water birds inhabiting the port terminal as its ecological indicator for environmental protection assessment, achieving coordinated development of the port and city with remarkable results. Guangzhou Port Group has also positioned its Nansha, Xinsha, Huangpu, and Inner Harbor port areas as ecological protection demonstration areas, clean demonstration areas, and other environmental protection functions, and continues to explore new ways of energy conservation and emission reduction, especially investing heavily in the newly built Nansha Port for "oil to electricity" conversion, green terminal lighting, container application of LNG refueling stations, and other facility and technology upgrades and transformations.

The following will mainly use Guangzhou Port as a case study to introduce its measures in the construction and development of green ports.

Due to the large-scale development of port construction, negative environmental effects have been brought about. In response to this, Guangzhou Port actively implements the spirit and requirements of higher-level departments, and has issued various green port-related regulations and systems such as the "Guidelines for the Construction of Green Ports in Guangzhou", the "2018 Green Port Implementation Plan", and the "Guangzhou Port Ship Emission Control Action Plan (2018–2020)", etc. in 2019. In the year, the "Notice on the Implementation Plan for the Subsidy Fund for Ship Emission Control in Guangzhou Port" was issued by the Guangzhou Port Authority. This provided certain economic subsidies to port enterprises and shipping companies using clean energy, guiding relevant enterprises to actively participate in the construction of green ports. This greatly promoted the construction process of green ports in Guangzhou and proposed a green low-carbon plan for all ports in the province, providing policy support for the construction of the Pearl River Delta ecological port cluster.

Specifically, Guangzhou Port is fully promoting the construction of wind and dust suppression walls at bulk cargo terminals, the transformation of enclosed systems for belt conveyors, the implementation of dry fog spraying, the use of dust suppressants, and the installation of online dust concentration monitors, continuously improving dust control levels. It is also fully promoting the construction of shore power, with all existing port-specific berths and barge loading and unloading berths equipped with shore power facilities, and 186 berths capable of providing shore power. It is actively promoting clean energy such as LNG and electricity, with the coverage rate of RTG "oil to electricity" at container terminals reaching 100%. It is also constructing photovoltaic power generation projects, purchasing a batch of LNG container tractors, electric forklifts, electric commuter vehicles, etc., and continuously expanding the application ratio of energy-saving lamps. The port is continuously improving its environmental technology level, independently developing a roll-on/roll-off ship loading and unloading vehicle cargo information system, a comprehensive logistics intelligent management platform, and other technology projects. It has built a new automated container terminal, and its port and shipping environmental protection company's testing laboratory has obtained a CMA qualification certificate issued by the Guangdong Provincial Quality and Technical Supervision Bureau, improving the environmental monitoring technical capabilities of Guangzhou Port.

The port is continuously improving its ability to prevent environmental risks. Relying on the port and shipping environmental protection company, it has established 3 joint defense bodies for preventing and controlling ship pollution of the marine environment, built multiple rapid mobile warehouses, shared anti-pollution materials and equipment, and improved the overall emergency response speed and efficiency of Guangzhou Port. It is continuously optimizing the conditions for collection and distribution, vigorously developing and promoting water-to-water transshipment business. In 2019, Guangzhou Port's "Shuttle Bus" domestic and foreign trade routes reached 67, completing 1.823 million TEU of container transportation, opening more than 160 direct water-to-water barge lines, covering the Pearl River Delta, Guangxi, Hainan and other regions, and the Pearl River system barge container transportation network is continuously improving. The port is continuously optimizing its industrial layout. Swire Warehouse Wharf has been transformed from "retreat two and advance three" into Guangzhou's "urban living room". Huangsha Wharf has now developed into the largest scale wholesale market for aquatic products in the country. Dashatou Wharf has become the Guangzhou Pearl River Tourist Distribution Center and the largest "home port" for Pearl River cruise ships. The Inner Harbor, Huangpu Hongshengsha Wharf has withdrawn from loading and unloading operations, and the old Xin Port Company has withdrawn from coal bulk cargo operations. The layout of the wharf operations is continuously optimized and upgraded.

10.2.4 Case of Coordinated Environmental Development of Southeast Coastal Port Cluster

The Southeast Coastal Port Cluster mainly serves the economic development of some areas in Fujian Province and inland provinces such as Jiangxi, and meets the needs of "three links" with Taiwan. According to the "Fujian Coastal Port Layout Plan" issued by the Fujian Provincial Department of Transportation in January 2021, the Southeast Coastal Port Cluster includes Fuzhou Port, Xiamen Port, Quanzhou Port, and Meizhou Bay Port, with a total of 25 port areas.

Taking Xiamen Port as an example, since 2010, Xiamen Port Group has invested more than 600 million yuan in the construction of green port projects, including environmental protection infrastructure construction and transformation, energy-saving and emission-reduction project construction, green technology equipment application, intelligent logistics information system construction, production process system optimization and upgrading, etc., achieving a green virtuous cycle of energy saving, consumption reduction, environmental protection, pollution reduction, and efficiency increase.

Strengthen environmental protection and build a green ecological port area.

Construction of ship anti-oil spill facilities, strengthening the equipment work of ship anti-oil spill equipment facilities. Purchase solid float type, PVC oil fence and other ship anti-oil pollution equipment to enhance the ship's oil spill prevention and control capabilities; new docks are required to establish anti-oil spill related facilities and anti-oil spill monitoring systems during design and construction. Increase the intensity of dust pollution prevention and control in the port area. For bulk cargo docks, invest in setting up air quality monitoring stations to track changes in air quality in the port area in real time; by using sprinkler facilities, building dust-proof nets, port area greening isolation belts, in-warehouse stacking, covering tarpaulins and other measures, reduce dock dust pollution and effectively reduce total suspended particles, soot and other indicators. Carry out sewage treatment and reclaimed water reuse work, Xiamen Port Group's docks have all built sewage treatment facilities with different treatment capabilities. Chemical docks are equipped with chemical washing water treatment facilities. This facility uses a combination of air flotation-anaerobic–aerobic-activated carbon filtration process, and the sewage treatment capacity can meet the use needs of docked ships.

Implement green port construction measures

Xiamen Port started the construction of shore-based power supply facilities in 2015, guiding ships that meet the access conditions to use shore power, and subsidizing shipping companies in accordance with the "Xiamen Port Ship Shore Power Use Management Interim Measures". In addition, dock companies also give moderate discounts to shipping companies using shore power in loading and unloading rates.

In terms of energy-saving technology transformation, Xiamen Port Group organizes member companies to carry out energy-saving technology transformation, including large-scale equipment energy feedback technology transformation, which improves energy efficiency, replaces small power generators with energy storage lithium batteries on the basis of "oil to electricity" for traditional gantry cranes, uses electricity for transshipment, and promotes the use of electric air conditioners on other internal combustion machinery. The port area's high pole lights use LED light sources, remote intelligent control, realizing automatic control, automatic detection and automatic alarm of high pole lights, transforming the static switch mode of "fixed time switch lights" into a "can automatically switch lights according to production operations and weather changes" dynamic management mode.

In promoting the use of clean energy, in order to increase the proportion of clean energy and optimize the energy consumption structure, Xiamen Port Group actively promotes the application of solar photovoltaic power generation systems, and has now built and put into use two small solar power generation systems, with an annual power generation exceeding 500,000 kW h. Xiamen Port Group has formulated a general plan for electric vehicle charging infrastructure, and implemented it in two stages: near-term and medium-long term. At present, 15 charging piles have been built in the port area, and it is planned to build 200 vehicle charging piles in the initial stage.

Through these measures, Xiamen Port Group, in the process of implementing green port construction, relies on information technology means, combined with the construction of smart ports, improves social logistics efficiency, realizes the green port ecosystem, and actively participates in the national power reform pilot, returning the benefits of reform to green port construction.

References

Lin Y, Liu C, Zhang H et al (2020) Comparison and reference of green port evaluation systems at home and abroad. Waterway Port 41(5):613–618

Tang X (2015) Lessons from foreign green ports. Times Finan 2015(27):153+155

Wang K, Li Y (2023) Review of the development of green port construction. China Navig Wkly 10:45–47

Zhang G (2018) The enlightenment of the construction and management experience of the new port in the United States to Wuhan new port. Yangtze Forum 01:22–26

Zhang N (2023) Foreign green port development strategy and its enlightenment to Shanghai Port. Containerization 34(05):1–5

Chapter 11
Policy Recommendations

11.1 Promote the Rational Allocation of Resources and the Coordinated Development of Land and Sea

Promote the green and low-carbon coordinated development of the entire supply chain with the port as the key hub. Coordinate the layout of inland ports and composite ports, vigorously develop container rail-water intermodal transport, and continue to deepen the promotion of container water-water transshipment. Promote the "public to rail" and "public to water" of bulk cargo, and increase the proportion of green transportation methods such as railways and waterways. Plan and layout international green low-carbon fuel refueling centers, enhance the refueling service guarantee capacity of low-carbon zero-emission fuels such as LNG, methanol, and hydrogen energy in our coastal ports, fully play the role of ports as key nodes of integrated transportation hubs, and jointly promote the decarbonization actions of the shipping industry and road transportation industry. Encourage port enterprises and shipping companies to jointly promote the application of low-zero emission fuels for transport ships, and jointly create a domestic "green shipping corridor". Promote the green and low-carbon coordinated development of regional port groups. The three world-class port groups of the Bohai Bay, the Yangtze River Delta, and the Guangdong-Hong Kong-Macao Greater Bay Area further optimize the layout of port facilities and the planning of feeder channels, save and intensively use shoreline resources, promote joint prevention and control of port ship pollution, systematically plan new energy clean energy supply systems, and accelerate the green and low-carbon coordinated development within the region, playing a demonstrative and leading role for the green and low-carbon development of ports nationwide. Strengthen the linkage between departments and provinces, enhance digital empowerment, and jointly promote green and low-carbon coordinated development. Strengthen structural optimization and achieve energy efficiency improvement. Comprehensively sort out and integrate port resources, promote the transformation of cargo owner terminals to public terminals,

B. Lu, *The Sustainable Development of Port Group*,
https://doi.org/10.1007/978-981-97-2378-2_11

traditional terminals to smart terminals, and general terminals to specialized terminals, and further improve the efficiency of shoreline use. According to the principles of "water where suitable", "road where suitable", and "rail where suitable", accelerate the adjustment of transportation structure, optimize the port feeder system, fully utilize the advantages of green transportation methods such as waterways and railways, steadily increase the proportion of bulk dry bulk cargo railway and waterway feeder, and reduce the carbon emissions and impact on urban environment caused by road transportation.

11.2 Strengthen Emission Monitoring in the Port Area and Improve the Compilation of Port Emission Inventories

(1) Carry out carbon footprint accounting for port enterprises

A carbon footprint refers to the total amount of carbon emissions directly or indirectly produced by corporations, activities, products, or individuals throughout their entire lifecycle of production or living. Identifying the driving factors of a port's carbon footprint is one of the most fundamental tasks in achieving carbon reduction, and it plays a crucial role in clarifying and improving the direction and specific strategies for reducing port carbon emissions. Currently, China's port industry has not yet calculated the total carbon emissions of the entire industry, and port companies have not carried out calculations of the port's carbon footprint. Port companies should carry out carbon footprint calculations, understand the main factors affecting port carbon emissions, such as energy structure, technological level, etc., and take effective emission reduction actions to promote low-carbon green development of ports.

(2) Clarify the carbon neutrality goals and paths for the port industry

At present, some port companies internationally have achieved carbon neutrality, and setting carbon neutrality goals is becoming a trend for sustainable development in the international port industry (Munim et al. 2021). However, Chinese port companies are significantly lacking in this regard. Currently, China's oil, chemical, coal, steel, power, automobile and other industries have all announced their own carbon peaking and carbon neutrality plans and roadmaps. Under the background of the "3060" carbon peaking and carbon neutrality goal, the port industry, as a high carbon emission industry, should actively respond to the call of national policy, set phased carbon reduction targets for the port industry, formulate carbon neutrality goals and implementation paths, to cope with climate change and achieve sustainable low-carbon development.

(3) Construct and improve the port environmental management system for port companies

Most port companies in China have established environmental management systems, but they all have problems to varying degrees. Port companies should improve their environmental management systems according to their own scale, throughput, business scope, etc., incorporate environmental management into daily business management processes, improve the organizational structure of environmental management, standardize environmental management operating procedures; strictly manage energy, strengthen centralized control of energy and information management of energy use; implement control over major loading and unloading equipment, control port energy use; and strengthen professional training for port staff, improve the professionalism of the environmental management team.

11.3 Improve Green Port Development Policies and Establish Energy-Saving and Emission-Reduction Mechanisms

Strengthen top-level design and achieve planning leadership. Based on the "dual carbon" strategy and the needs of building a strong transportation country, the transportation authorities should take the lead in formulating the "dual carbon" work action plan or implementation opinions for the port industry, formulate low-carbon or "zero carbon" development implementation paths that match the national "dual carbon" strategic goal time nodes and specific task measures, clarify timetables and roadmaps, scientifically formulate related plans for port low-carbon development, equipment development, facility development, technology development, low-carbon standards, port-city integration, etc., enhance the standardization, scientific nature, and digital level of energy-saving and carbon reduction, and provide guidance for the construction of "near-zero carbon ports".

Strengthen overall coordination and achieve multi-party governance. Strengthen policy support, ensure project funds and reasonable sea and land use needs, strengthen departmental communication and coordination, and form a departmental consultation mechanism for promoting the construction of "near-zero carbon ports". Innovate port green development investment and financing mechanisms, introduce social capital to participate in port low-carbon construction, form a joint construction effort led by the government, with enterprises as the main body, and social participation (Guo 2020). Steadily advance the revision of port carbon emission monitoring statistical accounting standards, carbon emission limit standards, and related equipment facility technical standards, and improve the port low-carbon development assessment and evaluation system.

11.4 Promote Industrial Structure Upgrade and Vigorously Develop Low-Carbon Clean Industries

Promote the coordinated development of port pollution reduction and carbon reduction centered on the clean low-carbon energy system. With the focus on electrification of terminal energy use and greening of electricity sources, promote the coordinated increase of pollution reduction and carbon reduction (Cao 2020). Promote the application of port distributed renewable energy microgrid with multi-energy complementarity, strive for the integrated development of ports and new energy, and achieve self-sufficiency of clean energy in ports with conditions. Form a linkage mechanism with the reform, ecological environment, energy and other departments to provide policy guarantees for the construction of new energy clean energy infrastructure such as wind power, photovoltaics, hydrogen energy, energy storage in ports. "Government, industry, academia, research, finance, and service" collaborate to innovate, carry out key technology research on low-carbon, zero-carbon, and negative carbon. Actively carry out low-carbon, near-zero carbon port creation actions. In the process of green and low-carbon, pay high attention to the relationship with port safety production. Promote the coordinated development of port green low-carbon technology and standards at home and abroad. Strengthen the construction of national-level technical standards, promote the internationalization of Chinese standards through IMO (International Maritime Organization), ISO (International Organization for Standardization), APEC (Asia–Pacific Economic Cooperation) and other international organizations, and contribute Chinese wisdom and Chinese solutions to the technology and standards of global port green low-carbon development. Relying on the Asia–Pacific Green Port Award Scheme (GPAS) mechanism of the Asia–Pacific Port Services Organization (APSN), international scientific and technological cooperation bases, international port and shipping technology alliances and other international cooperation and exchange platforms, strengthen the exchange and sharing of Chinese experiences and solutions in green and low-carbon port construction.

11.5 Improve the Level of Port Informatization and Empower Green High-Quality Development

At present, the transformation of our country's ports to smart ports is just starting, and the construction and development pace of each port is different, but the common problem they face is still the bottleneck of insufficient informatization construction. Some useful experiences can be obtained through the analysis of the current situation of advanced port informatization abroad:

(1) Unified standards are the basis for information sharing

The construction of basic databases should be uniformly planned so that the database information sharing between various ports, departments, and national information centers can be smooth, avoiding phenomena such as each doing its own thing, disconnection from each other, and repeated data entry, to achieve low investment and high efficiency (Ayfantopoulou et al. 2015). Unified standards are the basis for interconnection, information sharing, and business collaboration. This functional play is reflected not only in the standardization of single technologies but also in a complete set of information standard systems. Therefore, a unified port information standard system is the basis for ensuring the accuracy of data between different departments and entities in the port. Standardize the databases built by various departments and entities, set unified standard connections for newly built databases, and integrate them into a unified standard information library. For example, Tianjin Port's one-stop external service platform, Jingangtong, interconnects the data of customs, national inspection and other regulatory units and dock companies based on unified standards, adding new convenient processes for users of the information platform, and using safer and simpler methods to execute electronic business functions.

(2) Establish and improve the rules and regulations for information resource sharing

Legislation related to information sharing is a prerequisite for successful information sharing among all entities. Information resources should be enjoyed by both the state and citizens, and there should not be a situation of independent monopoly. Under the premise of ensuring national and citizen interests, relevant information resources should be fully shared among all entities. Information resources exclusively owned by various departments and entities should be circulated and shared through standardized regulations, which will promote the dissemination of information resources throughout society. It is necessary to formulate and issue management regulations on port information sharing as soon as possible, and to confirm them in the form of laws, regulations, and policy provisions. From the perspective of top-level design, and considering the nationwide interconnection and network intercommunication, effective legislation should be carried out to establish a comprehensive and perfect sharing legal system, protect the rights and obligations of information resource owners, coordinate their interests, and provide a platform with better confidentiality. When local governments are building port informatization and formulating local policies, they should fully consider the informatization characteristics of different levels, departments, and entities, use the regulation, guidance, and intervention of policies, and standardize the activities and behaviors of government information resource sharing.

(3) Improve industry standards

Cross-departmental and cross-entity information resource sharing is not something that a single department can accomplish independently; it can be said that this is a long-term construction project for society. According to the current construction model, any information integration in the port area requires the establishment of a complete set of industry standards to provide a basic framework for information sharing. After the EDI data exchange platform developed by Ningbo Port unified the port operation standard system of port units and dock enterprises, it brought more convenient services to different departments and different customers. When port cargo transport customers upload standardized information to this system, related docks, shipping companies, ship agents, customs, border inspections, maritime affairs, national inspections, and other related entities will be able to obtain complete information, and each entity will also input the cargo information they handle into this system through electronic data exchange services, and standardized information will circulate in the system. Due to the unification of industry standards, the regional delivery capacity of Ningbo Port has been significantly improved, not only realizing one-stop declaration, but also adding dozens of value-added service functions such as sea-rail intermodal transit and international transit.

(4) Informatization provides full-chain support for green development

The essence of informatization empowering green development is to fully utilize data in various fields, optimize machine and production process efficiency through the comprehensive application of massive data, improve energy efficiency, and reduce emissions. Informatization provides full-chain support for improving equipment connectivity, production efficiency, and policy precision in green development.

Firstly, digital technology improves the connectivity of the physical world and establishes a closed-loop channel for information collection and feedback in green development. Internet of Things technology uses QR codes, RFID, and various sensors to capture ubiquitous information in the physical world, and through 5G, the Internet, and other heterogeneous networks, it realizes efficient information interaction between machines and between machines and people. This establishes a two-way data flow channel for the closed-loop optimization of green intelligent production processes, achieving real-time, refined equipment management and production control, effectively reducing energy consumption and carbon emissions.

Secondly, the information technology industry's solutions enhance energy use efficiency, empowering green transformation through data value mining. Information technology solutions, by connecting technology, data, and industry knowledge, use real-time monitoring data collected by end-user digital technology and virtual models based on application scenarios to optimize energy use and production operation plans, promoting efficient and low-carbon production processes. Looking at specific industries, information technology solutions are crucial for major emission sectors such as industry, transportation, and construction to achieve green development. In the industrial field, the industrial internet, as a comprehensive information technology solution for vertical fields, not only helps individual enterprises to achieve information tracking, monitoring, and analysis in all aspects such as research and design, production and manufacturing, logistics and transportation, recycling and reuse, but also realizes on-demand supply, efficient production, and carbon emission reduction, achieving energy-saving and efficiency improvement for enterprises. At the same time, it enables capacity sharing and element sharing based on data connectivity between enterprises, improving resource utilization efficiency in the upstream and downstream of the industrial chain, and reducing industry carbon emissions. In the construction field, modules such as 5G and sensors distributed in building walls, air conditioning systems, and elevator systems optimize the operation of building equipment, reduce idling rates, and reduce energy consumption and emissions. In the transportation field, intercity high-speed railways, intercity rail transit, charging pile networks combined with artificial intelligence, big data, cloud computing, and other technology applications can greatly improve the efficiency of traffic flow, reduce resource consumption, and enhance system safety and sustainability. According to calculations by CICC, digital technology can significantly reduce the empty load rate of logistics, reduce the annual invalid mileage by 147.2 billion kilometers, and reduce carbon dioxide emissions by 69.508 billion kilograms.

Thirdly, information technology improves the accuracy of carbon emission monitoring and management, providing strong support for the implementation of green development policies and the optimization of corporate carbon asset management. China is currently launching a national carbon trading market, and digital technology will greatly improve the real-time and accuracy of carbon accounting during the carbon trading process. Taking the online monitoring system for carbon emission accounting as an example, digital technologies such as the Internet of Things, cloud computing, and big data will strongly support the data collection, recording, transmission, and processing of this monitoring system, and then help enterprises better plan carbon quotas through data model analysis. In addition, in the green financial services industry, digital technologies such as the Internet of Things, blockchain, and big data help financial institutions form a real-time monitoring network for corporate carbon emissions, identify truly "green" enterprises, and improve the accuracy of financial support. For the government, through energy and carbon information monitoring and management, it can help governments at different levels to timely grasp the progress and trend prediction of the "carbon peak" and "carbon neutrality" goals, providing a basis for the scientific decision-making of government departments' emission reduction policies. Digital technology can also provide support in areas such as ecosystem health management, carbon sequestration potential assessment, carbon sequestration site optimization, and improving carbon capture and storage efficiency, enhancing carbon sink potential.

11.6 Unleashing the Integration Efficiency of Ports, Realizing Intensive and Economical Development of Ports

Promoting port resource integration is an important measure to promote the quality and efficiency upgrade of ports, resolve excess capacity, optimize resource allocation, and improve functional layout. It is of great significance to promote the construction of a strong transportation country, build world-class ports, and serve economic and social development. Resource integration and regional port integration are important contents of port transformation and development during the "13th Five-Year Plan" period. In 2017, a new wave of port resource integration was set off in China, and cross-administrative region port resource integration has become a new direction for the development of China's port industry. Although China has rich practical experience in port resource integration and has achieved initial results, there are still some problems that need to be solved under the new situation.

(1) Do a good job in the integration planning of ports at the provincial level

Led by provincial governments, it is urgent to compile port planning at the provincial level to provide guidance for port resource integration. Fully leverage the guiding and controlling role of planning, and based on this, implement adjustments and controls on the increment of natural resources in ports, achieve the optimal allocation of port natural resources, formulate regional port integration development plans, and achieve coordinated management of port resources.

Set up provincial port authorities. The responsibilities of city-level port management should be taken up to the provincial government level, and a provincial port authority should be established to focus on resolving the core issue of inconsistent interests of city governments during the integration of port resources. The provincial port authority is authorized by the provincial party committee and the provincial government to exercise provincial economic management authority, oversee port development-related work, such as coordinating comprehensive coastline management, coordinating port relations, promoting port integration development work, and after the establishment of the provincial port group, oversee the work of the provincial port group, and carry out work according to the principle of "unified management, hierarchical review".

Establish a provincial port group. The integration of port resources should be a market-oriented process and should not overly rely on government regulation, otherwise it will lead to low participation of port companies and low efficiency of resource allocation. Therefore, mature port resource integration should be guided by market operation rules, linked by capital, and use government macro-control as a means to fully stimulate the initiative and enthusiasm of port companies, and establish a provincial port group based on existing port companies in the region, as a platform for port resource integration, to scientifically and reasonably complete the integration of port resources in the region.

(2) Strengthen the construction of the supporting mechanism system for port resource integration

China's port development has moved from monopoly operation to market-oriented development, and while ports are developing rapidly, some problems have also accumulated, which have affected the integration of port resources. To ensure the smooth integration of port resources, it is necessary to strengthen the construction of the supporting mechanism system for port resource integration.

Improve laws and regulations to standardize port resource integration. At present, the highest law in China's port management is the "Port Law", but the Port Law only requires "one city, one port" and does not explicitly stipulate the integration of port resources at the provincial level. At the national level, it is recommended to improve the laws and regulations for port management to provide a legal basis for port resource integration; at the provincial government level, it is recommended to issue guiding opinions on port resource integration to provide support for port resource integration. At the same time, it is necessary to improve and optimize the port management system, establish a strict port planning approval mechanism and a long-term accountability mechanism, to provide institutional and organizational guarantees for port resource integration.

Exercise government regulatory functions to create a healthy and orderly market environment. Most of the berths in China's ports are composed of public wharves and owner wharves. Many ports have a large number of small, scattered, weak owner wharves and some black wharves that do not have business qualifications. These wharves adopt low-price competition strategies to grab cargo sources and disrupt market order, and public wharves often cannot compete with them. To optimize the market environment, government departments need to fully exercise government regulatory duties, clean up illegal operators, establish a healthy and orderly market environment, and ensure the orderly progress of port resource integration.

Strengthen coastline management and coordinate the use of coastline resources. It is recommended that the provincial port authority formulate and supervise the implementation of policy measures and management systems for comprehensive management of port coastlines. On the one hand, improve the approval system for the use of wharf coastlines, strictly control the input of new coastlines, handle the relationship between the stock and increment of coastlines, and achieve the optimal allocation of coastline resources; on the other hand, design a reasonable paid use system for coastlines, increase the cost of coastline use with the principle of rewarding the good and punishing the bad, force low-efficiency coastline occupying companies to exit, and reduce the difficulty of port resource integration.

Improve the statistical survey system and enhance the level of informatization. Port companies are improving their statistical survey systems, making detailed statistics for each type of cargo throughput data, striving to report the most accurate throughput data to the competent authorities, thereby providing a basis for business optimization adjustments during port resource integration. At the same time, they are strengthening the construction of information technology, networking port statistical data, achieving data sharing, and improving the decision-making level of all ports involved in resource integration (Dai 2023).

(3) Gradually release the integration efficiency by fully drawing on successful experiences

At present, both domestically and abroad, there are rich experiences in port resource integration, and there are mature port resource integration models for provinces in our country that are currently integrating port resources. Internationally, the New York-New Jersey Port provides valuable experience for the development of combined ports, and the integration of port resources in Tokyo Bay in Japan and in Germany and the Port of Hamburg provide references for regional port resource integration. Domestically, the Ministry of Transport has issued the "Zhejiang's Strong Promotion of Regional Port Integration Reform Experience", clearly stating that our country's port resource integration should learn from Zhejiang's integration experience and truly achieve deep integration of port resources.

Port resource integration is a time-consuming system project, and it is difficult to complete in one step due to the involvement of many stakeholders and the difficulty of coordination. Therefore, it is recommended to gradually implement port resource integration in a step-by-step manner. At present, the marketization level of our country's ports is not high, and the leading role of provincial port authorities should be fully utilized. Strictly in accordance with the national port layout plan, the provincial port development plan should be formulated, the ports in the region should be reasonably positioned and divided, the formation of provincial port companies should be promoted, and they should be responsible for port resource integration related affairs. When the marketization level of the port gradually matures, the leading role of the provincial port authorities should be downplayed, the role of market resource allocation should be played, and more state-owned enterprises or private capital (port companies or dock operators) should be encouraged to participate in regional port resource integration. In terms of development sequence, first achieve "one port, one city", gradually transition to "one province, one city", and finally achieve cross-regional port resource integration, fully releasing the potential of the port group.

11.7 Promote Port Energy Transformation and Build a Low-Carbon Port Energy System

In March 2021, General Secretary Xi Jinping proposed at the ninth meeting of the Central Financial and Economic Committee that achieving carbon peak and carbon neutrality is a wide and profound economic and social systemic reform. We need to incorporate carbon peak and carbon neutrality into the overall layout of ecological civilization construction, and strive to achieve the goals of carbon peak by 2030 and carbon neutrality by 2060. The report "Ports: Green Gateways to Europe—Ten Transformations of Ports into Decarbonization Centers" released by DNV GL in July 2020 pointed out that by 2050, the total electricity consumption of ports will increase more than tenfold, of which at least 70% will come from renewable energy, while the current proportion is only 5%. Therefore, achieving carbon peak and carbon neutrality in the port industry is not only a need for the adjustment of the national energy strategic layout, but also a need for industry transformation and development.

From carbon peak to carbon neutrality, developed countries have a transition period of 60 to 70 years, while our country only has about 30 years. This means that the difficulty and intensity of China's greenhouse gas emission reduction are much greater than those of developed countries. To achieve this goal, all industries need to come up with measures suitable for themselves, accelerate research, implement as soon as possible, and make active efforts to achieve the goal.

(1) Conduct serious research, analyze and judge.

All ports should comprehensively carry out carbon emission data surveys, collection, and analysis, propose scientific peak carbon emission path suggestions, and systematically establish a peak carbon and carbon neutral data system to meet the specific requirements of the country, industry, and region for carbon emission data monitoring, reporting, and verification. The basic research includes the requirements of the country (region), industry, and the company's own carbon reduction foundation (Song 2020). Through the analysis of basic research information, the boundary range of carbon peaking is determined, and a suitable accounting method for the company is selected to quantify greenhouse gas emissions and predict future emission trends.

(2) Categorized measures, focus on breakthroughs

For multiple fields such as port operations, port logistics, port construction, port services, port real estate, resource development, and capital operations, considering the situation faced by each port, strengthen the research and development of cutting-edge technologies, and carry out long-term key research around the key directions. In the implementation process, the construction of green ports is the focus, continuously strengthening the promotion and application of existing green low-carbon technologies, supporting the rapid advancement of industrial greening transformation.

(3) Determine the scope and boundaries

The dual carbon goals and paths should be analyzed and judged based on recent historical data, and future carbon emissions should be predicted, with short, medium, and long-term stages for emission trend analysis. Based on model prediction, carry out pre-assessment, calculate the total emissions of the baseline scenario, analyze the gap with the peak target, consider proposing the peak path and measures taken in the low-carbon scenario and technological breakthrough scenario; analyze the maturity of each type of technology, emission reduction contribution, economic acceptability, regulatory completeness, etc., and preferentially select emission reduction technologies at each stage; analyze the peak path and measures, screen out technical means suitable for different stages, and compile a peak roadmap.

(4) Adopted reference standards and guidelines

When carrying out greenhouse gas emission accounting for each port and its branches and subsidiaries, ISO 14064–1 and the greenhouse gas accounting guidelines/standards published by the national climate change authority can be referred to for corporate greenhouse gas emissions. All coastal and inland port companies can refer to the "Greenhouse Gas Emission Accounting Method and Guide for Land Transportation Companies" issued by the National Development and Reform Commission to calculate corporate greenhouse gas emissions and compile corporate greenhouse gas emission reports. The direct carbon emission sources of port companies mainly come from the combustion of fossil fuels, such as gasoline, diesel, natural gas, and coal; the main energy-consuming equipment includes loading and unloading equipment, lifting tools, transportation tools and facilities, etc., and the main types of greenhouse gases are CO_2; indirect carbon emission sources mainly include the use of purchased electricity and heat.

(5) Widely use photovoltaic power generation, wind power, solar energy

Firstly, consideration should be given to increasing the proportion of clean energy and renewable energy in ports. It is necessary to optimize port energy utilization, reduce the consumption of diesel and gasoline mainly from fossil fuels, and electricity from fossil fuels, combine the resource endowment of the port, and give priority to the use of distributed photovoltaics and dispersed wind power in the port. Support port companies to carry out energy-saving renovations of existing facilities and vigorously promote the application of new energy-saving products and technologies.

(6) Electrification of mobile machinery and tugboats

The electrification of mobile machinery and tugboats is an inevitable trend in future development. Combining the current operating area and the overall planning of the future port area, a design can be made with battery replacement as the main operation, and the whole vehicle power system and battery system can be combined with the needs of different vehicles and equipment to achieve the universalization of the battery replacement system, reducing the construction cost and management cost of battery replacement stations.

(7) Application of Hydrogen Energy

Hydrogen energy is clean and highly efficient, suitable for use in heavy-duty, long-distance, and long-duration devices. It can be widely applied in traditional fields, as well as in emerging areas such as hydrogen-powered vehicles and hydrogen power generation. By 2050, it is estimated that hydrogen energy will account for about 10% of China's energy system, with a demand of nearly 60 million tons. In future development, we should adhere to strategic guidance to ensure the orderly development of the hydrogen energy and fuel cell industries.

(8) Shore Power Systems for Port Ships

"Shore power" refers to the practice of ships stopping the use of their diesel generators and switching to land-based power supply systems while docked or anchored, achieving "zero fuel consumption, zero emissions, and zero noise", effectively reducing ship pollution. Using shore power when ships are docked is an effective measure to reduce atmospheric pollutants and CO_2 emissions, and is an important means to promote the pollution reduction, carbon reduction, and green transformation of the water transport industry. Port groups should further increase the construction of shore power, improve shore power technology, increase power efficiency, and strengthen communication with shipping companies, guiding them to actively connect to shore power, increase the use of shore power, and make greater contributions to the construction of green, low-carbon ports.

11.8 Strengthen the Propagation of Green Port Concepts to Build a Good Development Environment

Fully leverage the initiative of port enterprises, strengthen the propagation and training of green concepts among port workers, encourage port enterprises to cooperate with governments and research institutes, cultivate innovative green port construction management professionals, and formulate phased green transformation plans.

Raising the environmental awareness of port service personnel is an important aspect of building green ports. With the advancement of the "green port" initiative and the gradual improvement of environmental regulations, it is necessary to gradually raise the environmental awareness of port service personnel, enabling them to consciously participate in the construction of green ports (Duan et al. 2017). Firstly, various forms of propaganda and education methods should be adopted, such as using port news media and port information bulletins, propaganda boards and other media forms, regularly or irregularly inviting experts to hold energy-saving knowledge lectures and arranging staff to participate in energy-saving and emission-reduction knowledge training, conducting energy-saving competitions, award-winning essay contests and other educational activities, strengthening environmental propaganda and education for port service personnel, making them truly aware of the importance of environmental protection. Secondly, while carrying out propaganda and education, it is also necessary to establish a mechanism for reporting, complaining about, and rewarding and punishing environmental pollution in the port area, and resolutely punish behaviors that harm the construction of green ports.

We can learn from the development experience of the New York-New Jersey Port, regularly evaluate the effects of port emission reduction and the situation of fund investment, find the key points affecting the effect of port emission reduction, and ensure the balance of effectiveness and economy of port emission reduction measures (Zu et al. 2020). Through the construction of green belts in the port area, ecological parks in the port, standardizing port operations, and transforming port operation equipment, we can reduce the impact of ports on the urban environment and practice the concept of green development.

References

Ayfantopoulou G, Tsoukos G, Stathacopoulos A, Bizakis A, Gagatsi E (2015) Greener port performance through ICT. In: Stylios C, Floqi T, Marinski J, Damiani L (eds) Sustainable development of sea-corridors and coastal waters

Cao Y (2020) Study on the inventory and characteristics of ship and port air pollutants emissions in typical regions. Shanghai University

Dai Q (2023) Research on the optimization of multimodal container transport network in Port Hinterland considering carbon emissions. Wuhan University of Technology

Duan X, Xu X, Feng J (2017) Research of the evaluation index system of green port based on analysis approach of attribute coordinate. In: Shi Z, Goertzel B, Feng J (eds) Intelligence science I. ICIS 2017. IFIP advances in information and communication technology, pp 510
Guo J (2020) Study on the formation mechanism and investment optimization of low-carbon ports. Dalian Maritime University
Munim ZH, Saha R (2021) Green ports and sustainable shipping in the european context. In: Carpenter A, Johansson TM, Skinner JA (eds) Sustainability in the maritime domain. Strategies for sustainability, pp 81–99
Song TL (2020) Research on the integrated energy system of ports considering demand response. Southeast University
Zu Q, Yan J (2022) Innovation framework for green ports. In: Zu Q, Tang Y, Mladenovic V, Naseer A, Wan J (eds) Human centered computing. HCC 2021. Lecture notes in computer science, pp 13795

GPSR Compliance

The European Union's (EU) General Product Safety Regulation (GPSR) is a set of rules that requires consumer products to be safe and our obligations to ensure this.

If you have any concerns about our products, you can contact us on ProductSafety@springernature.com

In case Publisher is established outside the EU, the EU authorized representative is:

Springer Nature Customer Service Center GmbH
Europaplatz 3
69115 Heidelberg, Germany

The manufacturer's authorised representative in the EU is Springer Nature Customer Service Centre GmbH, Europaplatz 3, 69115 Heidelberg, Germany. If you have any concerns regarding our products, please contact ProductSafety@springernature.com

Printed and bound by CPI Group (UK) Ltd, Croydon, CR0 4YY
01/10/2026
02225850-0012